Encyclopedia

of Taboos

Encyclopedia of Taboos

Lynn Holden

ABC-CLIO
Oxford, England
Santa Barbara, California
Denver, Colorado

British Library Cataloguing in Publication Data

Holden, Lynn
    Encyclopedia of taboos
    1. Taboo – Encyclopedias
    I. Title
  390'.03

ISBNs 1–85109–348–6 (Paperback)
      1–57607–069–7 (Hardback)

ABC-CLIO Ltd,
Old Clarendon Ironworks,
35A Great Clarendon Street,
Oxford OX2 6AT, England.

ABC-CLIO Inc.,
130 Cremona Drive,
Santa Barbara,
CA 93117, USA.

Typeset by ABC-CLIO Ltd., Oxford, England.
Printed and bound in Great Britain by
MPG Books Limited, Bodmin, Cornwall.

Contents

Acknowledgements

For suggestions and advice on topics as diverse as forbidden musical chords, Japanese bean feasts and the realm of the senses, I would like to thank Gidon Bahiri, Dr Frances J. Fischer, Rebekah Gronowski, Ruth Holden, Eri Ikawa, Koert Linde, David Ward Maclean, Dr Karen Ralls-MacLeod, Malika Natley, Dr Roy Willis and Dr Wei Zhengwei. I am also indebted to Dr Margaret A. Mackay, director of the School of Scottish Studies, University of Edinburgh, for a research fellowship that allowed me access to valuable resources. Finally, permission to quote is gratefully acknowledged as follows:

Material from *Totem and Taboo* by Sigmund Freud, translated by James Strachey. Copyright 1950 by Routledge and Kegan Paul, Ltd. Used by permission of W. W. Norton and Company, Inc. (USA).

Material from *Totem and Taboo* by Sigmund Freud, translated by James Strachey. Copyrights 1953 by Angela Richards, The Institute of Psychoanalysis and the Hogarth Press. Used by permission of The Random House Group Ltd (UK).

Material from *Purity and Danger: An Analysis of the Concepts of Pollution and Taboo* by Mary Douglas. Copyright 1966 by Routledge and Kegan Paul. Used by permission of Cambridge University Press, Cambridge, UK.

Material from *The Savage Mind* by Claude Lévi-Strauss. Copyright 1966 by Weidenfeld and Nicolson. Used by permission of The Orion Publishing Group Ltd (UK).

Material from *The Savage Mind* by Claude Lévi-Strauss. Copyright 1966 by Weidenfeld and Nicolson. Used by permission of The University of Chicago Press (USA).

Material from *The Laws of Manu* translated by Wendy Doniger O'Flaherty with Brian K. Smith. Copyright 1991 by Wendy Doniger O'Flaherty and Brian K. Smith. Used by permission of Penguin Books Ltd, London.

Material from *The Rites of Passage* by Arnold van Gennep, translated by Monika B. Vizedom and Gabrielle L. Caffee (Routledge and Kegan Paul). Copyright 1960 by Monika B. Vizedom and Gabrielle L. Caffee. Used by permission of The University of Chicago Press.

Material from *Taboo: A Sociological Study* by Hutton Webster. Copyright 1940 by Stanford University, Stanford University Press. Used by permission of Stanford University Press.

Material from *The Concise Encyclopedia of Islam* by Cyril Glassé. Copyright 1989 by Stacey Publications, London. Used by permission of Stacey Publications.

Preface

The word *taboo* derives from the Tongan *tabu* and is related to the more general Polynesian word, *tapu*, and the Hawaiian *kapu*. It became a familiar term in Europe after it was mentioned by Captain James Cook in his journal describing his third voyage around the world. He was introduced to the expression in 1777 in the Tonga, or Friendly, Islands. The literal meaning of the word is simply "marked off", or "off-limits", possibly a combination of *ta* (to mark) and *pu* (exceedingly). Unfortunately, the term was interpreted by early anthropologists such as William Robertson Smith and James Frazer as a form of superstition, or magic, and became a repository for all that remained inexplicable in preliterate cultures. It took later scholars like Mary Douglas and Edmund Leach to show how taboos are just as prevalent in the industrialised West. Far from being remnants of a distant time or place, a product of supposedly "primitive" thought, taboos are a crucial part of our, or indeed any, society, determining how people must and must not behave.

Perhaps because of the low esteem in which the evolutionary theories of earlier writers are held today, contemporary anthropologists have often shied away from using the term in the earlier sense, avoiding the conceptual complications of "sacred" versus "polluting", preferring to focus on the context, reason and agents of specific avoidances. As a result no comprehensive encyclopedia or dictionary on taboos has been published in recent years and the last attempt at a general survey of the topic dates back to 1956. This means that there is no overview of either the many excellent monographs on prohibitions within individual cultures or of current theories on the importance of specific taboos.

The present book, therefore, is intended as a preliminary guide to taboos, examining some aspects of their meaning, use, and importance in religion, economics, politics and society. It draws on a wide range of disciplines, including anthropology, folklore, psychology, art, literature, music and the natural sciences. The time-frame ranges from the origins of human culture, with evidence of animal remains found in ancient Chinese tombs, to ancient law codes from India, Iran and the Near East and proscriptions against pollution in Greece and Rome from the classical era, and extends to 20th-century society with the application by surrealist artists and film-makers of the controversial psychological insights into the subject made by Sigmund Freud. Because the aim of the encyclopedia is to be as diverse as possible, the use of taboos in traditional literature and folklore, such as the importance of the *geis* in medieval Irish texts, is also included.

Those topics naturally associated with the concept of taboo such as incest, cannibalism, food, sex, pollution and death are discussed in detail with theoretical analyses by major scholars in the field, while there are also separate entries for the foremost writers on the subject, including Sigmund Freud, Mary Douglas, Edmund Leach, Franz Steiner and Frederick Barth. This makes the encyclopedia useful for students and those with a specialist interest while at the same time introducing the general reader to the background and context of some familiar present-day taboos, such as table manners, dress and pornography. But not all entries are entirely serious in their aim: there is plenty to discover within these pages of an imaginative and fanciful nature, customs and prohibitions that betray a playfulness at work quite at odds with the gravity normally associated with taboo.

Entries are listed in an alphabetical order and are followed by cross-references and a bibliography.

List of Headwords

A

Art in China

Taboos in Traditional Chinese Art

Traditional Chinese painting had its Twelve Taboos (*shih-er chi*) as listed by Jao Tzu-jan (Yuan dynasty 1280-1368 CE). No painting should contain any of the following:

1 Cramped Layout (*pu-chih p' o-sai*)
2 Distances Undifferentiated (*yuên-jin pu-fen*)
3 Mountains Lacking Vital Energy and Underlying Veins (*shan wu ch' i-mai*)
4 Streams Lacking Sources and Flow-Direction (*shui wu yuên-liu*)
5 Terrains Lacking Plains and Steeps (*ching wu yi-hsien*)
6 Roads Leading and Coming from Nowhere (*lu-wu ch' u-ju*)
7 Rocks having Only One Face (*shih-chih yi-mien*)
8 Trees Lacking Full Branchage (*shu shao ssu-chih*)
9 Figures Hunched (*jên-we yu-lou*)
10 Buildings Jumbled Together (*lou-kê ts' o-tsa*)
11 Thickness and Thinness of Ink Inappropriate (*nung-tan shih-yi*)
12 Detail and Colouring-in Lacking Method (*tien-jan wu fa*)

Taboos on Painting the Eyes in Buddhist Art

In many Buddhist regions, painting the eyes is tantamount to bringing an image to life. The Theravada Buddhists of Ceylon have a rite named *netra pinkama* (eye ceremony) where the eyes of a statue of Buddha are painted in. It is a consecration of the figure which imbues it with life. An Englishman, Ronald Knox, was a prisoner in Ceylon from 1660 to 1679 where he witnessed the *netra pinkama*:

> The ceremony is regarded by its performers as very dangerous and is surrounded with tabus. It is performed by the craftsman who made the statue, after several hours of ceremonies to ensure that no evil will come to him. This evil ... is imprecisely conceptualized, but results from making mistakes in ritual, violating tabus, or otherwise arousing the malevolent attention of a supernatural being, who usually conveys the evil by a gaze (*bälma*). The craftsman paints in the eyes at an auspicious moment and is left alone in the closed temple with only his colleagues ... Moreover, the craftsman does not dare to look the statue in the face, but keeps his back to it and paints sideways or over his shoulder while looking into a mirror, which catches the gaze of the image he is bringing to life. As soon as the painting is done the craftsman himself has a dangerous gaze. He is then led out blindfolded and the

covering is only removed from his eyes when they will first fall upon something which he then symbolically destroys with a sword stroke (Freedberg, p. 85-86).

In Thailand and Cambodia the Buddhists prick the pupils with needles in order to "open the eyes" of the statue, a ritual also practised by the Hindus where a golden needle is used to open the eyes in the *netra moksa* ceremony.

The dangers of opening, or painting in, the eyes of an image are recounted in several traditional Chinese tales. The legendary Ku K'ai-chih only painted in the eyes of his dragons at the end as this would animate them. Chang-Seng-Yu, working in the temple in Chien-K'ang, refused to complete the eyes of his Four White Dragons lest they fly away. After persistent harassment by the crowd, he finally agreed, but he only dotted the pupils of two of the dragons. Immediately thunder and lightning tore the walls apart and the two dragons flew up into the sky leaving their eyeless companions alone in the temple. The wiser Wei-Hsieh refrained from painting in the eyes. Perhaps the French primitive painter, Henri Rousseau (1844-1910), who was said to be frightened by his own paintings, would have been less terrified of his tigers if he had followed Wei-Hsieh's example (Freedberg, p. 86, 458 n.19).

See also

Evil Eye; Iconoclasm; Looking or Seeing

References

Dolby, William. 1993. "A Preliminary Look at 'Twelve' in Chinese Traditions". *Shadow: The Journal of the Traditional Cosmology Society*, no. 10, p. 38-39. (trans. from Morohashi. 1960. *Dai Kan-Wa jiten*. Tokyo).

Freedberg, David. 1989. *The Power of Images*. Chicago, Illinois: University of Chicago Press.

B

Barth, Fredrik (1928-)

The ideas of the Norwegian anthropologist, Fredrik Barth, on taboo are largely derived from his fieldwork among the Baktaman of New Guinea. The Baktaman represent the notion of taboo by the term *eïm* which encompasses both restraints on behaviour and those things to which access is restricted. The cult leader is known as *Kinun-eïm* (*eïm* man). A breach of a taboo has magical and supernatural repercussions: wasting sickness or skin disease. From his research, Barth concludes that the Baktaman use taboo as a means of classification, not simply to create binary codes that reveal oppositions between the sacred and profane, or the strong and the weak, but by combining these codes they construct a complex network that embraces all important facets of the culture.

Although Baktaman taboos apply to many things, few have universal application. Things that are absolutely forbidden include the flesh of the *eiraram* marsupial, the domestic variety of rat, certain snakes and things grown within the village. Most taboos are related to status and may be permanent (restrictions on food, marriage, killing, touch, sight and knowledge are all subject to social status), or temporary (during menstruation, initiation, after eating wild pig, while in a temple or garden). Knowledge is carefully guarded. Within Baktaman society there are seven levels of initiation; at each level new

secrets are revealed and the neophyte learns that previously learned rules are false. The taboos on knowledge, which is unveiled in rituals, serve to impress upon the participants the importance of the forbidden. The anthropologist Radcliffe-Brown has argued that secrecy is a means by which sacred events and artefacts acquire their ritual and social value. Barth mentions the secret marsupial hunt, conducted during the third initiation, as an example of this, but finds that Radcliffe-Brown's proposition does not account for the disparities between junior and senior men in Baktaman society.

Barth also considers the theories of Ralph Bulmer and Edmund R. Leach. Bulmer argues that the closer to the ground an animal is, the "dirtier" it is, and therefore the more unsuitable for a person of a higher status. Among the Baktaman, men in a higher state of ritual purity must abstain from dirty foods like lizards and crayfish but the patterns of food avoidance are not so simple. Leach sees taboo as a convenient tool for creating clear distinctions between opposing categories: those ambiguous things that cross the boundaries are forbidden. One problem with applying Leach's theory to the Baktaman is that their taboos involve many different factors. Although there is a division between garden, village and forest, anything is allowed in the forest even if its proper place is in the temple. Few animals defy categorisation and those that do are not taboo to everyone: wild pigs live in the forest and rummage in the gardens yet they are only taboo to women and juniors and are eaten with impunity by senior men. Similarly, although the swallow, which flies through the air yet sleeps underground, transgresses the air-earth-subterranean divisions and is taboo to all, the cuscus (a marsupial) which burrows into the ground may be eaten by everyone.

Baktaman taboos, whether concerned with location, status, name or food avoidance, defy easy categorisation. Certain things must not be combined: pork fat and water, first-degree initiates and fire, the fire stones for cooking cassowary and those for cooking marsupials, pigs and man. Women are subject to fewer taboos than young males and the most extensive taboos concern eating and drinking. Many taboos surround initiates, who are particularly vulnerable at this time. Some taboos concern freedom of movement: women may not enter the houses of men or temples and men may not enter women's houses at night or menstrual huts; moreover, all are temporarily debarred from the whole village during the seventh initiation. On the basis of his observations Barth realises that for the Baktaman:

> Taboo is used to differentiate and separate objects and acts that are supposed to affect each other adversely. We may think of it as purity and pollution, but if so in the chemical sense whereby any basic substance may be purified and the presence of any and every other substance in the mixture is then an impurity or pollution.

The Baktaman clearly express the idea that things hedged by taboo are "strong" ... taboo both protects this strength and protects potential victims *from* the strength (Barth, p. 170).

Things may be separated because of the danger of pollution through dirt (like men in a higher state of ritual purity needing to avoid certain "dirty" foods) or the risk of knowledge being acquired too soon. Certain red and black birds represent knowledge which is not suitable until the sixth initiation. These are therefore taboo to lower-degree initiates who have only an inkling of the truth, but not to women, who know nothing, or fully-initiated men, who know all. Sexuality is another powerful force that needs to be contained:

> light-coloured and long-furred marsupials embody power of sexuality and growth which is too strong for 1st degree novices in their present precarious phase, and so they are taboo to them – but not to adult men and women, or to small children (Barth, p. 170).

Similarly, sexuality and strength are separated by a series of taboos. In this way, a structure can be created that encompasses all the particular dichotomies so that the Baktaman can generate "both a conceptual distinction and clarification, and an actual store of concentrated power of a certain kind" (Barth, p. 170).

See also

Food Taboos; Red

References

Barth, Frederick. 1975. *Ritual and Knowledge among the Baktaman of New Guinea*. Oslo: Universitetsforlaget; New Haven, Connecticut: Yale University Press.

Bulmer, Ralph. 1963. "Why the Cassowary is not a Bird". In Mary Douglas ed., *Rules and Meanings*, p. 167-193. Harmondsworth, Middlesex: Penguin.

Leach, Edmund. 1964. "Anthropological Aspects of Language: Animal Categories and Verbal Abuse". In Eric H. Lenneberg ed. *New Directions in the Study of Language*, p. 23-63. Cambridge, Massachusetts: MIT Press.

Radcliffe-Brown, Alfred Reginald. 1952. *Structure and Function in Primitive Society*. London: Cohen and West.

Bataille, Georges (1897-1962)

The French archivist and librarian, Georges Bataille wrote novels (often under pseudonyms), poetry and essays. His most famous novel, first published in 1928, is *The Story of the Eye*, a wild tale of sexual deviation and excess; other fiction includes *Madame Edwarda, The Blue of Noon, L'Abbe C, The Dead Man* and *My Mother*. The themes of Bataille's essays often echo those of his novels: eroticism and desire, religion and sacrifice, transgression and death. In 1957 he published both *Literature and Evil* and *Eroticism*.

The Story of the Eye was published in four versions (the first three appearing under the pseudonym "Lord Auch"); after the edition of 1928, versions appeared in 1940, 1941 and 1967. In the first narrative, the protagonist expresses his desires:

> I did not care for what is known as "pleasures of the flesh" because they really are insipid; I cared only for what is classified as dirty ... My kind of debauchery soils not only my body and my thoughts, but also anything I may conceive in its course, that is to say, the vast starry universe, which merely serves as a backdrop (p. 16 website)

Certainly, the novel revels in the breaking of taboos, including as it does scenes of masturbation, fellatio, cunnilingus, orgies, urination, coprophilia (sexual desire related to excrement), sacrilege, suicide, insanity, theft and murder. Themes are linked through a series of correspondences so that the eye of the title, essentially the eye of the voyeur, reappears in the eye of the suicide, the dead matador and the murdered priest, and is identified with eggs, testicles and the "eye" of the vagina.

Bataille's philosophical theory is developed in *La part maudite* (The Accursed Share: An Essay on General Economy), which appeared in 1949 and contains volumes devoted to consumption, eroticism and sovereignty, and in *Eroticism: Death and Sensuality,* which was originally published under the title, *Death and Sensuality: A Study of Eroticism and the Taboo. Eroticism* is the work in which Bataille most fully exposes his thoughts on taboo. In it he discusses the Marquis de Sade's concept of the "sovereign" man, Pomeroy and Martin Kinsey's reports on human sexuality, Sigmund Freud, eroticism, incest, prostitution, war, murder, sacrifice, death and religion. He is concerned to find the origins of taboo, religious ecstasy and the erotic impulse. Like Freud, Bataille believes that the tabooed object evokes both desire and repulsion. To satisfy a desire, it is necessary to overcome an initial anguish and break the taboo. The greater the initial anguish, the more satisfying the transgression. Exploring the relationship between fear and desire, eroticism and death, he shows how violence underlies not just sexual urges but also religious experience. Sacrifice has a pivotal role in religious experience and Christianity itself is founded on the notion of redemption through Christ's sacrifice on the Cross.

See also

de Sade, Marquis D.A.F; Freud, Sigmund; Necrophilia; Pornography; Surrealism

References

Bataille, Georges. [1957] 1987. *Eroticism*. trans. Mary Dalwood. London; New York: Marion Boyars.

Bataille, Georges. [1949] 1988-1991. *The Accursed Share: An Essay on General Economy*. trans. Robert Hurley. New York: Zone Books.

Bataille, Georges. [1928] 1977. *The Story of the Eye by Lord Auch*. trans. Joachim Neugroschel. New York: Urizen Books.

Bataille, Georges. 1989. *My Mother; Madame Edwarda, The Dead Man*. trans. Austryn Wainhouse. London; New York: Marion Boyars.

Bataille, Georges. 1983. *L'Abbé C*. trans. Philip A. Facey. London; New York: Boyars.

Bataille, Georges. 1986. *The Blue of Noon*. trans. Harry Mathews. London; New York: Boyars.

Georges Bataille in America Website: http://www.phreebyrd.com/~sisyphus/bataille/

Gill, Carolyn Bailey. ed., 1995. *Bataille: Writing the Sacred. Warwick Studies in European Philosophy*. London; New York: Routledge.

Hoyles, John. 1979. Georges Bataille 1897-62: "Jouissance and Revolution". In F. Barker, et. al., *The Sociology of Literature, Volume One The Politics of Modernism*. The University of Essex.

Beans

Although the Greek philosopher, Pythagoras, was credited with the placing of food taboos on carcass-meat, eggs and oviparous animals (those that produce young by means of eggs), it was the Pythagorean injunction against the eating of beans, an injunction that has also been attributed to another philosopher who followed his teachings, Empedocles, that captured the imagination. In Greece, beans were proscribed not only by the Pythagoreans but also by followers of Orphism. Outside Greece, according to the Greek historian, Herodotus, Egyptian priests would neither eat nor look at beans and in Rome the Flamens Dialis (priests) refused to utter their name.

Cicero tried to rationalise the taboo by pointing out that beans cause flatulence and that this would upset the tranquillity of mind necessary for prophetic dreams. While caution is always necessary when dealing with "rational" explanations for taboos, it is true that a primary aim of the Pythagoreans was to contact divinities, initially those of the underworld, and that the preferred method of contact involved "incubation", awaiting a dream or vision while asleep. Iamblichus, in *Pythagorean Life*, claimed that Pythagoras "rejected all foods that produce flatulence or cause disorder … all foods which interfere with divination … anything that conflicted with ritual cleanliness and rendered turbid the various purities of the soul – especially the purity of the visions it sees during dreams" (Kingsley, p. 283-286).

Certainly, beans and the world of the dead were linked in some way. Kingsley surmises that the connection between beans and the chthonic (underworld) realms led to interpretations of the taboo that tied it in with the doctrine of reincarnation and that the statement of Iamblichus was proof of a continuing link between the taboo and divination in later Pythagoreanism (Kingsley, p. 286). Beans played a role in the Eleusinian Mysteries held near Athens in honour of Demeter and her daughter, Kore or Persephone, who was abducted by Hades and carried off to the underworld. Besides the world of the dead, beans, in the Pythagorean tradition, were associated with "human flesh and male semen, the female womb and a child's head; eating beans was considered cannibalism" (Burkert, 1983, p. 285).

The connection between beans, death and cannibalism is explained by the Roman writer, Pliny the Elder. He noted that beans, for the Pythagoreans, served as abodes for dead souls which was the reason they were used in memorial services for dead relatives. To eat the bean would be equivalent to eating the human soul and would deny that soul the opportunity for reincarnation.

Aulus Gellius, writing in the 2nd century CE, thought the whole taboo surrounding beans was a mistake and that Pythagoras had loved the laxative qualities of beans. The mistake arose, he claimed, because of a line supposedly written by Empedocles: "Wretches, utter wretches, keep your hands from beans". Empedocles, here, was not referring to beans but to testicles, called beans because they are the cause of pregnancy (*kuein* in Greek means "to be pregnant" and the word for beans is *kuamos*). Therefore, argues Gellius, Empedocles was calling for sexual restraint rather than a ban on bean-eating (Barnes, p. 205-207).

The French anthropologist, Claude Lévi-Strauss, has discovered several parallels between the Pythagorean views on broad beans (*faba*) and the symbolism of the native American bean (Lévi-Strauss, p. 32-41). Both in Greece and the New World beans have been associated with death or, more precisely, as Marcel Detienne puts it, they have been regarded as intermediaries between the dead and the living, life and death. The native American Pawnee of Missouri relate a story that is reminiscent of the

Greek myth of Orpheus and Euridice. In their version, the hero, having succeeded in rescuing his wife from the underworld, halts at the dwelling of his supernatural helper whom he had visited on his outward journey. She presents him with some red beans which, if eaten, will enable the people of his village to commune with the dead. A variant of this tale supposes that the beans would, on the contrary, serve to bewitch the living.

Lévi-Strauss sees links between the role of beans in this myth and Ovid's description of the festival of Lemuria or Lemuralia which took place over three days, 9, 11 and 13 May. The purpose of the festival was to bring offerings to the ghosts of ancestors who returned to their old homes during the days of the festival. During the ceremony, the head of the family had to walk barefoot, making the mystic sign with his first and fourth fingers extended and with the other fingers turned inward and with the thumb crossed over them, so that he should not be harmed if he inadvertently bumped into a ghost. He then washed his hands and threw black beans over his shoulders, saying "with these beans I buy back myself and my family". He repeated this nine times without looking behind him at the ghost who was thought to have followed and picked up the beans. Then the master of the house washed once more, clashed bronze, and requested the ghost to leave, repeating nine times "Spirits of my ancestors, depart!". He then looked round and concluded the ceremony as the ghosts would not return for another year (Ovid V, 436ff. in Lévi-Strauss, p. 35).

Beans are also used to exorcise demons in the Japanese feast of Setsubun, just before the coming of spring. The beans, usually soybeans, are scattered about the house to scare away the demons with the chants, *Oni-wa soto* (Out with the evil demons) and *Fuka-wa uchi* (In with good luck). Then family members eat as many beans as the years they have lived. In Nagoya, the ceremony is performed in certain shrines and people queue up to be purified by the priest. The term *setsubun* was originally used to designate the eve of the first day of any of the twenty-four divisions of the solar year known as *setsu*. Later it was specifically applied to the last day of the *setsu* named *daiken* (great cold), which corresponded to the eve of Risshun (the first day of spring), the New Year's Day of the ancient solar calendar.

Besides the association with the spirit realm, beans in the New World also have a sexual symbolism in common with classical Greece. In a creation myth of the Kaingang of Southern Brazil, beans are formed from the testicles of the primal ancestor (Lévi-Strauss, p. 37). Lévi-Strauss speculates that just as the coconut in New Guinea represents both the male testicles and the female breasts, so beans may denote not only testicles but the swellings of nubile girls. They therefore mediate between the female and the male, and, by extension, between the states of life and death. However, there is no indication of any rules forbidding the consumption of beans in the New World and Lévi-Strauss himself confesses to being mystified by the friezes of Mochica (pre-Inca Peruvian Indian) ceramics that represent half-human, half-bean figures. These figures, once interpreted, should shed more light on the meaning of beans in the New World.

See also
Food Taboos

References

Barnes, Jonathan. [1988] 1997. *Early Greek Philosophy*. London: Penguin

Burkert, Walter. [1972] 1983. *Homo Necans*, trans. Peter Bing, Berkeley; Los Angeles; London: University of California Press.

Burkert, Walter. 1972. *Lore and Science in Ancient Pythagoreanism*. trans. E. Minar, Cambridge, Massachusetts: Harvard University Press.

Detienne, Marcel. 1972. *Jardins d'Adonis (La mythologie des aromates en Grece)*. Paris: Gallimard.

Felton, D. 1999. *Haunted Greece and Rome: Ghost Stories from Antiquity*. Austin, Texas: University of Texas Press.

Kingsley, Peter. 1995. *Ancient Philosophy, Mystery and Magic. Empedocles and Pythagorean Tradition.* Oxford: Oxford University Press.

Lévi-Strauss, Claude. 1979. "Pythagoras in America". In R. H. Hook ed. *Fantasy and Symbol. Studies in Anthropological Interpretation*, p. 32-41. London: Academic Press.

Begging

While begging is promoted as a spiritual ideal in certain religious traditions such as Hinduism and Buddhism, under Islamic law it is discouraged, although the giving of alms (*sadaqah*) is a religious duty. For those who still have provisions for a day and a night it is forbidden to beg. Despite this injunction, certain dervishes collected alms and the Sufi holy man al-Hujwiri gave three permissible reasons for begging:

> First, for the sake of mental liberty, since no anxiety is so engrossing as worry about getting something to eat; second, for the soul's discipline: Sufis beg because it is so humiliating and helps them to realise how little they are worth in other men's opinion, so that they escape self-esteem; third, to beg from men out of reverence for God, regarding all as his agents – a servant who petitions an agent is humbler than one who makes petition to God himself ... I once saw a venerable old Sufi who had lost his way in the desert come starving into the market-place at Kufah with a sparrow perched on his hand crying "Give me something, for the sparrow's sake". "Why do you say that?", people asked. "I can't say 'for God's sake'", he replied, "one must let an insignificant creature plead for worldly things" (Glassé, p. 70).

Animals are commonly associated with beggars. In North Africa the beggars' order of the Heddawa treats cats as humans, although this does not prevent them from being ritually slaughtered on occasion. Within Britain it is not illegal to beg if one is completely destitute as long as there is no harassment of potential donors. However, rather than sparrows or cats, dogs often accompany the supplicants, favoured perhaps for their large appealing eyes.

See also

Necrophagy and Asceticism

Reference

Glassé, Cyril. 1989. *The Concise Encyclopedia of Islam.* London: Stacey Publications.

Blue

Although blue is the colour of the clear summer sky, the colour of heaven and of the robes of the Virgin in Renaissance paintings (the azure pigment, lapis lazuli, being extremely valuable), it also has a more sinister side. Marina Warner mentions the tale of Bluebeard, in which a brutal murderer, who forbids his new bride to enter a certain room (frequently a blue chamber), is distinguished by the unnatural hue of his luxuriant beard:

> The colour blue, the colour of ambiguous depth, of the heavens and the abyss at once, encodes the frightening character of Bluebeard, his house and his deeds ... The chamber he forbids his wife becomes a blue chamber in some retellings: blue is the colour of the shadow side, the tint of the marvellous and the inexplicable, of desire, of knowledge, of the blueprint, the blue movie, of blue talk, of raw meat and rare steak (*un steak bleu*, in French), of melancholy, the rare and the unexpected (singing the blues, once in a blue moon, out of the blue, blue blood) (Warner, p. 243).

Predictably, Bluebeard's bride enters the forbidden room and discovers the hanging bodies of his murdered wives. Also to be avoided are "The Blue Men of the Minch" who swim out to wreck ships in the waters around the Shiant Islands off the north-west coast of Scotland, candles that burn blue (without a red flare) which portend death or signal the presence of ghosts, and the "blue devils", apparitions seen when suffering *delirium tremens*.

"Blue" is also used to denote the obscene. Blue movies, which contain sexually explicit scenes, have frequently been banned by film censors. In 1922 the Hays office was established in the United States of America to monitor the sexual content of films, a move that followed the establishment of the British Board of Film Censors in 1912. No doubt the script was subjected to the "blue pencil", that erased the forbidden. The ultimate blue movie, however, contains no scenes of sex (or of anything else). Called *Blue*, it was made by the British film-maker, Derek Jarman, shortly before his death from AIDS. Throughout the film, the screen remains a uniform blue, while the narrator, now blind as a result of the disease, describes all things blue.

In New Haven, Connecticut, severe puritanical laws, enacted in the 18th century, were known as "blue laws". The physiological dangers of the colour are indicated by Kandinsky, who proposed that blue light can cause temporary paralysis to the heart, while Goethe states in his *Theory of Colours* that blue "brings a principle of darkness with it, gives an impression of cold, reminds us of shade, affinity to black, the appearance of objects seen through a dark glass is gloomy and melancholy" (Goethe, p. 310-311).

References

Goethe, Johann Wolfgang von. [1810] 1973. *Theory of Colours*. trans. Charles Lock Eastlake. Cambridge, Massachusetts: MIT Press.

Kandinsky, Wassily. [1914] 1977. *Concerning the Spiritual in Art*. trans. M. T. H. Sadler. New York: Dover Publications.

Warner, Marina. 1994. *From the Beast to the Blonde: On Fairytales and Their Tellers*. London: Chatto and Windus.

C

Camels

Camels are forbidden within Judaism because, according to *Leviticus*, they are ruminants that do not have the requisite cloven hoofs (11:4). Although camels differ anatomically from true ruminants, they do ferment, regurgitate and chew the cud and are the only true cud-chewers whose flesh is tabooed. (The Levite priests erroneously classed hares as cud-chewers.) Marvin Harris identifies pragmatic motives for the ban. Although ideally adapted to survival in harsh conditions, the camel is less efficient than the sheep or goat at converting cellulose into meat and milk. Moreover, it only ruts once a year, and then, not until the age of six, and gestation takes twelve months. Though the patriarchs might have valued the beasts for desert transportation, they would not have been an important source of food. On the other hand, the camel is ideally suited to desert regions; capable of conserving fat within its hump and withstanding sandstorms, it can also bear great weights and is invaluable to the nomadic Bedouin for both transport and, when occasion demands, food. Before their conversion to Islam, Arabs ate camel flesh and the animal has been traditionally revered throughout the Islamic world. The public slaughter of camels on ceremonial occasions was banned in Iran as recently as 1933. Before this time, flesh from the sacrificed animal was given to the sick and the 13th-century Spanish naturalist, Ibn al-Baytar extols the medic-inal and magical uses of camel milk, meat and urine within the Islamic world (Simoons, p. 88).

However, while Harris may have illustrated why camel flesh was more important to the desert nomads than to the Israelite pastoralists, he fails to explain the necessity for a biblical injunction if the animal was, in any case, rarely eaten – the taboo remains enigmatic.

Certain Christians have rejected camel meat, most notably the 5th-century hermit Simon Stylites, who forbade the flesh to his Saracen converts and the Coptic Christians of Egypt and Ethiopian Christians who are subject to excommunication if they ignore the ban. It is also proscribed to the Zoroastrians of Iran and the Mandaeans of Iraq and Iran, and Hindus neither eat its flesh nor drink its milk. In China, there is no general ban. In the north, the Bactrian camel, known as both a wild and domesticated animal, was much appreciated during the T'ang dynasty (618-907 CE). The hump, in particular, was a favourite ingredient in stews, if the poets Tu Fu and Ts'en Shen are to be believed, and later recipes mention spit-roasting. Camel fat was also used to cook rice-cakes – sold by Iranian street vendors – with the interesting virtue of curing haemorrhoids (Schafer, p. 99, 117-118).

References

Schafer, Edward H. 1977. "T'ang". In *Food in Chinese Culture: Anthropological and Historical Perspectives*, ed. K. C. Chang, p. 85-140. New Haven, Connecticut; London: Yale University Press.

Simoons, Frederick J. [1961] 1967. *Eat not This Flesh: Food Avoidances in the Old World*. Madison, Wisconsin: University of Wisconsin Press.

Cannabis Sativa L.

Cannabis sativa, the cultivated hemp, was named by Linnaeus in 1753. In Morocco and along the North African Coast, it is known as kif; in the Middle-East, Egypt and Iran as hashish; in India, the drink made from brewing cannabis is called bhang while the resinous material that is smoked is known as ganja – a name also used in Jamaica where the plant was introduced by Indian workers. The Mexican name, marijuana, is used in the United States and Canada, along with many other nicknames. Although it is surrounded by taboos, and is actually illegal in most Western countries, it has been around for a long time. There is evidence that it may have already been gathered in the Late Neolithic Age and, apart from Egypt, it was widely cultivated – for rope or cloth – during the Bronze and Iron Ages.

An early use of cannabis was medical. A Chinese pharmacopoeia, the *Pen T'sao Ching,* ascribed to the legendary Emperor, Shen-Nung ("Divine Cultivator") of the 3rd millennium BCE, but probably compiled about the 1st century CE during the late Han Dynasty, recommends the ingestion of cannabis for "female weakness, gout, rheumatism, malaria, beriberi, constipation, and absent-mindedness" (Emboden, p. 217). Its resin, mixed with wine, was used as an anaesthetic in 220 CE by the surgeon, Hua-T'o, who claimed to perform pain-free operations. A more magical medical application is contained in the *Shu-King*, written in 500 BCE. It speaks of a rod, with a serpent coiling around it, that is carved from the woody plant and used in curing rituals: beaten on the bed of a sick person, it drives away evil spirits.

Cannabis as an hallucinogen, to induce delirium and visions, was known by the pre-Socratic Greek philosopher, Democritus, (c. 460 BCE) as *potamaugus.* It was drunk with wine and myrrh and kindled, he observed, "immoderate laughter". That it was also smoked, or at least inhaled, is indicated by the Greek term, *cannabeizein,* which means to smoke cannabis. Mixed, as a resin, in an incense burner together with the resins of myrrh, balsam, frankincense and perfumes, its vapours were inhaled. The Greek botanist, Theophrastus (371-287 BCE) gives an accurate account of the plant, which he names *dendromalache,* and the Roman writer, Lucilius (c.100 BCE) describes its use. One person to mention both the medicinal and the social applications of cannabis is the famous physician, Galen (130-200 CE): mixed with wine and drunk at the end of banquets, it promoted warmth, pleasure and excitement.

The Greek historian, Herodotus (born in 484 BCE) records in his *Histories* that the Scythians, a nomadic tribe occupying an area from northern Iran to central Siberia and to the north and west of the Black Sea, threw hemp seeds on red-hot stones and the smoke made them "so happy that they howled in joy" (4.75). Aeschylus (525-456 BCE) also mentions hemp being thrown on the fire, and the smoke inhaled, and archaeologists excavating burial mounds at Pazaryk, in the Altai, have discovered bronze vessels containing the stones which were heated to produce the potent hemp-seed vapours and also the seeds themselves. S. I. Rudenko surmised that these objects were used for purification ceremonies following a funeral (Emboden, p. 223). It is possible that the use of cannabis in Scythian funeral rituals is a result of their brief domination by the Thracian Getae in the early 6th century BCE. The Getae shamans used hemp smoke to induce a visionary trance during their healing which involved an arduous journey to the realm of the spirits to retrieve lost souls.

The intoxicant was most likely transmitted to India by the Iranian tribes. The resins were extracted and used to treat dysentery, sunstroke, phlegmatic tempers, indigestion and muddled intellect. Drunk as bhang by Hindus, it aided devotion, elevated consciousness and fostered closer union with the divine. It is still used in present-day India. The British anthropologist, Colin Turnbull, recalls living in an ashram in Banaras (now Varanasi), and celebrating the feast of Holi which commemorates the life of the god, Krishna. It is celebrated by spraying brightly coloured water and consuming drinks and delicacies laced with bhang. Participating fully, Turnbull experienced leaving his body and floating above the clouds until he reached the Himalayas and found the frozen source of the sacred river Ganges, emerging from a black cavern. Returning to his body and the ashram, he was told that many Hindu sages used bhang to separate mind from body but it was dangerous; far wiser was the traditional way of training body and mind together.

Hashish is named after the Persian, al-Hasan ibn-al-Sabbah (1124 CE), whose full name was Hashishin ibn-al Sabbah. He was raised in the Ismailite tradition, an esoteric movement which advocated an allegorical interpretation of the Koran. Personally ambitious and charismatic, he attracted young men who were dissenters from orthodox Muslim thought and who came to be known as hashishin. The term is anglicised as "Assassins". In 1090 al-Hasan and his followers took possession of the high mountain fortress Alamut, near the towns of Baghdad and Basra. The sect grew till it had more than 12,000 members with Hasan designated as "Grand Master", and his companions as "Grand Priors", "Spreaders of the Faith", or "Fiad'is", the lowest order, whose duty was to execute all those who were considered a threat to the faith. By plundering the caravans from the East heading for Baghdad, the hashishin were able to amass great wealth and transform the fortress, constructing elaborate palaces and gardens. Passing through the region in 1271, fifty years after al-Hasan's death, Marco Polo describes the Grand Master's court:

> He kept at his court a number of the youths of the country, from twelve to twenty years of age, such as had a taste

for soldiering ... He would introduce them into his garden ... having first made them drink a certain potion which cast them into a deep sleep ... When therefore they awoke and found themselves in a place so charming, they deemed it was Paradise ... and the ladies and damsels dallied with them to their heart's content. When the Old Man would have any prince slain, he would say to such a youth: "Go thou and slay So and So; and when thou returnest my angels shall bear thee into Paradise" (Emboden, p. 221-222).

Unfortunately, as William Emboden explains in his detailed study of the ritual use of cannabis, Marco Polo was not adverse to a little slander. There is no evidence that hashish was used to intoxicate the Assassins; neither is it certain that the slaughter attributed to the sect was as bloodthirsty as claimed (although it is perhaps callous to suggest that killing can be anything else). As all the books and documents of the cult were destroyed when Alamut was seized by the Mongolian Hulagu, grandson of Ghenghis Khan, in 1256, and as most of the information about the Hashishin comes from Hulagu's descendants, a suspension of credulity is probably wise.

Hashish is mentioned in another Oriental source. *The Thousand Nights and One Night*, a medieval collection of tales composed between 800 and 1400 CE, gives important insights into Oriental folklore and the court life of Persia, Arabia, India and Egypt. In "The Tale of the Two Hashish-Eaters", a Sultan, disguised as a merchant, is amused by two men who "swallow enough hashish to destroy a hundred-year-old elephant", undress completely, dance, sing, and attempt to urinate on the disguised ruler. As the tales, whether erotic or scatological, delight in the violation of taboos, it is difficult to know whether hashish was acceptable at the time. Certainly, there is a note of irony when the storyteller, Shahrazad, declares "Allah had willed that the Kadi [a minor magistrate] should also be addicted to the use of hashish", considering that intoxication results in the cheerful flouting of Allah's laws.

Kif is the name by which the resin of *Cannabis Sativa* is now known in North Africa. It is not clear how cannabis entered the African continent; it probably came from Saudi Arabia or India. Cultivated in the Valley of the Zambezi before 1500 CE, it was initially thrown on burning coals and inhaled through hollow reeds but the tribes of the Upper Zambezi later made pipes from gourds, bamboo stalks and coconut bowls in which they smoked both the resins and the leaves. It was in North Africa that the water pipe was developed. In this region too, the Islamic injunction against alcohol has led to the widespread use of kif although the substance is officially discouraged.

When Napoleon conquered Egypt in around 1800, the use of hashish was widespread. He banned its use throughout the country, as much to protect his own soldiers as the indigenous population, but with limited success. In Europe, in the mid-19th century, Cannabis intoxication became a source of inspiration for the literary Romantic movement. The Parisian poet, Theophile Gautier, described his hallucinations after ingesting an extract:

> It seemed that my body had dissolved and become transparent. I saw inside me the hashish I had eaten in the form of an emerald which radiated millions of tiny sparks ... I heard the shattering and crumbling of multi-coloured jewels ... Millions of butterflies, with wings beating like fans, continuously swarmed in a faintly luminous atmosphere. I heard the sounds of colours: green, red, blue and yellow sounds in successive waves. An overturned glass echoed through me like thunder ... I became entirely disengaged from myself, absent from my body, that odious witness which accompanies you wherever you are (Nahas, p. 16-17).

Gautier prefaces his novel about a transvestite, *Mademoiselle de Maupin*, with a declaration that abandonment to the senses is the will of God. In 1844 *Le Club des Haschischins* was founded by Gautier and his friends to further this aim. One of the members was the leading French decadent poet, Charles Baudelaire.

Gautier's observations were used in the appendix of publications by the medical practitioner, Jacques Joseph Moreau, regarded by many as the founder of clinical psychopharmacology. Moreau had been experimenting with common medieval potions in the treatment of mental illness in his patients. In 1841 he substituted hashish, after testing it on himself, and experiencing euphoria and hallucinations. Another Western physician, Sir William O'Shaughnessy Brooke, who served with the British East India Company, published an article in Calcutta in 1839 which described how he had found cannabis successful in the treatment of rabies, rheumatism, epilepsy and tetanus.

Marijuana was first imported into the United States from Mexico in 1910. In Mexico itself, it was not known until the Spanish Conquest. The indigenous population has its own powerful narcotics including the hallucinogen, peyote, derived from the cactus. But *Cannabis sativa*, known as "The Herb Which Makes One Speak", has been known to replace peyote in sacred rituals when the native intoxicant was scarce. Before it was imported from Mexico, hemp had been cultivated in the United States for its fibres, used in the production of rope, twine, sailcloth and sacks. In 1857 Fitz Hugh Ludlow, an amateur psychopharmacologist, published *The Hasheesh Eater*, an account of his experiences after taking huge quantities of Tilden's Extract of *Cannabis sativa indica*, a drug used at the time to treat epilepsy and rheumatism. Initially terrified, he later experienced visions of a heavenly Paradise in which he heard celestial chords. The harmony of the spheres convinced Ludlow that he was a reincarnated member of the school of Pythagoras that had existed in Greece from the

6th century BCE and that Pythagoras himself must have partaken of this elixir.

When, in the 20th century, marijuana entered the United States from Mexico it was smoked in the form of cigarettes by poor black and Mexican workers in Texas and Louisiana. After the First World War it was incorporated into the emerging jazz culture and its proliferation so worried the Federal Bureau of Narcotics that it prompted Congress to pass the Marijuana Tax Act of 1937. This outlawed the cultivation, possession and distribution of hemp plants. Already in 1925 Egypt had asked the International Opium Conference to place cannabis in the same category as the opiates in an attempt to curtail its use in the Middle East.

Nonetheless, *Cannabis sativa* enjoyed a resurgence of popularity in the 1950s and 1960s in Britain, the United States and the rest of the Western World with the emergence of rock music, subcultures and an inquisitive and questioning youth. Dr John Kaplan, a distinguished professor of law at Stanford University, argued that banning marijuana constituted a new Prohibition; being less harmful than alcohol or tobacco, it should, he claimed, be commercially available.

The debate over its legalisation continues. Meanwhile it has again become a sacred substance for the Rastafarians of Jamaica. Taking their name from Ras (Prince) Tafari Makonnen, who became Emperor Haile Selassie of Ethiopia in 1930 and whom they venerate as the Messiah, the Rastafarians refer to ganja as a mystic herb, divinely sanctioned, and claim it as the "seed-bearing plant" of *Genesis* 1. 11-12. Ganja is smoked in "spliffs", longer than American joints, and is a means of attaining illumination and spiritual inspiration.

References

De Ropp, Robert S. 1958. *Drugs and the Mind*. London.

Emboden, Jr., William A. 1972. "Ritual Use of *Cannabis Sativa L.*: A Historical-Ethnographic Survey". In *Flesh of the Gods: The Ritual Use of Hallucinogens*. ed. Peter T. Furst. p. 214-236. London: George Allen and Unwin.

Fackelmann, Kathy. 1993. "Marijuana and the Brain". *Science News*, no. 143, p. 88-94.

La Barre, Weston. 1977. "Anthropological Views of Cannabis". *Reviews in Anthropology*, no. 4, p. 237-250.

Nahas, Gabriel G. [1976] 1979. *Keep off the Grass: A Scientific Enquiry into the Biological Effects of Marijuana*. Oxford: Pergamon Press.

The Book of the Thousand Nights and One Night. vol. 3. 1986. Tale of the 797 and 798 Nights, p. 520-523. London: Routledge and Kegan Paul.

Turnbull, Colin. 1961. "While I Was Always Conscious ..." In *The Drug Experience*. ed. David Ebin. New York: Orion Press.

Usdin, Earl and Daniel H. Efron. 1979. *Psychotropic Drugs and Related Compounds*. Oxford: Pergamon Press.

Cannibalism

Cannibalism or anthropophagy (man-eating) has always been, as anthropologist Lévi-Strauss would say, "good to think". Those who are distant in time or place are commonly perceived to be cannibals. In the 5th century BCE the Greek historian, Herodotus, recorded *Anthrophagi* (man-eaters) living next to the Scythians, a people on the eastern rim of Greek civilisation. The popular term "cannibal" is a derivation, via Spanish, of Caribs, the name of a native race which occupied the southern islands of the West Indies at the time of their discovery by the Spanish at the end of the 15th century. Christopher Columbus confused Caribs with *cani-ba* and the "*canine*" great Khan of China, and coined the term "cannibal" (White, p. 63). He is responsible for the proliferation of the rumour that Caribs were cannibals: although he had personally witnessed no flesh-eating he mentions man-eating Caribs in a letter that was printed and disseminated throughout Europe (Arens, 1980, p. 44-46). Since the time of Columbus, travellers and, later, anthropologists, have reported the existence of cannibals in almost every part of the globe. Curiously there are remarkably few eye witness accounts of the actual deed; usually the ethnographer merely repeats a statement concerning the habits of a neighbouring tribe (which, in the best traditions of calumny, tends to be incestuous as well as flesh-devouring). This lack of reliable data, added to the disconcerting fact that he himself was accused of being a cannibal, has prompted the anthropologist, William Arens to question the very existence of cannibals in his book *The Man-Eating Myth*.

Whether or not anthropophagy is a myth, myths certainly contain anthropophagy. In Hesiod's *Theogony*, composed around the end of the 8th century BCE, the father of Zeus, Kronos, swallows his own children as they are born from Gaia, until he is tricked into swallowing a stone instead. In another Greek myth of roughly the same date (which appears in Book Nine of Homer's *Odyssey*), Odysseus encounters the Cyclops who lives in a cave on a distant island inhabited by his fellows: wild, lawless giants with no knowledge of agriculture. Ignorant of table manners, the Cyclops systematically eats the companions of Odysseus until blinded and duped by the wily hero. With the idea of man-eating firmly planted in his imagination through tales such as these, it is not difficult to imagine Herodotus' description of a people living beyond the Scythian borders:

> The anthrophagi have the most savage customs of all men; they pay no regard to justice, nor make use of any established law. They are nomads, and wear a dress like a Scythian; they speak a peculiar language; and of these nations are the only people that eat human flesh (*The Histories* 4.18).

The anthropophagi were just one among the many unusual races reported by Herodotus and other Greek travellers such as Ktesias of Knodos (beginning of the 4th century BCE), Megasthenes (4th century BCE) and conquerors like Alexander the Great. Strabo, a geographer of the 1st century CE, criticised his predecessors for their naive belief in monstrous races and was sceptical of cannibalism. About Ireland he writes:

> Concerning this island I have nothing to tell, except that the inhabitants are more savage than the Britons, since they are man-eaters, ... and since they count it an honourable thing, when their fathers die, to devour them ... but I am only saying this with the understanding that I have no trustworthy witnesses for it (Arens, 1980, p. 14).

Others have not been so scrupulous. St. Jerome needed no trustworthy witnesses to claim that the pre-Christian Scots and Picts were cannibals, an accusation that was also levied at the Christians by the Romans in the 2nd century. Jews in Alexandria in the 1st century BCE were said to worship a donkey's head and consume the corpses of those they had ritually murdered (Ginzberg, p. 74). Sadly for the Jews, allegations that the blood of Christian children was necessary for their rituals continued throughout the Middle Ages and persisted into the 20th century, providing a pretext for pogroms and expulsions. Another European group persistently denounced for infanticide and cannibalism is that of witches, or at least those indicted for witchcraft. In the 15th century, during the Inquisition, the Bernese judge, Peter von Greyerz, condemned several witches to death at the stake. During interrogation they revealed that it was their practice to attack unbaptised children or those not protected by a crucifix:

> The corpses of the children, killed with magical ceremonies, were removed from the graves in which they had been buried: the witches put them in a pot to cook until the flesh turned to pulp and fell off the bones. The more solid part was used as an ointment for magical practices and metamorphoses; the more liquid part was poured into a flask or a leather bottle and, in conjunction with certain ceremonies,

given to those wishing to become teachers of the sect to drink (Ginzburg, p. 70).

The unspeakable appetites of the witches extended to the sexual sphere: witches were generally depicted as females and subsequent accounts of witches' sabbaths describe orgies in which naked women copulate with the devil. A correlation between cannibalism and sexual deviancy remained in the minds of the European explorers and was projected onto those in the New World whom they encountered (Mason, p. 54-59).

In fact, just as the myths of Hesiod and Homer coloured Herodotus' accounts of foreigners, so the European legends of anthropophagy provided a model for travellers to the New World in the 15th century (Arens, 1980, p. 95). Over the following centuries, not only the Caribs and their neighbours, but the Aztecs, Africans, Native Americans, Fijians and other groups in the Pacific, the Australian Aborigines, the Maori of New Zealand, and virtually every group encountered, was believed to eat its fellows. The study of anthropophagy was refined: scholars defined different types of cannibalism such as exocannibalism (the eating of enemies, slaves or prisoners-of-war), endocannibalism (devouring relatives), autocannibalism (ingesting parts of one's own body), ritual cannibalism (for religious purposes), nutritional cannibalism (to provide an added source of protein or to prevent starvation) and medical cannibalism.

Michael Harner and Marvin Harris are materialists who adhere to the idea of nutritional cannibalism. This, they claim, was the reason for the extensive human sacrifice of the Aztecs. Harner argues that a diet based on maize in an area depleted of wild game and lacking domesticated herbivores would suffer a severe protein deficiency. The protein was supplied by eating prisoners-of-war, the flesh of which served as a reward for Aztec soldiers unused to eating meat. As evidence of the widespread practice of cannibalism, Harner cites reports by conquistadores such as Hernando Cortés, Bernal Díaz and the priest, Fray Bernando de Sahagún. He accuses his professional colleagues of underestimating the number of humans sacrificed which he estimates to be a quarter of a million annually. Marvin Harris similarly sees a substantial increase in population in the Valley of Mexico and a corresponding lack of animal protein as the explanation for Aztec cannibalism.

Marshall Sahlins rejects such a utilitarian view. He sees Aztec cannibalism as a religious phenomenon: consuming human flesh in a ritualistic setting was a sacred event. Eating the consecrated victim created a link with the divine and the human sacrifice re-enacted the original sacrifice of the gods that set the sun in motion.

Others, such as Donald Tuzin study the psychological aspects of cannibalism. Tuzin observed that the Arapesh of New Guinea were horrified by the Japanese during the Second World War, who resorted to cannibalism as a result of their extreme hunger. Tuzin thinks the intense fear of anthropophagy among the Arapesh may be due to a past period when famine caused parents to eat their own children and that the fear of the cannibal monster may be based on the oral-aggressive fantasies of early childhood (Tuzin, p. 70).

Peggy Reeves Sanday, in her evocatively titled book, *Divine Hunger*, conducts a cross-cultural survey of cannibalism to discover how its function changes to accommodate the world-views and symbolic systems of different societies. For instance, in ritual cannibalism, the victim may symbolise the evil or chaos that has to be overcome to maintain social order. Besides this, certain acts of mortuary cannibalism (where the dead are ritually consumed), like those performed by the Hua and the Bimin-Kuskusmin of Papua New Guinea, recycle the vital forces of the newly dead to the living and provide a sense of social continuity. Sanday does not question the existence of cannibalism in the regions she studies, relying on the reports of ethnographers, but in *The Man-Eating Myth* William Arens indicts the anthropologists for their gullibility and argues that most reports of anthropophagy are merely myths.

His suspicions, as mentioned earlier, were first aroused during fieldwork in Tanzania in 1968 when he himself was suspected of "blood-sucking". Europeans were believed to kill and drain the blood of local Tanzanians; this was taken by fire engine to a local hospital to be converted into pills which were necessary if white people were to survive in Africa. The question arose: if Africans had constructed such erroneous stories about Europeans, could western tales of African cannibalism be equally spurious? On inspection, there turned out to be few first-hand accounts of cannibalism and those that did exist were often implausible. A German, Hans Staden, had described his capture by Tupinamba Indians on the South-American coast in the 16th century and reported dialogues between the Indians even though it is unlikely that he understood their language, especially during the first encounter when they discussed his potential as meat (Arens, 1980, p. 22-27). Records of Aztec cannibalism are similarly difficult to substantiate: Cortéz and his colleagues never claimed to have actually witnessed the eating of prisoners and a description by an officer of Cortéz of "roasted babies" found among the provisions of captured Aztecs was probably a calculated attempt to malign the Indians. The arguments of Harner and Harris, namely that Aztecs needed the human flesh for nutritional purposes, has proved unfounded – any protein deficiency suffered by the Indians was the result of Spanish intervention which banned certain protein-rich crops such as amaranth and prevented food importation (Arens, 1980, p. 55-80).

Arens thinks that political and economic considerations played a considerable role in the spread of the man-eating myth. Christopher Columbus never actually visited the island of the Caribs but based his evidence on the neighbouring Arawaks (Mason, p. 54). However, he saw the possibility of using the Caribs as slaves to work in mines and on plantations. Official Spanish royal policy prohibited the enslavement of the islanders; only those of the Cannibal race were exempt, a clause that naturally led to the identification of ever more Cannibals in hitherto uncharted territory (Arens, 1980, p. 44-54). The depiction of foreigners as uncultured man-eaters helped palliate the guilt of the colonisers who could claim they were bringing civilisation to savages.

What has made Arens' book controversial is his accusation that 19th- and 20th-century anthropologists have perpetuated the myth of anthropophagy, misinterpreting data and believing second-hand accounts, reconstructing a cannibalistic past from untenable evidence and failing to grasp the intense hostility towards, or fear of, "the other" that has caused tribes to accuse other tribes of man-eating, whether they be literate or non-literate, African or European. When Lieutenant James King, an officer on Captain Cook's ship, questioned the Hawaiians as to whether they had eaten part of the Captain's body after he was killed, they were horrified. Not partaking of human flesh, they could only come to the logical conclusion: that Europeans did (Obeyesesekere, p. 138).

Since the book's publication, anthropologists have made a sustained effort to find concrete, or at least, tangible, evidence of anthropophagy. Tim White has carried out excavations in the Four Corners region of Arizona and discovered arm and thigh bones broken open for their marrow. He concludes that the Anasazi, ancestors of the Hopi and Pueblo Indians used cannibalism to terrorise the neighbouring Polacca Walsh tribe. Bones from Mancos, an Anasazi village on the Colorado plateau, when examined with an electron microscope, had marks of butchering and gnawing and an abrasion indicative of pot boiling (White, p. 1992). This corroborates earlier findings of anthropologist Christy

Turner who is in no doubt that the 400-year-old bones of the Polacca Walsh tribe that he examined in 1967, which had been burnt, broken open and cut, were the debris left from a cannibalistic repast (McKie, p. 1998). Palaeontologists have also looked for evidence of prehistoric man-eating: digging at Atapuerca in Spain, an 800,000-year-old settlement, has uncovered human bones, stripped of their flesh, and mixed with animal bones that had been eaten (McKie, p. 43). Arens does not categorically deny the existence of prehistoric cannibalism, conceding that he has not yet studied the Anasazi evidence in detail, but he thinks that the eating of one's fellows has generally been condemned, not condoned, by human societies (Arens, p. 1997). The British archaeologist, Paul Bahn, agrees, claiming that the cuts and scrapes on the bones could be the result of mortuary practices: in many societies flesh was scraped from bones which were then buried elsewhere or stored in ossuaries (McKie, p. 44).

Another source of evidence for cannibalism that does not rely on oral reports is medical documentation. The medical scientist, D. Carleton Gajdusek, received the Nobel Prize for his work linking the transmission of the disease, *kuru* (the word means "trembling" and is related to Creutzfeld-Jacob's disease) to the ingestion of human brains. His research was based on the Foré tribe of New Guinea where *kuru* was endemic in the 1950s. Curiously, those affected were predominantly women and, to a lesser extent, children, from which it might be surmised that females had a greater proclivity to cannibalism, a view perpetrated by the local, somewhat misogynous, males. Arens thinks this unlikely and, given the lack of any direct observation of anthropophagy among the Foré, considers the traditional living arrangements of the tribe, in which the married woman lived together with her children, in a setting conducive to the spread of viral infection, the more likely cause of disease. He also reveals that a photograph depicting Gajdusek

sharing a meal with a group of Foré beneath a picture of a *kuru* victim and accompanied by a description of the preparation of endo-cannibalistic meals is not all it appears to be. It was not a human the group were devouring, but roast pork (Arens, 1980, p. 114-115).

Of course no-one would totally deny the existence of cannibalism. Sometimes it is necessary for survival – in 1972 survivors of a plane crash in the Andes ate the flesh of the dead victims and a recent documentary on Anne Frank, a Jewish victim of Nazi persecutions, revealed the presence of this practice in German concentration camps. A Chinese writer, Zheng Yi, has written about the pattern of cannibalism against class enemies in the Guangxi province of China in the Cultural Revolution of 1966-76, and the use of human parts for their supposed medical benefits is well attested. Mummy, or "mumia", a medicinal preparation consisting of the embalmed or dried human body, was included by the English College of Physicians in the official London Pharmacopoeia in 1618 and the Roman writer, Pliny the Elder, recommended the warm, living blood from the wounds of gladiators as a cure for epilepsy (Gordon-Grube, p. 1998). Criminal trials where a murderer has partially eaten his victim have occurred sporadically and an anthropologist was accused of autocannibalism when he accidentally cut his finger and sucked the blood from the wound (Gell, p. 1979). But it is unlikely that cannibalism, in any form or for any purpose, whether nutritional, ritual or medical, has ever been widespread; although Lévi-Strauss speaks of boiled and roast human, Arens points out that no actual recipes have been found, an indication that human cuisine did not include humans (Arens, p. 1997).

See also
Food Taboos; Necrophagy and Asceticism

References
Arens, William [1978] 1980 *The Man-Eating Myth*. Oxford: Oxford University Press.

Arens, William. 1997. "Man is off the menu". *Times Higher Education Supplement*, no. 12, December 1997.

Dundes, Alan. ed. 1992. *Blood Libel Legend: Casebook in Anti-Semitic Folklore*. Madison, Wisconsin: University of Wisconsin Press.

Gell, Alfred. 1979. "Reflections on a Cut Finger: Taboo in the Umeda Conception of the Self". In *Fantasy and Symbol: Studies in Anthropological Interpretation*, p. 133-148. ed. R. H. Hook. London: Academic Press Inc.

Ginzburg, Carlo. [1989] 1991. *Ecstasies. Deciphering the Witches' Sabbath*. trans. Raymond Rosenthal. London: Penguin.

Gordon-Grube, Karen. 1998. "Anthropophagy in Post-Renaissance Europe: The Tradition of Medicinal Cannibalism". *American Anthropologist*, no. 90, p. 405-409.

Harner, Michael. 1977. "The Ecological Basis for Aztec Sacrifice". *American Ethnologist*, no. 4, p. 117-135.

Harris, Marvin. 1977. *Cannibals and Kings: The Origins of Cultures*. New York: Random House.

Hesiod. *Theogony* in *Hesiod and Theognis* trans. Dorothea Wender. [1973] 1979. Harmondsworth, Middlesex: Penguin.

Mason, Peter. 1990. *Deconstructing America Representations of the Other*. London: Routledge and Kegan Paul.

McKie, Robin. 1998. "The People Eaters". *New Scientist*, no. 2125, 14 March 1998, p. 42-46.

Obeyesesekere, Gananath. 1992. *The Apotheosis of Captain Cook. European Mythmaking in the Pacific*. Princeton, New Jersey: Princeton University Press.

Sahlins, Marshall. 1978. "Culture as Protein and Profit". *New York Review of Books*, no. 26, vol. 4, p. 45-53.

Sanday, Peggy Reeves. 1986. *Divine Hunger*. Cambridge: Cambridge University Press.

Strabo. 1939. *The Geography of Strabo*. trans. H. L. Jones. Book 4. London: Heinemann, quoted in Arens. [1979] 1980.

Tuzin, Donald. 1983. "Cannibalism and Arapesh Cosmology: A Wartime Incident with the Japanese". In *The Ethnography of Cannibalism*, ed. Paula Brown and Donald Tuzin, p. 61-71. Washington, DC: Society for Psychological Anthropology.

White, David Gordon. 1991. *Myths of the Dog-Man*. Chicago, Illinois: University of Chicago Press.

White, Tim. 1992. *Prehistoric Cannibalism at Mancos*. Princeton, New Jersey: Princeton University Press.

Zweng Yi. 1996. *Scarlet Memorial: Tales of Cannibalism in Modern China*. trans. T. P. Sym. Boulder, Colorado: Westview Press.

Carnival

Carnival is the time of wild excesses and the breaking of taboos – sometimes with official approval – for the vast consumption of food before the austerity of Lent when *carne*, flesh, ceased to be eaten, hence the name of the festival, which is also known in France as *Mardi Gras*, fat Tuesday, or, in Britain, Shrovetide. Still celebrated in Catholic countries in Europe and South America, it was one of the major festivals from medieval times to the 17th century. While *Mardi Gras* (*Fastnacht* in Germany) refers to the day immediately preceding Lent, the festival of carnival sometimes began in January or as early as late December. In its wider, figurative, use, the word carnival denotes any festival that is characterised by licentious behaviour and as the ceremonies often manifest identical features, it is wise to consider the phenomenon in its entirety.

Carnival was a time when the population took to the streets, wearing masks, dressed as clerics, fools or devils or in clothes of the opposite sex or costumes from the *commedia dell'arte*. It was a time of liberation from repressive ecclesiastical, feudal and political constraints, from the denial of the flesh (lovemaking was forbidden during Lent), a time of parody, political and religious satire, but also a time of violence and hostility (in Rome, Jews were made to race through the streets while being pelted with mud and stones).

The violation of religious taboos was originally enjoyed by the clergy themselves: from medieval times onwards, monks wrote parodies of learned treatises – Mikhail Bakhtin mentions "Cyprian's supper", a travesty of the whole Scripture – and composed liturgies with such titles as "The Liturgy of the Drunkards" and "The Liturgy of the Gamblers" (Bakhtin,

p. 13). On individual feast days, the Feast of St Stephen, New Year's Day or the Feast of the Holy Innocents, the minor clergy organised mock festivals including the "Feast of the Ass" (which commemorated Mary's flight to Egypt with Jesus but had an ass as protagonist and was accompanied by a comic braying) and the "Feast of Fools" described by Peter Burke:

> During the Feast of Fools a bishop or abbot of the fools would be elected, there would be dancing in church and in the streets, the usual procession, and a mock mass in which the clergy wore masks or women's clothes, or put their vestments on back to front, held the missal upside down, played cards, ate sausages, sang bawdy songs, and cursed the congregation instead of blessing them. The 'indulgences' proclaimed in the south of France … might go like this: "My lord, who is here present/ Gives you 20 bags of toothache/ And to all you others also/ Gives a red bum" (Burke, p. 192).

At the end of the Middle Ages these sacrilegious "feasts" were banned from churches but continued in taverns and on the streets and are mentioned in texts from the 16th to 18th centuries. Bakhtin argues that their purpose was not primarily to express contempt for spiritual life but to celebrate the joys of earthly existence, carnal pleasures, fecundity, obscenity and laughter (Bakhtin, p. 75). Certainly these were quintessential carnival traits. The theme of abundance is evident in King Carnival of the Shrovetide celebrations – a huge bellied figure with game birds, rabbits and sausages hanging from him – and there is ample testimony to the enormous quantities of food and drink consumed, as if by these means the arrival of Lent (generally depicted as an emaciated old woman) could somehow be delayed.

The relaxation of sexual restraints meant that lewd songs and lechery were the norm – the costumes of the revellers, with their long-nosed masks, the inflated bladders of the fools, the sausages draped over King Carnival, the Fastnacht custom of harnessing an unmarried woman to the plough (mentioned in a Hans Sachs poem), all spoke of sex or sexual innuendo. Not surprisingly, speech was translated into action and conception increased at this time, as 18th-century records testify (Burke, p. 186).

Aggression was often sublimated and diffused through contests and games, but verbal insults were condoned at this time and real violence did occur. On Shrove Tuesday in 1376, the celebrations in Basel turned into a massacre; in Bern in 1513 there was a peasant revolt and riots have been well documented in London, Dijon, Madrid and Catalonia on carnival days (Burke, p. 204).

While the ecstatic excesses of carnivals were considerably repressed in Europe, even in Catholic countries, after the Reformation, features of carnival behaviour including transvestism, sexual license and riotous behaviour continued in Europe and elsewhere. This has led anthropologists to examine the social need to break taboos and defy conventional restraints. An early argument, proposed not by an anthropologist, but by the Paris School of Theology in 1444, suggested that such ceremonies as the "feasts of fools" acted as a safety-valve for suppressed energies:

> … so that foolishness, which is our second nature and seems to be inherent in man might freely spend itself at least once a year. Wine barrels burst if from time to time we do not open them and let in some air. All of us men are barrels poorly put together, which would burst from the wine of wisdom, if this wine remains in a state of constant fermentation of piousness and fear of God. We must give it air in order not to let it spoil. This is why we permit folly on certain days so that we may return with greater zeal to the service of God (Bakhtin, p. 75).

The theme of transgression and rebellion in ceremonies, in an entirely different culture in a different part of the world, has been the subject of an enquiry by the anthropologist, Max Gluckman. The Swasi *incwala*, or first fruits, ceremony, is characterised by an expression of hatred towards the king who is normally held in high esteem. The people sing songs of rejection, "King, alas for your fate, king, they reject thee, king, they hate thee" (Gluckman, p. 121). Similarly, during the Nomkubulwana festival of the Zulu, in the "little ceremony", the women exhibit unusually assertive behaviour: they wear male clothes and herd and milk the cattle which are normally taboo to them, deriding passing males and uttering obscenities. Like the Paris School of Theology, Gluckman emphasises the cathartic function of the transgressions, which allow popular resentments towards the king or the dominant male population to surface, but within a ritual framework which keeps any rebellion within bounds. Moreover, the transgressions actually help to delineate the status quo: "To ritually act out conflicts, either directly or by inversion, emphasises the social cohesion within which conflicts exist" (Gluckman, p. 192). While this may be true of traditional societies, in more recent times, as we have seen, the freedom from work, large gatherings and lack of inhibitions made festivals the ideal crucible for social revolt and change.

Nonetheless, carnivals may be characterised by harmony rather than dissent. Roger Abrahams and Richard Bauman studied carnival behaviour in St. Vincent and "belsnickling", a form of Christmas mumming, in the La Have islands, Nova Scotia. They found that those who practised transvestism and exhibited licentious behaviour during the festival were the same people who engaged in riotous behaviour the rest of the year. Whereas under normal conditions these people were to a certain extent separated from the rest of the community (or confined to a separate area in which they could indulge their behaviour) during the festival they were incorporated within the community and all could "participate together within a unified event" (Abrahams and Bauman, p. 206).

See also

Excrement; Liminality; Transvestism

References

Abrahams, Robert and Richard Bauman. 1978. "Ranges of Festival Behaviour". In *The Reversible World*. ed. Barbara Babcock, p. 193-208. Ithaca, New York; London: Cornell University Press.

Babcock, Barbara A. 1978. ed. *The Reversible World: Symbolic Inversion in Art and Society*. Ithaca, New York; Cornell University Press.

Baktin, Mikhail. [1965] 1984. *Rabelais and his World*. trans. Hélène Iswolsky. Indiana: Indiana University Press.

Burke, Peter. [1978] 1979. *Popular Culture in Early Modern Europe*. London: Temple Smith.

Davis, Natalie Zemon. 1982. *Society and Culture in Early Modern France*. Stanford, California: Stanford University Press.

Gluckman, Max. 1963. "Rituals of Rebellion in south-east Africa". *Order and Rebellion in Tribal Africa*, p. 110-136. London: Cohen and West.

Stallybrass, Peter and Allon White. 1986. *The Politics and Poetics of Transgression*. Ithaca, New York: Cornell University Press.

Cereals

Cereals and grain products like rice are the most pernicious foods for a Taoist in search of longevity and spiritual well-being. This is because they are the principal food of the Three Cadavers or Worms, malicious spirits inhabiting the body who, together with the Nine Worms and the *p'o* ("bone souls" or spirits of the skeleton), aim to destroy human beings. One function of these spirits is to report back to the August Emperor of Heaven, on appointed dates throughout the year, the transgressions and misdeeds of the person whose body they inhabit. While good deeds lead to an increase in the allotted life-span, bad deeds or a blank record mean that Destiny's Attendant will cross them off the Book of Life. (Other, more benevolent, god-souls are just and although they also report back to Heaven, they only mention a sin if it is particularly heinous.) Therefore, the Taoist, by abstaining from cereals, hopes to starve the Three Cadavers to death.

Legends report that the Chinese Immortals also practise *tuan-ku*, "cutting oneself off from grains", although ancient texts, including that attributed to the Taoist master, Chuang Tzu, refer to the Immortals as *ku-hsien* "Immortal of grains", implying that they are instrumental in their production.

Taoists have explained the taboo on cereals as due to the intensive cultivation methods that were adopted in the central and western provinces of China in the 3rd century BCE which ended hunting and resulted in an increasing dependency on agriculture. When crops failed, or some other calamity occurred, the peasants retreated to the mountains where they survived on roots and nuts (Schipper, p. 167-170). This diet was thought to be healthier and to prolong life. Ko Hung, The Master-Who-Embraces-Simplicity (383-443 CE), relates the tale of a woman forced to flee to the mountains. Agile, wild and naked, she is finally caught by hunters and enthuses over her diet:

I am a servant at the court of the Ch'in (221-207 BCE). When I learned that rebel troops from east of the Pass were coming, that the heir to the empire had capitulated and I saw the palace in flames, I fled in fright to these mountains. I was famished and had nothing to eat. I was on the verge of dying of hunger when an old man taught me to eat the needles and nuts of the pine tree. In the beginning, I found all that very bitter and not to my taste, but little by little, I got used to it. As a result, I was never hungry or thirsty. In winter, I did not suffer from the cold, nor from the heat in summer (Schipper, p. 169).

Had she continued with the diet, The Master-Who-Embraces-Simplicity explains, she would have become Immortal – she was already more than 200 years old. But on her return to the village she began, once more, to eat cereals even though the smell alone initially repulsed her. She aged rapidly, lost all her hair, and died within two years.

Taoism is not unique in its alertness to the dangers of agriculture, identified already in myths from Sumeria (such as the descent of Inanna) with death and the underworld. In an African myth of the Masai people, Kintu, the only man on earth, ascends to heaven where he marries the daughter of heaven. They return to earth with some animals and plants, but Kintu suddenly realises that he has forgotten the corn. He returns to heaven, but the god of Death is there waiting and follows him to earth, where he has remained ever since.

See also

Taoism – Japanese

References

Lévi, Jean. 1989. "The Body: The Daoists' Coat of Arms". trans. Lydia Davis. In *Fragments for a History of the Human Body*. Part One, ed. Michel Feher, p. 104-126. Cambridge, Massachusetts.

Schipper, Kristofer. [1982] 1993. *The Taoist Body*. trans. Karen C. Duval. Berkeley; Los Angeles: University of California Press.

Chinese Food Taboos

Certain Chinese food taboos derive from Buddhism which entered China during the 1st century CE. Buddha himself, who died around 500 BCE, did not specifically forbid beef but he banned cannibalism as well as the consumption of certain animals such as elephants, dogs, horses, lions, tigers, panthers, bears, hyenas and snakes. Curiously, Buddha did allow a monk to eat fish and meat if he had neither seen nor heard the animal being slaughtered, and did not suspect that it had been killed on his account. Later, when the Indian King Asoka (who reigned from 274-236 or, according to another calculation, from 268-234 BCE) was converted to Buddhism he condemned animal sacrifice and the injuring of all living things. Buddhism also traditionally banned the "five strong-odoured foods" (*wu hun*) which included members of the *Allium* genus such as garlic, onions and scallion. One effect of Buddhism on the diet was the relative unpopularity of beef but the dietary strictures of Buddhism were often ignored, sometimes even by the monks themselves. The monk Huai-su wrote in the 7th century that "an old monk eats fish in Ch'ang-sha, but when he comes to the walled city of Changan – he eats meat in abundance" (Schafer, 1977, p. 128). Taoism also had a list of prohibited food but the abstinence from grains that Taoism prescribed proved unpopular, especially since it was more expensive to practise than the vegetarianism advocated by Buddhism.

A major motivation for taboos in Chinese tradition arose from the notion that food is also medicine and that certain foods have a *yin* quality while others are *yang*; to be healthy a person needed to achieve an equilibrium between the *yin* and *yang* forces within his body. In a healthy person, overeating one kind of food would result in an excess of either *yin* or *yang* and cause disease. On the other hand, eating a particular food could help a patient to regain the equilibrium necessary for health (Chang, p. 10). Generally, drinking was *yang*, eating was *yin* but certain dishes including meat cooked by fire tended to be *yang* while food and drink from grain (which represented the earth) were probably *yin*. The principle of duality goes back at least to the Chou dynasty (12th century BCE to 221 BCE) and includes the concepts of "hot" (*jê*) and "cool" (*liang*) food. Among "hot" foods may be listed oily and fried food, pepper hot flavouring, fatty meat and oily plant foods like peanuts. Water plants, crustaceans and especially crabs, mung beans and certain other legumes are "cold". "Cold"

foods such as crabs would aggravate a common cold while "hot" foods were bad for a fever. Chia Ming, writing in the 14th century about the principles of correct diet, gives specific warnings on the dangers of certain foods. About spinach, a typical "cold" food, he notes:

Its flavour is sweet, and its character cold and slippery. Eaten to excess it may cause a weakening of the feet and will bring about pains in the waist and arouse chills. If a person who has previously been afflicted by stomach chills should eat spinach, it will certainly rupture his stomach. It must certainly not be eaten together with eels for that can induce cholera. If northerners, after eating meat and noodles cooked over a coal fire, should then eat spinach, that will neutralise the [bad] effects. If southerners eat moist fish with rice and then eat spinach, that will gain a cooling effect. Spinach makes the small and large intestines cold and slippery (Chia Ming. 1368. *Yin-shih hsü-chih* [Essential Knowledge for Eating and Drinking] Quoted in Mote, p. 231-232).

Distilled spirits [*shao chiu*] on the other hand are "hot" and must be avoided by those who have a tendency to *huo cheng*, localised fevers. Consumed together with ginger, garlic or dog-meat, distilled drinks can cause haemorrhoids. Fortunately there are antidotes to an alcohol-induced fever; these include being placed in water freshly drawn from a well, drinking cold salt water with green-pea flour and imbibing enough black-bean soup to induce vomiting.

As well as the divisions into hot and cold foods, Chinese food was classified according to five flavours: sweet, sour, bitter, pungent (piquant, hot) and salty. The flavours were in turn related to the five agents or elements: earth, wood, fire, metal and water.

Chia Ming's *Yin-shih hsü-chih* is divided into eight chapters and is filled with warnings and taboos on everything from fish, foul and meat to vegetables, seasonings and grains. It even includes a chapter on water and fires (forty-three kinds including rainwater that falls on the beginning of spring, winter frost and water from a stalactite cavern). Heeding all the injunctions would make eating impossible but the Chinese were generally pragmatic and adjusted their diet according to need. Ming's book was condemned during the Ch'ing dynasty (1644-1911 BCE) by the compilers of the imperial library catalogue (*Ssu-k'u ch'üan-shu tsung-mu t'i-yao*) who claimed it lacked originality. It is true that by the 2nd century BCE the three classical texts on ritual, the *Chou li*, *I li* and *Li chi* had already been substantially composed and included large sections devoted to food but, as the sinologist Frederick Mote remarks, Ming's book is important "as a reflection of Chinese beliefs about foods as active agents in the cosmic processes of generation and decay" (Mote, p. 233). The 14th century produced another influential work relating diet to disease and its cure: the *Yin-shan cheng-yao* (Principles of Correct Diet), written by Hu Ssu-hui in 1330.

Earlier, in the 7th century during the T'ang dynasty, the pharmacologist Meng Shen wrote on the medicinal use of food. He warned against the prolonged drinking of rice wine which injured the spirit and shortened the life-span. He also advised against mixing certain types of food: quail was not to be eaten with pork, pheasants could not be eaten with walnuts and chukar (*che-ku; Alectoris*) could not be eaten with bamboo shoots. Some animals, though, were not to be eaten at all because they were believed to be poisonous. Meng Shen particularly warned against devouring the flesh of the dhole, or wild dog (*ch'ai; Cuon*), the common yellow ox and the black ox.

Also during the T'ang dynasty (618-907 CE) Ch'en Ts'ang-ch'i classified certain tabooed animals which included:

the flesh of a black ox or goat with a white head, a single-horned goat,

domestic animals that had died facing north, deer spotted like leopards, horse liver and meat that a dog had refused to eat (Schafer, p. 131-132).

Some of these injunctions have a long pedigree. Already in the Han period (206 BCE-220 CE) the liver of a horse was considered to be deadly poisonous, although the rest of the horse was relished. The Emperor Wu who reigned from 140-187 CE reputably told the court necromancer, Luan Ta, that Luan's predecessor, Shao-weng, had died as a result of eating horse-liver (Ying-Shih Yü, p. 58). Horse-liver is also absent from the extensive food lists from the Han tombs. As for the black animal with a white head, the deer spotted like leopards and the single-horned goat, it is clear that they contravene the requirements for sacrifice, since, traditionally, animals to be offered needed to be free of blemish, of one colour and unmarked by spots or patches. In the *Huang Ming tsu-hsün-lu* (Ancestral Admonitions) of 1381 there is specific mention of the inclusion of "40 young bullocks of one colour" in a levy to be sent to the Forbidden City (Mote, p. 214). Animals that had died facing north were inauspicious in Chinese thought because this was the direction which the heads of the dead were traditionally placed. Edward Schafer finds many of these taboos essentially magical in character:

comparable, but opposite, to the prescriptions which advocated, for instance, the ingestion of the flesh of the goshawk reduced to ashes, as a defence against wild foxes and goblins. It was believed that the power and ferocity of the hawk were transferred to the man who ate its flesh (Schafer, p. 132).

Some dietary taboos were transient, such as the imperial injunction of 18 March 833 forbidding wine-drinking on days of national mourning. Others applied to specific persons: the food of the Son of Heaven was regulated according to the passage of the seasons and he himself was not permitted to eat, drink, or listen to music in the company of visiting foreigners. Still other proscriptions were founded on a cultural or regional abhorrence of certain foods. Frogs were detested by the residents of northern China during the T'ang dynasty. Po Chü-i, in his poem, *Frogs*, discusses those animals which are suitable as temple offerings: "But what is unusable is the frog – filthy in form, rank of skin and flesh" (in *Ch'üan T'ang shih*. Quoted in Schafer, p. 131). In the far south however, and especially in the Kuei-yang region, frogs were a delicacy. Live frogs were added to a cauldron containing a root and bamboo-shoot soup. Agonised, they clutched the stems and were served in this position.

Food taboos persist in present-day China; each religion has it own injunctions with Muslims rejecting the pork that is such a feature of Chinese cuisine while the Buddhists remain wary of beef. Even a secular ideology such as Communism is not adverse to food regulations. In an effort to counter the discrepancies between the eating habits of the rich and poor (or exploiter and exploited) the following rules were made by the Communist-led Peasants Association from their base in Hunan:

In Shao-shan, Hsiang-t'an county, it has been decided that guests are to be served with only three kinds of animal food, namely, chicken, fish and pork. It is also forbidden to serve bamboo shoots, kelp and lentil noodles. In Hengshan county it has been resolved that eight dishes and no more may be served at a banquet. Only five dishes are allowed in the East Three District in Li-ling county, and only meat and three vegetable dishes in the North Second District, while in the West Third District New Year feasts are forbidden entirely. In Hsiang-hsiang county, there is a ban on all "egg-cake feasts", which are by no means sumptuous ... In the town of Chia-mo, Hsiang-hsiang county, people have

refrained from eating expensive foods and use only fruit when offering ancestral sacrifices (Mao Tse-tung. 1927. Quoted in K.C. Chang. 1977, p. 15. Introduction. *Food in Chinese Culture*).

Though frugality has not been a popular export, the concepts of *yin* and *yang* and cold and hot foods, and their medicinal qualities, have aroused interest, and sometimes enthusiasm, in the West.

See also
Food Taboos

References

Anderson, E. N. 1997. "Traditional Medical Values of Food". In *Food and Culture: A Reader*. ed. Carole Counihan and Penny van Esterik, p. 80-91. New York; London: Routledge.

Chang, K. C. 1977. "Introduction". In *Food in Chinese Culture: Anthropological and Historical Perspectives*. ed. K. C. Chang, p. 1-21. New Haven, Connecticut; London: Yale University Press.

Goody, Jack. 1982. *Cooking, Cuisine and Class: A Study in Comparative Sociology*. Cambridge: Cambridge University Press.

Mote, Frederick W. 1977. "Yüan and Ming". In K. C. Chang ed., *Food in Chinese Culture: Anthropological and Historical Perspectives*, p. 193-257. New Haven, Connecticut; London: Yale University Press.

Ying-Shih Yü. 1997. "Han". In *Food in Chinese Culture: Anthropological and Historical Perspectives*. ed. K. C. Chang, p. 53-83. New Haven, Connecticut; London: Yale University Press.

Chopsticks

In Japan it was taboo to serve a bowl of rice with chopsticks in except when the rice was prepared as a gift for the dead. In this case, a pair of chopsticks was thrust upright into the bowl. Chopsticks were originally a Chinese invention, widely adopted in the country around 500 BCE at the time that the scholar replaced the warrior as the ideal type of citizen, although bronze chopsticks have been unearthed from royal tombs dating back to

1500 BCE. Food was prepared in small pieces before reaching the table and then eaten with chopsticks, a custom that was preferable to the savage habits of Europeans who used knives at table, or, as the Chinese put it, "ate with swords".

That a taboo, like that imposed on chopsticks in Japan, should be reversed at the time of death is not unusual. In Japan, as in most other cultures, a corpse was traditionally thought to be dangerous and certain rituals needed to be followed to mitigate the harm. Just as food offerings for the dead differed from those of the living, a bedside screen was erected upside down near the head of the deceased and instead of cold water being added to hot to wash the corpse, hot water was poured onto cold.

See also

Table Manners

References

Farb, Peter and George Armelagos. 1980. *Consuming Passions: The Anthropology of Eating.* Boston, Massachusetts: Houghton Mifflin Company.

Natley, Malika. Personal communication.

Clitoris

The discovery of the clitoris, as Thomas Laqueur reveals in his article on the topic, has been claimed by Renaldus Columbus. In 1559 Columbus writes from Venice in his *De re anatomica*:

> Therefore, since no-one has discerned these projections and their working, if it is permissible to name things one has discovered, it should be called the love, or sweetness of Venus ... And this, most gentle reader is that: pre-eminently the seat of women's delight ... (Laqueur, p. 91).

It is perhaps the seat of women's delight, but it is also a part of the body considered so taboo that many cultures have seen fit to remove it in a clitoridectomy or excision. Columbus' claim to be the first to discover the organ, however, has been fiercely contested. Bartholinus, an early 17th-century anatomist remarks that the clitoris has been "known to everyone from the second-century physicians Rufus of Ephesus and Julius Pollux to the Arabic anatomists Albucasis and Avicenna" and fifty years later Regnier De Graaf traces its history back to Greek anatomists. Hippocrates knew it as *columnella*, little column, he says. It was better known to the Greeks as *kleitoris*, and the verb form, *kleitorizein,* is first recorded by Rufus who gives its meaning as "to touch [the *nymphe*] lasciviously" and Gabriello Fallopius, the 16th-century Italian anatomist who discovered the fallopian tubes, speaks of the "lewd verb", from which "to touch the clitoris" is derived (Laqueur, p. 109-110).

Certainly the clitoris has been known of for a long time, and not just in Europe. A 19th-century ethnographic work, *Das Weib* (woman) by Hermann H. Ploss, tells of clitoral excision in Egypt in the 2nd century BCE, and then speaks of the practice in Muslim East Africa, in parts of Central, Northern and Western Africa and in the South-East as well as in South America among the Peruvian Indians – and in Equador and Malaysia (Weideger, p. 68-77). Nici Nelson, who conducted field research among the Kikuyu of Mathare Valley, Kenya, offers a motivation for the operation:

> Medical doctors and Kikuyu women to whom I talked agreed that circumcision ... would limit women's sexual pleasure since the most sensitive tissues of the female genital organs, the clitoris and the labia minora, are excised. Old women interviewed during a return visit in 1984 confirmed this. They said that girls were circumcised to limit their sex drive and to keep them under control ... sex was for procreation only rather than for pleasure (Nelson, p. 221).

In Western Europe clitoridectomy is rare although in the 1870s certain operations were performed to counter what many considered the most abhorrent of vices: masturbation. However, the example Thomas Laqueur gives of a 17th-century excision is not a punishment for onanism; the transgression in this case is the crossing of sexual boundaries and counterfeiting the male. Henrica Shuria, as the protagonist of this tale is named, dressed as a soldier and went to war, fighting at the siege of Sylva Ducis under Frederick Henry. It was only when she left the army and took up with a widow, "who burned with immoderate lusts", that she was reprimanded and sentenced to death. This was later repealed and, after the clitoridectomy, she was sent into exile (Laqueur, p. 115-116).

Henrica Shuria was credited with having an unnaturally long clitoris, an anatomical feature also attributed to Egyptian women by the 6th-century Byzantine physicians, Aetius of Amida and Paulus Aegineta. The Greek geographer, Strabo, mentions circumcision of both sexes by the Mediterranean Jews (without any reference to size) and also by an Arabian people known as Creophagi. Certainly among men, the clitoris has been known to arouse both fear – especially if, in a state of hypertrophy, it resembles too closely a penis – and a voyeuristic excitation. The French surgeon, Ambroise Paré, tells an *Arabian Nights* tale of demons and exorcism, lust and excision. In Fez, in North Africa, he declares, lives a band of female prophets or exorcists who claim to have demons as familiars. The wily women imitate the voices of the spirits, live from the presents that people bring for the djins and, more lasciviously, "rub one another for pleasure, and in truth they are afflicted of that wicked vice of using one another carnally" (Laqueur, p. 117). Moreover, they request the beautiful women who come to be healed to pay for their services with sex, and the practice so delights their visitors that illness is feigned in order for the "payment" to be exacted. To prevent innocent husbands from being duped by their lecherous wives, there exist in Africa, so we are told, "castrators" who "make a trade of cutting off such caruncles" (Laqueur, p. 117).

By the 19th century, it was claimed that "Clitorisme", the solitary excitation of the clitoris, would lead to the collapse of the social order and was the mark of the prostitute. In 1905, the psychoanalyst Sigmund Freud also argued against the clitoris, not because it induced lust but because it denoted an infantile form of sexuality; in adult females, orgasms were to occur in the vagina, not through clitoral stimulation. In his *Three Essays on the Theory of Sexuality*, Freud is not unaware of the power of the clitoris:

> The leading erotogenic zone in female children is located at the clitoris, and is thus homologous to the masculine genital zone of the glans penis. All my experience concerning masturbation in little girls has related to the clitoris and not to the regions of the external genitalia ... I am even doubtful whether a female child can be led by the influence of seduction to anything other than clitoridal masturbation (Freud, p. 142).

This is hardly surprising: long before Freud's research, medical evidence had revealed an abundance of sensitive nerve endings in the clitoris with a corresponding paucity in the vagina itself, and the later clinical findings of William Masters and Virginia Johnson confirm this, showing that all female orgasms originate in the clitoris (Masters and Johnson, 1966). Nevertheless, Freud postulates that at puberty a girl experiences a repression of her libido, which principally affects her clitoridal sexuality. Her sexual restraint and denial of the "masculine" aspect of her sexuality only serves to heighten the libido of the male. (Freud retains the image of man as the hunter chasing his coy prey.) The prowess of the pursuer is finally rewarded, but for the woman the location of her gratification has changed:

> When at last the sexual act is permitted
> and the clitoris itself becomes excited,

it still retains a function: the task, namely, of transmitting the excitation to the adjacent female parts, just as – to use a simile – pine shavings can be kindled in order to set a log of harder wood on fire. Before this transference can be effected, a certain interval of time must often elapse, during which the young woman is [vaginally] anaesthesic ... When erotogenic susceptibility to stimulation has been successfully transferred by a woman from the clitoris to the vaginal orifice, it implies that she had adopted a new leading zone for the purposes of her later sexual activity ... The fact that women change their leading erotogenic zone in this way, together with the wave of repression at puberty, which, as it were, puts aside their childish masculinity, are the chief determinants of the greater proneness of women to neurosis and especially to hysteria (Freud, p. 143-144).

So the erotic zone of woman migrates, as Thomas Laqueur amusingly puts it, "like a Bahktiari tribesman in search of fresh pastures" (Laqueur, p. 92). Freud is not the first to suggest this. In the 1890s, Richard Freiherr von Krafft-Ebing, a neurologist specialising in sexual pathology, had written of the transference, supposing it to occur after "defloration", although he did not deny the existence of other erogenous zones. But as Thomas Laqueur's essay shows, there exists no basis in physiology for such a view. Rather, it is cultural or social considerations that recognise, in the unruly and excitable clitoris, a barrier to reproductive intercourse and a concomitant, settled, family life. Moreover, as Freud has shown, humans are latently bisexual so a rejection of the "male" clitoris in favour of the "female" vagina helps to differentiate the sexes. But as the vagina is relatively insensitive, a sense of pleasure can only be achieved through a feat of imagination – in much the same way that an amputee might experience pain in a missing limb or, as in hysteria, symptoms are manifested which have no physical cause. The move from clitoris to vagina, therefore, is hysterical:

> Like the missing limb phenomenon, it involves feeling what is not there. Becoming a sexually mature woman is therefore living an oxymoron, becoming a lifelong "normal hysteric," for whom a conversion neurosis is termed "acceptive" (Laqueur, p. 122).

Freud may not have advocated clitoral excision but he nonetheless designated the clitoris a forbidden zone. His rejection of clitoral orgasm led to a reaction later in the century when feminists, such as Helena Wright, once again claimed to have discovered the seat of women's delight.

See also
Vagina

References
Freud, Sigmund. [1905] 1977. *Three Essays on the Theory of Sexuality.* The Penguin Freud Library. Vol. 7. trans. James Strachey. London: Penguin.

Laqueur, Thomas W., [1989] 1990. "Amor Veneris, vel Dulcedo Appeletur". In *Fragments for a History of the Human Body.* Part Three. ed. Michel Feher, p. 90-131. New York: Zone.

Masters, W. and Johnson, V. 1966. *Human Sexual Response.* New York: Little, Brown and Co.

Nelson, Nici. [1987] 1996. "'Selling her kiosk': Kikuyu notions of sexuality and sex for sale in Mathare Valley, Kenya". In *The Cultural Construction of Sexuality.* ed. Pat Caplan, p. 217-239. London: Routledge.

Weideger, Paula. [1985] 1986. *History's Mistress: A New Interpretation of a Nineteenth-century Ethnographic Classic.* Harmondsworth, Middlesex: Penguin.

Cook, Captain James (1728-79) and Taboo in Polynesia

Captain Cook, the British naval captain, navigator, explorer and astronomer is responsible

for introducing the word *taboo* into European languages, where it has been used as an adjective, noun or verb. It is first mentioned in 1777 in a journal charting his third voyage around the world as the captain of HMS *Resolution*. Describing the indigenous people of Atui, one of the Sandwich group of islands, he writes:

> The people of Atooi ... resemble those of Otaheite [Tahiti] in the slovenly state of their religious places, and in offering vegetables and animals to their gods. The *taboo* also prevails in Atooi, in its full extent, and seemingly with much more rigour than even at Tongataboo. For the people here always asked, with great eagerness and signs of fear to offend, whether any particular thing, which they desired to see, or we were willing to show, was *taboo*, or, as they pronounced the word, *tafoo*? The *maia*, *raa*, or forbidden articles of the Society Islands, though, doubtless, the same thing, did not seem to be so strictly observed by them, except with respect to the dead, about whom we thought them more superstitious than any of the others were (Steiner, p. 22).

Cook realised that the term *taboo* was common throughout Polynesia and could be applied to many different things, both animate and inanimate, living and dead. It could mean something, or someone, that was set apart, or consecrated for a special use or purpose: in Tahiti, the victim of human sacrifice was *Tataa-taboo*, a consecrated man. The term also applied to restrictions placed upon certain members of the society, often women: in Tahiti females were forbidden to eat in the company of men and the Polynesian *Mories*, places of worship and sacrifice, could never be entered by women. In Tonga, *tabu or tapu,* indicated all things that must not be touched. Cook also mentioned the "mysterious significance" of the notion of *tabu* and the "mixture of religion" in a ceremony that had been designated *taboo*.

Unfortunately James Cook's investigations into the subject came to an abrupt end when an argument with some Hawaiians (who employed the term *kapu*) over a cutter that had been stolen ended with him being killed on the beach at Kealakekua. Cook's journal was continued by his successor, King, who continued his research into the meaning and application of *taboos*. Upon receiving Cook's remains, King requested of the Hawaiians that the area surrounding the spot where the crew were to bury Captain Cook's bones should be tabooed for that day, a request that was zealously adhered to, with no inhabitants venturing close. Moreover, the field of sweet potatoes which the Europeans wished to use as an observatory was consecrated, and thereby rendered taboo, by the priests. To do this, the priests fixed their wands around the wall that enclosed the field. After the consecration, the men of the island would only approach the site when specifically invited and the women refused absolutely, stating that their chief, Terreeboo, would punish them with death for such a transgression. Another spatial taboo that King observed was the consecration of the bay on the day preceding the arrival of Terreeboo.

King also remarked upon the use of taboo as a means of social stratification in Polynesia. Among the *Erees*, or chiefs, of each district, one was superior and at Owhyhee he was named *Eree-taboo* and *Eree-moee*. The first part of his name indicated his absolute authority while the latter part expressed the fact that everyone had to prostrate themselves in his presence. Taboos also applied to certain foods and eating habits: pork, turtle, certain types of fish and species of herbs were forbidden to women and women who had assisted at a funeral or touched a dead body were tabooed and not allowed to feed themselves. Such women relied on others to place food in their mouths. King concluded that the word taboo had many applications and could be used to describe anything "sacred, or eminent, or devoted" (Steiner, p. 27). Just as the king of Owhyhee was called *Eree-taboo* and the king of Tonga was named *Tonga-taboo*, so a human victim on Owhyhee was *Tangata-taboo*.

Later ethnographers, visiting the Polynesian islands in the early 19th century, continued to explore the concept of taboo. In 1802 a Russo-German expedition commanded by Adam Johann Ritter von Krusenstern sailed to the area with Captain Urey Lisiansky and the naturalist George H. van Langsdorff on board. George von Langsdorff was interested in the social aspects of taboo; he compiled a list of taboo customs and translated the word as "forbidden". Adam von Krusenstern emphasised the religious implications of taboo while Urey Lisiansky defined taboo as a "sacred prohibition". The difficulties of an adequate definition were reiterated by Otto von Kotzebue who commanded the *Rurik* in 1821. Louis de Freycinet, who had accompanied Kotzebue on an earlier expedition in 1817, decided that the word meant "forbidden or prohibited" and that the custom of taboo was "an institution, simultaneously civil and religious" (Steiner, p. 29).

The anthropologist Roger Keesing points out that by suggesting that the Oceanic Austronesian word *tapu/tabu* could also be interpreted as a noun (instead of as a stative verb which is how the indigenous islanders used it), Cook initiated the problems that later ethnographers had in interpreting the term. Franz Steiner, in his book, *Taboo*, supplies a Polynesian etymology in which the word *tabu* is derived from *ta* (to mark) and *pu* (thoroughly), indicating something that is "marked off" or, as Keesing puts it, "off-limits".

See also

Keesing, Roger M.

References

Keesing, Roger M. 1985. "Conventional Metaphors and Anthropological Metaphysics: The Problematic of Cultural Translation". In *Journal of Anthropological Research*, no. 41, p. 201-217. Alburquerque, New Mexico: University of New Mexico

Steiner, Franz. 1956. *Taboo*. London: Cohen and West.

Cows

For Hindus, cows are a sacred species, protected by India's federal constitution. Article 48 of the government's *Directive Principles of State Policy* recommends a prohibition on the slaughter of cows and calves and many religious Hindus are agitating for a total ban on the killing of cattle. The champion of Indian independence, Mohandas Gandhi, was an ardent advocate of cow protection, a feature that endeared him to the Hindu masses, and the protection of cows has a marked political dimension, separating Hindus from the beef-eating Muslims. Gandhi's treatise, "How to Serve the Cow", articulates the general principle of *ahimsa,* or "non-injury," a doctrine whose foundation lies in the practices of the *sramanas* "world-renouncers" of the 6th century BCE and which was adopted by the composers of the Upanishads and by Buddhists and Jains.

The sanctity of the cow is well attested in myth. In Vedic tradition, Tvastr, the architect and artisan of the gods, possesses a magic cow capable of yielding *soma*, the potent ambrosia of the gods (which is stolen by the god, Indra). Hymn 10.101 of the *Rig Veda* invokes the cow as a symbol of divine inspiration and a Vedic theory of the rain cycle interprets the sun's rays as a cow, drinking up the waters of the earth and then returning them in the form of milk or rain (*Rig Veda* 1.164). Hindu festivals celebrate the merciful Krishna, protector of cows, while Shiva, the divine avenger, rides on a bull. All that the cow produces is holy, whether milk, urine or excrement and ghee, clarified cow's butter, is burned in lamps in the temples.

Yet the taboos on killing cattle have not always existed. Texts of the Vedic period (1200-900 BCE) focus on the *yajna,* the fire sacrifice, an essential rite necessary for maintaining cosmic order. The Brahmins (the priestly caste) were responsible for the sacrifice and cattle, held in such high esteem, were considered an eminently suitable offering. Sacrificed animals were consumed and Brahmins viewed beef as the finest meat. The sacrifice of cattle was once widespread, practised in Babylonia, Greece, and among many pastoral peoples. In Iran, the sacrifice of a bull was an essential cult of Mithraism. What is puzzling in India is the reversal in ideology: in Vedic times a philosophy of *himsa*, the desire to inflict injury, prevailed, and the Brahmins, as sacrificers, relished beef; but in the Hindu period this was gradually replaced by an adherence to *ahimsa* and the purity and status of Brahmins was enhanced by their rejection of flesh.

According to the anthropologist, Marvin Harris, the Hindu ban on beef was a purely pragmatic move: the animals were of more use alive, pulling ploughs, providing milk and milk products and dung (for fuel), than dead. Harris speculates that a population growth, combined with a reduction in grazing areas, meant that the ratio of cattle to humans had considerably declined by around 600 BCE. The poor no longer received donations of beef from the Brahmins and resented the fact that Brahmins and Kshatriyas (the ruling warrior chiefs) still indulged in feasts. Succeeding centuries saw an increase in the popularity of Buddhism and Jainism, with their policies of non-violence and self-renunciation, and eventually the Brahmins realised that the best course would be to integrate these observances and adapt their teachings. This was an auspicious decision because crops can feed larger populations than beef-cattle, cows can be grazed on waste land that is unsuitable for cultivation, and the initial investment on a pair of oxen is far less than on a tractor. Harris' views are highly controversial and debates have raged over the significance of the "holy cow" (see the anthropological journal *Current Anthropology* from 1966 onwards).

Of course the taboo on killing and eating cows was not always absolute. Buddhists could eat meat as long as they did not kill the animal and conflicting opinions are evinced in the Hindu text, the *Laws of Manu* (c. 1st century CE), which advocates vegetarianism as a Brahmanic ideal (recognising that no meat can be obtained without violence) yet asserts that "killing in a sacrifice is not killing [if] ... sanctioned by the Veda – that is known as non-violence" (*Manu* 5, p. 39, 44). On the other hand, in the *Rig Veda,* despite the allusions to sacrifice, cows are referred to as *aghnya*, "beings not to be killed".

The Sanskrit scholar, Wendy Doniger, argues along the lines of B. R. Ambedkar, namely, that Brahmins adopted the doctrine of *ahimsa* to prove their moral superiority over other social groups. During the Vedic period, Brahmins controlled the all-important sacrifice but vied with the more powerful Ksatriyas. The *Veda* (which they composed) validated their status. As the creed of world-renunciation gathered momentum, the Brahmins saw the need to "re-invent" themselves, in the words of Doniger:

> by rewriting the rules of the game ...
> with the introduction of non-violence
> as the criterion for 'purity' and as the
> paradigmatic practice for social standing (*Manu*. xxxviii).

Though they could not compete with the Ksatriyas in terms of physical force, they could commandeer the moral high ground.

An aversion to the sacrifice of cattle is not confined to India. The Greek philosophers, Pythagoras and Empedocles were opposed to the Athenian *Bouphonia*, or ox-slaying. Moreover, myths warn of the dangers of inadvertently killing protected cattle: in the Sumerian *Epic of Gilgamesh*, the ill-fated Enkidu is condemned to death for slaying the Bull of Heaven and the Homeric *Hymn to Hermes* tells how Hermes stole and killed some cattle belonging to his brother and had to pay him restitution.

See also

Food Taboos; Foods Forbidden to Brahmins; Laws of Manu

References

Ambedkar, B.R. 1948. *The Untouchables*. New Delhi: Amrit Book Company.

Brown, W. N. 1957. "The Sanctity of the Cow in Hinduism". *Journal of the Madras University*. Sect. A. Humanities. 28, p. 29-49.

Detienne, Marcel and Jean-Pierre Vernant. [1979] 1989. *The Cuisine of Sacrifice among the Greeks*. trans. Paula Wissing. Chicago, Illinois; London: University of Chicago Press.

Harris, Marvin. [1985] 1986. *Good to Eat: Riddles of Food and Culture*. London: Allen and Unwin.

The Laws of Manu. trans. and introduction Doniger, Wendy and Brian K. Smith. 1991. London: Penguin.

Lincoln, Bruce. 1987. "Cattle". In *The Encyclopedia of Religion*, vol. 3, p. 123 127. ed., Mircea Eliade. New York: Macmillan.

O'Flaherty, Wendy Doniger. 1984. *Dreams, Illusions and Other Realities*. Chicago, Illinois: University of Chicago Press.

The Rig Veda, trans. Wendy Doniger O'Flaherty. [1981] 1983. Harmondsworth, Middlesex: Penguin.

Simoon, Frederick J. [1961] 1967. *Eat Not This Flesh: Food Avoidances in the Old World*. Madison, Wisconsin: University of Wisconsin Press.

Cross-roads

Cross-roads are places of danger; haunted by spirits, demons, ghosts and gods, they can not be crossed with impunity. Almost every society in the world has at some time treated them with apprehension, as repositories of all that is polluted or all that is magical, and requiring special rituals if they are to be traversed safely. Greek and Roman writers identified the convergence of paths with Hekate, a goddess who had to be supplicated by means of rituals and meals, or "suppers", if she was to keep the uncanny ghosts of the cross-roads at bay and allow the traveller safe passage. The suppers were taken to the *hekataia* – shrines of Hekate situated at cross-roads – at the time of the new moon. If her desires were thwarted and she was denied homage, she could turn vengeful and summon up the wrathful spirits to do her bidding.

Sarah Johnston suggests that it is the indeterminate nature of cross-roads that makes them so threatening:

The Greeks, Romans, and many other ancient civilisations regarded both natural and man-made liminal points of all kinds – doors, gates, rivers and frontiers, as well as cross-roads – as uncertain places, requiring special rituals … because of their lack of association with either of two extremes, liminal points eluded categorisation – a threshold was neither in nor out of the house, a cross-road was part of neither road A nor road B nor road C. On the one hand, liminal points and boundaries structured the world … on the other hand … the liminal point … because it didn't belong to either of the two extremes it separated, was a sort of permanent chaos (Johnston, p. 217-218).

This is certainly true; ambiguity and periods of transition – twilight, midnight, midsummer, Mayday Eve and Halloween (turning points of the year in the Celtic calendar) – are all seen as hazardous. Moreover, cross-roads can cause confusion, especially to the traveller unsure of the route. In Voodoo rituals in Haiti, Legba/Elegba, God of the cross-roads, also known as Legba-Carrefour, performs a similar function to that of Hekate in Greece. Legba must appear before any other god, or *loa*, can descend. He is the:

Master of the mystic "barrier" which divides men from spirits, Legba is also the guardian of the gates and of the fences which surround houses and, by extension, he is the protector of the home … He is also the god of roads and paths. As "Master of Cross-roads" he is the god of every parting of the way – a favourite haunt of evil spirits and propitious to magic devices; and it is at cross-roads that he receives the homage of sorcerers and presides over their incantations and spells. Many magic formulae begin with the words, "By thy power, Master of Cross-roads" (Métraux, p. 101-102).

Although Legba appears pitiful, dressed in rags and leaning on a crutch, he is extremely strong and anyone whose body he possesses is thrown to the ground and struggles violently.

In Voodoo mythology, and also in that of the Greeks, cross-roads exist on a vertical as well as a horizontal plane; they are the place where the gods descend to earth, where the ghosts appear, where the upper and lower worlds, the living and the dead, meet. Certainly the road junctions were a place for spirits to congregate. The Greek philosopher, Theophrastus (4th-3rd century BCE) wrote that a superstitious man will anoint stones at cross-roads to appease the ghosts thought to gather there. A Chinese Buddhist text from the 6th century, the *Cheng-fa nien-ch'u chung*, includes under the thirty-six subspecies of hungry ghosts those that stay at cross-roads. The Aztecs believed that the spirits of women who had died in childbirth, the Ciuapipiltin, descended at the cross-roads at intervals of fifty-two days. They were greatly feared; under their spell, a person's mouth became twisted and filled with foam, the face contorted and the feet numb and misshapen (Baquedano, p. 190). In European folklore, witches haunted the intersections, a belief that may derive from the association of Hekate with witchcraft. In Wales and Germany witches danced with the devil on May Day Eve at cross-roads (Puhvel, p. 168).

Besides being a magnet for ghouls, cross-roads have also served as a dumping-ground for things that society sees as polluted or tabooed. In ancient Greece the polluted remains of household purification rituals were taken to junctions – places at the intersection of private or public lands but owned by nobody. The pollution of the city caused by parricides was also expelled at the cross-roads. Plato mentions how the body of a parricide, after execution, must be taken to a cross-roads outside the city and stoned by all the officials, to expel the dangerous blood-guilt, before being cast out beyond the boundary of the state (*Lg.* 873b-c. In Johnston, p. 222). This is not so different from the European tradition of burying the bodies of homicides or suicides (once a heinous offence carrying the death penalty) at cross-roads. Disposal of suicides at intersections has even been reported among the Baganda of Central Africa. Fearful of the evil ghosts of these suicides, the Baganda burned the corpses on waste land or at cross-roads together with the tree used for the hanging or the house in which the person had killed himself (Puhvel, p. 177 n.58).

Diseases, also, could be safely left at these junctures. A 19th-century cure for a stye involved going to a cross-roads and repeating "Stye! Stye! go out of my eye,/ And go to the stranger who next passes by". In Japan, the ill-luck accruing to those who had reached an unlucky year (*yaku-toshi*) could be banished if those at risk gathered beans, one for each year of their lives, and wrapped them in paper together with a coin that they had rubbed over their bodies. The misfortune would then be transferred to the bundle which could be placed in a bamboo tube and thrown away at the cross-roads (Puhvel, p. 176 n.38).

The cast-off illnesses, which could often affix themselves to the next passer-by, as well as the baleful ghosts and other malcontents, made cross-roads dangerous, especially at inauspicious times of the day or year. But because of the spirits lingering there, who could be summoned up by a sorcerer to perform magic, they also had their uses. Love-spells in the Greek magical papyri require the enamoured lover to shape a figure in wax or dough and to bury it at the cross-roads or to inscribe a spell on a sherd picked up at the cross-roads. Obviously the meeting of the paths was deemed auspicious for the meeting of the lovers.

See also

Beans; Miasma; Suicide

References

Baquedano, Elizabeth. 1989. "Aztec Earth Deities". In *Polytheistic Systems. Cosmos: The Yearbook of the Traditional Cosmology Society*, vol. 5, p. 184-198. Edinburgh: Edinburgh University Press.

Johnston, Sarah Isles. 1990. "Cross-roads". *Zeitschrift für Papyrologie und Epigraphik*, no. 88, p. 217-224.

Métraux, Alfred. [1959] 1972. *Voodoo in Haiti*. trans. Hugo Charteris. New York: Schocken Books.

Puhvel, M. 1976. "The Mystery of the Cross-Roads". *Folklore*, no. 87, p. 167-177.

Cunnilingus

Cunnilingus, the oral stimulation of the female genitals (from *cunnus* "vulva" and *lingere* "lick"), though until recently not spoken of openly in Western society, is accorded a revered place in Chinese Taoism. This is because the aim of Taoism is to achieve immortality, or at least longevity, and the loss of semen, vaginal, and other, bodily liquids is believed to bring about a corresponding loss of vitality. However, conversely, by either semen retention or ingesting the secretions from the vagina, a male can conserve and increase his *ch'i*, or original vital breath. In Taoism:

> The *Great Medicine of the Three Mountain Peaks* is to be found in the body of the woman and is composed of three juices, or essences: one from the woman's mouth, another from her breasts, and the third, the most powerful, from the *Grotto of the White Tiger*, which is at the *Peak of the Purple Mushroom* (the mons veneris) (Paz, p. 97).

According to Philip Rawson (Rawson in Paz, p. 97), these half-poetic, half-medicinal metaphors explain the popularity of cunnilingus among the Chinese: "The practice was an excellent method of imbibing the precious feminine fluid" (Paz, p. 97). But the Taoist ideal is not just about the male being enriched by female secretions; the female also benefits from her communion with the male, a feature that has led the sinologist, Kristofer Schipper, to denounce the ancient handbooks on the "Art of the Bedroom" as embracing a "kind of glorified male vampirism", that is not truly Taoist at all (Schipper, p. 148). Ideally, by mingling the male and female liquids, the Taoist aims to reconcile opposites and to recapture the mythical time that existed before the division of the sexes, the primordial time of the original *ch'i*.

The religious historian, Mircea Eliade, speaks of a similar desire to transcend old age and death, and achieve a state of *nirvana*, in the Hindu practice of Tantric yoga. In Tantric yoga, the same emphasis is placed on the retention and absorption of vital liquids and Sanscrit texts describe how the male semen must not be emitted if the yogin is to avoid falling under law of time and death (Eliade, p. 267-268).

See also

Onanism

References

Eliade, Mircea. [1954] 1973. *Yoga, Immortality and Freedom*. trans. Willard R. Trask. Princeton: Princeton University Press.

Girardot, N. J. [1983] 1988. *Myth and Meaning in Early Taoism*. Berkeley; Los Angeles; London: University of California Press.

Maspero, Henri. 1937. "Les Procédés de 'nourir le principe vital' dans la religion taoiste ancienne". *Journal Asiatique*, no. 228.

Paz, Octavio. [1969] 1975. *Conjunctions and Disjunctions*. trans. Helen R. Lane. London: Wildwood House.

Rawson, Philip. 1968. *Erotic Art of the East*. New York: G. P. Putnam's Sons.

Schipper, Kristofer. [1982] 1993. *The Taoist Body*. trans. Karen C. Duval. Berkeley; Los Angeles; London: University of California Press.

Van Gullik, R. H. 1961. *Sexual Life in Ancient China*. Leiden, the Netherlands: Brill.

D

De Sade, Marquis D. A. F. (1740-1814)

Sadism, defined by the Oxford dictionary as "a form of sexual perversion marked by cruelty", is named after a count, Donatien Alphonse François, Compte de Sade, usually called the Marquis de Sade, who is infamous both for his crimes and his erotic writings. His most renowned works are *Les 120 journées de Sodome* (One Hundred and Twenty Days of Sodom), written after he was imprisoned in the Bastille in 1784, *Les Infortunes des la vertu*, later to be revised as *Justine, ou les malheurs de la vertu* (Justine; or, The Misfortunes of Virtue), and *Juliette* (or, The Prosperities of Vice). The writings of de Sade are still officially banned by the French courts and sadism is still regarded as perverse and surrounded by taboos although in 1995 the Law Commission for England and Wales recommended that it should no longer be regarded as a criminal offence for consenting adults to indulge in acts of sado-masochism.

Deriving pleasure from the infliction of pain is certainly perplexing and it is difficult to imagine anyone not being disturbed by the cruelty and violence in de Sade's books. A typical response to the marquis' works is that of Jules Janin, writing in the *Revue de Paris* in 1834:

There are bloody corpses everywhere, infants torn from their mothers' arms, young women with their throats slit after an orgy, cups full of blood and wine, unimaginable tortures. Cauldrons are heated, racks set up, skulls broken, men flayed alive; there is shouting, swearing, blasphemy; hearts are ripped from bodies ... When the author has committed every crime there is, when he is sated with incest and monstrosities, when he stands panting above the corpses he has stabbed and violated, when there is no church he has not sullied, no child he has not sacrificed to his rage, no moral thought on which he has not flung the foulness of his own thoughts and words, then at last this man pauses, looks at himself, smiles to himself and is not frightened (Bataille, p. 1987)

What is surprising, given their contents, is the way in which de Sade's writings have been acclaimed by artists and writers including the French poet, Apollinaire, the surrealists and even the champion of feminism, Simone de Beauvoir. To understand this is it necessary to look a little closer at the life and times of the marquis, writing as he was at a time of social and political revolution.

The Marquis de Sade was born into an aristocratic family and, after abandoning a military career, he married the daughter of a magistrate, Renée-Pélagie de Montreuil, in 1763. Four months after the marriage, he was imprisoned in Vincennes; the charges included blasphemy, sacrilege and immorality. After two weeks in jail he was released and resumed his dissolute life, living with prostitutes and falling into debt.

Then, in 1768, a scandal arose over an encounter between de Sade and a young German woman named Rose Keller. According to Rose Keller, the marquis met her in Paris on Easter Sunday and offered her domestic work. However, once back at his house in Arcueil, de Sade threatened her with a knife, tied her to the bed and beat her with a leather whip. She managed to escape and some village women, horrified by her account, took her to the authorities. As a result, the marquis was once again imprisoned, this time near Lyon in the Pierre-Encise.

He was released but was in trouble once again in 1772 when he was charged with the attempted poisoning of several prostitutes: three girls and a woman, Marguerite Coste. The women had been procured in Marseilles by the marquis' servant, Latour. It has been established that de Sade never intended to kill the girls but, in an orgy that included sodomy, homosexuality and flagellation, he passed around chocolates that were laced with cantharides, soft-bodied beetles known as "Spanish flies", which were once thought to have an aphrodisiac effect. Subsequent abdominal pains and vomiting convinced the women they had been poisoned and the marquis and Latour, forewarned of the serious charges levelled at them, fled towards Italy and were arrested by the king of Sardinia. In their absence, the pair were found guilty of sodomy and immorality as well as attempted poisoning and were burned in effigy in the central square of the town of Aix after the Parliament of Provence had confirmed the judgement of the judges in Marseilles.

The marquis, after escaping from prison, continued his sexual extravagances in his house at La Coste, together with his wife and local youths he had abducted. When the parents of the latter objected, he fled to Italy and took along his sister-in-law whom he adopted as a mistress, thereby arousing the anger of his mother-in-law. His incensed mother-in-law was instrumental in having de Sade detained in the prison of Vincennes in 1777 after he returned to La Coste.

Much of the marquis' writing was carried out in jail; it provided an outlet for his rage against incarceration and helped to relieve the boredom. In 1782 he completed *Dialogue entre un prêtre et un moribund* (Dialogue Between a Priest and a Dying Man), in which he declared his atheism, and after his transfer to the Bastille in Paris in 1784 he wrote *One Hundred and Twenty Days of Sodom* or *The School of Libertinage*.

The plot of this novel is simple. Four exceedingly rich people – the Duke of Blagnis, his brother and two other men – decide to seclude themselves in an impregnable castle to experience all imaginable forms of sexual perversion. They hire four old procurers, former prostitutes, who must recite all the perversions of which they are aware, ranging from "simple" perversions and "rare and complicated aberrations" (including those which require multiple participants), to perversions that lead to bodily tortures and might end in murder, and finally, violence itself. Young boys and girls are engaged as "objects of debauch", victims upon whom the duke and his partners enact all the vices of which they have heard.

The manuscript of the novel, written in a tiny script on sheets of paper joined end to end, was lost for some time after the storming of the Bastille on 14 July 1789. The marquis' next novel, *Justine*, exists in at least three versions, an early version of which, *Les infortunes de la vertu* (The Misfortunes of Virtue), was completed during his stay in the Bastille. In 1788 de Sade wrote the short stories which were later published as *Les crimes de l'amour* (Crimes of Passion). A few days before the French Revolutionaries stormed the Bastille, de Sade tried to stir up passers-by to rebellion by shouting that the prisoners' throats were being cut. For this he was imprisoned in a psychiatric institution in Charenton until 1790.

Upon his release, he began to live with an actress, the widow Quesnet, and offered several plays to the Comédie Française. He also wrote a version of his famous novel, *Justine*. As with *The 120 Days of Sodom*, the plot is less important than the excesses it describes. The novel relates how an innocent orphan girl is dismissed, at the age of fourteen, from the convent in which she had been educated. She retains her principles and refuses to sell herself for sex, finding service in the house of an avaricious man..The man tries to induce her to steal from a neighbour and when she refuses she is falsely accused of theft. She is imprisoned but escapes after becoming an accomplice in an arson which kills several prisoners. Once outside, in the woods of Bondy, she is raped, and is further maltreated when she takes refuge in the castle of the Count of Bressac. He tries to persuade her to help him poison his mother, arguing that the power to destroy a human being is merely illusory as nothing in nature is destroyed, merely transmuted into a different form. Justine contends that after a crime one is tormented by feelings of remorse but the count replies that habit dulls remorse and that continued crime hardens the criminal. Justine refuses to help Bressac and he sets his mastiffs on her. The narrative continues with accounts of the terrible cruelty evoked by the girl's virtuous behaviour: she is branded with a hot iron, kidnapped by perverse abbots who further abuse her and is finally struck by lightening.

As soon as de Sade completed his allegory on the "misfortunes of virtue", he started on its complement, *Juliette, or The Prosperities of Vice*. This is the story of Justine's sister, Juliette, who embraces vice with the same zeal that her sister displayed for virtue. She becomes a poisoner for a murderous politician, joins the Society of the Friends of Crime, travels through Italy prostituting herself, indulging in necrophilia and all manner of sexual deviancies, enters the richest courts and even the pope's mansion, and

becomes rich and respected. In one version of *Justine*, the two sisters meet and, after Justine has related all her woes, Juliette, now a beautiful noblewoman, tells how her life of vice has led to nothing but roses.

Though the writings of the Marquis de Sade are filled with horrendous cruelty and corruption, he himself was revolted by the excesses of the Reign of Terror. As an enemy of the old régime, he had supported the Revolution and was appointed secretary of the Revolutionary Section of Les Piques in Paris in 1792. But he was outspoken in his criticism of the brutality of the revolutionaries. In the midst of the terror he managed to rescue his father-in-law, Montreuil, and his wife from the guillotine even through they had been responsible for his imprisonment on several occasions. Because he denounced their methods, the partisans condemned de Sade to the guillotine which he escaped by chance just before Robespierre was overthrown.

The marquis' final period of imprisonment began after he was arrested at his publishers in 1801. Copies of *Justine* and *Juliette* were found and he was sent once more to Charenton. From there he made appeals to Napoleon but the emperor proved unsympathetic. His final novel, *Les journées de Florbelle ou la nature dévoilée* (The Days of Florbelle or Nature Unveiled) was begun in Charenton; it was burned by his elder son after his death.

Since his death, the marquis' books have been both reviled and revered. On the surface, it seems difficult to see anything to celebrate in his inventory of vice. He has, of course, been acclaimed for his defence of absolute liberty and the individual's right to give free reign to his instincts. Yet the French literary critic, Roland Barthes, has argued that de Sade is essentially a grammarian of the erotic, more concerned with recording, describing and choreographing the deviancies than practising them. Records exist of the marquis interrupting a man who was whipping him in Marseilles so that he could mark the number of lashes in notches above the fireplace and he was meticulous in the orchestration of his orgies. Besides, the carnal scenes in the novels are interspersed with cool philosophical reflections, hardly likely to inflame the passions.

The actual events of the novels are totally implausible, calling to mind the wild excesses of Rabelais. But in his writings he describes deviancies that are known to exist and explains the pathological phenomenon known today as sadism. In this way he has been influential in the realm of psychoanalysis. His attitude towards taboos is also revealing; he thinks those things that most repel the mind must be brought to the surface of the conscious mind as they are part of human nature. Only through self-knowledge is it possible to control one's own depravity. The surrealists, influenced by Freud, took a similar view, aiming to destroy all censorship and liberate man's libidinal and anarchistic compulsions; in this way they hoped to undermine bourgeois sensibilities.

Georges Bataille points out that violence often underlies not just sexual urges but also religious experience. Sacrifice has played a pivotal role in many religions and even Christianity has its roots in the Crucifixion, the divine sacrifice through which man is redeemed. Secular life is also suffused with violence, but this is often hidden or ignored, a fact that may explain Simone de Beauvoir's defence of the marquis:

> The merit of de Sade is not only to have cried loudly what all confess shamefully to themselves: it is to have taken sides. Instead of indifference, he chose cruelty. And that is why he finds so many echoes today, when the individual is aware of being the victim not so much of the malice of men, as of their good conscience (Gonzalez-Crussi, p. 93).

At first, de Beauvoir appears to support the idea that anything is better than indifference; the existential philosopher, Jean-Paul Sartre, has argued that one hurts other people anyway, therefore it is better to do it consciously. But she is also denouncing human hypocrisy which proclaims the brotherhood of man while turning a blind eye to genocide.

References

Barthes, Roland. 1971. *Sade, Fourier, Loyola*. Paris: Editions du Seuil.

Bataille, Georges. [1957] 1987. *Eroticism*. trans. Mary Dalwood. London: Marion Boyars Publishers.

Carter, Angela. 1979. *The Sadeian Woman*. London: Virago.

de Beauvoir, Simone. 1955. *Faut-il brûler Sade?* Paris: Gallimard.

Gonzalez-Crussi, Franz. [1988] 1989. *On the Nature of Things Erotic*. London: Picador.

Lynch, Lawrence W. 1984. *The Marquis de Sade*. Boston, Massachusetts: Twayne Publishers.

Michael, Colette Verger. 1986. *The Marquis de Sade: The Man, His Works, and His Critics*. New York; London: Garland.

Schaeffer, Neil. 1999. *The Marquis de Sade: A Life*. London: Hamish Hamilton.

Death

Death, and all that surrounds it, is steeped in taboos. Certain myths, such as those of *Genesis*, tell how death itself came into the world through the violation of a taboo. More often, though, tales trace the origin of death to a meaningless accident or an unfortunate choice: God sends a chameleon with a message of life and a lizard with a message of death to the ancestors, but the chameleon pauses on the way and the lizard arrives first; or man, given the choice between a stone and a banana, chooses the banana and, like it, is doomed to perish, forfeiting the permanence of stone. An African myth from the Luba of Zaire is closer to the biblical story; here it is the eating of bananas, unwisely stolen from the creator, that causes man to sicken and die.

The corpse and mortuary rites

A fear of the corpse – considered to be a major source of danger and pollution – is almost universal. Among Hindus, it was left to that despised group known as "untouchables" to carry out the cadavers of those dying without relatives; within Judaism the priestly caste is forbidden contact with a corpse; in the Titicaca region of Bolivia the corpse is strangled, in order – it is said – to prevent the stench from escaping; while among the Cantonese of rural Hong Kong menial labourers, employed to handle the body and dispose of its clothing, were considered so contaminated by their task that villagers would not even speak to them. As the anthropologist, Robert Hertz, remarks:

> Death … by striking the individual, has given him a new character; his body, which … was in the realm of the ordinary, suddenly leaves it; it can no longer be touched without danger, it is an object of horror and dread. (Hertz, p. 38).

The relatives of the deceased are also affected by the funerary contagion and are banned for a time from participation in normal social life: their diet and dress is restricted and clothes may be deliberately torn, their hair shorn or, conversely, it may be forbidden to trim the hair and beard, the movement of close kin may be curtailed and a widow or widower may be forbidden to remarry during the period of mourning.

The manner of disposal of the pernicious corpse varies according to the society and often involves considerable effort and ingenuity:

> Corpses are burned or buried, with or without animal or human sacrifice; they are preserved by smoking, embalming or pickling; they are eaten – raw, cooked or rotten; they are ritually exposed as carrion or simply abandoned; or they are dismembered and treated in a variety of these ways (Metcalf and Huntington, p. 24).

The cadaver is considered most dangerous during the period of putrefaction and the function of a mortuary ritual may be to deny the process of decay, either by embalming or burn-ing the corpse, to hide it through a (often temporary) burial, to delay it through the use of formalin so that mourners have time to gather the food for a final feast, or to accelerate it by allowing scavenging birds to devour the flesh. The technique of embalming reached its apotheosis in Egypt in dynastic times but mummification of the body may occur naturally – a result of the desiccating qualities of the earth or air. However, smoking or embalming the corpse is a deliberate attempt to fight corruption. In the elaborate embalming practices of the Egyptians, the corpse became a god through identification with Osiris. A lengthy and meticulous religious ritual attended every movement of the embalmers and only when it was complete, and the body became imperishable, was it taken to the grave. In the Hindu Indian cremation ceremony, the body is burned on a funeral pyre and the purified, burned bones are then buried. The burning:

> … spares the dead and the living the sorrows and dangers involved in the transformation of the corpse; or at least, it shortens that period considerably by accomplishing all at once the destruction of the flesh and the reduction of the body to immutable elements (Hertz, p. 43).

Endocannibalism, in which members of a tribe dine upon the flesh of a dead kinsman, similarly spares the corpse the horror of a slow decomposition. The flesh is "buried" in the stomachs where it is quickly digested. The Zoroastrians of Iran allowed vultures to devour the exposed body, a custom still practised by the Parsi in India. According to the sacred texts of the Zoroastrians, the corpse is the essence of impurity and the earth must not be polluted by its burial. To avoid this, the body is taken to "tower of silence" or *dakhma*, a rock tower built in an isolated location. Inside the tower is a platform that slopes down to a central pit and it is here that the corpses are laid. Formerly, after the flesh had been devoured, the bones were taken to an ossary but now the bones are merely thrown into the depths of the pit where the lime that has been spread out there slowly transforms them to dust.

The social dimension of mortuary rites

It may be logical to attribute taboos surrounding the dead to a natural human aversion to the processes of bodily decay, the odour of putrefying flesh and the fear of disease. But Hertz rejects explanations based on hygiene:

> This is not a matter of hygiene (as we understand the word), nor even, exclusively, a concern to ward off foul smells: we must not attribute to these people feelings and scruples about smell which are foreign to them (Hertz, p. 32).

Indeed, Hertz describes how in Bali it was the custom to keep the corpse in the house for many weeks before cremation with the liquids produced by decomposition drained through a hole in the coffin and collected in a dish which was ceremoniously emptied each day. In Borneo a bamboo tube was used to drain the liquid from fermenting jars – in which the body was pickled – and this was then mixed with rice and eaten by close relatives during the mourning period. Moreover, the anthropologist, Peter Metcalf, noticed in his fieldwork among the Berawan of Borneo in 1987 that while not exactly indifferent to the smells of decomposition, "Rotting does not have the wholly negative connotations for them that it does for us" (Metcalf and Huntington, p. 73-74). Clearly the death pollution is understood to be supernatural – hence the common belief in the contamination of objects surrounding a dead man, things he has touched, the river in which he has fished, the fruit from his orchard.

But social factors, such as the status of the deceased, also play a part in the contamination of death. Hertz noticed how, within a single society, the death of a chief would arouse intense revulsion and dread while that of a child or slave would go practically unnoticed. The degree of kinship with the dead person is also important: the closer the relationship, the longer the mourning and the separation from the rest of community.

Even the time of death is commonly determined by social convention rather than medical evidence. When Nigel Barley visited a Torajan family in Indonesia he was introduced to a grandmother. Unfortunately, the grandmother was dead – wrapped in layers of cloth to absorb the liquids of putrefaction – and she could not return the greeting. Enquiring as to how long she had been dead, Barley breached the rules of etiquette and appalled his host: "We don't say that ... She won't die until she leaves the house. She's been sleeping for three years now". Noticing that her body acted as a handy shelf for storing tapes, the anthropologist remarked sagely, "You'll miss her when she dies" (Barley, p. 54-55).

On the other hand, among the Lugbara of Uganda, a dying man is considered dead as soon as he has spoken his last words and had them accepted by his successor. The latter then steps outside the hut and calls the *cere* – the personal cry – of his predecessor who is no longer regarded as alive even though he may linger on. Similarly disconcerting is the fate of those presumed dead, but actually still living, among the Dogon of the Sudan. Once the funeral rites have been performed a person is considered dead and, should he reappear later, not even his closest relations will acknowledge him and he will be forced to remain a nameless beggar for the rest of his life.

The social dimension of death and mortuary rituals was investigated by the Frenchman, Émile Durkheim, in an early essay of 1895 and in *The Elementary Forms of the Religious Life*, published in 1912. Analysing a description of a death among Australian aborigines – in which gashed thighs and heads, fighting and frenzy, would seem to point to overwhelming grief – Durkheim shows how the degree of emotion manifested, and the level of self-mutilation, is assigned according to kinship roles (mother's brother and brother, respectively). Moreover, the outward expression of grief is a prescribed duty and this public manifestation of sorrow affects those in the community not directly experiencing loss, so that a feeling of solidarity is evoked. The careful orchestration of grief in this way means that intense emotion can be utilised to foster social cohesion.

Hertz, a pupil of Durkheim, agrees that the emotions and conceptions of death are socially determined and that rituals can manipulate private emotions. Moreover, grafted onto each physical individual is a social being in whom the society has invested considerable energy:

> Thus, when a man dies, society loses in him much more than a unit; it is stricken in the very principle of its life, in the faith it has in itself (Hertz, p. 77-78).

This explains why the death of a ruler or someone of high status is so much more traumatic than the death of a child who has yet to be invested with a social role. It takes time for a society to recover from the crisis of losing an important member; gradually, "society" must reclaim what it has invested in the deceased and graft it onto a new member. To accommodate this process, typical mortuary rites are characterised by two distinct rituals: rites of separation, the purpose of which, as the Mossi of Burkina Faso proclaim, somewhat paradoxically, is to "kill the dead" by which they mean to destroy what remains alive in a dead person by sundering the emotional bonds that link him to the community; and rites of integration and the cessation of mourning when the soul is deemed to have been incorporated into the world of the ancestors and the mourners are reintegrated into society. The roles once occupied by the deceased are reallocated and order is re-established. An important monograph analysing the way in which the roles and property of a deceased LoDagaa of West Africa are redistributed has been written by the anthropologist, Jack Goody.

The liminal period

The period between the actual death of a person and the time when mourning ceases, between the rites of separation and those of integration, is known as the liminal period. It may vary from a few weeks to several years and is often demarcated by a double disposal of the dead. First the body is incarcerated (in a temporary grave, or a "Tower of Silence", or in fermenting jars, as in Borneo) while the flesh decomposes, then a great feast is held and the remains of the corpse are recovered and buried or stored elsewhere, in a place free from the taint of decay. While the underlying function of the burial customs may be social, the corpse itself is deemed dangerous and subject to taboos because, until its dissolution and reconstruction in the realm of the dead, part of its spiritual essence remains behind where it can menace and endanger the living. To free the soul, the body must be destroyed:

> The same belief applies to the soul and body of the deceased ... death is not a mere destruction but a transition: as it progresses so does the rebirth; while the old body falls to ruins, a new body takes shape, which with the soul – provided the necessary rites have been performed – will enter another existence, often superior to the previous one (Hertz, p. 45-48).

During the transitional, or liminal, period the status of the individual is undetermined and he is a danger to himself and others. The intermediate period is determined by the rate of decay: only when the putrefaction is complete and the bones are dry may the final celebrations commence. Hertz has argued, somewhat ingeniously, that even when the aim of the mortuary rituals is to avoid putrefaction, through embalming the body, burning it or ingesting the flesh, a twofold process is evident. In the first case, the embalming gradually renders the putrefaction inert and the mummy can then be taken to the grave; while in the second, cremation destroys the flesh but the burned bones are later buried; and as for endocannibalism, the flesh is "interred" in the stomach of the eater while the bones are kept for a certain time by the relatives until their final burial.

Throughout the transitional period, the corpse is in great danger from evil spirits and must be protected by ritual acts such as ablutions, the closing of the eyes and other orifices – common entry points for the spirits – with coins, vigils over the body and the beating of gongs to frighten the demons. Meanwhile, the soul, homeless and formless as the decaying corpse, is an object of both pity and dread and elaborate precautions are necessary to deflect its malevolence:

> In its present distress it remembers all the wrongs it has suffered during its life and seeks revenge. It watches its relatives' mourning sharply and if they do not properly fulfil their duties towards itself, if they do not actively prepare its release, it becomes irritated and inflicts diseases upon them, for death has endowed it with magical powers which enable it to put its bad intentions into practice (Hertz, p. 36-37).

Though the soul may be directed to the land of the dead on the day after death, it can return at will until the time of the dissolution of the corpse and the final rites. After this, it may return only on specified dates and by official invitation.

Other scholars who have examined the distinct phases (of separation, transition and integration) in funeral rituals include Arnold van Gennep, a contemporary of Hertz, and Victor Turner. In 1904 van Gennep published *Tabou et totemisme á Madagascar* and in 1909 *Les Rites de Passage*. Van Gennep was surprised that the rituals that separate the deceased from the living, his social roles, and the rest of the community are less elaborate than those joining him to the realm of his ancestors and those rites which re-incorporate the bereaved into the community. Concerning the rites of incorporation into the other world, he writes:

> They are equivalent to those of hospitality, incorporation into the clan,

adoption, and so forth. They are often alluded to in legends whose central theme is a descent to Hades or a journey to the land of the dead, and they are mentioned in the form of taboos: one must not eat with the dead, drink or eat anything produced in their country, allow oneself to be touched or embraced by them, accept gifts from them and so forth. On the other hand, drinking with a dead person is an act of incorporation with him and the other dead, and it consequently allows one to travel among them without danger, as does the payment of a toll (coins, etc.) (van Gennep, p. 165).

About the transitional, liminal, rites, van Gennep has stated that their duration and complexity is so great that they can be granted a certain autonomy. Victor Turner, writing of liminality, describes it as a mediatory movement between past and future, marked by ambiguous, equivocal, ambisexual allusions; a time when social distinctions are often blurred, when conventions are discarded and taboos transgressed. During the liminal stage, those affected are imbued with symbols of death, invisibility, darkness and decomposition followed by rebirth, vegetative growth, new dress and renaming.

Sexuality and death

Themes of regeneration and rebirth, expressed in allusions to agricultural and human fertility in the intermediate stage of funeral ceremonies, were observed by Hertz and van Gennep. However, Peter Metcalf and Richard Huntington were not satisfied with the conclusions of their predecessors, whom they judged not to have adequately explained the prevalence of such motifs. For instance, as they explain in *Celebrations of Death*, not all societies have eschatological beliefs that include a long journey of the soul to the afterlife as the flesh rots. It is also unclear why certain funerals, such as those of the Bara of Madagascar, should be characterised by drunkenness, sexual licence, bawdy songs and the violation of taboos rather than solemn hymns and a respectful show of solidarity. However, upon closer inspection, Metcalf and Huntington discover a dualism in Bara thought that opposes vitality – identified with the female, mother, blood, flesh, fecundity, birth and the womb – to order, represented by the male, father, semen, bone, sterility, dying and the tomb. A human is conceived by a conjunction of opposites when the fertile blood of the mother's womb is united with, and ordered by, the sperm of the father. Death upsets the delicate balance of life with a surfeit of order: the sterile order of bone overpowers the waning vitality of the decomposing flesh. If the deceased is to muster the strength to enter the afterlife, the balance must be restored: there must be a symbolic increase in vitality. Vitality is expressed by behaviour which the Bara would normally view as tabooed but which, at this precarious time, is absolutely essential: cattle-riding, ostentatious feasting, the wild, erotic dancing of hired dance troupes, the lascivious songs of the women, sexual encounters, drunkenness and allusions to incest.

Sexuality as a symbol of regeneration may seem indisputable but Maurice Bloch and Jonathan Parry (perversely, as they themselves admit) dispute it, proposing that sexuality may be antithetical to fertility. Essentially, they find a logical inconsistency in the analysis of Metcalf and Huntington. If the Bara place such a high value on the female element of vitality, and this is manifest in the flesh, why are the people so insistent that, at its first burial, the corpse should be denuded of all flesh? Surely all effort should be extended to preserve this precious resource, as is the case with the Merina, another Malagasy society, who are careful to retain both the bones and flesh (in the form of dust). Bloch and Parry therefore offer an alternative explanation, after carefully perusing the Bara data:

Immediately after death two huts are cleared: one for the men and one for the women ... The corpse is secluded in the latter for a period of three days and two nights. During the daytime the people mourn, while the nights are given over to promiscuous sexual pairing initiated by the erotic dancing and provocative singing of the girls ... [then] The men go to the women's hut and forcibly remove the corpse over the anguished protests of the female mourners. Relays of young men run with the coffin towards the mountain of the ancestors, pursued by a group of young girls – hair dishevelled and clothes in disarray, who try to hinder their progress ... Having reached the tomb, the deceased is reborn (head first like a foetus) into the world of the ancestors.

All this suggests a ritual drama in which women are given the role of an unacceptable obscene sexuality, in which they deliberately endeavour to implicate men, which takes place at night and which must be broken through during the day – as the obstructive cordon of girls must be broken through – in order to attain a proper rebirth into the world of the ancestors. In other words, it is the necessary defeat of women, sexuality and biology which is enacted, rather than their indispensable part in the recreation of life ... [sexuality] is associated with flesh, decomposition and women, while true ancestral fertility is a mystical process symbolised by the tomb and the (male) bones (Bloch and Parry, p. 21).

Among the Lugbara of Uganda, female sexuality is associated with the wild bushland which is opposed to the sacred fertility of the village with its ancestral shrine under the control of the men. At funerals, women shave their heads and cover their bodies with white chalk and ashes as a mark of their pollution and association with the barren wilderness. But during the death dances, whose function is to restore an equilibrium after death's disruption, couples make love freely in the fields outside the compound, an act which would normally pollute the crops. Even incest is permitted. No children may result from these unions but the unrestrained sex, like death itself, represents an intrusion of the wild into the ordered world of the homestead (Middleton, p. 148-149).

Bloch and Parry include the article on the Lugbara in their collection of essays on death rituals, and it is perhaps not surprising that many of these papers validate their thesis which identifies women with sexuality and sexuality with death. In his examination of death pollution in Cantonese society, James Watson is startled by the community's horror of the putrefying corpse although the bones, once stripped, enhance fertility in the descendants. Men, in particular, are contaminated if they handle the corpse, which depletes their *yang*, or male essence, and if they are unwise and repeat the process several times, the pollution will be indelible. Yet a woman is not subject to such strictures and married daughters and daughters-in-law (but not the sexually inactive unmarried daughters) of the deceased rub their unbound hair against the coffin – symbolically absorbing the pollution – then leave it unwashed until the cessation of mourning seven days later (Watson, p. 172-173).

Bloch and Parry also draw attention to Pina-Cabral's study of the cults of the dead in contemporary north-western Portugal. In this region, the flesh is seen as a sign of mortality, binding the soul to the material world. Spiritual perfection is reached when the bones are disinterred and cleaned a few years after the initial burial. If, at this time, decomposition has not occurred, the priests conclude that the priest is still in a state of sin. However, the laity have a completely different interpretation of an uncorrupted corpse: a female with inviolate flesh is considered a saint – putrescence is a result of concupiscence (Bloch and Parry, p. 22).

This denigration of female sexuality in the death rituals of so many communities is seen by the authors as a deliberate ploy to ensure that social control remains in the hands of the male elders; by controlling the rituals necessary for the reproduction of the lineage, social rather than biological reproduction is paramount, nature has been subdued by culture, woman by man. Predictably, every theory has its limitations. It may be questioned whether a woman's hair can absorb and annul pollution if she herself is a source of it. Also suspect are the easy dichotomies of nature/culture, male/female, life/death; such discrete categories may owe more to the taxonomic inclinations of the scholar than to social reality.

Secular death

Essentially, the aim of funeral rites is to reorganise the society that has been disrupted by death and to console the mourners. In a modern, urban setting many of the rituals have been abandoned, mourning itself is virtually tabooed, and an inevitable sense of isolation and alienation results. As Louis-Vincent Thomas argues so eloquently:

> Consider, for example, today's laying out of the dead: for the impurity of former times, the pretext of hygiene is substituted; for respect for the corpse as subject, obsession with or horror of the corpse as object; for family deference, the anonymity of an indifferent wage. In the same way, the signs of mourning have fallen into disuse – we have passed from "mourning clothes in twenty-four hours" to twenty-four hours of mourning – and it is unseemly to show one's sorrow. People care less and less about the deceased, who sink into the anonymity of the forgotten; fewer and fewer masses are said for the repose of their souls, while the scattering of ashes eliminates the only physical support for a cult of the dead ...
>
> Without a doubt, man today is condemning himself to a dangerous

cultural void concerning rites and their symbols. We may well ask if our funerals, expedited in the "strictest intimacy", do not dangerously deprive us of a ritual that would help us to live (Thomas, p. 450-459).

See also

Necrophagy and Asceticism

References

Barley, Nigel. 1995. *Dancing on the Grave: Encounters with Death*. London: John Murray Ltd.

Bloch, Maurice and Jonathan Parry. [1980] 1982. "Introduction: death and the regeneration of life". In *Death and the Regeneration of Life*. ed. Maurice Bloch and Jonathan Parry, p. 1-44. Cambridge: Cambridge University Press.

Goody, Jack. 1962. *Death, Property and the Ancestors: A Study of the Mortuary Customs of the Lodagaa of West Africa*. London: Tavistock Publications.

Hertz, Robert. [1907] 1960. "A Contribution to the Study of the Collective Representation of Death". In *Death and the Right Hand*, p. 25-113. London: Cohen and West.

Metcalf, Peter and Richard Huntington. [1979] 1995. *Celebrations of Death: The Anthropology of Mortuary Ritual*. Cambridge: Cambridge University Press.

Middleton, John. [1980] 1982. "Lugbara Death". In *Death and the Regeneration of Life*. ed. Maurice Bloch and Jonathan Parry, p. 134-154. Cambridge: Cambridge University Press.

Thomas, Louis-Vincent. 1987. "Funeral Rites". *The Encyclopedia of Religion*. vol. 5. ed. Mircea Eliade, p. 450-459. New York: Macmillan and Free Press.

van Gennep, Arnold. [1909] 1960. *The Rites of Passage*. London: Routledge and Kegan Paul.

Watson, James L. [1980] 1982. "Of Flesh and Bones: the Management of Death Pollution in Cantonese Society". In *Death and the Regeneration of Life*. ed. Maurice Bloch and Jonathan Parry, p. 155-186. Cambridge: Cambridge University Press.

Deformity

Many religions add to the sheer misery and pain that accompany disability and deformity by forbidding a disabled person to participate fully in rituals. Among Hindus, physical perfection is a sign of moral transcendence and priests, as Jonathan Parry relates, must therefore be perfect:

> A one-eyed man or a hunchback has no right to perform "the work of the gods". A Brahman who has black teeth, bad nails or is excessively corpulent should be excluded from the feast for Brahmans held on the thirteenth day after death; and nobody with an open wound should act as chief mourner … and it is a sin to worship an image of a deity that is broken or cracked (Parry, p. 502).

Parry deduces that it is this premium placed on physical perfection that lies behind the throwing of sulphuric acid at one's enemies in an effort to disfigure them, a tactic employed by the powerful Pilgrimage Priests in India and also by aggrieved or rejected Hindu suitors who wish to take revenge on their women (Parry, p. 502).

The bible, too, has a taboo on the deformed or the disabled performing sacrifices. *Leviticus* 21: 17-24 states:

> None of your descendants, in any generation, must come forward to offer the food of his God if he has any infirmity – no man may come near if he has an infirmity such as blindness or lameness, if he is disfigured or deformed, if he has an injured foot or arm, if he is a hunchback or a dwarf, if he has a disease of the eyes or of the skin, if he has a running sore, or if he is a eunuch. No descendant of Aaron the priest must come forward to offer the burnt offerings of Yahweh if he has any infirmity … he must not go near the veil or approach the altar, because he has an infirmity and must not profane my holy things.

Curiously, Moses, who was entrusted to bear this message to his brother, was himself afflicted with a speech impediment making him "slow of speech" (*Exodus* 4: 10-12), a feature which had made him unwilling to be God's mouthpiece. The patriarch Jacob, too, at the moment he is blessed and receives the name "Israel", walks with a limp, wounded from his encounter with the sacred. Moreover, to prove to the Israelites that he has been chosen by Yahweh, Moses is commanded to place his hand within his breast and bring it out leprous. Generally, though, biblical stories mention leprosy as a punishment, a token of spiritual as well as physical impurity, and this view remained prevalent in Europe throughout the Middle Ages. Like AIDS today, leprosy was associated with moral turpitude and degeneracy. Unfortunately, even in what we consider to be enlightened times, all too often physical imperfection continues to be seen as a "stigma".

References

Brody, Saul Nathaniel. 1974. *The Disease of the Soul: Leprosy in Medieval Literature.* Ithaca, New York: Cornell University Press.

Holden, Lynn. 1991. *Forms of Deformity: A Motif-Index of Abnormalities, Deformities and Disabilities of the Human Form in Traditional Narrative.* Sheffield: Sheffield Academic Press.

Parry, Jonathan. [1989] 1990. "The End of the Body". In *Fragments for a History of the Human Body*. Part Two. ed. Michel Feher, p. 490-517. New York: Zone.

"Degenerate" Art

A major characteristic of totalitarian regimes, and one of the ways in which absolute control is maintained, is the application of rigorous censorship of both overtly political tracts and less obviously political, or even apolitical, writing, music and art. One prominent example of direct censorship of the visual arts is manifest in the notorious exhibition of "*Entartete Kunst*" (Degenerate Art) organised by Hitler's National Socialist regime and held in Munich in 1937. The exhibition included works by all the major contemporary German artists and other Europeans such as Gauguin, Van Gogh, Munch, Picasso, Braque, Matisse and Chagall. The aim of the exhibition was to thoroughly discredit modern art (viewed as a conspiracy by Bolsheviks and Jews to undermine traditional German culture) by mixing these works, by artists who were now banned in Germany, with inferior pieces and paintings by the incurably insane. The paintings were badly hung and subjected to ridicule and attack by the controlled press. At the same time another show opened in Munich which, in a dull, academic style, showed portraits, landscapes and genre scenes extolling the virtues of the Nazis and their ideals of heroism, family duty and work on the land. It was at the opening of this exhibition, the "Great Exhibition of German Art", that Hitler denounced the paintings of "*Entartete Kunst*":

> I have observed among the pictures submitted here, quite a few paintings which make one actually come to the conclusion that the eye shows things differently to certain human beings than the way they really are, that is, there really are men who see the present population of our nation only as rotten cretins; who, on principle, see meadows blue, skies green, clouds sulphur yellow, and so on ... in the name of the German people, I want to forbid these pitiful misfortunates who quite obviously suffer from an eye disease, to try vehemently to foist these products of their misinterpretation upon the age we live in, or even to wish to present them as "Art" (Chipp, p. 480).

Abstraction, Cubism, Fauvism, Expressionism, Dadaism and Surrealism were all forbidden; only naturalistic portrayals of "uplifting" subjects, expressing "Germanic" values, were allowed. (Ironically, posters advertising "*Entartete Kunst*" employed the very techniques of geometric abstraction and expressionism that the Nazis eschewed.) Joseph Goebbels, the Minister for Propaganda,

ordered 16,550 works of modern art to be confiscated from German museums. Some were
sold at a public auction while others were sold
to private dealers and sent abroad or secretly
burned in Berlin. Innovative art schools, such
as the Bauhaus, were already closed in 1933
and academics dismissed. The *Malverbot* (prohibiting painting) led to the inspection of
artists' studios for evidence of 'subversive'
painting, an act which caused the expressionist,
Emil Nolde, to paint in odourless watercolours,
less easily detectable than oils. Another piece of
legislation, the *Ausstellungsverbot*, forbade
artists to exhibit their work. Before the Third
Reich, Germany had been a pioneer of modern
art but the régime left the country spiritually
and culturally barren as the best artists fled to
America and elsewhere. What remained was
insipid propaganda inspired by dangerous theories linking art with racist supremacy: *Kunst
und Rasse* (Art and Race) written by Paul
Schultze-Naumburg in 1928 and Alfred
Rosenberg's *Myth of the Twentieth Century* published in 1930.

See also
Surrealism

References
Chipp, Herschel B. 1968. *Theories of Modern Art*,
p. 473-483. Berkeley; Los Angeles: University of
California Press.

Hamilton, George Heard. [1967] 1978. *Painting
and Sculpture in Europe 1880-1940. The Pelican
History of Art*. Harmondsworth, Middlesex: Penguin.

"Degenerate" Music

In May 1938, an exhibition of *"Entartete
Musik"* (Degenerate Music) was held in
Düsseldorf, Germany, as part of the national
music festival, the *Reichmusiktage*. Inspired by
an exhibition of "degenerate art" held the previous year in Munich, it was the most direct
expression of musical censorship during the
Nazi régime. Its aim was to castigate the "mod-

ernist" tradition in music which it held to be
contrary to the Germanic spirit, "bolshevist",
"internationalist", "degenerate" and controlled
by Jews. Particularly attacked was the "atonal"
(having no reference to a key or tonic) music
and twelve-tone compositions exemplified by
the German composer, Arnold Schoenberg,
and Jazz. "The atonal movement in music is
against the blood and the soul of the German
people", declared Alfred Rosenberg, editor of
the Nazi newspaper *Völkischer Beobachter*, in
May 1935. But Nazi confusion as to what actually constituted "atonality" led to composers as
stylistically diverse as Paul Hindemith, Ernst
Krenek, Kurt Weill, Igor Stravinsky, Arnold
Schoenberg and Hermann Reutter all being so
designated. Experimental musical forms,
together with theatre, design, the visual arts
and architecture, had flourished in Germany
during the preceding Weimar Republic. Just as
the Third Reich was to denude Germany of its
major artists, so the repressive and reactionary
attitude to music led to the loss of prominent
musicians including the composers, Arnold
Schoenberg, Kurt Weill, Hanns Eisler and
Ernst Toch (who were forbidden because they
were Jewish as well as for their music) and Paul
Hindemith, as well as the conductors Otto
Klemperer and Hermann Scherchen.

Hans Severus Ziegler, the theatre director
who organised the exhibition of "degenerate
music", favoured diatonic (tonal) harmony and
simple melody. Similar tastes were prevalent at
the time in Stalinist Russia where the radical
composer Dmitri Shostakovich was suffering
condemnation. Ziegler's opening lecture
defined the music he abhorred:

> The *Entartete Musik* exhibition pres-
> ents a picture of a veritable witches'
> sabbath portraying the most frivolous
> intellectual and artistic aspects of
> Cultural Bolshevism ... and the tri-
> umph of arrogant Jewish impudence
> ... Degenerate music is thus basically
> de-Germanised music for which the
> nation will not mobilise its involve-

ment ... it is the last measure of snob-bist adoration or pure intellectual consideration (Ziegler in Levi, p. 96).

Foreign influences were blamed for suffocating such German music as the late romanticism of Richard Wagner. The racist overtones of the speech echoed those expressed at the exhibition of "degenerate art" the previous year. Jews had been consistently excluded from German musical life, whether as composers, performers or teachers, since Hitler became Chancellor in 1933.

The show itself consisted of portraits and photographs of those contemporary composers Ziegler considered to be the most pernicious for German music. They included Arnold Schoenberg, Igor Stravinsky, Paul Hindemith, Anton von Webern and Ernst Krenek. One omission was the contemporary Hungarian composer, Béla Bartók, who had openly showed his contempt for the Nazi régime and wrote a letter of protest to the Ministry of Propaganda complaining that his portrait had not been displayed (Levi, p. 101). Accompanying each picture was a caption attacking the character and racial origins of the musician. Also exhibited were theoretical texts by the composers and six booths were erected so that visitors could listen to recordings of works by Weill, Hindemith and others.

Curiously, for various reasons, the Third Reich's attack on music was not as successful as their campaign against the visual arts. Certain forms of music, such as jazz, were too popular with the people to be totally excluded despite the ludicrous attempts at depreciation, such as the caricatured negro playing a saxophone with a Star of David on his lapel displayed at the exhibition of "degenerate art" (Levi, p. 96). Political expediency also played a role: after Hitler signed a pact of non-aggression with Stalin in 1939, modern Soviet composers such as Sergey Prokofiev were suddenly accepted, and as Italy was an ally, contemporary Italian music was not censored even though its foremost proponents, Alfredo Casella and Gian

Francesco Malipiero, were strongly influenced by Stravinsky. Moreover, the Minister for Propaganda, Joseph Goebbels, was far more interested in film, art and literature, focusing his attention on these areas rather than on music.

See also

"Degenerate" Art; Musical Harmony

References

Levi, Erik. 1994. *Music in the Third Reich*. Basingstoke; London: Macmillan.

Ziegler, Hans Severus. 1938. *Entartete Musik. Eine Abrechnung*. Düsseldorf, quoted in Erik Levi *Music in the Third Reich*. Basingstoke; London: Macmillan.

Diminished Fifth, The

The diminished fifth (or augmented fourth) was proscribed by medieval musical theorists as *diabolis in music* (the devil in music) because its sound was considered flawed. To understand this taboo, it is necessary to know a little about musical harmony. Harmony, in music, is a succession of notes that sound simultaneously. Harmony derives from a natural phenomenon known as the harmonic series. The intervals, or distance between pairs of notes, in a piece of music determine the harmony; some intervals are consonant, of equal tension, causing the two notes to blend together, others are dissonant, with the two notes clashing, but with the expectation that they will resolve to a consonance. The earliest form of harmony in Western Europe began in the 9th century with the introduction of *organum*, which moved in parallel fifths and fourths. Fifths are so called because of the interval between two notes; for example, if the first note is a C on the treble clef, its companion is a G. D is linked with A, E with B, and so forth, with the tension between the notes remaining the same. These are called "perfect fifths". However, the fifth that is formed from a B and an F does not correspond to any of the simple tensions of the harmonic series. Viewed as dissonant and imperfect, this diminished fifth, also known as the Tritone, was avoided as the *diabolus in musica*. When it was sung, the B was flattened (a procedure known as the *musica ficta*) to produce a perfect fifth. Alternatively, the F could be sharpened.

By about the 12th century, a three-note chord, called a triad, was established. The three notes of a triad are known as the root, third and fifth. The third lies at an interval of a third above the root, midway between the root and the fifth. There are four types of triad: two are consonant, containing only consonant intervals; the other two are dissonant. The dissonant triads are the diminished triad, containing a dissonant diminished fifth, and an augmented triad containing a dissonant augmented fifth. Triads can be built on any note of a scale; the diminished fifth, in this case, can be created by flattening the final note.

Because the diminished fifth (which is the same as the augmented fourth) was traditionally considered to destroy all sense of ordered tonality, a system of keys was introduced to "correct" the "flaw" in the harmonic series. A key consists of a tonic note, together with its scale and the triads constructed on that scale's notes. This allows the dissonant notes to be integrated, as "inessential" notes, resolving on the tonic, and major, third.

Sometimes, however, a composer wishes to deliberately create an air of dissonance and exposes the *diabolus in musica*, without any resolution, in order to destroy the integrity of a tonic key. For obvious reasons, it is often utilised to represent the devil. Deryck Cooke, in *The Language of Music*, gives several examples. He begins with a scene from Mozart's *Don Giovanni*:

> the Statue offers the Don his hand – "Here it is" – and the Don grasps it and cries out in horror, moving to the diminished fifth. The chord accompanying his cry the chord of the dimin

ished seventh – is ... made up of two interlocking diminished fifths (Cooke, p. 87).

Cooke goes on to cite Weber, a composer who also employs the diminished fifth in his opera, *Der Freischütz*. In the scene, the Wolf's Glen, the music moves from F sharp minor (as the clock strikes midnight) via the diminished fifth A to E flat (as Casper invokes the Black Huntsman, Samiel) to C major (in anticipation of the arrival of Samiel ten bars later). Berlioz chooses the *diabolus in musica* for the opening of the Dream of a Witches' Sabbath in his *Symphonie Fantastique*. In *The Damnation of Faust* Berlioz again summons the note for the entrance of Mephistopheles and his call to spirits of fire. Other demonic applications include Gounod's *Faust* (with Mephistopheles standing in a pillar, in the Church Scene, inducing the praying Marguerite to despair); the Inferno scenes at the beginning of the Dante Sonata and Dante Symphony of Liszt and the beginning of his Mephisto Waltz No. 2; episodes from Wagner's *Ring* cycle, including the cursing of the ring by the diabolical Alberich, the call to arms by his son, Hagen, and the appearance of the dragon, Fafnir; Saint-Saëns' *Danse macabre*, where Death tunes his fiddle and calls the skeletons from the graves; the Walpurgisnacht scene from Boito's *Mefistofele*; Stravinsky's penultimate phrase of the Triumphant March of the Devil in *The Soldier's Tale*; Satan's Dance of Triumph in Vaughan William's *Job*; and phrases from Bartók's *Cantata Profana*, in which nine boys are enchanted and turned into deer.

The diminished fifth, or augmented fourth, can create not just a demonic, but an alien or hostile world. Deryck Cooke expresses this eloquently:

> Vaughan Williams employed it for the frozen wastes of his *Sinfonia Antartica*; Britten for the icy winter which opens his *Spring Symphony*; Holst for his "Mars, the Bringer of War" in *The Planets*. In as much as these forces are

inimical to mankind, they may be regarded as springing from the "negative" principle of the universe. With regard to Mars, nothing need be said in this age; as for the spirit of cold, we may remember that Mephistopheles, in Goethe's Faust, expresses a desire that life shall dissolve into nothingness; and, as we know, when that happens, the sun will have burnt out, and cold will conquer all (Cooke, p. 89).

If the 20th century was indeed an age of discord, as Cooke suggests, it created a fitting music. Between 1912 and 1922, the composer Arnold Schoenberg introduced a musical structure which was not primarily based on harmony and the diatonic scale. His atonal compositions, such as *Pierrot Lunaire* (1912), utilised a chromatic scale of twelve equidistant semitones, replacing the one or two tones which had previously served as the main focus points for an entire composition (the keys of tonal music). Harmonic cadences were replaced by melodic-rhythmic tensions and resolutions, resulting in a music of great emotional intensity. Though his detractors derided what they saw as a triumph of dissonance (no doubt the *diabolus in musica*), he, and his fellow composers, including Anton von Webern, Alban Berg, Luigi Dallapiccola and Hans Werner Henze, have had a radical influence on 20th-century music.

See also
Musical Harmony

References
Cooke, Deryck. 1959. *The Language of Music*. London: Oxford University Press.

Dogs

Eating a dog is believed to have dire consequences in many parts of the world and consuming the canine species is widely eschewed.

There are several reasons for this. Religious conviction lies behind many of the bans. Buddhism abhors the killing of any living being. In the *Nagarakrtagama,* sent in 1365 CE to King Hayam Wuruk of Majapahit in Java, the Buddhist Prapañca explains that ancient scriptures forbid dog-meat and institute punishments for transgressors (Simoons, p. 100). Muslims consider dogs ritually unclean and the Maliki school of law states that touching one causes *hadath*, or impurity, which must be cleansed by the lesser ablution (*wudu*) (Glassé, p. 102). In Moroccan tradition, the killing of a dog pollutes a man, and any subsequent animals he slaughters will be unfit for consumption, and he himself barred from certain religious rituals (Simoons, p. 104 n.12). Hunting dogs, though, are not unclean and it is lawful to eat game caught by trained hunting dogs provided it is released with pronunciation of the *basmalah* (in the name of Allah). Hindus consider the animal a filthy scavenger. Within the Hindu caste system those designated as "Untouchables" (who were lower than even the lowest caste) were also disparagingly called "dog-cookers".

On the other hand the Zoroastrians of ancient Iran refrained from eating dog-flesh because they held the animal sacred and used it in cleansing rituals. The historian Herodotus, writing in the 5th century BCE (*Historia* 1.140) relates how Xerxes had a great number of Indian hounds in his army when he invaded Greece and he discusses the cultic importance of dogs in Iran where the dead were exposed to dogs and scavengers. In his article "Zoroastrianism and the Body", Alan Williams describes a Zoroastrian purification ceremony in which a priest tethers a dog. The gaze of the canine is purifying to the *riman* (polluted one), who has been tainted by contact with a corpse or through a miscarriage, but anathema to the corpse demoness who is exorcised by the rite (Williams, p. 163).

A ban on canine flesh is also found in mythology. In an Irish tale, dogs are the downfall of the hero, Cuchulainn. Cuchulainn's name means "Dog of Culann" (dog is *cu* in Gaelic). He becomes the guard-dog of the smith Culann (the "Dog of War") to atone for having killed Culann's hound, in self-defence, at the age of six. He is under an injunction not to eat the flesh of his namesake and dies when he violates this *geis* or taboo by accepting meat from three crones. This is a personal taboo and is not unlike the injunction in many cultures on eating the totemic animal of one's clan.

Where there is no religious check on eating dogs, they may yet be spared because they are more useful living than dead or because there is other, more succulent, flesh available. This is a view endorsed by the anthropologist, Marvin Harris. Among certain groups including the Tahitians, Hawaiians and the Maori of New Zealand, dogs were kept before the arrival of Europeans and were an important source of food. The Tahitians and Hawaiians also kept pigs and chickens, and actually preferred pork to dog-meat, but as the pigs needed to be fed on cooked taro, raising them proved as time-consuming as rearing dogs, who were also fed cooked vegetables. With an absence of large game on these islands, the dogs were not needed for hunting and were of most use in the pot. Among the Maori, dogs were the only domesticated animal and although they helped in the hunting of the flightless birds known as kiwis, they were of more value when they themselves were the prey. Harris contrasts the lives of these islanders with those of the Hare, an Athabaskan-speaking people who live north of the Arctic Circle near Colville Lake in Canada's Northwest Territories. The Hare live by hunting and trapping caribou, moose, marten, mink, fox, beaver, muskrat and ermine and by fishing for trout, whitefish and pike. In this environment, teams of dogs are essential to pull equipment and traps and to transport furs and supplies. A hunter and his dog may travel up to 2,500 miles in a single winter and as well as pulling sleighs, the canines help in the hunt. Together, hunters and dogs can produce a sur-

plus of meat which they both share. The grateful Hare would never eat their dogs and find it painful even to kill the sick or lame animals (Harris, p. 179-190).

Of course, there are other reasons for consuming dogs beyond nutritional needs. Among certain groups in Nigeria, including the Amo, the Angas, the Berom, the Efik, the Ibibio, the Igara, the Igbo, the Kagoro, the Magazawa and the Yoruba, dogs are valued for their therapeutic and magical qualities. Canine fat is used in preparations against syphilis and fever and dog-flesh is eaten to protect against *juju* (harmful magic); Nigerian clairvoyants grind the eyes into a powder so that they may see like a dog and discern distant spirits; dog meat increases sexual potency and is used in love philtres and to cure infertility; and the Yoruba use a dog's head to prepare a soap which, if used regularly, guarantees success in business (Ojoade, p. 219). Even when the dog is used for food, it undergoes a mysterious transformation:

> the dog itself is called '404 station wagon' (after the Peugeot 404) ... the head is called 'gearbox' or 'loudspeaker', the legs are known as '404 wheels', the tail is referred to as 'telephone', the intestine 'roundabout' and the feet are called 'tyres'. The ears are called 'headlamps', and the water with which the dog is cooked is called 'penicillin' (Ojoade, p. 218).

In China, the eating of dogs goes back to the earliest times. Archaeologists have unearthed the remains of large numbers of dogs at the neolithic Yangshao (c. 5000-3200 BCE) and Lungshan (3rd-early 2nd millennium BCE) sites and dogs have been found at all Shang (c. 18th-12th century BCE) and Chou (12th century-221 BCE) sites. In a country where the major source of protein comes from the soybean, dogs were an important addition to the diet as they contain more protein than any other animal. The 7th-century pharmacologist, Meng Shen, believed dog flesh to be beneficial for the kidneys and during the Yuan and

Ming dynasties (1271-1644 CE) a lust for dog-meat signified hot-blooded, animal energy. Since the middle of the 20th century, however, the consumption of dog-flesh in mainland China has rapidly declined. A fear of disease and the competition for scarce food resources has led to a widespread culling of dogs in urban areas.

Evidence of the importance of canines in Southeast Asia can be found in the *Hou Han shu* myth written by Fan Yeh in the 5th century CE but probably deriving from earlier oral sources. The myth relates how Kao-hsin, the White Emperor, was threatened by the Dog Jung and offered his daughter and, as an added inducement, much gold, to whoever could bring him the head of Dog Jung's formidable chieftain, General Wu. Some time later, the emperor's pet dog, a magnificent creature with a pelt of five colours, returned with the head of General Wu between his teeth. This dog, named P'an Hu, happily married the emperor's daughter and returned with her to a stone chamber in Nan-shan ["Southern Mountain", in the Lu-chih district of Hunan province]. Here his wife disrobed and, in deference to her spouse, made a *pu-chien* (dog-coiffure) hairstyle and dressed in a *tu-li* (dog-tailed) robe. After three years twelve children were born, six of each sex. These married incestuously and retained the sartorial tastes of their parents: they liked five-colour clothing and always cut their clothes with a tail. Their descendants became known as *Man-i* (barbarians), and the present day Man people of Wu-ling in Ch'ang-sha [Hunan] are reported to be a branch of these (White, p. 141-142).

This tale, in which a race of humans is believed to have descended from dogs, touches on one of the most salient reasons for the avoidance of dog-flesh: dogs are too close to humans. As domesticated animals, they have hunted with man and lived in his homestead. To eat the flesh is akin to cannibalism.

See also

Food Taboos

References

Glassé, Cyril. 1989. *The Concise Encyclopedia of Islam*. London: Stacey Publications.

Harris, Marvin. 1986. *Good to Eat: Riddles of Food and Culture*. London: Allen and Unwin.

Ojoade, J. Olowo. 1990. "Nigerian Cultural Attitudes to the Dog". In *Signifying Animals: Human Meaning in the Natural World*. ed. Roy G. Willis, p. 215-221. London: Unwin Hyman.

Simoons, Frederick J. [1961] 1967. *Eat not This Flesh: Food Avoidances in the Old World*. Madison, Wisconsin; London: University of Wisconsin Press.

White, David Gordon. 1991. *Myths of the Dog-Man*. Chicago, Illinois; London: University of Chicago Press.

Williams, Alan. 1997. "Zoroastrianism and the Body". In *Religion and the Body*. ed. Sarah Coakley, p. 155-166. Cambridge: Cambridge University Press.

Dolls and Puppets

Dolls

Although dolls and puppets are often thought of as mere toys, innocent instruments of childhood pleasure, they are in essence simulacra and have in the past been invested with the powers and taboos of idols and effigies. Idols are consistently condemned in the bible, evidence of the popularity of idolatry, and effigies are commonly believed to contain part of the spirit of the person they represent. This explains their role in magical rituals where they can be used both to harm and to heal. In Japan dolls were used as scapegoats to rid the emperor of ritual pollution, a practice that began in the Nara imperial court (710-782 CE) and continued through the Muromachi period. For the rite, known as *nanase o-harai* (purification at the seven shallows), a Taoist diviner would make a small doll (*hitogata*, "in the shape of a human") of paper, straw or wood. On the first night of each lunar month the doll would be sent to the court where it was presented to the emperor. Using the doll like some kind of sacred soap, he would rub his entire body with it and the doll absorbed all his sins and transgressions. Then the doll was laid in a box and taken to one of seven river locations from which it would float out to sea. It is also possible that the *hitogata* were used magically to curse people as they were credited with the power of capturing a human spirit and conducting it to the afterlife. Because the effigy could embody the human spirit, *hitogata* of wives and family members were placed in the coffins of the nobility to provide company beyond the grave (Law, p. 33-35).

It is a small step from imagining that an effigy can capture the human spirit to believing the doll capable of human motion, alarmingly animate and menacing. In a story by Algernon Blackwood, a doll is delivered by a "dark-skinned" man to the house of a colonel who is guilty of crimes committed during his colonial stay in India. The colonel recognises the doll as a kind of fetish, capable of extracting retribution, and orders it to be destroyed but it escapes this fate and finally attacks him:

> Fast it came, supernaturally fast, its velocity actually shocking, for a shock came with it. It was exceedingly dreadful, its head erect and venomous and the movement of its head and arms, as of its bitter, glittering eyes, aping humanity. Malignant evil, personified and aggressive, shaped itself in this otherwise ridiculous outline. It was the doll … Savagely, its little jaws of make-believe were bitten deep into Colonel Masters' throat, fastened tightly (Blackwood, p. 31).

The doll is terrible because it can "ape" humanity. Animate dolls haunt literature; in E. T. A. Hoffman's nightmarish tale, *The Sand-man*, a beautiful woman who captivates the hero turns out to be nothing more than a mechanical doll. However, Sigmund Freud finds that the terror in *The Sand-man* cannot be totally explained by the eeriness of a living doll. The story makes constant reference to eyes and in one horrifying sequence the hero imagines his eyes being pulled out, a fear, Freud suggests, that is akin to the fear of castration. The hero's obsessive love for the automaton, named Olympia, is, in this reading, the projection of his own ego (and, in this instance, his eyes) onto an external object – the doll – which is symptomatic of the narcissistic stage of human development. Generally one outgrows this stage but the hero, Nathaniel, remains incapable of loving a real woman because he is still fixated upon his father through his castration complex (Freud, p. 348-358).

Curiously, it is also because dolls are so innocent, creatures of the nursery, that they are such suitable candidates for subversion. In 1913 the German artist Lotte Pritzel presented a series of elongated and emaciated dolls, constructed from wire and wax, at a gallery in Munich. Dressed in extravagant costumes, their postures suggested dance, decadence and melancholy eroticism. When her dolls were shown at the Munich Puppet Theatre Museum in 1987, the exhibition was entitled "Dances of Vice, Horror and Ecstasy", a title used previously by dancers in the 1920s who had impersonated her dolls.

Another German artist who has been criticised for his "decadent" dolls is Hans Bellmer. In 1933, as a protest against the National Socialists seizing power, Bellmer gave up his work as a technical draughtsman and directed his attention towards the construction of a wooden doll, a "purposeless" creation of art in praise of playfulness as well as the methodical representation of all the possible erotic experiences with a woman/child. The doll was constructed with an "axis of reversibility" at its navel, thus allowing the artist to identify the buttocks with the breasts and the mouth with the vagina. A second wooden doll was constructed in 1937; this one turned around a central ball and was inspired by the anatomical marionettes or lay figures used as models for art in Dürer's time. Bellmer's dolls could be manipulated, the limbs twisted and organs pulled askew. The brutal dislocation of the female body appears sadistic but Bellmer always stressed the psychological importance of his work and maintained that the disarticulation and dismemberment of the body was not a sign of brutal indifference to feminine beauty, but a token of desire in which attention to the constituent parts paid a sincere tribute to the attractiveness of the whole. He did, however, admit that the doll could help to liberate suppressed, aggressive, desires which could then be safely channelled into an illusory object. Essentially, Bellmer saw himself as the interpreter of dreams:.

> the body, just like the dream, can displace the centre of gravity of its image capriciously. Inspired by a curious spirit of contradiction, it superimposes on some what it takes away from the others, the image of the leg, for example, over that of the arm, that of the sex over the armpit, to make them "condensations", "proofs of analogies", "ambiguities", "play upon words", strange anatomical "calculations of possibilities" (Matthews, p. 27).

In 1938 Hans Bellmer left Germany for France and his works, like those of so many innovative German artists, were confiscated by the National Socialists. Another artist, the Austrian expressionist, Oskar Kokoschka, had trouble with a doll. While living in Dresden, he had a full-size, lifelike doll constructed and bought Parisian clothes and underwear for it. The doll was an effigy of Alma Mahler with whom he had enjoyed a passionate, if turbulent, relationship. Rumours circulated about outings and opera visits with the doll but during a wild party the doll lost its head and was doused in red wine. The "crime" was soon discovered. Early the next morning the police arrived at the door investigating a report that a headless body had been seen in the garden.

For the poet, Rainer Maria Rilke, the unsettling aspect of the doll does not lie in its capacity to assume human characteristics. On the contrary, what is disturbing is its very insentience. Suffused with love, it makes no response. This can only evoke a feeling of bitterness and of the ultimate loneliness of human existence:

> It was silent, and the idea did not even occur to it that this silence must confer considerable importance on it in a world where destiny and indeed God himself have become famous mainly by not speaking to us. At a time when everyone was concerned to give us prompt and reassuring answers, the doll was the first to make us aware of that silence larger than life which later breathed on us again and again out of space whenever we came at any point to the border of our existence. Sitting opposite the doll as it stared at us, (or am I mistaken?) that hollowness in our feelings, that heart-pause which could spell death, did not the whole gentle continuum of nature lift one like a lifeless body over the abyss (Rilke, p. 33).

Puppets

Unlike the doll, the puppet is animated by an external force. Sometimes the animator is thought to be a divinity, a spirit of the dead or a soul of the living. An Indian myth tells how the deity, Shiva, and his wife, Parvati, were so enchanted by some wooden dolls that they entered their bodies and danced around the doll-maker's shop, a frolic that inspired the dolls' creator to attach strings and make the first marionette. In the Japanese *Shiki Sanbaso* (ceremonial Sanbaso) rite, enacted to encourage prosperity, fecundity and a successful rice crop, a puppet serves as a surrogate body and is possessed by the deities of the rice field. The deities summoned are too powerful to inhabit a human being and the puppet acts as a kind of mediator, or shaman, bridging the gap between the human and the divine. The ritual begins with the Sambaso puppet covering his face to indicate submission to a greater spirit; then, after purifying the surrounding space, he shakes a rattle and begins to dance. As the dance becomes more and more frenzied, the eyes of the puppet change, becoming round, rolling and frantic and the puppet waves his arms and stamps his feet to drive out all evil and to convoke powers from the earth. The actual moment of possession is marked by a mask being placed on the puppet. Just as the lifeless puppet is animated in the ritual, so, it is hoped, new life will be conferred on the crops and the community (Law, p. 31, 176-178).

Puppets also assume the mantle of the gods in Taoist rituals and are considered crucial aids in the battle against evil influences. Natural disasters such as droughts, floods, plagues and famines all require the expulsion of evil and the puppets are also used in the purification of temples and new houses and the sanctification of offerings. The Taoist puppeteers consecrate the string dolls, or marionettes, in the same way as they hallow the statues of the gods and the sacred tablets of the ancestors. A marionette ensemble consists of 108 puppets (using combinations of bodies with detachable heads) which is the number of the constellations. This means that the puppets represent all the essences of the universe. Because the marionettes are so sacred, they are also dangerous and the demons they expel are especially so:

So fearsome is their strength that when they chase away demons with their chants and dances, and assail invisible devils with their miniature weapons, no one dares to look. The orchestra plays, the master puppeteer recites sacred formulas, the puppets move about, but the place in front of the stage remains empty and the common people stay home behind closed doors afraid that, in a panic, the demons might take refuge in their homes, or even in their bodies (Schipper, p. 44-45).

While it is easy to see why taboos may surround the puppets in a liturgical performance, the banning of secular plays is not always so easy to explain. In fact, for a long time puppet plays in England escaped the censorship that the Puritans placed on standard plays, which were banned because they presented illusions and were deemed immoral. But in the 18th century the Englishman Geoffroy Fenton wrote that plays using marionettes were just as pernicious as those that employed living actors. In France and Germany at this time there was competition between the supporters of marionette theatres and those who loved large-scale operas. French puppeteers were forbidden to use artificial voices for their acts and the situation got still worse at the time of the French Revolution. The guillotine, so instrumental in the reign of terror that followed the uprising, found its way into the plays and a leading character, Polichinelle, an anarchistic street hero, was solemnly beheaded. More sinister yet was the beheading, in 1794, of a couple of puppeteers merely because the authorities condemned their Polichinelle, previously a hero of the proletariat, for being too aristocratic (Boehn, p. 111, 122).

A similar situation was evinced by the Soviet authorities after the Russian Revolution. Petrushka, the Russian Polichinelle, had been popular with the audiences of street theatres throughout the 19th century. He was loved for his defiance, his subversive ridiculing of both figures of authority and the prevailing mores of decency and morality; he broke taboos yet enjoyed immunity because, like the carnival heroes, he was considered harmless. Although the ecclesiastical authorities in Russia were opposed to all popular entertainment and disliked puppet theatres, the revolutionaries realised that Petrushka was a useful vehicle for political satire which they could use to their advantage. By using humour as a cover, the plays could examine social and sexual taboos and express social unease in such a way that the censor would be deceived while the intended audience would be enlightened. After the Revolution of 1917 all this changed. Petrushka's irreverence was now levied at representatives of Soviet authority who were sensitive to criticism and intolerant of protest. Moreover, leaders tended to agree with V. I. Lenin that while spectacles are fine, "we mustn't forget that spectacles are not genuine great art; they are, rather, a more or less attractive type of entertainment" (Kelly, p. 12). With the ostensible aim of promoting "high" art, the authorities could demean and sanitise the subversive puppet plays.

Nowadays puppets are still used as instruments of satire and subversion. Embracing new technologies, television programmes such as the British "Spitting Image" include repertoires of life-size latex puppets, moulded to caricatures of political and royal figures, which are animated and broadcast to millions of viewers.

See also

Mirrors

References

Blackwood, Algernon. [1962] 1971. "The Doll". In *Tales of the Uncanny and Supernatural*. London: Spring Books.

Boehn, Max von. 1929. *Puppenspiele*. Munich: F. Bruckmann AG.

Freud, Sigmund. [1919] 1990. "The 'Uncanny'". In *The Penguin Freud Library, vol. 14. Art and Literature*. trans. James Strachey, p. 335-376. London: Penguin.

Kelly, Catriona. 1990. *Petrushka: The Russian Carnival Puppet Theatre*. Cambridge: Cambridge University Press.

Kokoschka, Oskar. [1971] 1974. *My Life*. trans. David Britt. London: Thames and Hudson.

Law, Jane Marie. 1997. *Puppets of Nostalgia: The Life, Death, and Rebirth of the Japanese Awaji Ningyo Tradition*. Princeton, New Jersey: Princeton University Press.

Matthews, J. H. 1977. *The Imagery of Surrealism*. Syracuse, New York: Syracuse University Press.

Reiniger, Lotte. 1970. *Shadow Theatre and Shadow Films*. London: B. T. Batsford.

Rilke, Rainer Maria. [1913/1914] 1994. "Dolls: On the Wax Dolls of Lotte Pritzel". trans. Idris Parry and Paul Keegan. In *Essays on Dolls*, p. 26-39. London: Penguin, Syrens.

Schipper, Kristofer. [1982] 1993. *The Taoist Body*. trans. Karen C. Duval. Berkeley; Los Angeles; London: University of California Press.

Douglas, Mary (1921-)

Mary Douglas is a British anthropologist, an Africanist who began her career by conducting fieldwork on the Lele of Kasai in the Belgian Congo (Douglas, 1963). She has since become known for her work on cultural anomalies – those things which evade simple classification – and the taboos adhering to them. Her most important works on the subject of taboos are *Purity and Danger: An Analysis of the Concepts of Pollution and Taboo* published in 1966, and *Natural Symbols* which appeared in 1970.

Purity and Danger

In *Purity and Danger* Mary Douglas examines the taboos surrounding that which is considered dirty and polluting, and the dangers of impurity from contact with people, objects or food considered unclean. Paying particular attention to Hindu prescriptions on ritual purity and the dietary laws of *Leviticus*, she concludes that things are often regarded as polluting, not because they are innately unclean, but because they are in the wrong place or because they defy classification. Both our contemporary concern with hygiene and the ritual imposition of taboos are symptomatic of a need for order, a desire to make the world conform to an abstract idea we have of it. Without clear lines of demarcation, without strict boundaries, it is feared the world will descend into chaos.

Douglas begins by showing how fluid our ideas on dirt really are. Although inhabitants of the industrialised world maintain that cleaning is a purely hygienic act, designed to kill germs and thereby reduce the risk of disease, it was only in the 19th century that the bacterial transmission of disease was discovered, and the obsession with cleanliness is much earlier than this. Many a visitor to the Netherlands of the 17th century expressed astonishment at the almost pathological attack on dirt by the citizens (Schama, p. 377-384). On the other hand, a Havik Brahmin in India must observe intricate rules to avoid ritual pollution but one of the techniques for purification, a daily bath, could also be considered hygienic. Modern hygiene would appear to share important characteristics with ritual purifications and undermine the assertion that: "… we kill germs, they ward off spirits" (Douglas, [1966] 1984, p. 32).There is also a question as to what constitutes dirt. Mary Douglas follows Lord Chesterfield's definition of dirt as "matter out of place" (Douglas, [1966] 1984, p. 35); shoes are dirty when placed on the table, cooking utensils are dirty when not in the kitchen, similarly the hair in the bath or the nail clippings:

> Dirt then, is never a unique, isolated event. Where there is dirt there is system. Dirt is the by-product of a systematic ordering and classification of matter, in so far as ordering involves rejecting inappropriate elements. This idea of dirt takes us straight into the field of symbolism and promises a link-up with more obviously symbolic systems of purity (Douglas, [1966] 1984, p. 35).

One "more obviously symbolic" system of purity that she considers in detail is the dietary code of the Jews derived from the biblical texts of *Deuteronomy* and *Leviticus*. She dismisses hygienic explanations for the food taboos – such as the famous prohibition on the eating of pork being due to the danger of trichinosis – and suggests instead that it is those animals, or categories of animals, which are in some way anomalies, that are considered unclean:

> In the firmament two-legged fowls fly with wings. On the earth, four-legged animals hop, jump or walk. Any class of creatures which is not equipped for the right kind of locomotion in its element is contrary to holiness … Thus anything in the water which has not fins and scales is unclean (*Leviticus* xi, 10-12) … The only sure test for cleanness in a fish is its scales and its propulsion by means of fins.

Four-footed creatures which fly (*Lev.*xi, 20-26) are unclean. Any creature which has two legs and two hands and which goes on all fours like a quadruped is unclean (*Lev.*xi, 27), or creatures endowed with hands instead of front feet, which perversely use their hands for walking: the weasel, the mouse, the crocodile, the shrew, various kinds of lizards, the cameleon and mole…

The last kind of unclean animal is that which creeps, crawls or swarms upon the earth (*Lev* xi, 41-44) … Whether we call it teeming, trailing, creeping, crawling or swarming, it is an indeterminate form of movement. Since the main animal categories are defined by their typical movement, 'swarming' which is not a mode of propulsion proper to any particular element, cuts across the basic classification. Swarming things are neither fish, flesh nor fowl. Eels and worms inhabit water, though not as fish; reptiles go on dry land, though not as quadrupeds; some insects fly, though not as birds … As fish belong in the sea so worms belong in the grave, with death and chaos (Douglas, [1966] 1984, p. 55-56).

Thus shellfish are prohibited as they have no scales and do not swim and pigs are forbidden according to the laws of *Deuteronomy* (xvi, 8) because although they have cloven hooves, they do not chew the cud, so they do not fit into the class containing oxen, sheep, goats and antelopes. Things which avoid categorisation, like matter out of place, disturb our sense of order; they are dangerous, polluting, taboo.

Similarly taboo are the orifices of the body, the body's boundaries, because they are the places of transition between the internal body and the outer world. Through the openings pass food and drink and out of them are expelled saliva, mucous, urine, faeces, and, at times, blood and milk. Together with fingernail and hair clippings, the excreta are both of the body and outside the body, they transgress boundaries and are therefore dangerous. But the physical body, Douglas asserts, has another dimension. It is also a model of human society: "We cannot possibly interpret rituals concerning excreta, breast milk, saliva and the rest unless we are prepared to see in the body a symbol of society" (Douglas, [1966] 1984, p. 115). The dangers of breaching the body's borders reflect the dangers (and powers) of transgressing social and moral norms. This means that the fear of pollution is essentially a moral fear, a fear of moral deviance.

Mary Douglas also argues that societies with more rigid social categories manifest a greater anxiety about pollution and bodily control. Among Hindus, the Brahmins have elaborate sanctions to protect the caste purity of their women. But pollution associated with sex can also arise because of a conflict of interests between men and women. This is the case with the Lele whose anxiety about the ritual dangers of sex arises because of the "distinct, mutually hostile spheres" (Douglas, [1966] 1984, p. 152) of males and females. This leads to sexual antagonism and a belief that the opposite sex constitutes a real danger.

If women are dangerous sexually, at the time of menstruation they are especially threatening. Taboos on menstruating women are extremely common and serve, Douglas observes, to separate male and female spheres although the "polluting" women are banned from handling not only the tools and hunting equipment – the attributes of the male – but also cooking implements and food. In this way the taboos also help to establish male superiority and dominance by denigrating the "impure" women and excluding them from the control of strategic resources like food and equipment.

Criticism of Mary Douglas' analysis of Jewish dietary laws has come from M. P. Carroll, who, while agreeing that it is generally anomalous things that are taboo, argues that in the case of *Leviticus*, the anomaly relates to the distinction between nature and culture. While humans (embodying culture) may eat meat, animals (nature) should be vegetarians. The pig, however, eats carrion and vermin, mould and mildew, belongs to nature yet invades the world of man/culture (Carroll, p. 339-346). Further criticism has come from R. Bulmer (Bulmer, p. 5-25) and S. J. Tambiah (Tambiah, p. 423-459) who studied Karam and Thai classification of animals and realised that the taxonomies of animals are governed by social rather than merely physiological criteria. While things that are out of place may be polluting, the Karam and Thai determine for themselves what is out of place and effectively organise nature so that it mirrors and fortifies their social rules. Mary Douglas has acknowledged their research and modified her views; she had already noticed that among the Lele, the pangolin, a scaly, tree-climbing ant-eater, though clearly seen as an anomaly by the Lele and transcending their system of classifications, was auspicious and revered. Turning to the Jewish prohibition on the pig, she quotes Bullmer who says it is just as valid to argue that the pig is accorded anomalous taxonomic status because it is unclean as to suggest that it is unclean because it is an anomaly (Douglas, [1975] 1979, p. 249-275). The pig is unclean, she decides, because it eats carrion but also because it was reared as a source of food by non-Israelites. Marriage with outsiders was forbidden to the ancient Israelites and they established strong boundaries between themselves and others; not eating the pig preserved their purity. By contrast, the Lele encourage transactions with others and have weak social boundaries; for them the pangolin, in defying classification or crossing boundaries, is sacred, not polluting (Douglas, [1975] 1979, p. 276-318).

Natural Symbols

In *Natural Symbols: Explorations in Cosmology*, written in 1970, Mary Douglas develops the analogy, begun in *Purity and Danger*, between the human body and the social system. She argues that different systems of bodily symbols reflect different social patterns and that there is a direct correlation between physical control of the bodily processes and the exertion of social control:

> According to the rule of distance from physiological origin (or the purity rule) the more the social situation exerts pressure on those involved in it, the more the social demand for conformity tends to be expressed by a demand for physical control. Bodily processes are more ignored and more firmly set outside the social discourse, the more the latter is important. A natural way of investing a social occasion with dignity is to hide organic processes (Douglas, [1970] 1978, p. 12).

This means that in a society marked by subordination of the individual to authority there will be severe restrictions on behaviour and dress, the formal and ritual element will be strong and there will be many taboos. The correspondence is as valid for western social and religious life as it is for primal societies: in the organised Roman Catholic Church ritual dominates, fasting is encouraged (during Lent, before receiving the sacrament, and with abstention from meat required on Fridays) and sins, like taboo violations, incur penalties and must be formally cleansed. Among the Protestants, by contrast, external symbols are less important, and religion is internalised.

To elucidate her ideas, Mary Douglas introduces the concepts of "group" and "grid":

> *Group* means the outside boundary that people have erected between themselves and the outside world. *Grid* means all the other social distinctions and delegations of authority that they use to limit how people behave to one another (Douglas, 1982, p. 138).

Where the group is strong, its boundaries must be protected from outsiders by magic and taboos. If the group is weak, the external world

is less threatening and magical protection is less important. The Mbuti pygmies of the Ituri forest in Africa typify the weak group. They live in small fluid groups, moving freely between camps and attaching little importance to the community. They have no concept of pollution and have no taboos relating to birth, menstruation or death. Besides this weak group, their social life demonstrates a weak grid: there is little differentiation of individuals on the grounds of sex, age or kinship. It is, of course, possible to have a weak group combined with a strong grid: the Hadza hunters in Tanzania have even freer groupings than the Mbuti but within the group there exists an intense hostility between the sexes which is expressed by the taboo on menstrual blood, and the male fear of pollution. If, on the contrary, the group is strong and the grid weak, magic protects the borders of the social unit.

While Mary Douglas' paradigm of group and grid has been criticised for being too reductionist and simplistic (Wuthnow, Hunter, Bergesen and Kurzweil, p. 119-128), her work has aroused interest in the relationship between anthropological material and contemporary religious and social practices. More recently, she has turned her attention to the American environmental movement, the sociology of perception, Biblical exegesis, pollution, menstruation, AIDS and contamination, continuing to analyse contemporary Western society in the light of information gleaned from Oriental and pre-literate cultures.

See also

Food Taboos; Jewish Dietary Laws; Menstruation; Pollution

References

Bulmer, R. 1967. "Why the cassowary is not a bird: a problem of zoological taxonomy among the Karam of the New Guinea Highlands". *Man*, no. 2, p. 5-25.

Carroll, M. P. 1978. "One more time: Leviticus revisited". *Archives européennes de sociologie*, no. 19, p. 339-346.

Douglas, Mary and Aaron Wildavsky. 1982. *Risk and Culture: an essay on the selection of technological and environmental dangers.* Berkeley: University of California Press.

Douglas, Mary. [1966] 1984. *Purity and Danger: An Analysis of the Concepts of Pollution and Taboo.* London: Ark-Routledge and Kegan Paul.

Douglas, Mary. [1970] 1978. *Natural Symbols.* Middlesex, England: Penguin.

Douglas, Mary. [1975] 1979. "Deciphering a Meal". In *Implicit Meanings: Essays in Anthropology by Mary Douglas*, p. 249-275. London: Routledge and Kegan Paul.

Douglas, Mary. [1975] 1979. "Self-Evidence". In *Implicit Meanings: Essays in Anthropology by Mary Douglas*, p. 276-318. London: Routledge and Kegan Paul.

Douglas, Mary. 1963. *The Lele of Kasai.* London: Oxford University Press.

Douglas, Mary. 1982. *In the Active Voice.* London: Routledge and Kegan Paul.

Schama, Simon. 1991. *The Embarrassment of Riches, An Interpretation of Dutch Culture in the Golden Age.* London: Harper Collins, Fontana.

Tambiah, S. J. 1969. "Animals are good to think and good to prohibit". *Ethnology*, no. 7, p. 423-459.

Wuthnow, Robert, James Davison Hunter, Albert Bergesen and Edith Kurzweil. 1984. *Cultural Analysis: the Work of Peter L. Berger, Mary Douglas, Michel Foucault and Jürgen Habermas*, p. 119-128. London: Routledge and Kegan Paul.

Wuthnow, Robert, James Davison Hunter, Albert Bergesen and Edith Kurzweil. 1984. *Cultural Analysis: the Work of Peter L. Berger, Mary Douglas, Michel Foucault and Jürgen Habermas*, p. 119-128. London: Routledge and Kegan Paul.

Dreams

"The Sleep of Reason Produces Monsters" runs the caption for an engraving by the Spanish artist, Goya. He was referring to the political tyranny which ensues when a society loses its reason, which he likened to the tyranny of nightmares that seize control once sleep takes over. Goya was not the first to notice how monstrous and tabooed deeds are enacted in the dream, when the conscious mind is sleeping. In the 5th century BCE Plato had observed:

The unnecessary pleasures and desires ... that wake while we sleep, when the reasonable and humane part of us is asleep and its control relaxed, and our fierce bestial nature, full of food and drink, rouses itself and has its fling and tries to secure its own kind of satisfaction. As you know, there's nothing too bad for it and it's completely lost to all sense of shame. It doesn't shrink from attempting intercourse (as it supposes) with a mother or anyone else, man, beast or god, or from murder or eating forbidden food. There is, in fact, no folly nor shamelessness it will not commit (*The Republic.* 9, p. 571).

Freud made a more complex statement on the mechanism of dreams. He agreed with Plato that the forbidden desires of the unconscious find an outlet in the dream. But because these tabooed longings are censored by the conscious self they must find a way to elude detection. They must, in other words, outwit the censor. One technique employed to escape notice is displacement: the dreamer may exaggerate a minor detail and play down the important topic or transfer feelings for one person onto a substitute. This is an interesting trick, akin to distracting an unruly child by diverting its attention. Then there is condensation, a form of shorthand which must be unravelled if one wants to disclose the dream's innermost secrets. Politicians employ a similar ruse when they claim that they have not lied but only been "economical with the truth". The dream is also filled with symbols and puns so that a dreamer may dream that he is being kissed by his uncle in an automobile (the manifest content) while the latent content is the dreamer's auto-eroticism. Freud's ingenuity in interpreting dreams so that they validate his theories is remarkable. Needless to say, a single dream analysed by Freud, Jung and Adler would evince three different interpretations.

While dreams may have an internal censor, regulating what is dreamt, the idea of an external censor belongs in the realm of fiction. A novel by the Albanian author, Ismail Kadare, describes an oppressive Empire ruled by a tyrannical Sultan who requires the citizens to submit their dreams for analysis. In *The Palace of Dreams*, all the dreams are carefully classified and interpreted in order to identify the "master-dreams" that will provide information on the future of the State. Those who have suspicious dreams, dreams that are potentially subversive or portend the downfall of the Sultan, are interrogated in the Palace of Dreams until the dreams are erased from their minds or until they themselves are erased from memory, carried out of the building in coffins. This parable of a dictatorship sustained by the ultimate thought-police was banned as soon as it appeared in Albania in 1981. The author acknowledged that the writer, like the authentic dreamer, is the natural enemy of dictatorship.

See also

Surrealism

References

Doniger O'Flaherty, Wendy. 1984. *Dreams, Illusions and Other Realities*. Chicago, Illinois: University of Chicago Press.

Freud, Sigmund. [1900] 1965. *The Interpretation of Dreams*. trans. James Strachey. vols. 4 and 5, *Standard Edition*. London; New York.

Kadare, Ismail. [1981] 1993. *The Palace of Dreams*. trans. Barbara Bray. London: HarperCollins, Harvill.

Plato. *The Republic*. trans. Desmond Lee. [1955] 1983. Harmondsworth, Middlesex: Penguin.

Durkheim, Émile (1858-1918)

Émile Durkheim was a French sociologist whose major publications include *The Division of Labour in Society* ([1893] 1933); *Suicide* ([1897] 1951); *Incest: The Nature and Origin of the Taboo* ([1897] 1963); and *The Elementary Forms of Religious Life* ([1912] 1915). In *Incest*, Durkheim claimed that members of the same totemic clan feared they would be polluted by the blood of the totemic spirit if they indulged in sexual intercourse. This theme of totemic taboos is elaborated in *Elementary Forms of Religious Life*, a work influenced by the theories of William Robertson Smith and which, dealing as it does with data from the Australian Aborigines, is of great interest to anthropologists.

Essentially, Durkheim saw the function of taboos as defining, protecting and isolating what he termed "the sacred", preventing its pollution by "the profane". Durkheim viewed both defilement and contagion as basic attributes of religious cult and the sacred. Besides being encompassed by taboos, religion (as opposed to magic) could be identified through its social manifestations:

> A religion is a unified system of beliefs and practices relative to sacred things, that is to say, things set apart and forbidden – beliefs and practices which unite, into one single moral community called a church, all those who adhere to them" (Durkheim [1912] 1915, p. 47).

Durkheim draws on Robertson Smith's idea that man's relation to the gods, and his religious behaviour, is an aspect of prescribed social behaviour. As an example of this, he mentions the way in which the food taboos of the Australian Aborigines, such as the ban on eating one's own totemic animal, cannot always have the function ascribed by the participants, namely the propagation of the species and the contribution of each clan to the common food supply. Sometimes, for instance, ceremonies such as the *intichiuma* are performed even when the totem is a non-existent snake, a *wollunqua*. A more feasible explanation for the ceremonies is based on social factors: gathering together for the rites, the individual becomes aware of the importance of group solidarity. In the same way, the taboos on marrying members of one's own totemic clan foster a sense of interdependence between clans. The totems themselves, worshipped as sacred, are both the symbol of the god or *mana* (vital principle) and the representation of society itself; in other words, god and society are indivisible and religion is essentially society worshipping itself through the manifest totem.

Because religion is no more than society itself, the dangerous powers attributed to the gods are merely the means employed by society to protect itself from the deviancy of its members. The taboos, emphasising the risks of transgression, serve to demarcate acceptable social behaviour. Criticism of Durkheim has arisen over the rigid dichotomy he envisages between the sacred and the profane – categories that are often so closely intermingled as to be almost inseparable (Douglas, p. 47-59; Evans-Pritchard, p. 51-77). Nor is the sacred always demarcated by interdictions.

See also
Food Taboos; Incest; Radcliffe-Brown, A.R.; Smith, William Robertson; Suicide

References
Douglas, Mary. 1975. "Pollution". In *Implicit Meanings: Essays in Anthropology*, p. 47-59. London: Routledge.

Durkheim, Émile. [1912] 1915. *The Elementary Forms of the Religious Life*. New York: Macmillan.

Durkheim, Émile. [1897] 1963. *Incest: The Nature and the Origin of the Taboo*. New York: Lyle Stuart.

Durkheim, Émile. [1897] 1951. *Suicide: A Study in Sociology*. Glencoe, Illinois: Free Press.

Durkheim, Émile. [1893] 1933. *The Division of Labour in Society*. New York: Free Press.

Evans-Pritchard, E. E. [1965] 1977. *Theories of Primitive Religion*. Oxford: Oxford University Press.

Giddens, Antony. 1979. *Emile Durkheim*. New York: Viking.

van Gennep, Arnold. 1904. *Tabou et totémisme à Madagascar: étude descriptive et théorique*. Paris: Leroux.

E

Eggs

Predating the chicken, humanity, and the universe itself, eggs feature in creation myths from Finland to China. The primal egg encloses the chaos from which the cosmos is formed and in which, very often, the culture hero crouches, waiting to be born. Eggs are therefore symbols of life and fertility but they are also subject to many taboos; like contemporary vegans, followers of Pythagoras and the Orphic tradition avoided eating eggs (and egg-laying animals) as did the Inuit in the Mackenzie Delta, who thought they caused disease, while the indigenous people of central Australia avoided the eggs of their totemic animal. Curiously, the Kelh Yegomawa of northern Nigeria believed the consumption of eggs caused infertility in young women as did the Konde of Tanganyika (Newall, p. 114-115).

Unusual or misshapen eggs were especially dangerous. In Hungary, an egg with a soft shell from a black hen was a death portent and was immediately crushed. Elsewhere in Europe, irregular eggs were thought to have been laid by a cock, and were an important ingredient in sorcerers' spells (Newall, p. 70-72).

Witches were commonly believed to use egg-shells as cups and plates and to travel to the Sabbath in them, a belief that explained the necessity for smashing egg-shells. Venetia

Newall quotes a charming tale of a grateful witch, told by a Slavonian gypsy:

... a girl noticed everyone smash the shell when they had eaten an egg. She asked why and was told, "You must break the shell to bits for fear Lest the witches should make it a boat, my dear. For over the sea, away from home, far by night the witches roam." "I don't see why the poor witches should not have boats as well as other people," said the girl, and she threw an egg-shell as far as she could, crying, "Witch – there is your boat!" To her amazement, it was caught up by the wind and whirled away until it was invisible. A voice cried out, "I thank you." Some time later the girl was on an island, when a great flood rose and washed her boat away. The island was almost swamped when a white vessel came in sight. It contained a "woman with witch eyes" rowing with a broom, and with a black cat perched on her shoulder. "Jump in," she called to the girl, and rowed her to dry land. Then she said, "Turn three times to the right and look each time at the boat." The girl did as she was told, and every time she looked the boat was smaller, until it was like an egg. Her rescuer sang, "That is the shell you threw to me, Even a witch can grateful be." Then she vanished, shell and all (Newall, p. 201).

In Belgium, Germany and England it was believed that an egg-shell left whole would cause epilepsy while the Faroese feared shipwreck. The Faroese also avoided eating eggs on 14 April, the day marking the end of winter; to do so would lead to an affliction with boils for the entire year. In Greece in the 5th century BCE the egg was a common offering to the dead and it was into this 'food for corpses' that the evil of a person was transferred during the rites of purification (Parker, p. 230). Eggs and their shells were used for magical charms (by humans as well as witches) but egg-shells could also be used for counter-charms. In Germany, people were advised to place the urine of a sorcerer in a shell and hang it, sealed, beneath the chimney. As the contents evaporated, his strength would wither. Similarly, in Haiti, an egg, together with white cotton thread tied with seven knots, was placed under the pillow of a voodoo *houngan* while he lay on his deathbed to prevent him turning into a zombie (Newall, p. 62-97).

See also

Knots; Urine

References

Newall, Venetia. 1971. *An Egg at Easter: A Folklore Study.* London: Routledge and Kegan Paul.

Parker, Robert. 1983. *Miasma.* Oxford: Clarendon Press.

Evil Eye

Whoever fell under the gaze of the Medusa, that terrible Gorgon of Greek myth, would turn to stone. Perseus managed to avoid her face, by watching instead her reflection in his shield as he raised his sword and lopped off her head. This tale exemplifies a folk belief found throughout the Indo-European and Semitic world: that certain individuals have the power to harm or destroy other people, their livestock and their crops, and even to stop their cows from producing milk and the milk from setting

into butter, merely by looking at them or by praising them or their belongings. Such people are said to possess the evil eye and their malign influence is shielded by the implementation of numerous rituals and taboos, charms and colours (generally in the Indo-European world, red has averted the evil eye while in Semitic regions it is blue).

Those accused of possessing the evil eye are often unusual in some way, they may be cross-eyed, squinting, or have eyes differing in colour; they may be strangers, travellers, the very old or the infertile, those who are feared as outsiders or those considered to have cause for jealousy. In most societies, envy is the principal cause of the evil eye (as Helmut Schoeck points out, the word *envy* derives from the Latin *invidia*, which is a combination of *videre* "to see" and *in*, which can mean "against" (Schoeck, p. 194). This explains the taboos against praising: to praise is to provoke envy and thereby to invoke disaster. The classicist, Eugene S. McCartney, relates a tale culled from modern Greek folklore in which the admiration is tinged with irony:

> ... I have heard of an ancient dame of Salonica who had the reputation of possessing an evil eye. Many of her achievements were whispered with becoming awe. One day, it was said, as she sat at her window, she saw a young man passing on horseback. He seemed to be so proud of himself and his mount that the old lady ... could not resist the temptation of humbling him. One dread glance from her eye and one short cry from her lips: "Oh, what a gallant cavalier!" brought both horse and horseman to their knees (McCartney, p. 18).

Praising a fruit tree, a lactating cow, or a child can cause misfortune even if no malice is intended by the remark.

Times of great vulnerability, such as pregnancy, childbirth and infancy, require special protection. The legendary precursor of Eve,

Lilith, was banished to the Red Sea for insubordination and was only allowed to procreate demons. Her jealousy of human children induced murderous inclinations and already in the 6th century CE earthenware bowls were inscribed with incantations in Aramaic (a language similar to Hebrew) prohibiting her from entering the house. Her ability to cause barrenness, miscarriages and complications during childbirth added to her unpopularity.

The taboo upon complimenting a child has been recorded from Scotland to Iran. The Rabbis of Palestine would insult their sons to avert the evil eye while in Turkey and Russia an admired child would be spat upon. But praise is not the only danger; in Scotland a woman nursing a child was not allowed in the room where a woman had just given birth as this could cause the milk to dry up in the newly-delivered mother. If this happened, the new mother had to secretly get the child of the one who had stopped her milk and pass it under her apron to bring back her milk. The best protection against the evil eye was to do nothing that could provoke it. Giving to beggars and sharing food, appeasing the angry, staining new clothes, and veiling the bride were good apotropaic devices, as was the use of phallic statues and amulets which distracted the evil eye.

Belief in the power of the evil eye is attested in the earliest recorded literature; a Sumerian "Incantation in the 'House of Light' Against the Evil Eye" dates back to the 3rd or 4th millennium BC and the malevolence of the gaze is mentioned by the writers of classical Greece and Rome. Theories of the evil eye range from those involving the infant's fear of the staring eye of the adult, considered "other" and therefore dangerous, through the concept of envy and Freud's elaboration of this (that the possessor of something valuable considers himself enviable and projects onto others the envy that he would have felt in their place), to those focusing on the relief of aggression and oral and phallic elements. Alan Dundes has attempted a comprehensive, if somewhat curious, theory in his essay, "Wet and Dry, the Evil Eye" (Dundes [1981] 1992). He begins with the common folk belief that there is only a limited amount of "good" in the world and that if one person gets more (of health or possessions), another person will get less. This inequality breeds envy in the poor and fear of envy in the rich. Furthermore, life is associated with wet things such as semen, blood, milk and saliva while dryness suggests emaciation and death. As receptacles of wet things, such as the breasts and the testicles, can be symbolically identified with an eye or eyes, it is natural to fear appropriation of the "life" contained in these organs by the eyes of others.

Today, in the western world, remnants of the belief remain in the tipping of waiters (so they will not envy the diners) and the blessing of those who sneeze (who are in danger of losing precious liquid). And staring is still considered impolite, if not exactly taboo.

See also

Looking or Seeing

References

Bennett, Margaret. 1992. *Scottish Customs from the Cradle to the Grave*. Edinburgh: Polygon.

Dundes, Alan. [1981] 1992. "Wet and Dry, the Evil Eye". In *The Evil Eye: A Casebook*. ed. Alan Dundes, p. 257-312. Madison, Wisconsin: University of Wisconsin Press.

Elseworthy, Frederick Thomas. [1895] 1958. In *The Evil Eye: The Origins and Practices of Superstition*. New York: Julian Press.

Krappe, Alexander Haggerty. 1927. *Balor with the Evil Eye. Studies in Celtic and French Literature*. Institut des Études Français, Columbia University.

McCartney, Eugene S. [1981] 1992. "Praise and Dispraise in Folklore". In *The Evil Eye: A Casebook*. ed. Alan Dundes, p. 9-38. Madison, Wisconsin: University of Wisconsin Press.

Schoeck, Helmut. [1981] 1992. "The Evil Eye: Forms and Dynamics of a Universal Superstition". In *The Evil Eye: A Casebook*. ed. Alan Dundes, p. 192-200. Madison, Wisconsin: University of Wisconsin Press.

Excrement

Excrement is a substance charged with taboos. Perhaps this is because it is an ineluctable sign of our animal nature; as the pathologist, Gonzalez-Crussi ruefully remarks, excreta could be vaporised and gently eliminated, molecule by molecule, but instead it collects in an offensive concentration (Gonzalez-Crussi, p. 127). The ancient Hindu moral code, *The Laws of Manu*, contrasts the pure orifices of the body above the navel with those impure organs of pollution that emit urine and excrement, so it is unsurprising that among Hindus the lowest social group, known as the Untouchables, were traditionally responsible for the disposal of excrement. Muslims only use the left, inferior, hand for cleansing after defecation and for the early Christian Church fathers, such as Saint John Chrysostom (c.349-407), excreta was the distasteful result of indulgence in delicacies – only fasting could redeem the soul.

The elimination of faeces is described in a plethora of euphemisms and the familiar Anglo-Saxon term "shit" is described in the Oxford English Dictionary as "not now in decent use". This word, also used as an expletive, is still taboo among broadcasters, although it has, since the 1970s appeared uncensored in the quality newspapers. An argument could be made for more imaginative synonyms. In the Canadian novel, *The Rebel Angels*, by Robert Davies, a doctoral student visits a scientist whose specialisation is human faeces, and muses on this theme. The Middle Ages had specific terms for the faeces of different animals:

> the Crotals of a Hare, the Friants of a Boar, the Spraints of an Otter, the Werderobe of a Badger, the Waggying of a Fox, the Fumets of a Deer (Davies in Gonzalez-Crussi, p. 129).

Why not have, the student muses:

> the Problems of a President, the Backward Passes of a Footballer, the Deferrals of a Dean, the Odd Volumes of a Librarian, the Footnotes of a Ph.D., the Low Grades of a Freshman, the Anxieties of an Untenured Professor? (Gonzales-Crussi, p. 129).

Given the contempt with which faeces is viewed, it is perhaps surprising that it has been identified with that which is held in the highest esteem: gold. The psychoanalyst, Sigmund Freud, postulates that the first "gift" an infant makes is that of his or her faeces. "Sacrificing" his faeces for one he loves, the child sublimates the auto-erotic satisfaction afforded by retention. Later, this gift is replaced by gifts of money or gold. Parsimony is thus an indication of a person who was formerly an anal erotic: unwilling to part with his money just as in his childhood he had withheld the "gift" of excrement. Freud typically links the connection between gold and excrement to earlier modes of thought:

> In reality, wherever archaic modes of thought have predominated or persist – in the ancient civilisations, in myths, fairy tales and superstitions, in unconscious thinking, in dreams, and in neuroses – money is brought into the most intimate relationship with dirt. We know that the gold which the devil gives his paramours turns into excrement after his departure, and the devil is certainly nothing else than the personification of the repressed unconscious instinctual life. We also know about the superstition which connects the finding of treasure with defecation ... Indeed, even according to ancient Babylonian doctrine gold is "the faeces of Hell" (Freud. 1995, p. 296-297).

While a sceptic might argue that the infant's "gift" owes more to a lack of muscular control than to generosity, it is true that gold is commonly linked to faeces – perhaps simply because the imagination delights in linking opposites. In a myth from West Ceram, the protagonist, Hainuwele, "Frond of the

Cocopalm", defecates valuable articles such as Chinese porcelain dishes, gongs, coral, bushknives, copper boxes and golden earrings. In alchemy the aim is to turn base material into gold, and although the base material is unspecified, the secret philosopher's stone is commonly concealed in dung or filth. Employing a more direct technique, a 19th-century artist, Piero Manzoni, hit upon the idea of selling his faeces in cans labelled "Merda Artista" (artist's shit) for the price of their weight in gold. This is described as a humorous acknowledgement of the subconscious alliance between art, money and excrement identified by Freud. In a conscious reversal, Thomas More, in *Utopia*, proposes the use of gold for chamber-pots in an attempt to expose the vanity of human desires.

Freud, as mentioned earlier, thinks that the development of an individual is not unlike the cultural evolution of a society. This has prompted Norman Brown, in *Life against Death* (London: 1959), to argue that the prevalence of defecation as a theme in the myths of pre-industrial peoples is an indication that they are still at the anal-erotic (pre-genital) stage and that they believe in a type of excremental magic. As opposed to the present society, he proposes, where sublimation of desire is the norm, the preliterate individual believes that the magical manipulation of the body and its effluvia is efficacious in fulfilling his desires. While it is true that the oral myths of North and South America contain delightful scatalogical tales, anthropologists no longer accept a cognitive difference between preliterate and literate societies. Mary Douglas is forceful in her rejection of Brown's ideas:

> the use of excrement and other bodily exuviae in primitive cultures is usually inconsistent with the themes of infantile erotic fantasy. So far from excrement, etc., being treated as a source of gratification, its use tends to be condemned. So far from being thought of as an instrument of desire, the power residing in the margins of

the body is more often to be avoided (Douglas, p. 118).

She is also sceptical about allegations of sorcerers using excrement for magical purposes. The accusations usually come from the victims, who have no substantial evidence. Moreover, the tale-cycles mentioned by Brown are also full of references to incest and cannibalism, topics that are known to be taboo, and it is quite likely that the humorous stories are playfully and deliberately flouting the social rules.

If excrement is considered dangerous and polluting, Mary Douglas asserts, this is because, like sweat, pus, spittle or blood, it breaches the margins of the body. For the body is a convenient symbol of human society. To breach the borders of the body is tantamount to transgressing social and moral norms. Excreta are both of the body yet outside it; they confuse the body's borders and are therefore polluting but they are also powerful. It is the individual culture that determines which effluents are considered dangerous:

> In some, menstrual pollution is feared as a lethal danger; in others not at all. In some, excreta is dangerous, in others it is only a joke. In India cooked food and saliva are pollution-prone, but Bushmen collect melon seeds from their mouths for later roasting and eating (Douglas, p. 121).

In India, Hindus consider themselves polluted if they touch excrement, and the latrine cleaners have been the most despised sect in the caste hierarchy, but the actual act of defecation is not hidden or shameful and squatting in public places is common. According to Douglas, this is definite proof that the faeces serves a symbolic role, helping to define the social order.

One aspect of Norman Brown's writings that is not discussed by Mary Douglas is his conviction that the "excremental" vision constitutes the symbolic essence of modern civilisation. He fuses Max Weber's theory of the relation between the Protestant ethic and the evolution of capitalism with Erich Fromm's idea that connects capitalism with anal eroticism. The condemnation of gold (excrement) by the Reformation is, Brown believes, the cause of capitalist sublimation: gold transformed into banknotes and stocks and shares. His explanation is that the Protestant ethic condemns the retention of gold/faeces as being worldly. The hoarding of worldly things is inconsistent with a spiritual life. At the same time, anal retention (the saving of gold) is consistent with a rational economy that calculates what it spends. It is not wasteful and does not squander its resources. Faced with the choice between hoarding and wasting, the only recourse is to sublimation. If the cellar where the gold/excrement is kept is transformed into a bank, the material can be saved and yet, at the same time, circulated and increased. Gold therefore disappears from the churches, palaces and paintings and becomes the invisible source of commercial society. The Mexican poet and philosopher, Octavio Paz, cites Karl Marx who perceptively described capitalism as "the domination of living men by dead matter" (Paz, p. 19-33). Though the material is sublimated, it retains its power of corruption.

Sublimation may be one method of countering the embarrassment evoked by excrement. Another solution is that encountered by the Dutch medical anthropologist, Sjaak van der Geest. His article, "Akan shit: Getting rid of dirt in Ghana" (van der Geest, p. 8-12), is a meditation on the confrontation of the Akan culture of Ghana with human faeces. Sjaak van der Geest is struck by an apparent paradox: while the Akan positively hate filth and especially human excrement, they have very crude methods of disposing of the substance so that they are constantly confronted by that which they most despise. For the Akan cleanliness is indeed next to godliness. To be clean and neat is to be respectable, attractive, beautiful, civilised and moral. Bathing twice a day is the norm and the immediate use of laxatives and enemas, if a day passes without emptying the

bowels, ensures that the body is cleansed both externally and internally. If the faeces remain in the body for too long, it is believed that the blood will be poisoned and that this will give rise to piles, ulcers, excessive phlegm, headaches and skin rashes.

Dirt is divided into different categories. *Efi* is dirt which has come from outside and which attaches itself to the body. This may be mud from a field or debris from a workplace. It has a temporary character and is less detestable than *atantaneè* (literally nasty or hateful things). *Atantaneè* is used to denote dirt coming from within the body: vomit, phlegm, menstruation, blood, urine or faeces. *Pòtoo* (dirty) can refer to both types of dirt. To be dirty is to trangress moral codes: the expression *Efi aka no* (literally 'dirt has stuck to him') is used when someone has committed evil or broken a taboo. To call someone dirty is a major insult. Expressions such as *Wo ho bòn sè oburoni motomu* (you stink like the body of a white man) are bad enough but others, such as *mene wo so* (I shit on you) or *mene w'anom* (I shit into your mouth) are truly offensive yet very common. The word *ebin* (shit) is as taboo as the thing itself.

Yet despite this hatred of dirt and emphasis on personal cleanliness, waste disposal is extemely primitive. In Kwahu-Tafo, a town with a population of 5,000, there are only four public toilets, each containing twelve squatting holes (six for each sex). In addition, there are about sixty private (mostly bucket) latrines, ten private pit latrines and ten water closets. The buckets in the private latrines are emptied once a week by a *Krufoò* (workers who formerly came from Sierra Leone, hence Kru people) who comes stealthily in the night and carries the container on his head to a dumping place on the edge of town. Frequently the buckets overflow and the combination of this detritus and the soiled toilet paper, which is deposited in a separate bin, make the latrines extremely unpleasant, not to say unsanitary, places to visit. Even the hospital in the capital, Accra, to which van der Geest was admitted in 1991 with severe diarrhoea, had atrocious toilets. The only conclusion the anthropologist can reach is that the Akan are so afraid of excrement that they try to remove it not only from their bowels but from their minds. They may pass through polluted places but they put it out of mind, just as greetings are not exchanged when they visit the latrine: although the physical need is imperative, they pretend that nobody sees them and that they see nobody.

The Akan would like to pretend that their excreta is spirited away. In medieval Japan the belief was real. 12th-century Japanese Buddhist texts describe the *gaki*, hungry ghosts, who practised coprophagy, the eating of excrement. Faeces and other effluvia seemed to discolour, pulverise and disappear quite rapidly when compared with many other substances, and as the workings of bacteria were unknown at that time, it was thought that they were eaten by these perpetually hungry spirits. The *gaki* originated in India where their Sanscrit name was *preta*. Their sorrowful condition was due to bad karma: having demonstrated moral turpitude in a previous existence. Though constantly famished, they had needle-thin throats which explained why the excrement took some time to vanish.

The *gaki* both explained a natural phenomenon and horrified Buddhists with the notion that they, too, might be reborn to eat dung should their behaviour fail to be exemplary. A 6th-century Chinese text (*Cheng-fa nien-ch'u chung*), translated from an Indian Buddhist commentary, mentions thirty-six subspecies of the hungry ghost including: those with needle-thin throats, vomit-eaters, excrement-eaters, nothing-eaters, eaters of the Buddhist dharma, water-drinkers, saliva-eaters, blood-drinkers, defecation-watchers, disease-dabblers, consumers of incense smoke, intensely burning ones, ones fascinated with colours, infant-eaters, semen-eaters, fire-eaters, poison-eaters, those living among tombs (and eating ashes),

ones that stay at cross-roads and those that kill themselves.

The diet could hardly be considered salubrious, consisting largely of substances regarded as polluting or repulsive. It is notable that fire-eating explains another natural phenomenon, namely, the extinguishing of flames, while water-drinking is the obvious cause of evaporation. Eating Buddhist dharma – social law or the ideal order of the world – may be more mysterious. The *Gaki zoshi*, two 12th-century Japanese scrolls, graphically depict the *gaki* as they feed, squatting next to mortals in latrines or consuming fireballs. One scene shows monks feeding *gaki* who come running, ravenous, from the woods. The accompanying inscription explains that the feeding of hungry ghosts was inaugurated by Ananda, a disciple of the Sakyamuni, and contains a formula for continuing the tradition. This is interesting because even today, *segaki*, a ritual of giving food to *gaki*, is performed, the food usually consisting of a few grains of cooked rice (Lafleur, p. 271-303).

The eating of excrement is not the sole preserve of spirits. Because of the natural human revulsion it inspires, consuming excreta can be a proof of spirituality, overcoming not only desires but also repulsions. Certain Taoist sects claim to eat dung and in India the Aghoris, Hindu ascetics who practise extreme austerities, claim to devour corpses and human waste. This is not the traditional Hindu practice; as mentioned earlier, excrement in India is perceived as polluting. An ideal death is preceded by fasting and drinking water from the holy river Ganges. Fasting not only weakens the body and releases the "vital breath", but it frees the corpse from faeces. Should someone die a "bad death", he suffers the indignity of his vital breath leaving his body via the anus in the form of excrement, or as vomit through another orifice. Yet, as Jonathan Parry observes in his study of the Aghori in Benares, conventional taboos are violated by the sect:

The "true" Aghori is entirely indifferent to what he consumes, drinks not only liquor but urine, and eats not only meat but excrement, vomit and the putrid flesh of corpses ... I myself have been present when an Aghori drank what was said to be the urine of a dog (Parry, p. 89).

Parry is convinced that foraging among the forbidden contributes significantly to the ascetic's powers:

By his various observances the Aghori acquires *siddhis,* or supernatural powers, which give him mastery over the phenomenal world and the ability to read thoughts. If he is sufficiently accomplished he can cure the sick, raise the dead and control malevolent ghosts. He can expand or contract his body to any size or weight, fly through the air, appear in two places at once, conjure up the dead and leave his body and enter into another. All this, of course, is exactly what one might predict from the Aghori's dealings with corpses and bodily emissions, for – as Douglas (1966) points out – that which is anomalous and marginal is not only the focus of pollution and danger, but also the source of extraordinary power (Parry, p. 92).

In this case the excrement may be powerful because of its marginal position *vis-à-vis* the body, but the ascetic is also trying to transcend all categories, to reach a state, both primordial and divine, in which the pure and the polluted, the divine and the human, are one.

Excreta have been linked to gold, to spiritual practices and also, in the realm of literature, to love. The poem of William Butler Yeats, "Crazy Jane talks with the Bishop", opens with the bishop imploring Jane, now old, to think of her soul: "Live in a heavenly mansion, Not in some foul sty". But Jane is wiser, realising that "Fair and foul are near of kin, And fair needs foul". Completeness can only arise from the embracing of opposites; beauty and ugliness, spirit and body, creation and destruction. For "Love has pitched his mansion in the place of excrement" and "nothing can be sole or whole That has not been rent" (Yeats, p. 294-295). The sentiment is not unlike that of the Aghori. Gonzalez-Crussi remarks on similar dualities in the work of the Spaniard, Don Francisco de Quevedo y Villegas (1580-1645) who alternates between sublime theological treatises and satires such as *Graces and Disgraces of the Eye of the Ass* (Gonzales-Crussi, p. 129-132). Satire is also the instrument of the Irish writer, Jonathan Swift, who relates excrement to moral perdition, and the French monk, François Rabelais (c.1494-1553), who, in *Gargantua* (1534), mocks theological education and the monastic ideal. In one much quoted passage, Gargantua debates the merits of different "arse-wipers" and expresses preference for the neck of a well-downed goose. This is far better than the fur of a cat whose claws "exulcerated my whole perineum" (Rabelais, p. 67).

It is no doubt because of the Christian distrust of the body, and the taboos with which it surrounds natural bodily processes, that scatological imagery appears so frequently in ecclesiastical satire. It also explains why medieval and early modern Carnivals witnessed scenes in which a mock priest would drape himself in sausages and throw excrement in place of blessings to the crowd: freed temporarily from the rigours of ecclesiastical ordinances, the crowd revelled in all that was most forbidden. Yet ultimately Carnival behaviour was not only an act of revolt but a celebration of our human nature which, like Crazy Jane in Yeats' poem, embraces the earthy along with the divine. All things are a necessary part of the whole.

See also

Douglas, Mary; Freud, Sigmund; Necrophagy and Asceticism; Pollution

References

Brown, Norman. 1959. *Life against Death: the psychoanalytical meaning of history*. Middletown, Connecticut: Wesleyan University Press.

Douglas, Mary. [1966] 1984. *Purity and Danger: An Analysis of the Concepts of Pollution and Taboo*. London: Routledge and Kegan Paul.

Freud, Sigmund. [1908]. "Character and Anal Eroticism". In *The Freud Reader*. ed. Peter Gay, p. 296-297. London: Vintage.

Freud, Sigmund. 1917. "On Transformations of Instinct as Exemplified in Anal Eroticism". In *On Sexuality: Three Essays on the Theory of Sexuality and other works*, p. 293-302. London: Penguin. 1977.

Gonzalez-Crussi, F., [1986] 1987. "The Anorectum". In *Three Forms of Sudden Death and Other Reflections On the Grandeur and Misery of the Body*. London: Pan-Picador.

Lafleur, William R. 1989. "Hungry Ghosts and Hungry People: Somaticity and Rationality in Medieval Japan". In *Fragments for a History of the Human Body. Part One*. ed. Michel Feher. trans. ed. Siri Hustvedt, p. 270-303. New York: Zone.

Lévi-Strauss, Claude. [1964] 1975. *The Raw and the Cooked*. New York: Harper and Row. trans. John and Doreen Weightman.

Parry, Jonathan. [1980] 1982. "Sacrificial death and the necrophagous ascetic". In *Death and the regeneration of life*. ed. Maurice Bloch and Jonathan Parry, p. 74-110. Cambridge: Cambridge University Press.

Paz, Octavio. [1969] 1975. *Conjunctions and Disjunctions*. trans. Helen R. Lane. London: Wildwood House.

Rabelais, François. [1955] 1977. *Gargantua and Pantagruel*. trans. J. M. Cohen. Harmondsworth, Middlesex: Penguin.

van der Geest, Sjaak. 1998. *Anthropology Today*, no. 3, vol. 14, p. 8-12.

Yeats, W. B. [1933] 1978. *Collected Poems*. London: Macmillan.

Fasting

For the duration of a fast, food, or certain selected foods, and drinking, are forbidden. To fast is to deny or mortify the body; in many cultures the denial of the body corresponds to the strengthening of, or approximation to, the soul:

> ... the less substantial the body becomes, the closer it gets to its shadow and soul: cosmic breaths and flashes, diaphanous shells, angelic figures – winged things, difficult to identify, that encompass physical quintessence and blissful sublimity ... a systematic inversion of all that is earthly (Tazi, p. 522).

Furthermore, abstaining from food can induce a visionary state; whether the person fasting is a Christian saint, a Hindu ascetic or a Siberian shaman, the aim is the transcendence of the mundane, or earthly, world. Fasting can also be a form of repentance for sins or transgressions, a means of petitioning the gods, a pathway to grace, a stage in a "rite of passage" marking a new status in life, or a prerequisite to a magical act – the body, through the denial of food, becoming a "pure" vessel. The reasons for fasting have long occupied scholars. W. Robertson Smith views fasting as a spiritual preparation for a sacred or sacrificial meal (Smith, p. 434, 673); Edward B. Tylor, in the 9th edition of the *Encyclopaedia Britannica*, mentions the visions aroused through the abstention from food; while Theodor H. Gaster considers its fecund aspects, as during times of human or natural infertility, fasting can be practised to induce fertility. It has also been proposed that the fasting of mourners (in traditional Tikopia society, for instance, mourners fast all day and are fed for three nights by kinsfolk) is a means of feeding the dead by denying the living. Other scholars, such as Rudolf M. Bell, have identified patterns in fasting that are manifest both in medieval Christian saints and in present-day sufferers of *anorexia nervosa*. The rejection of food in the 20th century has often had political motives: suffragettes have rejected food in the cause of women's political enfranchisement and political prisoners have fasted, sometimes with fatal consequences, in a bid to be recognised as such.

Fasting, though common, is not universal. In Zoroastrianism, fasting and asceticism are condemned in the religious texts as demonic tendencies. The *Gathas* of the prophet Zarathustra envisage the body as part of man's ultimate nature rather than as a mortal coil to be discarded once a complete, incorporeal state has been achieved. Created by the divinity, Ahura Mazda, the body reflects the inner nature and bodily sickness is a sign of spiritual malaise. Adequate food is necessary to maintain a healthy, fecund body that reflects a healthy spirit; indeed, Zoroastrian eschatology envisages a resurrected "Future Body" (Pahlavi *tan i pasen*) at the end of time when the spiritual world combines with a renewed material world which has been cleansed from the evil of Angra Mainyu, the "Hostile Spirit" (the Pahlavi Ahriman) (Williams, p. 155-157).

Preliterate Societies

In many preliterate societies fasting is a crucial element in the "rites of passage" which mark a change in the status of an individual within society, whether from child to man or woman, from unwed to wedded, during mourning, or in transitions from the secular to the sacred domain. A particularly gruelling ordeal is endured by those wishing to become shamans; they must symbolically die to this world and be reborn as shamans. Arnold van Gennep describes the procedure among the Caribs (a native race occupying the southern islands of the West Indies at their discovery):

> To be initiated as a *peai* among the Caribs, the novice goes to live with an "elder", sometimes for as long as ten years, and for twenty-five to thirty years thereafter he subjects himself to repeated tests, such as a prolonged fast. The old *peais* seclude themselves in a hut, where they whip the novice and make him dance till he falls in a faint; he is "bled" by black ants and made to "go mad" by being forced to drink tobacco juice. Finally, he is subjected to a three-year fast which gradually becomes less rigorous, and from time to time he imbibes tobacco juice. The inner meaning of this sequence of rites emerges from the descriptions by von den Steinen: (1) the novice is exhausted and brought to a state of abnormally high sensitivity; (2) he goes to sleep and dies; (3) his soul rises to the sky and descends again; (4) he awakens and revives as a *peai* (van Gennep, p. 109).

Hinduism

Fasting is an important part of the austerities and physical mortifications of the body prac-tised by Hindu ascetics in order to obtain *tapas,* a ritual "heating". *Tapas* is credited in the Rig Veda with playing a part in Creation and the heat produced by the ritual activity of the Vedic priest emulates the primeval ascetic heat of the Creator. Prajapata, the "Lord of Creatures", is himself the product of *tapas* and through *tapas* the ascetic becomes clairvoyant, has revelations of esoteric knowledge, and obtains supernatural powers. As well as fasting, *tapas* is generated by keeping watch in front of a fire, standing in the sun, and, occasionally, by taking intoxicants.

Hinduism generally views asceticism favourably. The Sanskrit text of Hindu law, the *Laws of Manu*, composed in the first centuries of the present era, counsels a serious student of the Veda to live by begging, which, while he is under a vow, is traditionally regarded as equal to fasting (2.188), and a Brahmin (priest) is required to fast if he has incurred "pollution" by, for instance, eating food that has been touched by a menstruating woman, or that has been in contact with the ground, the bodily fluids of another person or an outcast. Pollution in Brahmanic culture is therefore closely related to food and polluted food contaminates the eater. The fear of pollution, through ritually impure food entering the body, is a major preoccupation of the *Laws of Manu*. If pollutions are not cleansed, through fasting or some other designated act, the karma of the individual can be affected and reincarnation will be to a lower caste or animal form.

Members of certain Indian ascetic sects, like the *Ajivika*, which disappeared in the 14th century, followed such strict dietary rules that they often ended their lives by starving to death (Eliade, p. 188). Mircea Eliade mentions various other ascetic groups described in the *Vaikhanasasmartasutra*, a 4th-century CE text that contains much earlier material. The sects listed include those hermits who retire to the forest such as the "Audumbaras, who live on fruits, wild plants, or roots"; the Valakhilyas, with matted hair and torn clothes; and the

Phenapas, ecstatics who survive on "what falls to the ground" and "practise the penance called *candrayana*", which means that their meals are determined according to the waxing and waning of the moon. The *Vaikhanasasmartasutra* also speaks of hermits who "live like pigeons" and "those who eat only what has been dried by the sun", not dissimilar from the present-day *sanyasi* or fakir. Other ascetics include the Kuticakas, travellers between monasteries, at each of which they "swallow only eight mouthfuls"; Bahudakas, who are dressed in red, carry a "triple staff", and beg for food only from Brahmans and the pious; Hamsas, who live on cow urine and dung; and Paramahamsas, who live in cemeteries or under trees, go naked, accept food from members of any caste, and, in many respects, anticipate the later yogic and tantric sects (see also Necrophagy and Asceticism) (Eliade, p. 139).

Of the Yogi, Marco Polo observed in the late 13th century:

[The] regular religious order ... of yogi ... carry abstinence to the extremes. They go without a stitch of clothing and when asked why they display their private parts, reply that they are not ashamed since we commit no sin with them. Not only will they not kill any animals, because they say that they have souls, but that they eat nothing fresh, either herb or root, for the same reason. They fast all the year round and never drink anything but water (Goody, p. 119).

Food injunctions occur in many Hindu texts including the *Bhagavadgita*, *Kamasutra*, *Smrtis* and *Puranas* but nowhere is the horror of the human body expressed as clearly as in the *Laws of Manu*:

[A man] should abandon this foul-smelling, tormented, impermanent dwelling-place of living beings, filled with urine and excrement, pervaded by old age and sorrow, infested by illness, and polluted by passion, with bones

for beams, sinews for cords, flesh and blood for plaster, and skin for the roof (6. 76-77).

The ascetic tries to shake off earthly evil by sublimating human appetites. Fasting today is especially evident prior to festivals and during pilgrimages. A feature of contemporary Indian fasts, which often advocate alternative diets rather than total abstention, is the rejection of foods raised by ploughing (*jota anna*) in favour of the food of fruits (*phalahar*). Typically, on one day in the week, fruit will be eaten in place of grain or cereal based foods. Other restraints may accompany the fruit-eating, such as meditation, silence and sleeping on the ground. The food is also an offering, portions being presented to the sacred cow and, sometimes, to the crow, to be taken by this intrepid traveller to the realms of the dead so that the ancestors may be fed. Through such restraint, it is hoped, ultimate reality will be revealed, or (for we are all human) material wealth and pleasure will be vouchsafed (Goody, p. 117-118).

Buddhism

Fasting is classed as one of the thirteen Buddhist practices that leads to a happy life and is a form of purification (*dhutanga*). It is traditional for Buddhist monks and nuns to eat only one meal a day and to fast on the new and full moon. In general though, the Buddha taught moderation rather than excessive abstinence and modern Buddhists commonly fast only four times per month. The life of the Buddha shows that he himself was capable of extreme restraint.

Siddhartha, who was to be the future *buddha* (awakened) was born in the 6th century BCE to a king, Suddhodana, and his first wife, Maya. After marrying at the age of sixteen and fathering a son, Rahula, he left his palace and renounced the world at the age of twenty nine. Early texts relate how Buddha told his disciples that by meditating on old age, sickness and death, he lost all hedonistic desire and determined to save mankind from such evils.

Legend is more colourful, claiming that Siddhartha's departure had been predicted by diviners. To forestall such an event, Suddhodana confines his son to the palace and pleasure gardens. However, on three successive trips to the pleasure gardens, Siddhartha sees an ancient man leaning on a stick, a sick man burning with fever and a dead man being carried to the cemetery.

His coachman tells him that this is the fate of mankind but on his final excursion Siddhartha encounters a serene mendicant monk and realises that religion can transcend the miseries of the human condition.

Siddhartha leaves the palace and becomes a wandering ascetic named Gautama – his family name in the Sakya clan. He masters the yogic techniques and, settling near Gaya, he indulges in severe mortifications, subsisting at one point on one millet seed a day and then fasting completely until he is reduced to a virtual skeleton. He earns the title of Sakyamuni (the ascetic among the Sakyas) but on the point of expiring he realises that fasting is useless as a means of deliverance. By accepting an offering of boiled rice from a religious woman, Sakyamuni horrifies his five ascetic disciples who abandon him (although he later converts them). The Buddha is "awakened" sitting under a pipal tree (*Ficus religiosa*), after being threatened by Mara, Death. He learns the four Noble Truths including pain and its termination and spends the rest of his life proselytising until he dies in 478, or, in another tradition, 487 BCE. For Buddha, physical mortification is of less importance than charity, self-mastery, freedom from superstitions and intellectual control.

Nonetheless Buddhism is not without its horror of the body. In India, it is commonly believed that the gods neither eat nor emit any bodily fluids, a state that is considered ideal. The Buddhist scholar, Paul Williams, tells of a pertinent myth regarding the beginning of a cosmic cycle. At first, it is said, beings were born spontaneously into a world without distinctions. They possessed an inner luminosity, were euphoric, and traversed the air without the need for food. Temptation came in the form of a scum that formed on the earth's surface. Some of the beings tasted it and found it exquisite. Then others succumbed, and with the eating of the food the beings lost their luminosity and joy. The heavenly spheres appeared, as did sexual differentiation, and concepts of arrogance. Other foods arose and were eaten, each bite coarsening the body and increasing the depravity of the consumer. Fortunately, there exists, if the commentator Asanga is to believed, a very subtle food that induces no effluents, neither faeces nor urine, and that neither corrupts nor pollutes (Williams, 1997, p. 218-219).

Jainism

Jainism celebrates Mahavira (Great Hero), a contemporary and rival of the Buddha, as the last in a series of saviours. Historically the son of Siddhartha, head of a noble clan, Mahavira was initially named Vardhamana and lived as a prince, marrying and having a child, until his thirtieth year. At this point he renounced his possessions and became an ascetic. After thirteen months he abandoned his clothes and wandered naked, fasting rigorously and meditating. Enlightenment came as he sat beneath a *sala* tree; he became a *jina* (conqueror), from which his disciples, the Jains, took their name.

The Jain canon was edited in the 4th and 3rd centuries BCE. Jainism is characterised by such strict asceticism that it regards suicide by starvation as the supreme death. Despite this, there is profound respect for all living creatures as Jainists believe that everything has a soul, even inanimate objects, and a monk will therefore sweep the ground before him, lest he inadvertently crush a creature. Another tenet of Jainism is that the cosmic cycles are endlessly repeated and that all things are governed by *karman*, except the liberated soul. As *karman* creates the "karmic matter" a type of psycho-organism that attaches itself to the soul causing it to transmigrate, fasting can reduce the "karmic matter" created by *karman* and help the soul to fly to the summit of the universe, where it can commune with other freed souls.

At the time of Mahavira's death (in 468 or 477 BCE) there were reputed to be around 14,000 monks and 36,000 nuns as well as a large lay community. Curiously, the nuns could not attain deliverance because, although the stringent asceticism posed no problems, they were forbidden to practise the monastic nudity prescribed by Mahavira.

Judaism

The Hebrew root for fasting is *zwm* but another term, *innah nefesh* (to afflict the body), can be used to describe general abstinence, including sleeping on the ground, not wearing shoes, abstention from washing and anointing the body, and from lovemaking. Fasting is well attested in biblical literature: when the death of King Saul and his sons is announced, David and his men fast until evening (II *Sam.* 1:12) while the inhabitants of Jabesh-gilead abstain for seven days (I *Sam.* 31:13).

One motivation for fasting in the Bible is to avert the wrath of God. Ahab, king of Israel, fasts to prevent the terrible disaster predicted by Elijah in retaliation for Ahab's idolatry. Ahab, ever pragmatic, dresses in sackcloth, fasts, and thereby prevents his family from being killed and eaten by dogs (in the cities) and birds (in the country) (1 *Kings* 21:27). Fasting is also a prelude to a sacred encounter: Moses eats no food for forty days during the revelation on Mount Sinai (*Ex.* 24:18) and Elijah, after being fed by an angel, refrains from food for forty days and nights while he walks to Horeb, the mountain of God, where he meets, and is instructed by, the divinity (1 *Kings* 19). Similarly, Daniel fasts before being granted visions of angels (*Dan.* 9:3; *Dan.* 10:3) and Saul fasts for a day and a night before the act of necromancy in which the witch of Endor conjures up the disgruntled ghost of Samuel from the earth (I *Sam.* 28:20).

Public fasts were also declared to prevent annihilation by an enemy, whether by the Babylonians (*Jer.* 36:3, 9) or the Persians (*Esth.* 4:3, 16); to seek God's intervention in wars, against the Philistines (I *Sam.* 7:6; 14:24) or Israel's Transjordanian enemies (II *Chron.* 20:3); or to end the famine caused by a plague of locusts (*Joel* 1:14; 2:12, 15), although in the latter case, the voracious insects left little to be eaten in any case.

It has been suggested that, before the Babylonian exile, fasting was a spontaneous and pragmatic reaction to exigencies (*Encyclopaedia Judaica*. 6, p. 1189-1196). Indeed, the only specified day of fasting was the Day of Atonement, Yom Kippur, which remains today the holiest day of the Jewish year, during which Jews refrain from eating and smoking, and pray for the forgiveness of their sins. The inauguration of the fast is described in *Leviticus* just after Yahweh has instructed Moses to institute the rite of the scapegoat. To purify the sins of the Israelites, two goats are to be selected; one is to be offered as a sacrifice to Yahweh, while the other, marked "For Azazel" (a Canaanite and Israelite desert demon), is to have the rite of atonement performed over it – with the priest, Aaron, laying his hands on its head and confessing all the transgressions of the people – and is then to be led out into the wilderness. On the Day of Atonement, "the tenth day of the seventh month", Yahweh commands:

> ... you must fast and refrain from work, the native and the stranger who lives among you. For this is the day on which the rite of atonement shall be performed over you, to purify you. Before Yahweh you will be clean of all your sins ... (*Lev.*16: 29-31).

But even Yom Kippur, the day on which the sins are rescinded, may originally have been a reaction to some calamity (*E.J.*: 1190).

After the Babylonian exile (in 587 BCE) four additional dates are prescribed for fasting to commemorate days on which disasters had prevailed; namely, the beginning of the siege of Jerusalem (the tenth of Tevet, the tenth month), the breaching of the walls (the seventeenth of Tammuz, the fourth month), the destruction of the Temple (the ninth of Av, the fifth month) and the murder of Gedaliah, governor of Judea (the third of Tishri, the seventh month). These fasts, according to the prophet Zechariah (*Zech.* 8:19), were to be turned into days of feasting and celebration, with the rebuilding of the Temple. However, the Second Temple was also destroyed, in 70 CE, and the Ninth of Av remains a major day of fasting within the Jewish calendar.

Asceticism was practised during the time of the Second Temple, for purification and in order to approach God. The Essenes, a Jewish sect that flourished from roughly the 2nd century BCE to the end of the 1st century CE and who, it is generally agreed among scholars, occupied the settlement in the wilderness at Qumran, prescribed fasting as a means of catharsis and preparation for the end of time. The lack of food also encouraged the visionary journeys, to the heavens and the throne of God, mentioned in the apocalyptic literature.

The Jewish fasts resembled those of their neighbours. Tertullian, writing at the end of the 2nd century BCE (*De jejuniis* 16), describes a public fast of the Phoenicians of Carthage that is almost indistinguishable from biblical and post-biblical Jewish accounts of fasting. From the Second Temple period, a public fast was accompanied by readings from the Torah (the Pentateuch) and the sounding of the *shofar* (ram's horn) or *hazozerot* (trumpets) and people tore their clothes, donned sackcloth and placed ashes or earth on their heads.

Fasting within Judaism has also been used to avoid the pernicious consequences of nightmares. The Talmud (*Berakhot* 31b) states that although it is forbidden to fast on the Sabbath, if a man has had a bad dream that disturbs him, he is allowed to fast on this day in order to counteract its baneful effects. He must, however, also fast on a weekday as a penance for

having offended against the principle of Sabbath joy.

Although the fast of Yom Kippur is essential for practising Jews, there is an ambivalent attitude towards asceticism within the texts. Maimonides (1135-1206) thinks that bodily gratification is in direct proportion to the soul's destruction; a Talmudic passage (*Taanit* 11a) includes both approval and condemnation of the fasting Nazirite; while a hedonistic tract in the Jerusalem Talmud (*Kiddushim* 66d) claims that a man will be obliged to give an account before God for every legitimate pleasure he has denied himself (Jacobs, p. 74).

Greco-Roman fasts

Fasting plays a role in the Eleusinian mysteries of ancient Greece which commemorate the abduction of Persephone and the mourning of her mother, Persephone, goddess of grain. After her daughter's rape, according to the *Homeric Hymn to Demeter* (possibly dating back to the 8th century BCE), the goddess tears the diadem from her head, wraps herself in mourning clothes and wanders for nine days, neither eating or washing, and carrying two burning torches. On the tenth day she meets Hekate and together they visit Helios, the sun, to learn the identity of Persephone's assailant. She then travels to Eleusis, which lies beyond Athens and close to the river Kephisos where her daughter disappeared, and sits and mourns by a well. Taken as a nurse to the queen Metaneira, Demeter remains silent, seated on a ram-skin covered chair, her head veiled. Iambe, the serving maid, makes her laugh with her obscene gestures and then offers Demeter sweet wine. Demeter refuses but institutes her own drink, *kykeon* ("mixture") made from barley, water and mint.

At Eleusis, the mysteries (*mystes*, initiate) devoted to the two goddesses were organised by the *polis* (city-state) of Athens and supervised by the king. Initiation culminated in an autumn festival called Mysteria; a procession left Athens for Eleusis, a distance of thirty kilometres, and there, in the final nocturnal celebrations in the *telesterion*, or hall of initiations, holy things, "unspeakable" things, or mysteries, were revealed. Though the nature of the revelations remains unclear, fasting is a necessary prelude:

> The Eleusinian *mystai* abstain from food, as Demeter did in her grief, and they end their fast when the first star is seen, because Demeter did the same; they carry torches, because Demeter lit them at the flames of Mount Aetna; but they do not sit on the well because Demeter sat there, mourning for her daughter (Burkert, p. 77).

It is assumed that sitting on a fleece-covered stool with the head veiled, keeping silent, and then laughing and drinking the *kykeon*, were also part of the initiation. Fasting was thought to last for nine days (although Demeter's fast was longer than this) preparing the initiates for the hierophany (a sacred revelation). It is not known whether the *kykeon* was intoxicating. There have been suggestions that it contained ergot and therefore induced hallucinations or that the mixture was fermented, or that the mint may have induced delirium, although the long fast by itself could have achieved the same effect (Kerényi, p. 177-180). It is also unclear what was seen; one possibility is an ear of wheat.

Because Persephone was allowed to leave Hades for a part of the year, the festival not only celebrated grain, but also a triumph over death, although resurrection was not emphatically stated in the ritual. Those who had seen the mysteries were promised a privileged life after death but the content of the promise was not explicit. The Homeric hymn states that because Persephone ate a pomegranate seed while in Hades, she was bound forever to death's kingdom and so, because of the bitter memories they evoked, pomegranates were forbidden during the Eleusinian mysteries and during the winter festival of Haloa, held in honour of Demeter, Persephone and Dionysos (Kerényi, p. 138).

Abstinence, and the avoidance of certain foods, was a characteristic of other Greek rituals and magical practices and is reminiscent of the abstinences and food taboos of the Pythagoreans. Pythagoreans were advised to:

> ... abstain from carcase-meat and flesh and mullet and black-tail and eggs and oviparous animals and beans and the other things forbidden by those responsible for performing the rituals in the temples (Kingsley, p. 283 n.19).

Not only does Pythagoreanism appear to have a ritual background, but its taboos are closely related, according to Peter Kingsley, to those specified for the use of dream oracles. To obtain an oracle it was necessary to enter a state of "incubation", awaiting a visionary dream while sleeping on, or in, the earth. From the gods of the lower regions, the prophecy would arise. The Greek writer, Iamblichus, in *Pythagorean Life,* said that Pythagoras rejected all foods that caused flatulence, interfered with divination (because they caused flatulence?), or upset the purity of the soul, especially the purity of its dream visions (Kingsley, p. 285-286).

Pythagoreans, though, were not all so abstentious. Those called the Pure rejected meat, both for eating and for sacrifice, offering the gods cakes made from grain, honeycombs and incense; others argued, with considerable sophistry, that certain animals such as the goat and pig, were deprived of their fleshly attributes as a punishment for eating food that the gods had reserved for man (Detienne, p. 6).

Another tradition of Greek mysticism, Orphism, considered the slaughtering of animals to be an act of murder, an attitude Orphic disciples attributed to their founder, Orpheus. By refusing the civic duty of offering blood sacrifices, Orphics, like the Pure Pythagoreans, alienated themselves from the city and political life and were destined to a marginal existence. For the Orphics, the very act of animal sacrifice, designed to forge a link between men and gods, only underscored their separation; men

81

ate the flesh which reminded them of their own mortality, while the gods received the smoke and scent of perfumed herbs – transmuted, incorruptible, spiritual food. The Orphics aspired to the condition of the gods by eating only pure foods such as honey or grains (Detienne, p. 6-8).

The dramatist, Euripides, similarly stressed the conflict between body and soul in his plays *The Bacchantes* and *Hippolytus* while showing the common allegiance between alimentary and sexual appetites. Plato expressed a contempt for the body, declaring in a Platonic text that "The soul is man" (*Alcibiades* 1, 130c). Even within the soul, it was only the highest, intellectual part (*logistikon, nous*) that possessed immortality. The intellect was temporarily imprisoned within the tomb of the body and only by disengaging from the physical world could it achieve its divine potential. Thus, though the body was necessary for earthly existence, its instincts needed to be strictly controlled. For the body is:

> A source of countless distractions by reason of the mere requirement of food, liable also to diseases which overtake and impede us in the pursuit of truth; it fills us full of loves, and lusts, and fears, and fancies of all kinds, and endless foolery, and in very truth, as men say, takes away from us the power of thinking at all. Whence come wars, and fightings, and factions? Whence but from the body and the lusts of the body (Plato. *Phaedo*. 66c).

Another philosopher, Aristotle, argued for reasoned moderation but later Platonists and Plotinus, the founder of Neo-Platonism in the 3rd century CE, remained pessimistic about the body. These views were to influence certain early Christian saints who practised extreme asceticism, often to the point of heresy.

Christianity

Although Jesus fasted for forty days and forty nights in the desert, where he was tempted by Satan to turn the stones into bread, he rejected dietary rules and denied that anything entering the body from outside could defile a man. He even plucked ears of wheat on the Sabbath for his hungry disciples to eat. Saint Paul also condemned false asceticism, self-abasement and severe treatment of the body in his letter to the Colossians (*Colossians* 2:16-23). Thus although certain desert monks of Syria, Palestine and Egypt practised excessive asceticism, the early Church generally pleaded for moderation, especially since, by the 4th century, Christianity was turning into an official institution. Excessive fasting was as pernicious as gluttony: in the late 14th century Saint Gregory of Nyssa proclaimed that either extreme could upset the delicate balance of body and soul – good Christians needed both spiritual food for the soul and "sensible food" to strengthen the body – and in the 5th century, John Cassion, whose *Cenobitic Institutions* linked Eastern and Western monasticism, was even more emphatic, pointing out that the early Church Fathers never abstained from bread, nor did the saints live on herbs and fruit alone (Bell, p. 119-121). In the 6th century Benedict of Norcia, founder of the Benedictine monasteries, allowed his monks fish, fowl, fruit, generous quantities of bread and even a pint of wine each day.

An added impetus to such moderation (especially within the early Greek Church) was a desire to counter the strong differentiation between body and soul that existed in the Hellenic-Platonist tradition and that had influenced the Gnostics – who considered the body evil by nature – and certain Christians. Saint Augustine had always railed against the sinful body and, although he did not view the body as evil, the early Christian, Origen, in *Against Celsus* (VII, 38), describes the body as a mere tool of the soul, with only the soul reflecting the Divine image (Ware, p. 97). The soul, he believed, only entered the body as a punishment after it had fallen into sin.

Though total abstinence was therefore discouraged, seasonal fasts did exist, and continue to exist, within the Eastern Orthodox, Russian Orthodox and Roman Catholic calendars, including Lent – the forty days before Easter, especially Ash Wednesday and Good Friday. Fasting involves abstention from meat, dairy products, and sometimes also from fish, wine and olive oil. Eastern Christians fast on Wednesdays and Fridays, for seven weeks before Easter, forty days before Christmas, with two short fasts in the summer. Married couples are required to refrain from sex on the night before a fast day and during the longer fasts. Fasting is not so much a means of subjugating an evil body as a process of purification: cleansing the profane body in preparation for the sacred. This is also why it is common practice to abstain from all food and drink for several hours before receiving the Eucharist in the Catholic and Orthodox traditions. Other traditional Christian fasts include Rogation Days in spring in supplication for good crops, and Ember Days, days of fasting and prayer during each of the seasons.

While even the monastic life encouraged a sensible diet, Christianity in the 13th, 14th and 15th centuries was gripped by a religious zeal characterised at times, especially among women, by fanatical fasting. A famous example is Catherine Benincasa, known as Saint Catherine of Siena, whose life was recorded by Raymond of Capua who became her confessor in 1374. In his *Legenda* he describes how, following her father's death and a vision in which Christ enjoined her to abandon her solitary ways, she gave up food. As Rudolf Bell summarises:

> By the age of twenty-five ... she ate "nothing" ... While dressing the cancerous breast sores of a woman she was tending, Catherine felt repulsed at the horrid odour of the suppuration. Determined to overcome all bodily sensations, she carefully gathered the pus into a ladle and drank it all. That

night she envisioned Jesus inviting her to drink the blood flowing from his pierced side, and it was with this consolation that her stomach no longer had need of food and could no longer digest (Bell, p. 25).

Besides food, Catherine had also rejected marriage, a trait she shared with Lidwina of Schiedam in the Netherlands, who prayed for a deformity when plans were raised for her betrothal. Lidwina escaped matrimony when a skating accident paralysed her, at the same time causing severe internal injuries. Moreover, her hagiographers report, her body putrefied and great pieces fell off, blood poured from her mouth, nose and ears, and she stopped eating. Though she herself rejected food, Lidwina could produce milk from her breasts to feed Catherine, a visitor who had envisaged the event, and she could sometimes miraculously multiply food to feed the needy. She died in 1433 at the age of fifty-three, subsisting towards the end on the holy Eucharist.

There has been a certain speculation as to why extreme emaciation during the late Middle Ages was so characteristic of female piety. Rudolf Bell speaks of 'holy anorexia': the saints deny the body in a similar way to sufferers of *anorexia nervosa*, not in a quest for thinness, but in the pursuit of piety. Another scholar, Caroline Walker Bynum, equates the alimentary control of the body with the repression of sexuality: not only was food believed to provoke lust, but without adequate food menstruation ceases and the female is no longer a candidate for marriage. Nonetheless, she does not view the fasting as a denial of corporeality. On the contrary, just as the male, in medieval thought, characterised the spirit, the female was equated with flesh and also, therefore, with Christ, who was the incarnation of God. Just as Christ suffered physically for the redemption of mankind, offering his body in the Eucharist, so the female suffered through her body to achieve salvation, sometimes manifesting the same miraculous ability to succour, and sustaining herself through the eucharist (Bynum, 1997, p. 138-158; 1989, p. 160-219).

While moderate fasting remains a characteristic of the Roman Catholic and Orthodox churches, Protestant denominations, with the exception of certain evangelical sects, have no specific rules concerning fasting.

Islam

Within the Islamic tradition *sawm* indicates fasting, a religious fast that comprises not only food and drink, but also smoking and an abstention from sex; indeed, sexual intercourse or seminal emission will invalidate the fast. *Sawm* begins when "the white thread of dawn appears ... distinct from the black thread" (Qur'an. surah 2:187) and lasts until sunset. Fasting was introduced by Mohammed in AH 1 (622 CE). He suggested that his followers should refrain from food on *Ashura*, the tenth day of the month of Muharram, but in AH 2 this was replaced by the fast of Ramadan, in celebration of the month of the Qur'anic revelation. The fast of Ramadan is one of the "Five Pillars" of Islam and all those who have reached puberty are required to fast, during daylight hours, for the entire month although exceptions are made for pregnant, nursing and menstruating women and for the elderly and incurably ill. A meal (*sahur*) is eaten before dawn and after sunset, *iftar*, the breaking of the fast, is marked by a light repast. Those who violate any of the *sawm* taboos are required to provide restitution (*qada*) or atonement (*kaffarah*). Restitution involves fasting for each of the invalidated days while for atonement one must free a slave, fast for two months or feed sixty of the poor.

Because the Qur'an was revealed in Ramadan the whole month is holy. Special prayers, *tarawih*, are recited each evening, charity and good deeds are encouraged as is seclusion, or *i'tikaf*, the withdrawal to a mosque. Most sacred of all are the final ten nights, especially Laylat al-Qadr, the Night of Power,

which is "better than a thousand months" for "angels and the spirits descend and it is peace till the rising of the dawn" (Qur'an, surah 97:4-6). The festival marking the end of the Ramadan fast, the 'Id al-Fitr, begins on the new moon. This is a time of celebration when prayer and charity is augmented by joyful reunions of relatives and friends.

Sawm is prescribed in the Qur'an as a means of enhancing piety and celebrating the divine revelation. Certain Muslim scholars have stressed the need for an inner spirituality that goes beyond the obvious manifestations of denial. Al-Ghazali, who died in 1111 CE, thought that fasting should approximate the divine attribute of *samadiyah*, the freedom from want, while in the 14th century Ibn Qayyim al-Jawziyah advocated fasting as a means of enhancing spirituality by denying carnal appetites. Similar themes of denying the bestial and promoting the angelic are found in the writings of the 18th-century theologian, Shah Wali Allah and the 20th-century Sayyid Abu al-A'la Mawdudi. As the latter succinctly put it, fasting:

> ... for a full month every year trains a man individually, and the Moslem community as a whole, in piety and self-restraint; enables the society – rich and poor alike – to experience the pangs of hunger; and prepares people to undergo any hardship to seek the pleasure of God (Ansari, p. 91).

Early Sufi literature similarly stresses the power of asceticism with fasting seen as a state of grace: approaching the angels who feed on Divine Light.

References

Ansari, Zafar Ishaq. 1987. "Sawm. 91". In *Encyclopedia of Religion*. ed. Mircea Eliade. Vol. 13, p. 90-91. New York: Macmillan and Free Press

Bell, Rudolf M. 1985. *Holy Anorexia*. Chicago, Illinois; London: University of Chicago Press.

Burkert, Walter. 1987. *Ancient Mystery Cults*. Cambridge, Massachusetts: Harvard University Press.

Bynum, Caroline Walker. 1989. "The Female Body and Religious Practice in the Later Middle Ages". In *Fragments for a History of the Human Body.* Part One. ed. Michel Feher, p. 160-219. New York: Zone.

Bynum, Caroline Walker. 1997. "Fast, Feast and Flesh: the Religious Significance of Food to Medieval Women". In *Food and Culture.* ed. Carole Counihan and Penny van Esterik, p. 138-158. New York; London: Routledge.

Detienne, Marcel. [1979] 1989. "Culinary Practices and the Spirit of Sacrifice". In *The Cuisine of Sacrifice among the Greeks.* ed. Marcel Detienne and Jean-Pierre Vernant, trans. Paula Wissing, p. 1-20. Chicago, Illinois; London: University of Chicago Press.

Eliade, Mircea. [1954] 1969. *Yoga: Immortality and Freedom.* trans. Willard R. Trask. New York: Bollingen Foundation; Princeton, New Jersey: Princeton University Press.

Encyclopaedia Judaica. "Fasting and Fast Days". vol. 6. 1971, p. 1189-1196. Jerusalem: Keter Publishing House.

Goody, Jack. 1982. *Cooking, Cuisine and Class: A Study in Comparative Sociology.* Cambridge: Cambridge University Press.

Henisch, Bridget Ann. 1976. *Fast and Feast: Food in Medieval Society.* University Park, Pennsylvania; London: The Pennsylvania State University Press.

Jacobs, Louis. 1997. "The Body in Jewish Worship: Three Rituals Examined". In *Religion and the Body.* ed. Sarah Coakley, p. 71-89. Cambridge: Cambridge University Press.

Kerényi, Carl. [1960] 1967. *Eleusis: Archetypal Image of Mother and Daughter.* trans. Ralph Manheim. Princeton, New Jersey: Princeton University Press.

Kingsley, Peter. 1995. *Ancient Philosophy, Mystery, and Magic: Empedocles and the Pythagorean Tradition.* Oxford: Clarendon Press.

The Laws of Manu.. trans. Wendy Doniger and Brian K. Smith. 1991. London: Penguin.

Plato. *Phaedo.* In *The Dialogues of Plato.* ed. and trans. Benjamin Jowett. 1953. Oxford: Clarendon Press.

Smith, William Robertson. [1889] 1927. *Lectures on the Religion of the Semites.* Edinburgh: Black.

Tazi, Nadia. [1989] 1990. "Celestial Bodies: A Few Stops on the Way to Heaven". In *Fragments for a History of the Human Body.* Part Two. ed. Michel Feher, p. 518-552. New York: Zone.

van Gennep, Arnold. [1909] 1977. *The Rites of Passage.* trans. Monika B. Vizedom and Gabrielle L. Caffee. London: Routledge and Kegan Paul.

Ware, Kallistos. 1997. "The Body in Greek Christianity". In *Religion and the Body.* ed. Sarah Coakley, p. 90-110. Cambridge: Cambridge University Press.

Williams, Alan. 1997. "Zoroastrianism and the body". In *Religion and the Body.* ed. Sarah Coakley, p. 155-166. Cambridge: Cambridge University Press.

Williams, Paul. 1997. "Some Mahayana Buddhist perspectives on the body". In *Religion and the Body.* ed. Sarah Coakley, p. 205-230. Cambridge: Cambridge University Press.

Fellatio

Fellatio, the sexual act in which the penis is orally stimulated, is banned in many states of the United States including Alabama, Arizona, Arkansas, North Carolina, South Carolina, Florida, Georgia, Idaho, Kansas, Louisiana, Maryland, Massachusetts, Mississippi, Missouri, Montana, Nevada, Oklahoma, Oregon, Tennessee, Texas and Virginia. The act was equated with cannibalism by the Christian theologian, Tertullian (ca. 160-225) (Thody, p. 58-60), an association that is not altogether absent in a description of cannibalism related by the Foré tribe of New Guinea (Arens, p. 99).

Because fellatio is considered shameful, if not actually illegal, in many societies, accounts of the practice are rare, although illustrations are not uncommon on Greek vases and in Indian sculptures. However, the anthroplogist Gilbert H. Herdt has studied its place in a male cult of the Sambia tribe of the highlands of New Guinea. In this tribe, boys are separated from their mothers between the ages of seven and ten and for the next ten to fifteen years, until they marry, they live in a homosexual relationship with other bachelor males, taking on the roles of fellator and, later, fellated. They are initiated into fellatio in a secret "Penis and flute" ceremony in which bamboo flutes, representing the penis and the female breast nipple, are placed between the lips of the neophyte. If a male does not swallow semen, it is thought he will not grow strong and women will have power over him. The ceremony, and the flutes themselves, are absolutely forbidden for women to hear as is the myth, summarised by Tali, a Sambia ritual expert, which tells how men begot humanity through homosexual fellatio:

> We know that Numboolyu's [fictitious ancestor] penis was sucked by his agemate who himself became pregnant. His fellator's breasts swelled; he changed into a woman. This "woman" then gave birth – but only after Numboolyu created her vulva by slitting open the pregnant pubic area. A girl was the firstborn, and so now, girls grow faster than boys … A boy must be initiated and [orally] inseminated, otherwise the girl betrothed to him will outgrow him and run away to another man … If a boy doesn't "eat" semen, he remains small and weak (Herdt, p. 1).

The myth relates how man alone is responsible for procreation – even the first woman is originally male. In order to become truly masculine, the Sambia believe, fellatio with fellow males must precede heterosexual intercourse.

See also
Flutes

References
Arens, William. [1978] 1980. *The Man-Eating Myth*. Oxford: Oxford University Press.

Herdt, Gilbert H. [1981]1987. *Guardians of the Flutes: Idioms of Masculinity*. New York: Columbia University Press.

Thody, Philip. 1997. *Don't Do It! A Dictionary of the Forbidden*. London: The Athlone Press.

Fetishism

A fetish is any object believed to have talismanic or apotropaic powers. Because it is credited with possessing compelling magical forces, or being animated by a spirit, a fetish is often dangerous and surrounded by taboos. The term fetishism comes from the Portuguese *feitiço* and means "made by art". To describe an object as a fetish means either that it has been constructed or that it is charmed. From the 15th to the 17th centuries, Portuguese seamen sailing along the west coast of Africa used the term *feitiços* to describe carved wooden figures used by African augurs in magical and religious rituals. When French sailors reached the coast of Guinea they translated the Portuguese word as *fétiche* and although the name was originally applied to objects used by the Bantu-speaking people of Zaire or the Congo Basin, it was later applied to any carved or sculpted figure in sub-Saharan Africa.

The term "fetish" has been used by anthropologists to describe anthropomorphic, animal or abstract figures that are carved from wood, bone or ivory, or modelled in clay or termite secretions as well as natural objects such as the gnarled roots and branches of trees, dried leaves, animal claws, nails, fur and horns, tortoise shells, sacred rocks and minerals. More recently, the word has been applied to objects of religious devotion such as the Christian crucifix, religious relics and icons, while it is also used to define something that is irrationally reverenced such as goods in a capitalist economy or substitutes for the sexual object.

Due to the magico-religious forces of a fetish, the one who controls the fetish has considerable power. Mesquitela Lima relates that the Chokwe of the Kasai Basin in north-east Angola believe that the legendary *nganga* (witch-doctor), who can unleash both the benign and malevolent energies of the cosmos, lives in the fetish. Only the augurs and shamans, who generally also make the fetishes, have access to the *nganga's* powers. Protected by their initiation rituals and other ceremonies, they are immune to the evil influences of the *nganga,* but if they violate any taboos attached to its use they may be hurt by their own fetishes

(Lima, p. 314-317). Fetishes are also referred to as "medicines". The Ga people of the Gold Coast also speak of fetishes as "medicines" prepared and distributed by the shamans. These medicines have healing properties, can help in hunting and protect against trespass or theft. However, they become polluted and lose their efficacy if taken to the latrine. Chiefs, shamans or those with enemies, who usually have protective medicines, are vulnerable in, and therefore tend to avoid, public latrines.

Often the taboos placed upon medicines are ethical: the owner must avoid sexual transgressions, larceny, or injustice, with any moral transgression evoking dire consequences. In his book, *Religion and Medicine of the Ga People,* M. J. Field mentions a female vendor who had a medicine that would protect her from thieves as long as she remained entirely honest. When she died she left the medicine to her daughter who was ignorant of the taboo and stole a banana leaf to protect herself from the rain. Immediately her finger became paralysed and, upon consulting a shaman, she was told that the pain was sent as a warning by the spirit and that further offences would be punished with death.

Although anthropologists would no longer use the word *fetishism* to describe religious practices, fetishist cults were once thought to underlie all religions. This view was first proposed in 1760 by Charles de Brosses in his work *Du culte des dieux fétiches: Parallèle de l'ancienne religion de l'Égypte avec la religion actuelle de Nigritie,* and elaborated by Auguste Comte (1798-1857) in his *Cours de philosophie positive.* Comte assumed that preliterate people, seeing a direct correspondence between man and the cosmos, regarded fetishes as living creatures. He believed that fetishism developed into polytheism and polytheism into monotheism. Influenced by Comte, the British anthropologist, Edward B. Tylor, proposed the theory of animism (a belief that all things possess a soul which is detachable and capable of existing independently), and theories of fetishism in their turn influenced the (also now discredited) notion of totemism.

While fetishism is no longer a term employed by anthropologists, fetishes, understood as objects invested with magical powers, are a characteristic of religious life. Christianity is replete with holy relics and legends of animated statues: a sculpture of the Virgin Mary that stretches out an arm to cure a sick woman; an image of Christ that weeps; and apotropaic gargoyles which guard the portals of the church. The dispute over idolatry, the worship of images, has caused controversy within Christianity and strict taboos also exist on representation in Jewish and Islamic art. Other traditions, such as Hinduism, delight in portraying the gods. On a secular level too, images can arouse passion. Art historian, David Freedberg, suggests in *The Power of Images* that the act of looking fetishises a picture; by allowing the eye to dwell on a painting of a beautiful woman the male viewer becomes a voyeur, and the painting a fetish.

In a different context, Karl Marx contends that within a capitalist economy, merchandise is a fetish. Marx envisages the roots of religion, the idea of "soul" or "spirit", as arising at a time of clan leaders or patriarchs, a time when the division of labour led to the segregation of administrative work. Religion begins with the worship of the social leaders and is: "a reflection of production relations (particularly those of master and servant) and the political order of society conditioned by them" (Bukharin in Evans-Pritchard, p. 76-77). Marx demonstrates that within the capitalist ethos the alienated workers, dominated by the products that they produce, express their alienation by worshipping the goods as a fetish.

However, it is probably not Karl Marx but the psychoanalyst, Sigmund Freud, who is responsible for a 20th-century interpretation of fetishism. The fetish, according to Freud, is a substitute for the penis. In early childhood, he proposes, the susceptible male child catches sight of the female genitals and is shocked to discover the lack of a penis. Fearing that this may be the result of castration, and terrified lest such a fate should be in store for himself, he imagines that the woman still has a penis but that it is not the same as it was before: it has been replaced by a substitute. Because the horror of castration is so great, he develops an aversion to the real female genitals and an overvaluation of the fetish.

A typical fetish is the foot or shoe, because the boy has presumably peered up at the woman's genitals from below. Moreover the feet, like the hair (another favourite fetish with its evocation of pubic hair) have a strong smell and appeal to the repressed coprophilic (excrement-loving) pleasure. Yet the fetish is not always a substitute for a lost penis; in some cases it comes to represent the castration itself. Freud interprets the cruel Chinese custom of mutilating the female foot and then revering it like a fetish as a token of gratefulness that the woman has allowed herself to be castrated.

Whether contemporary obsessions with leather and rubber are a result of their resemblance to human skin, Freud does not say. Neither does he explain the use of these materials by homosexuals who, presumably, would have no need to compensate for a lost penis; on the contrary, Freud thinks the use of a fetish should preclude the need for homosexuality as it gives women the attribute that makes them acceptable as sexual objects. This is not to say that the use of fetishes is necessarily a mark of sexual deviancy: an obsession with the fetish (like desiring the handkerchief that has been held to the beloved's breast) may be a prelude to obtaining the real thing.

References

Bukharin, N. 1925. *Historical Materialism. A System of Sociology.* quoted in Evans-Pritchard. [1965] 1977. *Theories of Primitive Religion.* Oxford: Clarendon Press.

Evans-Pritchard, E. E. 1965. *Theories of Primitive Religion.* Oxford: Oxford University Press.

Field, M. J. 1937. *Religion and Medicine of the Ga People.* Oxford: Oxford University Press.

Freedberg, David. 1989. *The Power of Images.* Chicago, Illinois: University of Chicago Press.

Freud, Sigmund. [1917] 1961. "Fetishism". In *The Standard Edition of the Complete Psychological Works of Sigmund Freud.* trans. James Strachey, Anna Freud. vol. 21, p. 149-157. London: Hogarth Press.

Freud, Sigmund. [1905] 1953. "Unusual Objects for the Sexual Object-Fetishism". In *The Standard Edition of the Complete Psychological Works of Sigmund Freud.* trans. James Strachey, Anna Freud. vol. 7, p. 153-155. London: Hogarth Press.

Lima, Mesquitela. 1987. "Fetish". In *Encyclopedia of Religion.* ed. Mircea Eliade. vol. 5, p. 314-317. New York: Macmillan and Free Press.

Marx. Karl. [1867] 1976. *Das Capital: A Critique of Political Economy, vol. 1.* trans. David Fernbach. Harmondsworth, Middlesex: Penguin.

Tylor, Edward B. 1871. *Primitive Culture.* London: Murray.

Fish

A Syrian taboo on eating fish has been well attested by the Greeks. The taboo did not, however, mean that fish could never be consumed. Reports from Mnaseas of Patara and Antipater of Tarsus describe how the priests of Atargatis, goddess of Askalon, would bring boiled and roasted fish to her temple and then eat it themselves. Atargatis had decreed that fish might only be eaten in her temple and in her presence, thus rendering the fish sacred and the meal sacrificial.

Not surprisingly, there are myths which tell how Atargatis achieved her aquatic role. Xanthus the Lydian, in the 5th century BCE, explained how Queen Atargatis was captured by Moxos the Lydian and drowned in the lake of Askalon because she was both evil and proud. She was then eaten by the fish. Her son, Ichthys, neither evil nor proud, unfortunately suffered the same fate. After such suffering, Atargatis became the local goddess and all the fish in the lake of Askalon became sacred to her. Another story is mentioned by the Greek traveller and physician, Ktesias from Knidos, who uses the goddess' Greek name, Derketo. In this tale, far from being devoured by the fish, Derketo is rescued by them and carried to the shore after she has tried to drown herself following the birth of her illegitimate daughter, Semiramis. Ktesias even describes the goddess who is, like mermaids, half-fish and half-human (Burkert, p. 204-205).

Another pond with sacred fish could be found in the temple of the Syrian goddess at Bambyke-Hierapolis. Here the fish were so tame, they would rise up at the sound of the priests. The classicist, Walter Burkert, finds in the myths of Atargatis a theme of sacrifice and relates the sea-trial of Atargatis to Mesopotamian, Ugaritic and Greek tales in which fish are either sacred or have a pivotal role in a divine drama. As fishing supplanted hunting, he supposes, the rites of the hunt were transferred to the sea and, at least in those areas bordering the Mediterranean, the fish were sanctified and became suitable candidates for sacrificial meals (Burkert, p. 204-212). In classical Greece, though, the only fish suitable for sacrifice was the tuna (the only fish to "bleed") which was occasionally offered to Poseidon. Reasons advanced for the rejection of fish include the fact that they are not domesticated and that, living as they do in the depths of the sea, they are more "chthonian" or "other-worldly" than the grain that grows in the earth (Detienne and Vernant, p. 221. n. 8).

See also

Chinese Food Taboos; Fishing; Food Taboos; Jewish Dietary Laws; Laws of Manu

References

Burkert, Walter. [1972] 1983. *Homo Necans: The Anthropology of Ancient Greek Sacrificial Ritual and Myth*. trans. Peter Bing. Berkeley; Los Angeles: University of California Press.

Detienne, Marcel and Jean-Pierre Vernant. [1979] 1989. *The Cuisine of Sacrifice among the Greeks*. trans. Paula Wissing. Chicago, Illinois; London: University of Chicago Press.

Fishing

Probably because fishing is such a dangerous and unpredictable occupation, it is subject to many taboos. In parts of Scotland it was deemed unlucky to whistle while at sea, and women, ministers, and pigs, as well as the mention of such things, was inauspicious on deck. The anthropologist, James Frazer, interprets the ban on mentioning pigs as a reminiscence of the biblical taboo on pork mentioned in *Leviticus,* and links the almost universal taboos attached to fishermen with those applied to hunters and manslayers: to kill, or take the soul of a living creature is never without its dangers (Frazer, p. 190-223).

While present-day fishing quotas, introduced to conserve diminishing stocks, mean that fishing is restricted at certain times, in the past fishing was curbed on more sacred grounds. In Japan, for instance, fishing was forbidden in the Shima district of Mie-ken when the sacred shark was thought to emerge from the deeps and attend the annual festival of the Isa-no-miya shrine at Isobe-mura. Just as certain times were too holy for fishing, so were certain places, such as the areas of water bordering a shrine. Sea bream could not, for this reason, be caught in the pool of Tanjo-ji Temple in Kominato-machi, on the Pacific coast of Chibaken, and anyone disobeying the taboo would incur misfortune for himself and his community.

Besides bans on fishing, particular foods were not to be carried on board Japanese boats. These included beef, bean paste, vinegar, rice boiled with red beans and *kayu* (rice gruel). It is possible that the rice and red bean dish, because it was eaten at a girl's first menses, carried the taboos attached to menstrual blood while several legends explain why *kayu* was proscribed. A tale from the Harima-nada coast, along the Seto Inland Sea, relates how boatmen began to boil and eat *kayu* at the moment when a boat carrying the deity of mercy, Kannon, entered the Harima sea. Because the fishermen were eating so noisily, they failed to hear the rising storm and only just survived the raging seas, to reach the shore at Ikeda. A variant, narrated by fishermen in the sea area of Munakata in Genkainada, Kyushu, tells of a bell brought by sea from China to Japan:

> When the vessel bearing the bell reached the sea of Munakata, some of the boatmen began to wash rice for boiling. This action made the sea water cloudy, and the boat ran aground upon a hidden shoal; the precious bell fell overboard. According to the legend, the sea water has remained darkened around the spot where the bell sank, and to prevent further mishaps of this kind, fishermen have placed a taboo on eating *kayu* at sea (Oto, p. 1963:116).

See also

Fish

References

Frazer, James George. [1911] 1935: *Taboo and the Perils of the Soul – The Golden Bough*. New York: The Macmillan Company.

Oto, Tokihiko. 1963. "The Taboos of Fishermen". *Studies in Japanese Folklore*. ed. Richard M. Dorson, p. 107-121. Bloomington: Indiana University Press.

Flamen Dialis

Though religious leaders of many faiths have been subject to taboos, whether sexual, dietary or mortuary, the ancient Roman priest, the Flamen Dialis, was particularly restricted. In *Taboo and the Perils of the Soul*, James George Frazer summarises the almost impossible regulations imposed upon this holy man:

> The Flamen Dialis might not ride or even touch a horse, nor see an army under arms, nor wear a ring which was not broken, nor have a knot on any part of his garments; no fire except a sacred fire might be taken out of his house; he might not touch wheaten flour or leavened bread; he might not touch or even name a goat, a dog, raw meat, beans and ivy; he might not walk under a vine; the feet of his bed had to be daubed with mud; his hair could be cut only by a free man and with a bronze knife, and his hair and nails when cut had to be buried under a lucky tree; he might not touch a dead body nor enter a place where one was burned; he might not see work being done on holy days; he might not be uncovered in the open air; if a man in bonds were taken to his house, the captive had to be unbound ... His wife, the Flaminica, had to observe nearly the same rules [moreover] ... She might not ascend more than three steps of the kind of staircase called Greek; at a certain festival she might not comb her hair; the leather of her shoes might not be made from a beast that had died a natural death but only from one that had been slain or sacrificed; if she heard thunder she was tabooed until she had offered an expiatory sacrifice (Frazer, p. 13-14).

See also

Beans; Death; Dogs; Hair; Horses; Knots

References

Frazer, James George. [1911] 1935: *Taboo and the Perils of the Soul – The Golden Bough*. New York: The Macmillan Company.

Flutes

Flutes, made from bamboo or from bone, are amongst the earliest musical instruments. Because of their typical long, narrow shape they are often identified with the male phallus and are forbidden to women. Several origin myths tell how the flutes were originally invented by women, or possessed by them, but later came into man's possession. The Tucano Indians of Columbia recount how a bird-cage is accidentally opened and the birds, once free, turn into *yurupari*, sacred flutes, which the women take possession of and which enable them to reduce men to slavery. Now, however, the men own the flutes which have become the instrument of female subjection to men: the mere sound of the flutes inspires terror in the women (Lévi-Strauss, p. 169).

Among the Sambia people of the Highlands of New Guinea the identification of flute and phallus is an intrinsic feature of male initiation rites. The flutes, which are owned by different phratries (clans), are supposed to be feared by the women, who flee at their sound. This is in part because of the terror of male violence should women discover the secret of the flutes but also because they are told that the men, in blowing down the bamboo tubes, activate a female spirit, who is in league with the men and hostile to women, and who animates the flutes with her cries.

The Sambian flutes are always played in pairs, one of which is longer, and is referred to as the "male" or "penis" while the shorter one is called the "female". At the male initiation rite known as the "penis and flute" ceremony, the tip of a "female" flute, protruding from an enclosing "male" flute, is placed into the mouth of the initiate. What he is in fact being initiated into, in this ritual, is the practice of fellatio: ingesting the semen of bachelors in secret homosexual ceremonies is credited with strengthening the masculinity of the initiates. Until he has achieved sexual potency and warriorhood, a boy is forbidden to play the flute or sound bull roarers (a bull roarer is a flat piece of wood fastened at one end to a string which, when swung round, produces a whirring or howling sound that is identified with the voices of animals, spirits, or totemic ancestors) (Herdt, 1987).

See also

Fellatio

References

Herdt, Gilbert H. [1981] 1987. *Guardians of the Flutes: Idioms of Masculinity*. New York: Columbia University Press.

Lévi-Strauss, Claude. [1968] 1978. *The Origin of Table Manners* trans John and Doreen Weightman. New York: Harper and Row.

Folktales, Eating in

Eating with others is an act of communion. For this reason, many societies only allow those of a similar caste, class, race, age-group or sex to eat together. In folktales and myths, eating with the wrong companions is especially dangerous. If one eats in the land of the dead or with the fairies, an indelible link may be established, making return impossible. Because Persephone eats a pomegranate while she is in the realm of Hades, she must return for part of each year.

On the other hand, disobeying an alimentary taboo and eating fruit from the Tree of the Knowledge of Good and Evil results in the expulsion of Adam and Eve from Paradise.

If breaking a food taboo does not lead to either imprisonment or expulsion, it may have other unusual effects. A Scandinavian tale tells how a man catches a magic fish which he is supposed to feed to his wife. Eating it himself, he becomes pregnant and the child, with no other means of egress, must be cut out of his knee (AT 705). In a North American scatological tale, the trickster is warned by a certain bulb that if he eats it, he will defecate. Stubbornly, he eats the bulb and produces such a quantity of excrement that he is forced to flee up a tree to escape it (Radin, p. 25-27).

Many food taboos in myths are identical to those existing in the society itself. Cannibalism, universally condemned in tales, is nonetheless rife. Most of the ogres, giants, witches and step-mothers, have a predilection for human flesh. In Greek myth, Kronos combines this with infanticide, devouring his own sons. Other Greeks ate human meat unwittingly: Tantalos offered a banquet to the gods serving up his son, Pelops, whose shoulder Demeter inadvertently ate, while Thyestes ate his infant sons which his evil brother had slaughtered and served to him (Burkert, p. 99-104).

See also

Cannibalism; Folktales, Taboos in; Food Taboos

References

(AT) Aarne, Antti and Stith Thompson. [1961] 1981. *The Types of the Folktale. FF Communications,* no. 184. Helsinki: Academia Scientiarum Fennica.

Burkert, Walter. [1972] 1983. *Homo Necans: The Anthropology of Ancient Greek Sacrificial Ritual and Myth.* trans. Peter Bing. Berkeley; Los Angeles; London: University of California Press.

Radin, Paul. [1956] 1976. *The Trickster: A Study in American Indian Mythology.* New York: Schocken Books.

Thompson, Stith. [1946] 1977. *The Folktale.* Berkeley; Los Angeles; London: University of California Press.

Folktales, Taboos in

Taboos are so common in folktales that when the Russian formalist, Vladímir Propp, defined what he termed the "Functions of Dramatis Personae" in Russian folktales, he included the delivery of an interdiction to the hero as an important function. According to Propp, it is the actions of a story that are important, not its characters. In the *Morphology of the Folktale* he lists thirty-one "functions", or actions, of the characters that propel the tale forward from the initial motivation to the final happy conclusion. The actions or "functions" are the essential components of a tale that serve as constant elements. The series of functions fit into one consecutive story and determine the morphology, or form, of the tale. In Propp's scheme, "An interdiction is addressed to the hero" is the second function and is paired with the third function, "The interdiction is violated". Thus a character who is warned not to look in the closet, or to speak, to leave the tower or to pick the apples invariably does precisely this forbidden thing, often with terrible consequences. While Propp was describing Russian tales, the violation of a taboo is not confined to Russian stories. Adam and Eve eat the forbidden fruit in paradise, Lot's wife cannot resist looking back (Orpheus has the same problem) and the wife of Bluebeard turns the key to the forbidden chamber.

Taboos also form an important part of Stith Thompson's *Motif-Index of Folk-Literature,* filling an entire chapter. A motif is any small detail of a story; it can be a person, animal, object or an event, such as a wedding, a magical flight or the telling of a lie. The American folklorist, Stith Thompson, began to collect and classify the motifs of traditional narratives, drawing on American, Oriental and European stories, oral narratives from around the world, tale-cycles, ballads, legends, folklore journals and other scholarly sources. The aim was to create a comprehensive collection, carefully organised with details of sources, which could be used as a tool in folklore research. Publication of the index began in 1932 and was completed in 1936. Since then, it has been updated as other scholars have added their contributions. Chapter C covers taboos, the consequences of breaking them and unique compulsions. Under the taboo (spelled *tabu*) section, the headings are numbered from one to nine hundred and ninety-eight with numerous subdivisions. Some of the interdictions, such as not eating certain foods or menstrual taboos, are familiar but others are purely magical: a forbidden casket is opened and trouble enters the world (C915.1); the breaking of a sexual taboo causes a child to be born without bones (C101); and the killing of an albatross causes misfortune to follow the killer (C841.10.1).

See also

Geis, Gessa; Propp, Vladimir

References

Propp, Vladimir. [1928] 1979. *Morphology of the Folktale.* Austin, Texas; London: University of Texas Press.

Thompson, Stith. 1955. *Motif-Index of Folk-Literature.* vol. 1. Bloomington, Indiana: University of Indiana Press.

Folktales, the Telling of

Many traditional narratives, whether myths or folktales, are regarded as sacred and may only be told at certain times of the day or year, or at a special time in a person's life, during a "rite of passage", and sometimes only certain privileged members of the society are allowed to hear them, or to tell them. While a culture remains conservative, preliterate and immune to external influences, the rules will not be breached but the situation changes when writing and other technology is introduced that allows the tale to be recorded and retold at will. The moral dilemma that this can cause to an ethnologist, who wishes to preserve material that is under threat while at the same time not abusing the trust of the community, is discussed by Barre Toelken in his article, "The Yellowman Tapes".

Toelken spent forty-three years recording Navajo Coyote stories, episodes from the Navajo Emergence Myth, Yeibichei songs, instructions for hunting rituals, details of the sacred deer hide and anecdotes from Navajo oral history, including the first encounters with the Pueblo tribes. His principle informant was Hugh Yellowman with whose family he established a close relationship. Toelken begins by explaining the difficulties of conducting fieldwork within a community for whom the spoken word is imbued with such power:

> For instance, certain stories and songs are to be orally performed only at certain times of the year: during winter (that is, between the first killing frost and the first lightning stroke), during solstices, and during eclipses – moments that are defined by the larger movements of nature, not by the immediate agendas of humans. Electronic recordings have complicated the normal observance of these

"rules", for tapes can be played anytime, especially if they are out of the control or purview of the person who recorded them. My ability to record – or, more properly, Navajo permission for me to record – was made possible for me by my promise that I would play the tapes only during the season in which they could properly be performed (Toelken, p. 381-391).

While the first lightning stroke heralds summer, a time when certain narrations must not be spoken, technology ensures that the tales may yet be heard. For although the taped sounds are extremely dangerous if released into the air, causing an exchange between a person's *nílch'i* (wind, spirit or soul) and the external *nílch'i* of nature (evidence of which can be seen in the whorls on the fingers and toes), the use of earphones restricts the vibrations.

Despite this proviso, Toelken was well aware of the dangers posed by the tapes, a concern that was aggravated by Yellowman's death. For many Navajos are careful to avoid any contact with the dead, and now the voice of a dead man could inhabit the land of the living. Moreover, without careful supervision, the tapes might be played at the wrong time of the year, or the Navajo sounds picked up by a stranger who would speak them without concern for "the Navajo concept that spoken words create the reality in which we all live" (Toelken. 1998, p. 383). Yellowman's widow expressed concern that a person could be injured if the tapes were heard at the wrong time of the year or spoken aloud in the wrong setting. Because Toelken could not be certain of the fate of the tapes after his own death, he finally returned them to Yellowman's widow, so that she could destroy the recordings and preserve the sanctity of the tales themselves.

Reference

Toelken, Barre. 1998. "The Yellowman Tapes, 1966-1997". *Journal of American Folklore*, vol. 111.

Food Taboos

Proscribed foods – forbidden for religious or social reasons to entire cultures or to specified individuals within the community – have been around a long time and are recorded in ancient texts. *Genesis* relates how Adam and Eve, having eaten the forbidden fruit, were expelled from Paradise while the *Homeric Hymn to Demeter* tells how Persephone, having tasted a single pomegranate seed in the land of the dead, was forever bound to Hades.

Anthropologists, trying to determine the cause of the prohibitions, initially turned their attention to totemic practices. Linguistically, the word *totem* comes from *dotem*, and is used by the Algonquin Ojibwa people to denote clan membership. In 1910, James G. Frazer published *Totemism and Exogamy*, a work that stresses the social and religious values of totemism which, he claims, unites members of the clan spiritually while conferring group identity. A totem, he describes as:

> a class of material objects which a savage regards with superstitious respect, believing that there exists between him and every member of the class an intimate and altogether special relation (Frazer, p. 3).

As man and totem are mutually dependent, a man shows his respect for the totem, which protects him, by not killing it if it is an animal, and by not cutting it if it is a plant. To discover the origin of such practices, Frazer turned his attention to food taboos in relation to the clan totem species in the Intichiuma rituals of the Aborigines of central Australia. W. E. Roth had shown how members of each exogamous class of the Queensland tribes were forbidden to eat several different types of animals. Commenting on Roth's findings, Frazer gives his own explanation for the food taboos:

> With the evidence as to the *Intichiuma* ceremonies of the Central Australians

before us, we may surmise that the animals which are thus tabooed to the various intermarrying classes of these Queensland tribes are … what I have proposed to call multiplex totems, and that the members of each of these classes are, or have at some time been, bound to perform ceremonies of the same sort as the *Intichiuma* for the multiplication of all the kinds of animals which they are forbidden to eat. The surmise is confirmed by the circumstance that, though the members of each class are forbidden to eat the animals in question, they are not forbidden to kill them. In other words, they are at liberty to provide their fellows with the food of which they may not themselves partake. This entirely agrees with the view of Totemism here suggested, that it is a co-operative system designed to procure for the community a supply, primarily of food, and secondarily of all the other necessities of life (Frazer, p. 137).

Although both Roth and Frazer agreed that the aim of the system was to ensure equal access to the available food, Roth believed that the rules of abstinence imposed on each clan served to leave food for the rest of the tribe, while Frazer asserted that the food taboos had a magical effect: by observing them each group would enhance its "magical powers for the multiplication and enticement of the game to which the tribe, as a whole, trusted for its supply of food" (Frazer, p. 137).

A different reason for the taboos on totemic animals and the prohibition on marriage to members of one's own totemic group is offered by Sigmund Freud in his essay "The Return of Totemism in Childhood". Freud, like Frazer, studied the complex totemic kinship and marriage systems of the Australian Aborigines whom he believed to be at an earlier stage of development. In his highly imaginative essay, Freud proposes that humans originally lived in small groups consisting of a single adult male with his wives and children and that, at maturity, the young males were driven off so as to prevent the dangers of inbreeding. In their frustration, the sons rebelled against the tyranny of the father who kept all the females for himself. They killed him and then ate him, in a cannibalistic feast (the idea of a cannibalistic feast derives from the work of W. Robertson-Smith) and by eating him they identified with him and he became deified as their totem. But having accomplished this primal crime the sons were consumed with guilt and laid taboos upon the killing of the totem. Thus the oedipal guilt was projected onto the totemic animal which became taboo and could not be eaten, while their kinswomen, the women of their own totemic group, were similarly denied to them.

The avoidance of tabooed foods by certain clan members for social and psychological reasons – to create a bond and sense of group identity – has been studied by Émile Durkheim and A. R. Radcliffe-Brown. Durkheim rejected the views of Frazer, and of clan members themselves, that the reason for the taboos on eating the totemic animals was to benefit other clan members and ensure the continuance of the food supply. He noticed that although each member of a clan shared with other members a special relationship to a sacred species, whether duck, rabbit, frog, worm or plant, which was not to be eaten, the species was not always edible in the first place. For instance, he observed that the *intichiuma* ceremonies were performed even when the totem, the *wollunqua*, was a non-existent snake. He concluded that the rites must have had a social, rather than nutritional, function, creating a sense of solidarity and inter-dependence within the clan, and that its totem represented not just god, or the vital essence, but society itself, which were one and the same thing:

> The god of the clan, the totemic principle, can therefore be nothing else than the clan itself, personified and represented to the imagination under

the visible form of the animal or vegetable which serves as its totem (Durkheim, p. 47).

Radcliffe-Brown, as a student of Durkheim, was similarly interested in the social function of food prohibitions which, he realised, served to remind a person of his dependence, not only on food but also on society. Among the Andaman Islanders of the Bay of Bengal, initiation rituals involved proscriptions on certain foods. In the course of the ritual, the initiates were released from the taboos but the link between transition to adult status and the awareness of dependency on the adult community was forcefully made. Like Durkheim, Radcliffe-Brown saw totemism (and its concomitant dietary taboos) as an important means of social organisation.

The French anthropologist, Claude Lévi-Strauss, set out, in two works, *Totemism* (1962) and *The Savage Mind* (1966), to demonstrate that food taboos are not intrinsic to totemism as they "may be organised into systems that are extra- or para-totemic" (Lévi-Strauss, 1966, p. 99) and that anthropologists have been mistaken to think that dietary prohibitions symbolise man's sense of identity with animals. Like Freud, Lévi-Strauss imagines a distant past, when man lived, not in a primal horde as Freud supposed, but in a natural state of harmony and affinity with the animal kingdom. All was to change when man made the "triple passage (which is really one) from animality to humanity, from nature to culture, and from affectivity to intellectuality" (Lévi-Strauss, 1962, p. 101). The transition came about when man, observing the diversity in the animal kingdom, came to perceive a corresponding diversity among humans and then, finally, to recognise his own uniqueness as a human being as opposed to animals:

> It is because man originally felt himself identical to all like him (among which, as Rousseau explicitly says, we must include animals) that he came to acquire the capacity to distinguish

himself as he distinguishes *them*, i.e., to use the diversity of species as conceptual support for social differentiation … The total apprehension of man and animals as sentient beings, in which identification consists, both governs and *precedes* the consciousness of oppositions between, firstly, logical properties conceived as integral parts of the field, and then, within the field itself, between "human" and "non-human" (Lévi-Strauss, 1962, p. 101-102).

Once man had developed the intellectual capacity to differentiate himself from the animals, the food taboos were introduced because of a refusal by men "to attribute a real animal nature to their humanity" (Lévi-Strauss, 1966, p. 108). The nutritional prohibitions are therefore not related to alimentary concerns but serve as symbols, providing a conceptual framework for humans to distinguish different animals from one another on the natural plane and, through a process of analogy, to differentiate between human groups at a cultural level. All this explains, says Lévi-Strauss, why a particular animal species is chosen as a totem: not because it is useful or edible but because certain characteristics that it possesses make it "good to think".

In *The Savage Mind* Lévi-Strauss addresses the question as to why the food taboos relating to totemic representations, which are, after all, symbolic, should be accompanied by rules of conduct such as eating prohibitions and exogamous marriage. He points out, first of all, that food taboos are not necessarily linked to the totem. Among the Bororo of Brazil, for instance, the only forbidden food is the meat of the red deer which is a non-totemic species. In fact, many eating proscriptions can be readily distinguished from totemic prohibitions as Victor Turner's field work on Ndembu divination demonstrates:

> The Ndembu sorcerer, who is primarily a diviner, must not eat the flesh of bush-buck because of its irregularly spotted hide, for if he did so his divination would stray from the main point. There is a prohibition on the zebra for the same reason, on animals with dark coats (which would cast a shadow over his clairvoyance), on a species of fish with sharp bones because they might prick the diviner's organ of divination, the liver, and on several sorts of spinach with slippery leaves because they might cause his powers of divination to slip away from him (Lévi-Strauss, 1966, p. 97).

In these cases it is a physical characteristic that renders a particular species unsuitable for food, but the behaviour of an animal may also be a determinant. Among the Fang of the Gabon, pregnant women are forbidden to eat squirrels because squirrels hide within the holes of trees and, should the mother eat this flesh, the child might similarly hide, refusing to leave the womb and thus causing a difficult birth. The Fang also refrain from eating mice because mice live near homes and are almost members of the family.

Just as eating taboos do not need to be connected to the totem, so totemic prohibitions are not necessarily associated with food. The central Algonkin forbid the Fish clan to build dams, the Eagle clan to wear feathers on their heads, the Beaver clan to swim across rivers and the Thunder clan to take off their clothes to wash. It also happens that sometimes, rather than a prohibition on eating the totem, there is an obligation to eat it. Among the Chippewa native Americans, if an insult is directed at the eponymous animal of another clan member, the offender is himself forced to eat the food of that totem until he can eat no more and is forced to recognise the totem's power.

Even when a totemic animal is forbidden, this is not because of an intrinsic quality that may be harmful, but in order to "introduce a distinction between 'stressed' and 'unstressed' species (in the sense that linguists give to these terms)" (Lévi-Strauss, 1966, p. 102), or, to put it more simply, to identify those species that may be useful in denoting significance in the symbolic classification of a particular culture. The taboos relating food taboos to rules of exogamy are similarly ways of stressing significance. It is therefore not surprising to find that the connection between nutritional taboos and rules of exogamy is not causal but metaphorical. Food and sex have long been bedfellows. The Fang forbid the consumption of the inside of elephants' tusks, not only because of the bitterness but because, being soft, it may slacken or deflate the penis. In Yoruba the same verb is used for "to eat" and "to marry" while *kuta* denotes both cannibalism and incest in the language of the Koko Yao of Cape York peninsula. Even the act of lovemaking is commonly described in terms of eating or devouring and, in many a myth, the unwitting male is in mortal danger from the *vagina dentata*, the lethally-toothed orifice of his partner.

Totemism, then, resembles language in that it is a convenient way of organising and communicating human experience. It is, however, only one schema among many and food taboos, like exogamous marriage rules, can exist beyond a totemic system.

Lévi-Strauss' writings on tabooed animals had a direct influence on the works of two other anthropologists, Edmund Leach and S. J. Tambiah. In "Anthropological Aspects of Language: Animal Categories and Verbal Abuse", Edmund Leach explores the relationship between animals that must not be eaten, humans that must not be married and words that must not be spoken. Although he restricts his investigation to animal categories within English culture and among the Kachins of north-eastern Burma, he assumes that his conclusions should apply to many, or indeed all, other cultures. Leach interprets language and naming as a process in an individual's early development as the child learns to identify himself as a distinct entity, separating self from other, and creating discrete categories to subdivide this "other", which, together with "self",

had previously formed a continuum within his consciousness. Taboos occur whenever there is a danger of the categories becoming confused; their function is to demarcate the boundaries:

> Taboo serves to separate the SELF from the world, and then the world itself is divided into zones of social distance corresponding here to the words farm, field and remote (Leach, p. 53).

It follows that animals (and by extension all types of food) may either not be eaten, or be subject to taboos, if they could cause a confusion in the taxonomy by being too close to "self" or by otherwise blurring distinctions. Animals that live in the house, for instance, are too close for comfort and are therefore tabooed, a feature that is often stressed through the use of a verbal term that is either obscene or abusive. It is an insult to call someone a "bitch" (female dog) or accuse them of being "catty". Farmyard animals may be eaten but still live close to the house and are therefore commonly subject to restrictions and may be given derogatory appellations. A prime example is the pig which lives in very close proximity to humans; kept in the backyard pigsty and eating leftovers from the household, it has given rise to such human insults as "swine" and "boar".

Leach suggests that animals in Britain can be divided according to distance from self: house pets, farm, field (game) and remote wild animals. House pets are never eaten and are classed as inedible. Farm animals, tame but not close, are edible when young or castrated. Field animals (game) are protected by humans (often only hunted during certain seasons) but are not tame. They can be eaten while sexually intact. Remote wild animals are not controlled by humans and are inedible. Some animals trangress categories and are therefore surrounded by taboos. The rabbit, "ambiguously game and vermin", was formerly known as "coney", deriving "from Latin *cuniculus*, ... the 18th century rabbit was a cunny, awkwardly close to *cunt*" (Leach, p. 50). The linguistic taboo did not, of course, mean that the rabbit could not be eaten with relish. Those remote wild animals that are classed as inedible, Leach regards as subject to unconscious taboos (though they could be eaten they are not thought of as food) which differ from conscious prohibitions such as those imposed on pigs, by Jews and Muslims, and cows by Hindus (though recognised as food, they are forbidden).

Having established animal categories, circumscribed as they are by proscriptions, Leach turns to the correspondence between interdictions on animals and those on sex. In the (predominantly British) human bestiary, sex between sisters is incestuous and taboo (as pets are inedible); between close kin such as first cousins, or "clan sisters" in many cultures which have unilateral descent and a segmentary lineage organisation (the farmyard animals), marriage is forbidden, but premarital sexual relations may be permitted or even expected; neighbours or friends are free game (field animals) and are the most desirable marriage partners; and distant strangers, known to exist but never encountered (like those exotic creatures of the wilderness, the elephant and the hippopotamus) cannot be married as no social relationships with them exist.

The Kachins classify their animals, and kin, slightly differently. Here animals are divided into house (inedible), farm (edible if sacrificed), forest (edible and subject to no rules) and remote (inedible). Animals of the house, the dog (*gwi*) and rat (*yu*), are only eaten in ritual situations. To call someone a dog is an obscenity, while *yu* also means witchcraft. Farm animals such as pigs and cattle are designated *wu,* while forest dwellers (*nam*) are subdivided into small deer that live closer to the village, *hkyi* (with the homonym meaning "faeces") and *stu* (homonym "spirit, ghost") and large deer, *shan* (ordinary, clean meat) and *shat* (ordinary clean food of any kind), which live deep in the heart of the forest. Here too, then, the taboos on eating particular animals decrease in proportion to the

distance of the animal from the homestead. Pejorative homonyms also fade with remoteness. As Leach predicts a correspondence between edible animals and eligible mates, and as, in this case, it is the forest-dwellers (*nam*) who may be consumed without sacrifice, one would expect the marriage partner to come from the category designated *nam*. This is in fact so, except *nam* in this case includes a particular first cousin, the mother's brother's daughter, who is considered the most desirable partner.

The influences of both Edmund Leach and Lévi-Strauss (and also Mary Douglas, see below) are evident in S. J. Tambiah's ruminations on tabooed animals in northeastern Thailand (Tambiah, p. 423-459). During his fieldwork in Baan Phraan Muan, which means the village of Muan the hunter, Tambiah recorded a division of animals into *sad baan* (domesticated animals) and *sad paa* (animals of the forest). Most of the forest animals – the wild buffalo, wild ox, wild boar, wild fowl, wild duck, deer, squirrel, hare and forest rat – are edible. Exceptions are those rarely seen inhabitants of the deep forest – tigers, elephants, leopards and bear (not considered food), monkeys and wolves. Elephants, tigers, leopards and lions are said to be included in a list of food taboos imposed by Buddhism. The domesticated chicken and duck are edible but there are conditions attached to the consumption of the domesticated buffalo, ox and pig. The cat is not eaten and the dog is positively taboo.

It comes as no surprise to learn that animals at a greater distance from the house are rarely proscribed. Notable exceptions are the wolf and the monkey; the former resembles too closely the house-dwelling dog and the latter is forbidden (a taboo said to derive from Buddhism) because it is a "friend of man" (*ling pen sieow manud*) and is "descended from man" (*ling maa chag khon*). An etiological myth explains the affinity between monkeys and humans:

There is a story called *Nang Sibsaung*, i.e., a woman with twelve children. This woman with so many children was too poor to support and feed them. The children therefore had to go into the forest in search of food, and they ate the wild fruits there. In the course of time hair grew on their bodies and they became monkeys (Tambiah, p. 441).

It is a curious reversal that apes are descended from men rather than men from apes; obviously to eat monkeys would amount to cannibalism.

The dog, allowed to roam freely within the house, is neither friend nor fiend. Its heinous habits of eating faeces and enjoying incest do not endear it to the Phraan Muan villagers and, unlike the cat, it performs no useful role as a rat-catcher. It is used in verbal abuse: to say that a dog has had intercourse with someone's paternal and maternal ancestors is a terrible insult (comparable to the English "son of a bitch"). Whereas the cat is inedible, the dog is positively taboo.

The ox, and especially the buffalo, are extremely important for agriculture: the buffalo ploughs the rice-fields and possesses *khwan* (spiritual essence). On the Buddhist sabbath the buffalo, too, is granted a day of rest – to make it work on this day would be sinful. The buffalo is primarily a ceremonial food; either a buffalo or an ox provides the meat for Buddhist calendrical festivals and family rituals. Once a year, before the ploughing season, the buffalo is sacrificed to propitiate the guardian spirit of a large swamp (Bueng Chuean). The buffalo is considered to be close to humans and sleeps beneath the most intimate area of the raised house, the sleeping quarters. Like the dog, it is used in insults with a sexual connotation, such as "your face is like the head of my penis" (*ii naa hua khooi* where *khooi* sounds like *khuay*, buffalo). Although the buffalo may be eaten on ritual occasions, no animal raised in the village may be killed for communal rites; the ox or

buffalo must be acquired from another village. Similarly, household rituals require the beast to come from another dwelling. The violation of these taboos has dire consequences: animals will fail to breed, contract diseases and die.

Although the pig is also a ceremonial meat, it is not the first choice for feasts, and although the pig is subject to the same restrictions as the ox and buffalo, it is mainly bred for commercial purposes, slaughtered by a middleman and sold in the marketplace. Its affinity with man is not as close as that of the ox and buffalo. The hen and duck may be freely killed by villagers but while there are no ritual prohibitions associated with the hen, a duck may not be eaten at weddings. This is because of the "laid back" nature of the duck who, having laid her eggs, does not bother to hatch them. Such reprehensible conduct could have a detrimental effect upon the bride: eating goose flesh could induce sloth and the neglect of spouse and offspring.

Tabooed animals are related to tabooed relationships; just as animals that are too close to man are either forbidden or need to be obtained from further afield, so the marriage partner must not be close kin. Marriage between second cousins is allowed but should the wife be older than her husband, and thereby transgress the relative age distinctions, the couple are made to eat rice from a tortoise-shell (in the manner of dogs who are also incestuous). Moreover, the same words are used to describe the consequences of animal and sexual violations: *liang yaag*, difficulty in rearing beasts, and *phae luug*, infertility.

Tambiah concludes that the dietary regulations of the Thai villagers offer a clue to their relationship with animals, expressing:

> … neither a sense of affinity with animals alone nor a clear-cut distinction and separation from them, but rather a coexistence of both attitudes in varying intensities which create a perpetual tension … They [link] eating rules with sex rules, to man, on the one hand drawing nature into a single

moral universe and also at the same time vigorously separating nature from culture (Tambiah, p. 445).

Tambiah adopts the concepts of metonymy and metaphor from Lévi-Strauss' *The Savage Mind* to explain the mechanics. As the dog lives in the house, it is almost human, and thus has a metonymical relation to human society. This means it cannot be eaten. Nevertheless, its incestuous behaviour and filthy habits render it subhuman. Should a couple transgress the sexual rules and act in an incestuous way, like a dog, they can imitate a dog metaphorically by eating from a shell and correct the moral consequences. The ox and buffalo also have a metonymic relation to man but there can be no real confusion with man so they are edible, according to certain rules. Animals which are not subsumed under the domestic or forest groupings (such as the otter, vulture, snake or toad) are also subject to dietary rules. If they intrude into the habitat of man, either by entering the house or by resembling a domestic animal, they may be seen as adopting a metonymic or metaphorical relationship with man; in this case they are dangerous, inauspicious, and tabooed.

Failure to fit within a clearly defined category may also be a reason for a creature being inedible. Tambiah here acknowledges the influence of the anthropologist, Mary Douglas. In *Purity and Danger* (1966) Douglas concentrates her attention on precisely those animals which are anomalies in a particular society; it is, she deduces, animals that for one reason or another defy classification that are tabooed. The Jewish dietary code, for instance, renders such animals as pigs and shellfish taboo. Hygienic explanations for the food taboos – such as the prohibition on the eating of pork being due to the danger of trichinosis – are inadequate to explain the complexities of the system. What a reading of *Leviticus* 11: 2-42 and *Deuteronomy* 14: 3-20 makes plain is that animals are forbidden if they do not "fit". Pigs, although they have cloven hooves, do not chew the cud like oxen, sheep and, goats, so they are not cloven-hoofed ruminants. Fish characteristically have fins and scales. Shellfish have neither; they are therefore only masquerading as fish and must not be eaten. Things which avoid categorisation, like matter out of place, disturb our sense of order, they are dangerous, polluting, taboo. Tambiah's article criticises Mary Douglas' analysis of Jewish dietary laws and R. Bulmer, who studied the Karam classification of animals, also has reservations (Bulmer, p. 5-25). In their respective research among the Thai and Karam, they realised that the taxonomies of animals are governed by social rather than merely physiological criteria. While things that are out of place may be polluting, the Karam and Thai determine for themselves what is out of place and effectively organise nature so that it mirrors and fortifies their social rules. Mary Douglas has acknowledged their research and modified her views; she had already noticed that among the Lele, the pangolin, a scaly, tree-climbing ant-eater, though clearly seen as an anomaly by the Lele and transcending their system of classifications, was auspicious and revered. Turning to the Jewish prohibition on the pig, she quotes Bullmer who says it is just as valid to argue that the pig is accorded anomalous taxonomic status because it is unclean as to suggest that it is unclean because it is an anomaly (Douglas, p. 249-275). The pig is unclean, she decides, because it eats carrion but also because it was reared as a source of food by non-Israelites. Marriage with outsiders was forbidden to the ancient Israelites and they established strong boundaries between themselves and others; not eating the pig preserved their purity. By contrast, the Lele encourage transactions with others and have weak social boundaries; for them the pangolin, in defying classification or crossing boundaries, is sacred, not polluting (Douglas, p. 276-318).

Anna S. Meigs agrees with Douglas' assertion that food taboos are a means of recognising and defining both social and religious categories and of stressing opposition and difference. In the Eastern Highlands of Papua New Guinea where she conducted her fieldwork, Meigs noticed that the Hua people commonly use food to differentiate between different groups, whether kinsman and stranger or male and female. Typically, a person is not allowed to accept food that is produced, prepared or served by a stranger and young male initiates must be wary of eating things associated with a female such as the *dguripa* mushroom (which resembles the female breast before childbirth) or the red *kito'* which women wear on their buttocks. Transgression can lead to sickness, lack of vitality and, in the case of initiates, stunted growth.

However, the Hua people also use food and its exchange as a means of establishing social solidarity. This is related to the Hua conception of *nu*, a kind of life force or vital essence that exists principally in the body fluids but also in the body itself and in cultivated foods which contain the *nu* of their producer:

> The association of foods with *nu* are multiple. Foods resemble *nu* substances and therefore participate in their power. Initiates may not eat red pandanus oil because it looks like menstrual blood, *zokoni* mushrooms because they smell like menstrual blood, and foods that are dark on the interior because they resemble female interiors, which are full of *nu* and therefore fertile ... snails are tabooed not because of their slime but because their slime resembles vaginal secretions ... Foods are also associated with *nu* through contagion. A mature male may not eat leafy green vegetables picked by his real or classificatory wife or firstborn child because these vegetables are contaminated by spots of menstrual blood, genital waste, sweat and body oils transferred from the hand to the food. Moreover, foods are permeated by the *nu* of their producers ... All

the foods [Hua] eat are produced by people they know and whom they either trust (in which case they eat the food) or distrust (in which case they do not). Finally, in Hua culture ... blood, flesh, semen, sweat, body oils, hair, fingernails, and saliva, are all *nu* substances, and all are ingestible, even edible, to the Hua (Meigs, 1984, p. 122-123).

Since all cultivated foods contain *nu*, which can be either life-enhancing or life-threatening, it is important to only accept food from friends as enmity can be transmitted through the food, and cause disease. The entire community is linked through *nu* and eating together becomes an affirmation of trust, a celebration of solidarity. Conversely, to refuse a food is to express distrust, to deny the link between self and others. Foods are tabooed if the *nu* within them can be detrimental to the eater because they come from a suspect source or because they have the power to deplete a person's *nu*. Food picked by close kin or pigs belonging to a real or classificatory child cannot be eaten: this is as physically repugnant as, the Hua say, "a dog licking its genitals", in effect, eating one's own *nu* (Meigs, 1997, p. 99). Crucial though the conception of *nu* is to the Hua, certain foods are prohibited for other reasons such as "contagion", the belief that contact can permanently contaminate a person. For this reason, a woman should avoid the *hakeri'a* (dry and hard) varieties of taro, yam and banana in the final months of pregnancy for fear their properties might be transferred to her body and cause her womb and birth canal to dry out (Meigs, 1997, p. 97).

Most of the previous analyses of alimentary prohibitions have concentrated on symbolic, structural or functional reasons for avoidance: the food itself is of less importance than its semiotic or social value within a society. Opposed to these are the more pragmatic approaches that can be loosely termed cultural-materialist; here the emphasis is on the nutritional or ecological effects of food taboos in particular cultures.

Under this rubric falls Marvin Harris, a strict adherent to utilitarian analysis. If ritual restrictions exist, he argues, they only reinforce good husbandry. In India, cows are protected from slaughter under Article 48 of the federal constitution's Directive Principles of State Policy, a piece of legislation that reflects Hindu religious law. The ban on beef might seem ill-advised in a country where masses are suffering from starvation but Harris argues that the cows are more useful living than dead; they provide milk and manure and are useful debris-eating scavengers, while oxen are needed to pull the ploughs (Harris, p. 47-66).

Similarly, the Old Testament prohibition on pig-flesh makes sense given the climate and vegetation of the Middle East. Pigs have no functional sweat glands and are therefore happier in damp shady forests, where they can forage for roots and cool off in mud-pools, than in semi-arid scrub. A pastoral nomadic people like the ancient Israelites would be hard-pressed to find sufficient shade and adequate supplies of water for these animals. Pigs have other disadvantages; they are difficult to milk and provide no wool, they cannot pull ploughs and because they cannot digest cellulose, they cannot eat grass and so need to eat things that humans may also find nutritious. Although pigs have been raised for meat in the Middle East for over 10,000 years, with bones being discovered by archaeologists in some of the oldest Neolithic villages such as Jericho in Palestine and Jarmo in Iraq, the forests that existed in Neolithic times and provided an ideal environment were replaced by olive groves and agricultural land. Even when the Israelites formed settlements, pigs remained an expensive option. The biblical injunction against the pig merely codified existing prejudice. When, much later, Jews began to live in Christian societies, the taboo on swine became a cultural marker distinguishing them from their neighbours.

The survival value of certain food taboos has been observed among the Tikopia of the Solomon Islands by Raymond Firth. The production and acquisition of food on the isolated island involves a sustained effort made more difficult by the threat of drought and hurricane and the increase in population. Revisiting the Tikopia after a cyclone, Firth noticed the wisdom of the chief's ban on the consumption of his produce and those items that were not yet ripe. On the other hand certain foods such as coconuts, which are generally taboo and reserved for the chief or those of high status, were eaten by others when food was in short supply. Firth did, however, notice that the most hallowed food taboos, on bats and certain birds, were not violated and the acknowledgement of the food obligations to the chief and the dead meant that it was possible for the Tikopians to recover their social values once the food supply returned to normal. D. R. McDonald and Eric Ross note the ecological value of prohibitions in the conservation of species that might otherwise be destroyed through overconsumption.

Anthropologists have also considered the deleterious effects of food controls: restricting food in an area which has limited supplies can lead to nutritional deprivation. Exponents of this view include Christian Wilson, who studied Malay food strictures surrounding childbirth and Judit Katone-Apte who focused on food avoidances in Tamiland, South India.

In 1994 Robert Aunger wrote a paper examining the effects of alimentary injunctions on the inhabitants of the Ituri forest of Zaire. Within the forest live Sudanic- and Bantu-speaking horticulturists and Efe and Tswa Pygmy foragers. Food restrictions are of various types: "slippery" animal taboos require a pregnant woman (and couvade-participating man, i.e., a man participating so fully in childbirth that after the birth he takes to his bed to recover) to abstain from juvenile or unborn animals as these will cause a miscarriage; other forbidden animals will result in a dangerous birth, cause the unborn child to acquire a characteristic of the banned beast or induce a malaria-like disease known as *Eke*.

Some bans are family based: the violation of a taboo which has been transmitted by a clan ancestor can cause the descendant to keel over and die and the class known as *njou* requires a person to refrain from the animal into which members of his kin group will transmute upon death. *Imbara* taboos are associated with a male cult or secret society; women and immature men are restricted by this cult from eating "strong" animals such as viverrids (ferrets and civet-cats) and carnivores. The consumption of certain animals causes a loss in sexual attractiveness rendering a marriage partner hard to find and those who overcome this hurdle face further difficulties: women, once married, may be forbidden certain types of fish or meat while living in their husbands' villages. Injunctions are also linked to male initiation ceremonies and other "rites of passage" while personal or cultural revulsion may render particular foods inedible. On top of all this, an animal may be banned because eating it can be dangerous; not only illness but also an attack by witches may befall those unwise enough to ignore the ban. The best advice is to avoid those creatures not known to be safe and many young Ituri residents forgo permitted animals simply because they are not sure.

In a series of structured interviews, Robert Aunger found that these comprehensive taboos involve "140 different animals that represent over 95 percent of the nutritionally significant animal species in the Ituri" (Aunger, p. 283). Curiously, though, the only group to be seriously affected nutritionally are the Sudanic women who suffer a reduction in fitness and fecundity and may manifest an increased morbidity. The pygmy foragers have fewer food restrictions than the horticulturalists (those that exist are mainly concerned with reproduction and are therefore of limited duration) and are less affected by seasonal variations in the food supply; they can always travel to find new supplies. Among the agriculturists, the Bantu have fewer restrictions than the Sudanics and among the Sudanic-speaking groups, it is the women who have

the hardest time. During pregnancy, their calorie intake can be reduced by up to 9 per cent (75 per cent of meat-based calories) and there is evidence of a decrease in ovulation among the Sudanic-speaking Lese during seasonal shortages. The women are also subjected to family-based taboos; as they live with their husbands' families they are subjected to both family taboos and those placed on them by their relatives when they become their kinsman's spouse. Moreover, separated at a relatively early age from their mothers, they often fail to learn which foods to avoid and deny themselves permitted animals.

Aunger concludes that:

Since these women live in a marginal environment and are subject to seasonal fluctuations in the availability of food, the loss of almost 10 percent of calories from food avoidance is likely to represent a significant biological cost ... For most of these individuals, the likely effect is probably less than a 10 percent reduction in fitness ... [but] It is important to recognise that fitness differences on the order of 10 percent between individuals can quickly result in considerable changes in the demographic and genetic composition of a population. From this more evolutionary perspective, then, the degree of maladaption is highly significant, especially when considered over a number of generations (Aunger, p. 302-303).

Nor can Aunger find any of the compensatory aspects of food taboos that anthropologists often uncover: the restrictions neither foster social relationships nor reduce social tensions; on the contrary, the fear of witchcraft for a Sudanic woman who violates family- and marriage-taboos leads to her subjugation at the hands of her husband and his kin. The women themselves complain about the food embargoes and their real hunger and misery is poignantly captured in their entreaty to the anthropologist to give them some food (Aunger, p. 304).

In the industrialised nations of the world, food restrictions continue to play a role. The motivation for avoidance may be based on religious precepts, cultural habits, a regard for health, personal revulsion or a feeling of affinity with an animal. There is also a growing concern for the welfare of animals; the conditions in which animals are "factory-farmed" has led to a sharp rise in the number of vegetarians and vegans.

See also

Beans; Camels; Cereals; Chinese Food Taboos; Cows; Dogs; Eggs; Fish; Foods Forbidden to Brahmins; Frogs; Halal; Horses; Jewish Dietary Laws; Milk; Mushrooms; Oysters; Pigs; Salt; Snails; Tortoises

References

Aunger, Robert. 1994. "Are Food Avoidances Maladaptive in the Ituri Forest of Zaire?" *Journal of Anthropological Research*, no. 50, p. 277-310.

Bulmer, R. 1967. "Why the cassowary is not a bird: a problem of zoological taxonomy among the Karam of the New Guinea Highlands". *Man*, no. 2, p. 5-25.

Douglas, Mary. [1966] 1984. *Purity and Danger: An Analysis of the Concepts of Pollution and Taboo*. London: Ark-Routledge and Kegan Paul.

Douglas, Mary. 1990. "The pangolin revisited: a new approach to animal symbolism". In *Signifying Animals: Human Meaning in the Natural World*. ed. Roy G. Willis, p. 25-36. London: Unwin Hyman Ltd.

Durkheim, Émile. [1912] 1915. *The Elementary Forms of the Religious Life*. New York: Macmillan.

Farb, Peter and George Armelagos. 1980. *Consuming Passions: The Anthropology of Eating*. Boston, Massachusetts: Houghton Mifflin Company.

Firth, Raymond. 1959. *Social Change in Tikopia*. London: Allen and Unwin.

Firth, Raymond. [1973] 1975. "Food Symbolism in a Pre-Industrial Society". In *Symbols: Private and Public*, p. 243-261. London: George Allen and Unwin.

Frazer, J. G. [1887] 1910. *Totemism and Exogamy: A Treatise on Certain Early Forms of Superstition and Society*. Vol. 1. London: Macmillan and Co. Ltd.

Freud, Sigmund. [1913] 1985. "The Return of Totemism in Childhood. Totem and Taboo". In *The Origins of Religion*. The Pelican Freud Library Vol. 13. trans. and ed. James Strachey, p. 159-224. London: Penguin.

Harris, Marvin. 1986. *Good to Eat: Riddles of Food and Culture*. London: George Allen and Unwin Ltd.

Katone-Apte, Judit. 1977. "The Socio-Cultural Aspects of Food Avoidances in a Low-Income Population in Tamiland, South India". *Journal of Tropical Pediatrics and Environmental Child Health*, no. 23, p. 89-90.

Leach, Edmund. 1964. "Anthropological Aspects of Language: Animal Categories and Verbal Abuse". In *New Directions in the Study of Language*, p. 23-63. Cambridge, Massachusetts: Massachusetts Institute of Technology Press.

Lévi-Strauss, Claude. [1962] 1966. *The Savage Mind*. London: Weidenfeld & Nicolson.

Lévi-Strauss, Claude. 1962. *Le Totemisme Aujourd'hui*. Paris: Presses Universitaires.

McDonald, D. R. 1977. "Food Taboos: A Primitive Environmental Protection Agency". *Anthropos*, no. 72, p. 734-748.

Meigs, Anna S. 1984. *Food, Sex, and Pollution: A New Guinea Religion*. New Brunswick, New Jersey: Rutgers University Press.

Meigs, Anna. 1997. "Food as a Cultural Construction". In *Food and Drink: A Reader*. ed. Carole Counihan and Penny van Esterik, p. 95-106. New York; London: Routledge.

Messer, Ellen. 1981. "Hot-cold classification: theoretical and practical implications of a Mexican study". *Social Science and Medicine*, no. 158, p. 133-145.

Messer, Ellen. 1997. "Food Taboo". In *The Dictionary of Anthropology*. ed. Thomas Barfield, p. 200-202. Oxford: Blackwell Publishers.

Radcliffe-Brown, A. R. 1922. *The Andaman Islanders: a Study in Social Anthropology*. Cambridge: Cambridge University Press.

Ross, Eric B. 1978. "Food Taboos, Diet, and Hunting Strategy: The Adaptation to Animals in Amazon Cultural Ecology". *Current Anthropology*, no. 19, p. 1-19.

Schieffelin, Edward L. 1976. *The Sorrow of the Lonely and the Burning of the Dancers*. New York: St Martin's.

Simoons, Frederick J. [1961] 1967. *Eat Not This Flesh: Food Avoidances in the Old World*. Madison, Wisconsin; London: University of Wisconsin Press.

Tambiah, S. J. 1969. "Animals Are Good to Think And Good to Prohibit". *Ethnology*, no. 8, p. 423-459.

Willis, Roy G. 1990. "Introduction". In *Signifying Animals: Human Meaning in the Natural World*. ed. Roy G. Willis, p. 1-24. London: Unwin Hyman Ltd.

Wilson: Christine. 1980. "Food Taboos of Childbirth: the Malay Experience". In *Food, Ecology and Culture*. ed. J. R. Robson, p. 67-74. New York: Gordon and Breach.

Foods Forbidden to Brahmins

The food strictures to which the Brahmin priests are subject are described in great detail in *The Laws of Manu*. Death tries to kill the brahmins by tempting them to disobey the laws. These are some of the food taboos that they must observe:

[5] Garlic, scallions, onions, and the things that grow from what is impure … [6]. The red sap of trees … the "phlegmatic" fruit, and the first milk of a newly-calved cow … [7] a dish of rice with sesame seeds, or a spice cake, made of flour, butter and sugar, or a cake made of rice, milk and sugar … if these are prepared for no (religious) purpose; or meat that has not been consecrated; or food of the gods, or offerings; [8] or the milk of a cow within ten days of calving, or the milk of a camel or of any animal with a whole, solid hoof, or of a ewe … [9] … the milk of women, the milk of all wild animals in the wilderness except the buffalo, and all foods that have gone sour or fermented. [10] But … yoghurt can be eaten. [11] … carnivorous birds or any birds that live in villages, or any whole-hoofed animals that have not been specially permitted; or little finches, [12] the sparrow, the aquatic bird, the goose, the waterbird, the village cock, the crane, the wildfowl, the moorhen, the parrot, and the starling; [13] birds that strike with their beaks, web-footed birds, the paddy-bird, birds that scratch with their toes, and birds that dive and eat fish; or meat, from a butcher … [14]

or the heron or the crane, the raven or the wagtail; or (animals) that eat fish, or dung-heap pigs, or any fish … [16] But sheat-fish and red fish may be eaten if they are used as offerings to the gods or the ancestors, and "striped", "lion-faced", and "scaly" fish can always be eaten. [17] You should not eat solitary or unknown wild animals or birds, nor any animals with five claws, not even those listed among the animals that may be eaten. [18] They say that, among the animals with five claws, the porcupine, hedgehog, iguana, rhinocerus, tortoise, and hare may be eaten, as well as animals with one row of teeth, except for the camel (The Laws of Manu, p. 99-101).

See also
Food Taboos; Laws Of Manu

Reference
The Laws of Manu. trans. Wendy Doniger and Brian K. Smith. 1991. London: Penguin.

Frazer, James George (1854-1941)

The British anthropologist, James George Frazer devoted an entire volume of the third edition of his monumental work, *The Golden Bough* (1906-1915), to *Taboo and the Perils of the Soul*. He also wrote the entry on taboo for the ninth edition of the *Encyclopaedia Britannica* (1875-1888) and, in 1910, *Totem and Exogamy* (London: Macmillan). In the *Encyclopaedia Britannica* he defines taboo as "the name given to a system of religious prohibitions which attained its fullest development in Polynesia, but of which under different names traces can be discovered in most parts of the world" (*Encyclopaedia Britannica*: 1875). He later modifies this statement, realising that taboo has a far wider application than he had originally proposed.

Like William Robertson Smith and Émile Durkheim, Frazer separates the notions of purity and pollution from the "sacred" ideas of deities and souls, arguing that an inability to make moral distinctions between the concepts of holiness and pollution is a sign of a "primitive" mentality.

Taboo itself, he identifies as a type of negative magic. Frazer sees magic as characterising an early stage in man's cultural evolution, preceding organised religion (which in turn precedes scientific thought). At this stage, he asserts, man believes in mechanical ideas of contagion and sympathy. Frazer is influenced by the anthropologist, Edward Tylor, who defines magic as a mistaken belief that things which are alike are somehow mystically linked to one another. The law of mystical sympathy explains the Dayak conviction that males must abstain from the flesh of the deer before a hunt lest it make them timid, and shun oil before a pig-hunt lest the pig "slip" through their fingers. This is what Frazer describes as negative magic because it involves ritual avoidance behaviour, or taboo. It is opposed to positive magic which may be used to achieve prosperity.

In *Taboo and the Perils of the Soul*, Frazer classifies taboos, dividing them into tabooed acts, persons, things and words. Under "acts" he subsumes: taboos on intercourse with strangers, on eating and drinking, on showing the face, on quitting the house and on leaving the remains of food on the plate. "Persons" includes: chiefs and kings, mourners, women at menstruation and childbirth, warriors, manslayers, hunters and fishers. "Tabooed things" comprises: iron, sharp weapons, blood, head, hair, ceremonies of hair cutting, disposal of cut hair and nails, spittle, foods, knots and rings. In the final category, the following "words" are found: personal names, names of relations, names of the dead, names of kings and other sacred persons, names of gods and common words.

The taboos exist to protect people from supernatural dangers that pervade the universe, that can be drawn towards certain persons and things, and that are highly contagious:

> … in primitive society the rules of ceremonial purity observed by divine kings, chiefs and priests agree in many respects with the rules observed by homicides, mourners, women in childbed, girls at puberty, hunters and fishermen, and so on … the common feature of all these persons is that they are dangerous and in danger, and the danger in which they stand and to which they expose others is what we should call spiritual or ghostly … To seclude these persons from the rest of the world so that the dreaded spiritual danger shall neither reach them, nor spread from them, is the object of the taboos which they have to observe. The taboos act, so to say, as electrical insulators to preserve the spiritual force with which these persons are charged from suffering or inflicting harm by contact with the outer world (Frazer, [1911] 1935, p. 224).

As mentioned earlier, no distinction is made between what is tabooed because it is holy and that which must be shunned because it can cause pollution. Thus the Syrians, Frazer observes, are uncertain as to whether pigs are avoided because they are unclean or because they are sacred.

Frazer's thoughts concerning contagion are based on the notion that things which have once been in contact continue to be linked even after the physical contact has been severed. Thus the nails or hair of a person retain his essence and may be used in rituals for beneficent or malevolent ends (which explains why it is so important not to let them fall into the wrong hands).

Though Frazer's methodology and comparative deductions have been severely criticised by scholars, notably Edmund Leach, and the notion of social evolution is thoroughly discredited, his ideas remained popular with writers and he influenced the work of T. S. Eliot, W. B. Yeats, Robert Graves and others.

References

Ackerman, Robert. 1987. *J.G. Frazer: His Life and Work*. Cambridge: Cambridge University Press.

Fraser, Robert. 1990. *The Making of "The Golden Bough": The Origins and Growth of an Argument*. New York: St. Martin's.

Frazer, James Georges. [1906-1915] 1935. *The Golden Bough: A Study in Magic and Religion* (3rd., 12 vols.). New York: Macmillan.

Frazer, James Georges. [1911] 1935. *Taboo and the Perils of the Soul. The Golden Bough: A Study in Magic and Religion*. New York: Macmillan.

Frazer, James Georges. 1910. *Totemism and Exogamy*. London: Macmillan.

Leach, Edmund R. 1961. "Golden Bough or Gilded Twig"? *Daedalus*, no. 90/2, p. 371-387.

Freckles

Pliny the Elder, in his *Natural History* (28.188), records that those who have freckles are not allowed to participate in magical rituals. This is because divine beings will not obey those who have freckles and are never seen by them (*NH* 30.16). Freckles are regarded as an imperfection, a blemish, and individuals so affected may pollute the divine. The ruling recalls the injunction in *Leviticus* (21:17-23) which forbids the Israelites to approach the altar if they are afflicted with any disease or infirmity.

More recently, in 1833, a freckle-faced boy was depicted in an engraving from the *Clinique de l'Hôpital Saint Louis*. Commenting on the illustration, Barbara Marie Stafford is impressed by the way in which:

> The systematic classification of spotted diseases in the early nineteenth century identified a host of maculated signs, variegated blisters, blotches, eruptions, and tumours. These pits and pocks constituted a loathsome compendium of the evil or comic disfigurements

punctuating the modern stigmatised skin (Stafford. [1993] 1994, p. 23).

It is curious that such innocuous pigmentation is treated as a disease and that freckles, so common in childhood, are linked to moral degradation.

References

Pliny the Elder. *Naturalis Historia*.

Stafford, Barbara Maria. [1993] 1994. *Body Criticism: Imaging the Unseen in Enlightenment Art and Medicine*. Cambridge, Massachusetts: MIT Press.

Stafford, Barbara Maria. "'Peculiar Marks': Lavater and the Countenance of Blemished Thought". *Art Journal*, no. 46 (Fall 1987), p. 185-192.

Freud, Sigmund (1856-1939) – Totem and Taboo

Between 1912 and 1913 the Austrian psychoanalyst, Sigmund Freud, influenced by the evolutionary theories of Charles Darwin and the anthropologist, James G. Frazer, published four essays collected under the title *Totem and Taboo* with the somewhat unfortunate subtitle "Some Points of Agreement between the Mental Lives of Savages and Neurotics". In these essays Freud draws parallels between the psychological development of an individual and the cultural development of society and surmises that the successive neuroses, conflicts and fantasies that an individual has to overcome in childhood are mirrored by those experienced by preliterate societies as they struggle towards civilisation. Though the idea that preliterate societies have a different mode of thought from highly technological ones has been discredited (by Claude Lévi-Strauss among others), the essays are important for their theories of taboo.

The first essay, "The Horror of Incest", shows how incest is avoided by the Australian aboriginal peoples who implement elaborate marriage rules, including laws forbidding marriage to members of the same totemic clan (totemism refers to the relationship between a group of people and an animal species), and impose severe penalties in order to discourage the practice. These cultural prohibitions are seen as echoing an individual's self-imposed censorship on his incestuous desires.

The second essay, "Taboo and Emotional Ambivalence", compares the ritual taboos of Polynesians and others with the prohibitions of obsessional neurosis. That which is tabooed, Freud states, is holy and awe-inspiring while at the same time it is dangerous, forbidden and unclean. This ambivalence is also a characteristic of obsessional neurosis: an affectionate relationship is undermined by an underlying hostility towards, and fear of, the object of desire. The fear, as with cultural taboos, is manifested in an aversion to physical contact:

> As in the case of taboo, the principal prohibition, the nucleus of the neurosis, is against touching; and thence it is sometimes known as 'touching phobia' or '*délire du toucher*'. The prohibition does not merely extend to immediate physical contact but has an extent as wide as the metaphorical use of the phrase 'to come in contact with'. Anything that directs the patient's thoughts to the forbidden object, anything that brings him into intellectual contact with it, is just as much prohibited as direct physical contact. This same extension also occurs in the case of taboo.
>
> The purpose of some of the prohibitions is immediately obvious. Others, on the contrary, strike us as incomprehensible, senseless and silly, and prohibitions of this latter sort are described as 'ceremonial'. This distinction, too, is found in the observance of taboo.
>
> Obsessional prohibitions are extremely liable to displacement. They extend from one object to another along whatever paths the context may provide, and this new object then

becomes, to use the apt expression of one of my women patients, 'impossible' – till at last the whole world lies under an embargo of 'impossibility'. Obsessional patients behave as though the 'impossible' persons and things were carriers of a dangerous infection liable to be spread by contact on to everything in their neighbourhood. I have already drawn attention to the same characteristic capacity for contagion and transference in my description of taboo. We know, too, that anyone who violates a taboo by coming into contact with something that is taboo becomes taboo himself and that then no one may come into contact with *him* (Freud, p. 80-81).

The prohibitions against contact are imposed to counter an intense desire to touch, which refers back to a child's desire to touch his own genitals. The child's masturbatory practices are forbidden but the instinct remains although it is repressed and banished to the unconscious. The conflict between the conscious prohibition and the unconscious desire to touch causes an emotional ambivalence towards the act which cannot be resolved. On the one hand the instinct is to search for alternative outlets for the repressed desire (which comes to include incestuous and murderous desires) but at the same time the prohibition extends to suppress them. This leads to a tension which can only be released by performing obsessive acts.

Freud concludes the essay by explaining the differences between a neurosis and a cultural taboo. In the case of a cultural taboo an automatic punishment is expected to fall on the transgressor and only when death or illness is not imminent does the community itself mete out punishment to prevent further violations. The neurotic patient, however, fears that gratifying an immoral desire will cause harm not to himself but to someone else, and that he himself is therefore dangerous. This is not, Freud is at pains to point out, due to altruism:

> Originally, that is to say at the beginning of the illness, the threat of punishment applied, as in the case of savages, to the patient himself; he was invariably in fear of his own life; it was not until later that the moral fear was displaced onto another and a loved person ... At the root of the prohibition there is invariably a hostile impulse against someone the patient loves – a wish that that person should die. This impulse is repressed by a prohibition and the prohibition is attached to some particular act, which, by displacement, represents, it may be, a hostile act against the loved person. There is a threat of death if this act is performed. But the process goes further and the original *wish* that the loved person may die is replaced by a *fear* that he may die. So that when the neurosis appears to be so tenderly altruistic, it is merely *compensating* for an underlying contrary attitude of brutal egoism (Freud, p. 129).

The relationship between the "savage" and the obsessional neurotic is continued in the third essay, "Animism, Magic and the Omnipotence of Thoughts". Freud's basic contention in this piece is that, in the case of both what he terms "savages" and obsessional neurotics, there is a belief in the omnipotence of thoughts: that a mere wish or desire for something to happen is sufficient to bring it about and that negative wishes should be punished as though they were bad deeds. In preliterate societies the connection between thought and deed is founded on a belief in animism and magic. Animism presupposes that not only animals, but also inanimate objects have life and even a soul. Because of this, they can be manipulated by the magical techniques known as homeopathic and contagious magic. Homeopathic magic is founded on the conviction that similar things affect one another so that if, for instance, pins are stuck in the wax effigy of an enemy, that person will feel the pain or that rain can be summoned during a drought merely by imitating the sound of thunder. Contagious magic is based on the principle that once two things have been in contact the contact cannot be severed, even if they are separated, so that if a sorcerer has something belonging to another, such as the fingernail clippings, he can use them to harm the owner. In the case of the neurotic, there is a similar desire to exert control and the frustration with conventional means induces the sufferer to relieve his tension by obsessive acts which are analogous to magical rituals. At the same time, believing that his unconscious, murderous wishes may happen merely because he has thought of them, the patient hopes, by his behaviour, to ward off disaster.

The final essay, "The Return of Totemism in Childhood", examines the relationship between totemism and exogamy (the practice of only marrying someone outside one's particular group). "The Return of Totemism" is inspired by an idea of Darwin, that humans originally lived in small groups consisting of a single adult male with his wives and children and that, at maturity, the young males were driven off so as to prevent the dangers of inbreeding. Freud proposes that at one point the sons rebelled against the tyranny of the father who kept all the females for himself. They killed him and then ate him, in a cannibalistic feast, and by eating him they identified with him and he became deified as their totem. But having accomplished this primal crime the sons were consumed with guilt and laid taboos upon the killing of the totem. Moreover, the women whom they had originally desired were also forbidden and the crime of incest was instituted. This, according to Freud, was the beginning of human culture, for the incest prohibition established exogamy while the guilt of the sons led to a new moral system. At the same time, the inauguration of the totem, which

Freud identified with God, was the beginning of religious worship.

Underlying the essays is Freud's theory of the Oedipus complex: that a child unconsciously desires, and wants to marry, his mother and is jealous of his father towards whom he has ambivalent feelings. He wishes for his father's death, but then feels guilty and fears retribution. The healthy adult has learned to overcome these incestuous and murderous inclinations, just as human society has overcome them and established taboos forbidding incest and the killing of the totem. The obsessional neurotic, however, is still battling with the problem, hence the self-imposed repressions and taboos, designed to protect the individual from the imagined consequences of his own desires.

Few social anthropologists would today accept Freud's theories of the origins of human society, which are considered farfetched. Neither do psychologists accept the parallels between the development of an individual and the process of civilisation. A notable exception to this general disdain is the work of the Frenchman, René Girard, who regards collective murder as the foundation of religion.

See also

Incest

References

Boyd, Robert and Peter Richerson. 1985. *Culture and the Evolutionary Process.* Chicago, Illinois: University of Chicago Press

Freeman, Derek. 1969. "Totem and Taboo: A Reappraisal". In *Man and His Culture: Psychoanalytic Anthropology after "Totem and Taboo"* ed. Warner Muensterberger, p. 53-78. London: Rapp & Whiting.

Freud, Sigmund. [1912-1913] 1985. "Totem and Taboo". *The Origins of Religion. The Penguin Freud Library vol.13.* trans. Albert Dickson, p. 45-224. London: Penguin.

Girard, René. [1972] 1977. *Violence and the Sacred.* trans. Patrick Gregory. Baltimore, Maryland: The Johns Hopkins University Press.

Marcuse, Herbert. 1956. *Eros and Civilization.* London: Routledge and Kegan Paul.

Paul, Robert, A. 1976. "Did the Primal Crime take Place?" *Ethos,* no. 4, p. 311-352.

Wallace IV, Edwin R. 1983. *Freud and Anthropology: A History and Reappraisal.* New York: International Universities Press.

Frogs

Frogs are taboo to the Hua people of New Guinea. Male initiates may not eat them because:

> frogs are like women's vaginas; ... [they] have no fat (they have skinny buttocks) ... [they] are *mnipina na* "water things" and will cause males to get water in their joints, preventing them from running fast in battle (Meigs, p. 156).

In Hua society, frogs are closely identified with women and a dream of a frog portends female offspring. Nonetheless, these forbidden creatures may be eaten by a male to protect him from sorcery.

Reference

Meigs, Anna S. 1984. *Food, Sex and Pollution: A New Guinea Religion.* New Brunswick, New Jersey: Rutgers University Press.

G

Geis, gessa

The word *geis* (plural *gessa*) is used in medieval Irish literature to denote both a personal prohibition, forbidding a person to do a certain thing, and an obligation, compelling a person to act. Failure to obey a geis, which is magical in character, results in misfortune or death. While personal honour helps to secure obedience, a problem arises when a protagonist is confronted with two conflicting gessa. The Book of Leinster tells how the warrior, CúChulainn, is forbidden to eat dog-flesh as his name means hound (cú) of Chulainn. However, another geis compels him never to pass a cooking hearth without sampling the fare. On a particularly inauspicious day he passes three crones, blind in the left eye, using poisonous spells to cook a dog on spits of rowan. Suspecting that they do not have his best interests at heart, he tries to speed past them. They stop him and implore him to eat with them. It is an offer that is not difficult to refuse but the crones are as wily as they are evil. Accusing him of disdaining their modest meal, "only a hound", and taunting him with unseemly pride, one of the women gives him the side of the hound with her left, or sinister, hand. CúChulainn eats the meat with his left hand and places it under his left thigh. Immediately the hand and thigh lose their strength, and it is thus impaired that the hero must fight his final battle in which he is killed.

Within the corpus of medieval Irish literature, the gessa have a fatalistic function. As long as the gessa remain inviolate, the hero is safe from harm. But as he nears his death, situations arise in which he cannot avoid breaking them. The eminent Russian folklorist, Vladimir Propp, has shown that interdictions and their violation are not restricted to Irish tales but are an important characteristic of the European "wondertale".

See also

Left Hand, The; Propp, Vladimir Jácovlevic

References

Rees, Alwyn and Brinley. [1961] 1978. *Celtic Heritage*. London: Thames and Hudson.

Reinhard, John Revell. 1933. *The Survival of Geis in Mediaeval Romance*. Halle, Germany: Max Niemeyer.

Gell, Alfred (1945-1997)

The British anthropologist, Alfred Gell, became fascinated by the concept of taboo when he lived among the people of Umeda village in the West Sepic District of Papua New Guinea. His curiosity was aroused when he inadvertently cut his finger with his knife, while peeling a stick of sugar cane, and instinctively raised his finger to his lips. When he glanced up he was startled to see expressions of shock and disgust on the faces of his companions from the village. he had broken a fundamental Umeda food taboo – the taboo on consuming self-killed game. Meditating on the implications of this transgression, Gell realised that there was a close connection between taboo and self in Umeda thought and that "taboo clarifies the phenomenology of self" (Gell, p. 136). Not only was his own auto-cannibalism (and any other cannibalism) unacceptable, but nail-biting, moustache-chewing, swallowing dried mucus and consuming the blood of a pig killed by oneself are all anathema to the Umeda. The same principle underlies the ban on children and ritual novices eating the river fish *pannatamwa* whose red markings are thought to resemble the red body paint worn at times by them. In fact, the observance of certain taboos identifies (or establishes) a person on both an individual and a social plane.

As an example of how this works, Gell looks at the system of *tadv* relations. The word *tadv* means, according to context, "biting", "striking", "shooting with an arrow", "copulating with" and "eating". Essentially, it refers to killing, eating and having sex but the categories are mutually exclusive: a man may not eat something he has killed (and neither may his closest blood-kin) but those who are sexually available – a man's wife, her family or members of his opposite hamlet moiety – may eat his game. His actions therefore follow a pattern whereby he first performs an active role (as pig-killer), then a passive one (he allows the meat to be given to others), then again an active role (sexual conqueror) followed by a passive one (as he, or his "self", is "softened" by his sexual partners). After this, he needs to recover his integrity through a period of withdrawal and asceticism:

> The hunter has consummated his vital interests in the realms of venery – in both senses of that convenient homophone – but only at the cost of placing himself in jeopardy from which the only escape is via asceticism, that is to say, via taboo (Gell, p. 145).

The voluntary denials during this period lead the individual back towards an active life. Gell concludes by explaining the importance of the dream in this transition:

> Our ascetic hunter, benighted, hungry, and solitary … dreams of the women from whom he has voluntarily absented himself in order to restore his integrity, and of gifts of food brought to him by his sister … Detached from the entanglements of worldly *tadv* relationships, the ascetic has access to the sublime, to symbolic truths … A spirit will guide his steps to the pig's lair in the forest, and a wonderful dream about women … will set the seal of ultimate success on his endeavours (Gell, p. 146).

Having restored his sense of self, revitalised, and with divine guidance, the Umeda sets out once more in his venal pursuits.

Reference

Gell, Alfred. 1979. "Reflections on a Cut Finger: Taboo in the Umeda Conception of the Self". In *Fantasy and Symbol: Studies in Anthropological Interpretation*. ed. R. H. Hook, p. 133-148. London; New York; San Francisco: Academic Press.

Green

Green is the colour of plants, leaves, grass, vegetables and young crops and epitomises the fervour and life of spring and regeneration. The Christian, Chinese and Muslim religions all agree on this. Mohammed is thought to have been attended by angels in green turbans at pivotal points in his life and a green banner was identified with the prophet. Under a former Turkish law, only Muslims were allowed to wear green. Yet green can also be a dangerous colour. Frédéric Portal says of it:

> Green, like other colours, had a nefarious meaning; as it had been the symbol of the soul's regeneration and of wisdom, it also signified, by opposition,

moral degradation and madness. The Swedish theosophist, Swedenborg, gives green eyes to the madmen in hell. A window in Chartres Cathedral depicts the temptation of Jesus – Satan has green skin and great green eyes … The eye, in the lore of symbolism, signifies intelligence, the light of the mind; man may turn it towards good or evil; Satan and Minerva, folly and wisdom, were both represented with green eyes (Portal, p. 212).

The sinister side of the colour is well documented within the British Isles and the Gaelic word for bright green, *uaine*, is unlucky (as well as uncomplimentary) in describing individuals. To wear green at a wedding has been perceived to be particularly unlucky: "Married in green, a shame to be seen" quotes an informant in Scotland and "Married in May, and kirked in green / Baith bride and bridegroom winna lang be seen" (Hutchings, p. 59).

One explanation for the taboo is that it is the colour of the fairies who are not always benign. C. McIntyre recalled "As a child on an Argyllshire farm, more than 70 years ago, I remember going into a hayfield wearing a green dress, and being greeted by one of the hay-workers with: 'Oh that's the fairies' colour you're wearing, they'll be after you!'" (Hutchings, p. 57). It seems that they claim the wearers as their own. Green is certainly a colour of ill omen for Muirchertach, the King of Ireland in a Celtic tale. While out hunting one day he is resting alone on a mound when a beautiful girl in a green mantel appears beside him. He is captivated and she offers herself to him on condition that he never utters her name and that neither the mother of his children, nor clerics should be in her sight. The king turns his wife and children from his door and asks her the name which must never be spoken. "It is Sigh, Sough, Storm, Rough Wind, Winternight, Cry, Wail, Groan", she wails. She is a mistress of magic and illusion, conjuring

enchanted pigs and a headless battalion, but one dark evening a storm arises and the king exclaims: "This is the sigh of a winter night". He has uttered her name and is doomed. Now the storm (Irish *sín*) sets his house on fire and he is attacked by phantoms. He climbs into a barrel of wine and is drowned while fire falls on his head and burns him (Rees, p. 214-217).

Here green is associated with the supernatural (*Sín* is an enchantress though she is not, in this tale, immortal) but also with the forces of nature, of awesome yet terrible beauty. The Green Knight, beheaded by Gawain at the court of King Arthur yet with remarkable regenerative powers, has a similar affinity with the natural world. He, too, is potentially lethal, awaiting Gawain's visit so that he can return the blow. The green of nature is God's colour, says Alec Gill, and that is the reason one should never burn anything green. Just as green-leafed trees are followed by black bark in winter, the wearing of green must be avoided if one is to escape death (Hutchings, p. 59).

Rationalist explanations for the taboo on the colour point to its association in Elizabethan times with the loss of virginity and pregnancy, and the fact that it is the colour of envy, mould, unripe fruit and putrefaction. Historical instances where green clothes or artefacts have proved particularly unlucky can also be cited but would not explain why the prohibition is so widespread within the British Isles.

References

Bruford, Alan. 1985. "Colour Epithets for Gaelic Chiefs". *Shadow: The Newsletter of the Traditional Cosmological Society*, vol. 2, no. 1.

Hutchings, John. 1997. "Folklore and Symbolism of Green". *Folklore*, no. 108, p. 55-64.

Portal, Frédéric. 1857. *Des Couleurs Symboliques Dans l'Antiquité, le Moyen-Age, et les Temps Modernes*. Paris: Treuttel et Wortz.

Rees, Alwyn and Brinley. [1961] 1978. *Celtic Heritage*. London: Thames and Hudson.

Reinhard, John Revell. 1933. *The Survival of Geis in Mediaeval Romance*. Halle, Germany: Max Niemeyer.

H

Hair

Taboos on cutting

The immense strength of Samson resided in his hair which, as a Nazarite, he was forbidden from birth to cut (although often the Nazarites, consecrated to God by a vow, had their heads shaved at the Tabernacle at the end of the period of their vow). Unfortunately Samson was also extremely naive so that even though the seductive Delilah had asked three times for the secret of his physical prowess, and then attempted to betray him to the Philistines, he finally revealed the truth and she sheared his seven locks. That a certain power, whether bestial, sexual or divine, dwells in the hair, which must therefore never be cut, is a common perception. In Samson's case, he may have had the force of a great beast but the source was clearly divine – *Judges* 16. 20 relates how when his head was shorn, Yahweh deserted him, and a rabbinical source describes how his hairs became stiff, and knocked against one another like bells, when the spirit of God was upon him (*Midrash Rabba to Leviticus* 8.2).

Prohibitions against religious individuals and priests cutting their hair are found on every continent. The anthropologist, James Frazer has noticed taboos against shearing among the Aztec priests, sorcerers in West Africa, rainmakers on the lower Zambesi, magicians of the Masai clan of the El Kiboron and the *Leleen*

(priest) of the Alfoors of the Celebes, to name just a few (Frazer, p. 258-264). Penalties for violating the injunction include crop failure, loss of rain-making powers, premature ageing, death and the loss of protective spirits. Among the major world religions, Sikh men, Punjabi women and traditional Muslim women never cut their hair. While Hindu men generally cut their hair, long, tangled, matted locks are a sign of holiness. In the case of Orthodox Jews and contemporary Chasidim, the men grow *Pais* (side-locks). The Christian Anabaptists and Amish of both sexes refrain from shearing and priests of the Greek Orthodox Church grow their beards.

Not surprisingly, there have been numerous attempts to explain the taboos on cutting hair, many of them focusing on the symbolism of hair within specific societies. To be hirsute, in most parts of the world, is to participate in some way in the natural, bestial or demonic realms. In the Sumerian epic of *Gilgamesh*, the hero meets the strong, hairy Enkidu who lives among the animals without them fearing him, sucks their milk and shares their grass. Lured away from this natural existence by a harlot, he rubs down the matted hair of his body, anoints himself with oil, and appears as a bridegroom but pays the price of alienation from the animal kingdom – the gazelle and all the wild creatures flee from him. The tradition of the "wild man" or "Green man", dishevelled but fecund, has survived in folk traditions throughout Europe. A myth of the Kukukuku of Papua New

Guinea tells how the ancestors had hair covering their entire bodies and, ignorant of fire, they cooked their food over the genitals of women. When they learned the secret of fire, and cooked their food over it, they became fully human and their hair fell off. Not surprisingly, hairiness is a common characteristic of nature-spirits and demons: in Greek myth, Pan is not only hirsute, but also half-beast, and in the near East, the seductive demon, Lilith, is covered in hair. Christopher Hallpike mentions the European belief of the sixteenth and seventeenth centuries that the power of witches resided in their hair. To render them powerless before execution, not only were their heads shaved, but their entire bodies were depilated (Hallpike. 1987, p. 155).

Another, not unrelated, tradition – implicit in the Papuan myth – identifies hair with sexual potency. The scholar, Edmund Leach, in his article "Magical Hair" applies the work of the psychoanalyst Charles Berg to anthropological theories. Berg, in the Freudian tradition, identified head hair with the genital organs. The analogy between the head and the "second face" of the genitals is not unfamiliar to myths or medieval iconography but Berg saw in the head a universal phallic symbol. Hair was equated with semen so that cutting the hair was a symbolic castration. There is some evidence to support this: Hallpike mentions a Greek and Roman belief that the head was the source of semen in the form of cerebrospinal fluid and the Punjabis of India maintain that true ascetics can store up their semen and concentrate it as spiritual power at the top of their heads, an essential technique of Yoga. However, it is salutary to remember that symbols are rarely universal.

That hair has can be used for magical purposes is due to a belief that a sympathetic connection exists between an individual and every part of his body, even after the physical link has been severed. To possess hair from a person means that one can use it in spells to exert power over that individual. Sacred people avoided the danger of their hair clippings falling into the wrong hands by not cutting their hair. Others were extremely careful about what happened to the pieces, as Raymond Firth observes:

> … until recently old Maori men who might go to a barber to have their hair cut often made a contract with him to have all the hair ends gathered up; the owner would then go and hide them away to avoid the possibility of having them used for sorcery against him. Conversely, a controlled hair of one's own could be launched against someone else. There is a story of a Maori in quite recent times who had begun to drink a glass of beer in a public house when he noticed a hair in the liquid. He reacted swiftly, not aesthetically in disgust but ritually in fear. Supposedly plucked from a sorcerer's head, the hair was a sign of evil power against him; he vomited, ejected the hair and so, he thought, escaped death (Firth, p. 295).

Leach confirms this belief. At the Hindu festival of lights, *Diwali*, a first-born child must be protected from the malice of the sorceress who tries to shear its hair with magic scissors so that it will die and its soul may be reborn in her womb. But Leach examines the power of hair in sorcery, not just in its connection with a particular individual, but as a substance in its own right. He finds its symbolic value relates both to the dynamics of the individual subconscious explored by Berg (aggression, jealousy and sexual impulses) and to the social consciousness of a particular group with its concern about purity and pollution, the sacred and the profane. In an article written in 1965, Leach, like Mary Douglas, argues that hair is viewed as "polluting" because it is at the boundary of the body, at the same time connected to it but capable of being detached. This anomaly causes a confusion in the child's conception:

> The dirtiness of things arises in the first place because, in the process of the

child's category formation, the substances are ambiguous, they are neither "me" or "not me"; they present the child with a basic uncertainty as to the boundary of the clean self, the true self (Leach, p. 173).

It is true that in the Punjab hair is considered both "dirty" and "polluting" and this explains the mandatory shaving of the Hindu male's head at the tonsure ceremony and during periods, such as mourning, when he is particularly vulnerable to impurity. The hair of Punjabi women is also polluting but in her case it must never be cut, and must be left tangled and untidy at funerals. The implication is that any loss of purity by the women leads to an increase of purity in the men. Jains allow no hair at all on the bodies of ordained holy men. But things are not quite so simple. While the Brahmin's hair is kept very short, with just a tuft left unshaven, the ascetic Hindu sadhu leaves his hair long and tangled, and it becomes the highest manifestation of the sacred, and uncut hair is one of the five symbols of Sikhism (the others being a bangle, shorts, a two-edged blade and a one-edged comb) proving membership of the mystical Sikh brotherhood, the Khalsa (the pure). Hair is also considered sacred by the Rastafarians, followers of Haile Selassie (*Ras Tafari*, "Lion of Judah") who cite biblical injunctions for not cutting their hair which they wear in long, matted dreadlocks. For Mary Douglas there is no contradiction between hair as a symbol of impurity and as a sign of the sacred: "It often remains true that religions sacrilise the very unclean things which have been rejected with abhorrence" (Douglas, p. 159).

Mary Douglas is right to stress the ambivalence of symbols and it is also true that the taboos on hair cutting cannot be studied outside the particular social contexts in which they occur. C. R. Hallpike regards long hair as a sign of being "outside society" while the cutting of hair means re-entering society or living under a disciplinary regime: to cut the hair means to

exercise social control over an individual. As with the previous theories, examples can be found to substantiate this view. The transvestites who play female roles in Javanese plays traditionally grew their hair long and practised homosexuality offstage but the Indonesian government has recently exerted considerable pressure on the actors to cut their hair and refrain from homosexual acts. Moreover, it is customary to shave the heads of prisoners, those one wishes to humiliate, or those entering certain religious orders. Yet among the Tikopia studied by Raymond Firth (Firth, p. 279), where the women cut their hair while the men allowed it to grow, there is no substantial evidence to suggest that the women were subject to greater restrictions (although women who allowed their hair to grow did so as a protest) and in western Europe suffragettes and feminists cut their hair to demonstrate their equality with men. It is probably true to say that those who wish to demonstrate their freedom (or are beyond worldly concerns) act in a way which defies prevailing social norms. In the case of hair this means wearing it in a manner that flouts the conventions, whether they dictate that it be worn long, short, dyed, shaven, plaited, curly, straight, tied up or loose. In the same way, members of a particular group can be identified by a similarity of hairstyle, or, in the case of the judges in British law courts, by bizarre, anachronistic wigs.

Taboos on washing

Because of the magical nature that is ascribed to hair in many societies there are often strict taboos on washing it. No Punjabi woman will wash her hair on a Tuesday (a particularly inauspicious day) unless she has malicious intent: should she, on this day, leave it loose and wet to drip on a child, it will kill the child, which will then be born again from her womb. Hair washing on Sundays or Thursdays can cause the house to lose money while shampooing on the day of the new moon will mean that the dirty water from the hair flows onto the heads of dead in-laws. Another bad time is the day of a man's funeral: should she wash her hair on this day, a married woman will marry the dead man in a future reincarnation.

Tying or knotting the hair

A Scottish ballad, *Willie's Lady*, tells of a woman who is bewitched by her mother-in-law, a "vile rank witch of vilest kind", so that she is unable to give birth to her child. She promises her mother-in-law treasures if she will only remove the spell, but nothing will satisfy the old woman who has taken such an intense dislike to her. Fortunately a household spirit, Belly Blind, is more compassionate and advises Willie to make a counterfeit baby from wax, invite his mother to the boy's christening, and listen well to what his mother says. Thinking that her spells have been broken, and the child born, the mother wonders who has loosened the nine witch knots that were among the lady's locks, as well as removing the combs of care, loosening the left-foot shoe, removing the kid goat from beneath the bed and taking down the woodbine bush that hung between the bowers of the two women. Willie immediately removes the witch knots and combs of care from his wife's hair, loosens her shoe, kills the kid and takes down the woodbine, freeing his wife to give birth to a bonny young son.

The witch knots in the hair are a clear sign that magic is afoot. As James Frazer points out: "On the principles of homeopathic magic knots are impediments which tie up the mother and prevent her from giving birth to the child" (Frazer, p. 295). The Lapps, Scots, Indonesians, and tribes in Sulawesi (Celebes), West Africa, North Borneo and countless other regions traditionally made sure all knots were untied at the time of childbirth. There are nine knots just as there are nine months of pregnancy. On the Indonesian island of Roti a cord used to be fastened around the waist of a new bride:

Nine knots are tied in the cord, and in order to make them harder to unloose, they are smeared with wax. Bride and groom are then secluded in a chamber, where he has to untie the knots with the thumb and forefinger of his left hand only. It may be from one to twelve months before he succeedes in undoing them all. Until he has done so he may not look upon the woman as his wife ... When all the knots are loosed, the woman is his wife ... we may conjecture that the nine knots refer to the nine months of pregnancy, and that miscarriage would be the supposed result of leaving a single knot untied (Frazer, p. 311).

The "combs of care", in binding the hair, similarly restrict the birth channels of Willie's lady as does the tightly bound shoe.

Just as binding the hair constricts the natural flow of things, loosening the hair releases power and energy. Among Punjabi women:

val khule (loose hair) is used of sorcery, also of a woman in mourning loosening her hair for the period of pollution, and lastly of a woman possessed who in a trance whirls her head with the hair flying free (Hershman, p. 277).

See also

Knots; Pollution

References

Berg, Charles. 1951. *The Unconscious Significance of Hair*. London: George Allen and Unwin Ltd.

Child, Francis James, ed., 1882-1898. *The English and Scottish Popular Ballads*. Boston, Massachusetts; New York: Houghton Mifflin.

Douglas, Mary. 1966. *Purity and Danger*. London: Routledge and Kegan Paul.

Firth, Raymond. [1973] 1975. *Symbols. Public and Private*. London: George Allen and Unwin Ltd.

Frazer, James. [1911] 1935. *Taboo and the Perils Of the Soul. The Golden Bough*. vol. 2, New York: The Macmillan Company.

Hallpike, Christopher R. Hair. *Encyclopedia of Religion*. ed. Mircea Eliade. vol. 6. New York: MacMillan.

Hershman, P. 1974. "Hair, Sex and Dirt". *Man*, n.s., no. 9, p. 274-298.

Leach, Edmund R. 1958. "Magical Hair". *Journal of the Royal Anthropological Institute*, no. 77, p. 147-164.

Leach. 1965. *The Nature of War in Disarmament and Arms Control*. Oxford: Pergamon Press.

Halal

A Muslim should partake of no meat that is not *halal*, the Muslim term for acceptable food. Certain animals, such as swine and scavengers, are not to be consumed and no meat is *halal* unless it has been ritually slaughtered. Cyril Glassé describes the procedure:

> A Moslem must consecrate the kill by saying the words *Bismi-Llah*; *Allahu Akbar*, and cut the throat (both windpipe and jugular vein) with one stroke. Game is *halal* if the words of consecration are spoken when it is shot, or when a trained dog is released to retrieve it. Fish are *halal* if caught when alive, but dead fish which have been gathered are not (Glassé, p. 133)

Cutting the throat drains the animal's blood; though an animal's blood must not be drunk it is permissible to consume the blood that remains in meat after draining.

Since Islam contains an injunction to be reasonable in all things, non-*halal* meat can be eaten in cases of necessity.

See also

Wine

References

Glassé, Cyril 1989. *The Concise Encyclopedia of Islam*. London: Stacey Publications.

Islamic Desk Reference: compiled from The Encyclopaedia of Islam. 1994. ed. E. Van Donzel. Leiden, the Netherlands: Brill.

Haram

The Islamic term *haram* means "restricted, forbidden, sacred", and, by extension, "sacred possession or place". The areas around the mosques in Mecca and Medina are designated *haraman* and, with the exception of dangerous animals, it is forbidden to kill in these vicinities and non-Muslims must not enter them. In Arabic the part of the house that is reserved for the women is called by the related word *harim* (hence: harem).

Another related word refers to things that are forbidden for revealed, or sacred, reasons. Under the terms of *fiqh* (Islamic jurisprudence) there are five categories: (1) that which is prohibited (*haram*); (2) that which is discouraged (*makruh*); (3) that which is neutral (*mubah*); (4) that which is recommended (*mustahabb*); (5) and that which is obligatory (*fard*).

References

Glassé, Cyril. 1989. *The Concise Encyclopedia of Islam*. London: Stacey Publications.

Hekmat, Anwar. 1997. *Women and the Koran. The Status of Women in Islam*. New York: Prometheus Books.

Islamic Desk Reference: compiled from The Encyclopaedia of Islam. ed. E. Van Donzel. 1994. Leiden, the Netherlands: Brill.

Wikan, Unni. [1982] 1991. *Behind the Veil in Arabia: Women in Oman*. Chicago, Illinois; London: University of Chicago Press.

Heliocentricity – Galileo

Scientific discoveries which challenge preconceived dogma sometimes provoke intense hostility and censorship.

Galileo Galilei (1564-1642) was born in Florence and is lauded as the founder of modern mechanics. However, as is well known, an accusation of heresy was levelled against him by the Church of Rome for his defence of the

Copernican model of the solar system which posited a heliocentric system, with the earth and other planets moving in a regular motion around a central sun. The idea was not new – Philolaos had proposed something similar 2,000 years previously and Aristarchos had conceived of a heliocentric system 1,800 years before. More recently, Johannes Kepler's (1571-1630) more accurate model (with the planet's orbit as an ellipse, not a perfect circle) had superseded that of Copernicus (1473-1543). Nevertheless, in 1616 the model of Copernicus was queried by Cardinal Bellarmino and Pope Paul V as it contradicted the religious dogma that placed the earth at the centre of the cosmos. The cardinal presented the two principal propositions of the Copernican astronomy to the Holy Office's theological board who submitted their refutations:

1 That the sun is in the centre of the world, and totally immovable as to locomotion.
Censure: All say that the said proposition is foolish and absurd in Philosophy, and formally heretical inasmuch as it contradicts the express opinion of Holy Scriptures in many places, according to the words themselves and according to the common expositions and meanings of the Church Fathers and doctors of theology.
2 That the earth is neither in the centre of the world nor immovable but moves as a whole and in daily motion.
Censure: All say this proposition receives the same censure in Philosophy, and with regard to Theological verity it is at least erroneous in the faith (Tolstoy, p. 153).

Even though Galileo formally denied his belief in the Copernican doctrine before the ecclesiastic authority in 1616 he was tried and condemned by the Inquisition in 1633.

According to the historian Ivan Tolstoy, Galileo's quarrel with the Papal authorities was

unnecessary – no scientific issue depended on its outcome and it was more a dispute over ideologies. In particular, Galileo's attacks on Aristotelian orthodoxy caused much antagonism.

For instance, in a series of public lectures Galileo showed that the supernova of October 1604 was situated in the heavens, a view that opposed Aristotelian cosmology with its belief in a perfect and unchangeable heavenly sphere. Then, in 1609 Galileo constructed a telescope (just invented in 1608 by Hans Lippershey of Middelburg, Holland) and in 1610 he published *The Starry Messenger* (*Sidereus Nuncius*) based on his observations. He noticed that Jupiter travelled at great speed around the sun without losing its four moons – a proof that the earth could do likewise. (Copernicus had thought that the earth would lose its moon at speed.) He also discovered the mountains of the moon, again angering defenders of the Aristotelian concept of smooth, perfect planets.

In 1612, Galileo published his *Sunspot Letters* in which he claimed to have discovered sunspots, having first observed them in 1611. Unfortunately for him, he was not the first: Thomas Harriot in Oxford had already remarked on them and a Jesuit astronomer, Christopher Scheiner, had written about them using the pseudonym Apelles. As an Aristotelian, Scheiner could not, of course, attribute any "blemishes" to the sun itself; they were, he said, tiny planets seen against the bright, perfect sun. In an appendix to the *Sunspot Letters*, Galileo endorsed the Copernican system for the first time in print. In order, he said, to make correct calculations for the eclipses of Jupiter's moon, it was necessary to take into account the earth's motion.

From 1613 to 1616, Galileo's ideas suffered sustained attacks, initially by professors rather than by theologians. In an attempt to help, a Carmelite, P. A. Foscarini, wrote a book which reconciled Copernicanism and the Bible. A copy of this was sent to Cardinal Bellarmino. The cardinal responded by saying that as long as the motion of the Earth was treated as a hypothesis rather than a fact, all would be well. Galileo ignored the advice and this prompted the edict of Pope Paul V. Galileo was prohibited from teaching or defending the theory of Copernicus although he could continue to use it as a working hypothesis.

As though to thwart his best intentions, in 1618 three comets appeared in the sky and Galileo was once again drawn into controversy. Accused by a Jesuit, writing under the name of Sarsi, of defending the Copernican system, he responded by publishing *The Assayer Saggiatore* (1623). In this counter-offensive Galileo attacked those who treated philosophy as though it were a work of fiction:

> Well, Sarsi, that is not how things are. Philosophy is written in this grand book the universe, which stands continually open to our gaze. But the book cannot be understood unless one first learns to comprehend the language and to read the alphabet in which it is composed. It is written in the language of mathematics, and its characters are triangles, circles, and other geometric figures, without which it is humanly impossible to understand a single word of it; without these, one wanders about in a dark labyrinth (Tolstoy, p. 154).

The Assayer also argued the case for atomism. Galileo hypothesised a corpuscular theory not only of heat, solids and fluids but also of light and all the other elements of nature and all perceptible phenomena with the exception of sound. This corpuscular theory offered a kinetic model of the structure of matter. Light was special in that it had instantaneous velocity and universal propagation. Light, Galileo thought, was a final stage in the resolution of matter: its atomic stage was its ultimate resolution to indivisible atoms. The theory of atomism, needless to say, was anathema to the Aristotelians.

Nevertheless, at first things appeared to improve for Galileo. In 1624 Pope Paul V died

and was replaced by Mafeo Barberini, an old friend of the scientist, who became Pope Urban VIII. The Pope granted Galileo permission to publish his theory of tides in 1632 in *Dialogue Concerning the Two Chief Systems of the World*. However, this failed to comply with the Inquisition's injunction against defending or teaching the Copernican system, as he was not using it merely as a hypothesis. Not only did the Pope ban the book, but he ordered Galileo to come to Rome and stand trial. Galileo produced the statement of Bellarmino, signed in 1616, which stated that Copernicanism could be used to construct a working model. But the Inquisition had forbidden the theory, even though its 1616 document was unsigned. Eventually Galileo was told that if he presented a written acknowledgement stating that parts of his *Dialogue* contained unacceptable propositions, he would be let off lightly. Though sentenced to life detention, Galileo was not actually imprisoned. At first he was given a flat in the Vatican, then he was put into the custody of a friend, the Archbishop Piccolamini of Sienna, and later he was allowed to stay at home.

Despite the persecution, and although closely scrutinised by the Inquisition, Galileo wrote the *Discourse on Two New Sciences*, which treated uniformly accelerated motion. After 1632 he was forbidden to publish anything but the manuscript was smuggled to Holland and printed in Leiden in 1638 by Elzevir.

Although it is widely accepted that it was the Copernican controversy that led to his trial, an Italian historian, Pietro Redondi, has discovered a new document in the archives of the Vatican, which predates the trial and which denounces Galileo by suggesting that his advocacy of atomism threatened the doctrine of the Holy Eucharist. The Catholic doctrine maintained that even after transubstantiation the sensory qualities (the taste, colour and smell) of the bread and wine remained unchanged even though they had been transformed into the body and blood of Christ. This was due to divine intervention. Galileo did not speak of the Eucharist in *The Assayer* but his detractors referred to his distrust of sensible appearances (his belief in their subjectivity) and his thesis that beneath the sensible phenomena are hidden corpuscular structures, objectively knowable by reason. Essentially, the sensible phenomena of the Eucharist could no longer be reconciled with Eucharist transubstantiation. According to Redondi, the Jesuits had advanced such arguments to secure Galileo's downfall and the charge of Copernicanism was set up in mitigation by Galileo's friends and the Pope to spare him from the more serious charge of heresy (punishable by death). Redondi's proposal is, however, dismissed by another scholar, Joseph Pitt, who thinks that too much is dependent on a single document (Tolstoy, p. 157).

Whatever the pretext for the trial, one can only sympathise with the thoughts of the embattled scientist, recorded in the margins of the *Dialogues*:

In the matter of introducing novelties. And who can doubt that it will lead to the worst disorders when minds created free by God are compelled to submit slavishly to an outside will? When we are told to deny our senses and subject them to the whim of others? When people devoid of whatsoever competence are made judges over experts and are granted authority to treat them as they please? These are the novelties which are apt to bring about the ruin of commonwealths and the subversion of the state (Tolstoy, p. 159).

References

Redondi, Pietro. [1983] 1988. *Galileo: Heretic*. trans. Raymond Rosenthal. London: Allen Lane, Penguin.

Schlagel, Richard H. 1995. *From Myth to Modern Mind. A Study of the Origins and Growth of Scientific Thought*. 2 vols. New York: Peter Lang.

Tolstoy, Ivan. 1990. *The Knowledge and the Power: Reflections on the History of Science*. Edinburgh: Canongate.

Horses

In 732 CE Pope Gregory III issued an edict to Boniface, his missionary among the Germanic tribes, forbidding the consumption of horse-flesh:

Among other things, you also mentioned that some of [the Germans] eat wild horse and even more eat domesticated horse. Under no circumstances holy brother, should you ever permit this to be done. Rather impose on them an appropriate punishment by any means with which, with the help of Christ, you are able to prevent it. For this practice is unclean and detestable (Harris, p. 96).

This attack on the consumption of horses is surprising considering that Christianity, from the first, had rejected dietary laws, maintaining that "What goes into the mouth does not make a man unclean; it is what comes out of the mouth that makes him unclean" (*Matthew* 15: 10-11). The pope's strident missive was most probably directed at the religious practices of the northerners, from the Poles to the Icelanders, who regularly sacrificed horses and ate the flesh. Significantly, the assault on heathen acts was delivered in the same year that the Muslims, who disdained horseflesh and were steadily conquering Christian domains, were defeated at Tours.

In their esteem for the horse, the Germanic peoples were following a long-standing Indo-European tradition. The horse is prominent in the ancient Sanscrit text, the *Rig Veda*, which was composed between 1200 and 900 BCE where it is a sacred animal identified with many gods including Indra, Dadhikra, Surya, Agni, Soma and the Dawn (Usas). In the *Rig Veda* the horse is celebrated as an invaluable animal that helped the Indo-Aryans to conquer Indo-European territories, a race-horse that competed in sacred and secular contests and an important victim for sacrifices. Hymn 1.162 of the *Rig Veda* describes the ancient Indian horse sacrifice in considerable detail. Before the horse is slain a goat is killed so that it may "announce the sacrifice to the gods" (Doniger O'Flaherty, p. 90). After the horse has been ceremonially staked and then cooked in a cauldron, the priests offer thirty-four of the horse's ribs to the sun, moon, planets and constellations. The flesh is eaten by the priests who request expiation for the killing and prosperity for the future:

> Let this racehorse bring us good cattle and good horses, male children and all-nourishing wealth. Let Aditi (female principle of creation) make us free from sin. Let the horse with our offerings achieve sovereign power for us (*Rig Veda*, p. 89-93).

Horses were also venerated by the pastoral nomads who inhabited the steppes from the Ukraine to Mongolia. The Yakut of central Asia believed that the horse was a gift from a benevolent deity who taught humans how to ferment the mare's milk to make the drink known as *kumiss*. They sang of the horse in their love songs and ate its flesh at feasts. Horses were also ceremonially killed and eaten by the Scythians of the Ukraine while the Mongols would kill a man's horse when he died and bury it in his grave. These Asiatic pastoralists, which included the Kazakhs and Kirghiz Tartars and the Kalmuck, depended on their horses for transport, to herd their cattle and sheep which grazed on the vast semi-arid grassland, and for sustenance. It was in this region that the horse was first domesticated between 4000 to 3000 BCE.

The first taboos on horseflesh appeared when the animals began to be imported by the settled agrarian civilisations of Asia and the Middle East and proved more useful as instruments of war than as food. Horse-drawn chariots were used by early Bronze Age warriors from China to Egypt and the use of horses for cavalry (around 900 BCE) coincided with the rise of the Assyrian, Scythian and Median Empires. In 300 BCE the construction of the Great Wall of China was begun to check the cavalry assaults of the Huns. The Romans employed foreign horsemen, Scythians or Huns, for war, and neither rode nor ate the beasts. In the 7th and 8th centuries CE, Muslims began to breed small, swift, hardy Arabian mounts to help them in their *jihad*, or holy war, to spread the faith. Later, the Mongol horsemen, under the command of Genghis Khan, conquered an area from China to the plains of Hungary travelling on steeds that could reach speeds of 100 miles per hour. Of course the importance of horses for warfare did not always prevent them from being eaten: the Scythians, Sarmatians and Huns would shoot arrows from their steed, eat the flesh, drink the mare's milk, and, when occasion demanded, slit a vein on the horse's neck and drink the blood.

Pope Gregory III's ban on horse-meat in the 8th century placed Christianity in line with all the major religions. Judaism forbade the animal because it did not chew the cud or have cloven hooves. In India horsemeat was proscribed by the Buddha and among Hindus it was only eaten by those social groups known as "untouchables". The prophet Mohammed never touched horseflesh and although it is not mentioned in the Koran, the founder of the Hanafite school of jurisprudence, Abu Hanifa (699-767 CE), declared it unlawful. Although certain Muslims rejected Hanifa's ruling, the Tadjik of Turkestan, who lived among horse-eaters, observed his injunction.

Before the Pope's edict, horses had been eaten in Europe since the Stone Age and their beautiful stylised forms were frequently depicted on cave walls. After his ruling, they rarely appeared for consumption until the time of the French revolution although old, unwanted horses were still eaten by the poor. However, there were exceptions: 11th century Swiss monks ate "wild" horses and a horsemeat feast was reported in Denmark in 1520 while the Spanish Navy relished the flesh which they called "red deer". Even without the religious injunction, horses would not have been the most popular type of meat as they need larger areas for grazing than sheep or cattle, they eat grain, which is also human food, and from the Middle Ages onwards they were more useful when pulling ploughs.

However, things changed in France around the time of the Revolution. A food shortage caused by the effects of industrialisation – urbanisation and a concomitant growth in population – meant that any meat was welcome. Despite this need, royal edicts in 1735, 1739, 1762 and 1780 reinforced the prohibition on horsemeat. On the eve of the Revolution there were fourteen million horses in Europe. It was therefore only natural that during the Reign of Terror of 1793-94, when the French people were starving, they would begin to eat them. Napoleon's army surgeon, Baron Dominique Jean Larrey, championed the meat and although some conservative politicians tried to reintroduce restrictions after Napoleon's defeat, the consumption of horsemeat grew. During the German siege of Paris in 1871, horses were to prove invaluable for sustenance and between 60,000 and 70,000 were devoured. Horseflesh was legalised towards the end of the 19th century in France, Austria, Germany and Scandinavia. It remained popular until after the First World War, when numbers dwindled as tractors began to replace horses, but in 1960 there were still 3,500 butcher shops in Paris specialising in horsemeat.

In Britain the situation was different. To relieve the food scarcity caused by urbanisation during the Industrial Revolution of the 18th and 19th centuries, an empire was developed which supplied cheap food such as beef, pork and mutton. In Scotland and Ireland forests were cleared and farms and crofts were replaced by grazing sheep, cattle and pigs. Another source of cheap meat was Argentina because British banks controlled their beef industry.

This meant that it was unnecessary to consume horses, especially since the Empire depended on its cavalry.

In the United States horses were never bred for meat or milk and while European countries were passing laws to repeal the ban on horseflesh during the 19th century, America was instituting prohibitions although unwanted horses were still secretly consumed. Because it was rarely eaten, the meat was not inspected for safety until 1920 when Congress authorised inspections by the Department of Agriculture. Perhaps a nostalgia for the "wild west" and its cowboys also helped instil an image of the noble steed in the minds of Americans; certainly horse-eating is not condoned there.

Japan has no such qualms. Horses were eaten by the Ainu tribesmen and horsemeat remains a popular ingredient in contemporary *sukiyaki* dishes. Its neighbour, China, bred warhorses to counter the threat of the Mongols but rarely ate them, although the people of Shansi used horse-liver as a medicine. Even this organ could be dangerous: during the Han period (206 BCE-220 CE), the liver was considered poisonous and the Emperor Wu, who reigned from 140-187 CE, told the court necromancer, Luan Ta, that Luan's predecessor, Shao-weng, had died as a result of eating horse-liver.

References

Farb, Peter and George Armelagos. 1980. *Consuming Passions: The Anthropology of Eating.* Boston, Massachusetts: Houghton Mifflin.

Harris, Marvin. 1986. *Good to Eat: Riddles of Food and Culture.* London: Allen and Unwin.

The Rig Veda. trans. Wendy Doniger O'Flaherty. [1981] 1983. Harmondsworth, Middlesex: Penguin.

Simoons, Frederick J. [1961] 1967. *Eat Not This Flesh: Food Avoidances in the Old World.* Madison, Wisconsin; London: University of Wisconsin Press.

Hunting Taboos in Japan

Hunters in Japan must observe language taboos when they are stalking game in the forest. The mountain speech (*yama-kotoba*) employed during the chase uses substitute terms to avoid uttering proscribed words. Often the banned word designates an animal: a snake (*hebi*) is called a *naga-mono* (long thing), and a monkey (*saru*) or bear (*kuma*) is called *oyaji* (father). Similarly, *magari* (curve) is used for cat *(neko)*, *takase* (high back) for horse (*uma*), *yase* (lean) for wolf (*okami*), and *yama-no-negi* (priest of the mountain) for hare (*usagi*). The anthropologist, James Frazer, explains such hunting taboos (which seem to be almost universal) as a tactic to obscure the hunter's intentions, "from a dread that [the animals] ... may understand his speech and know what he is about, when he happens to be engaged in that which, if they knew of it, would excite their anger and fear" (Frazer, p. 417). More recently, other scholars, such as Edmund Leach, have offered different reasons for taboos on naming animals (Leach, p. 23-63) but, in this instance, Frazer's explanation seems to make sense.

See also
Food Taboos; Naming

References
Frazer, James, G. [1911] 1935. *Taboo and the Perils of the Soul. The Golden Bough*. New York: Macmillan.

Leach, Edmund. 1964. "Anthropological Aspects of Language: Animal Categories and Verbal Abuse". In *New Directions in the Study of Language*. ed. Eric H. Lenneberg, p. 23-63. Cambridge, Massachusetts: University of Massachusetts Press.

Oto, Tokihiko. 1963. "The Taboos of Fishermen". In *Studies in Japanese Folklore*. ed. Richard M. Dorson, p. 107-121. Bloomington: Indiana University Press.

I

Iconoclasm

Iconoclasm (from the Greek words *eikon* (image) and *klaein* (to break)) is any movement that involves the breaking or destroying of images and especially of images and pictures set up as objects of veneration. The most famous example of iconoclasm is that which troubled the Byzantine Empire during the 8th and 9th centuries CE, but its roots go back to antiquity and the 20th century can testify to its continued tenacity. The impetus for iconoclasm comes from an inherent belief in the power of images which must be destroyed to counter their efficacy (although this is not always the reason given by the iconoclasts). Usually the destruction is prompted by religious beliefs but political, social and psychological forces have also played a role, especially in more secular times.

Ancient Greece

The rejection of images is found already in the works of the early Greek pre-Socratic philosophers. Heraclitus, who lived from the 7th to the 6th century BCE, claimed that his compatriots praying to their statues was just as ludicrous as carrying on a conversation with a house and Xenophanes (6th-5th century BCE) ridiculed the fact that people believed the gods were born and had clothes, speech and bodies like their own. Zeno the Stoic (also known as

Zeno of Elea, 5th century BCE) insisted that nothing made by human hands and formed from a material substance could be worthy of the gods.

Plato himself (428-347 BCE) denigrated the material world while Antisthenes the Cynic (5th to 4th century BCE) denied the possibility of a material image representing the divine. The argument that it is impossible to circumscribe the divine, which is immaterial and without limits, can be found in the writings of Philo of Alexandria (20 BCE-50 CE), and in early Christian writers. It was to play a crucial role in the debates of the Iconoclast Council of 754 CE, held in the palace of Hieria, which condemned artists for "having attempted to delineate the incomprehensible and uncircumscribable divine nature of Christ" and because they had "confused the unconfusable union of the uncircumscribable Godhead in the circumscription of created flesh" (Freedberg, 1989, p. 403). Obscure as the arguments of Byzantine theologians may seem today, the heresy into which artists might fall was considered serious indeed.

Judaism

Jewish, Christian and Muslim taboos on idolatry stem from passages in the Old Testament. In *Exodus* 20, 3-5 God declares: "You shall have no gods except me. You shall not make yourself a carved image or any likeness of anything in heaven or on earth beneath or in the waters under the earth; you shall not bow down to them or serve them". Unaware that this command was being issued to Moses on Mount Sinai, the Israelites below were worshipping a molten calf made from their golden jewellery, an act that so angered the patriarch he destroyed the tablets on which this command was written. However, despite being officially aniconistic (having strictures on image making) and refraining from portraying the deity, Judaism is not without its images. Moses was instructed to make two golden cherubs for the ark (*Exodus* 25, 18-22) and figurative decorations appear in the Jewish catacombs in Rome and in Vigna Rondanini, the Villa Torlonia, while painted stucco figures adorn the Jewish sepulchral chambers of Gamart near Carthage (Freedberg, 1991, p. 451 n. 3). Jewish manuscripts of later times, such as the late 15th-century Kennicott Bible, contain animals and naked humans in the armature of the letters and a late 19th-century portrait of the scholar and rabbi, Moses Gaster, is formed entirely of words.

Christianity

In the Christian tradition, the Old Testament injunctions against idolatry merged with the Platonism of antiquity. The 2nd-century theologian, Origen, argued that painters make images which attract the attention of foolish men and drag down the soul from God to earth. He maintained that the best images of God were in the heart, formed by the word of God. Similar views were expressed by other Church fathers such as Epiphanius (ca 315-403 CE) and Eusebius (ca 260-340 CE) who thought the man-made colours of artists could never match the brilliant colours of Christ, while Tertullian (ca 160-225 CE) believed art to come from the devil: God did not choose false colours for nature or make-up for women, hence these must have come from the other, infernal, regions (Freedberg, 1991, p. 396-397).

Not everyone agreed. Pope Gregory the Great (ca 540-604 CE) thought that paintings could have a didactic function and in October 600 CE, he criticised the bishop of Marseilles, Serenus, for having removed the images from the churches: "Images are to be employed in churches, so that those who are illiterate might at least read by seeing on the walls what they cannot read in books" (Freedberg, 1991, p. 113). Images were not to be worshipped but were permissible only to teach illiterates the Sacred Word, a view that was to be repeated by the Protestant reformers, Luther, Calvin and, to some extent, Zwingli, in the 16th century. Pope Gregory's stance went some way towards accommodating images within the Latin church.

However, within the Greek-speaking Byzantine Empire, which was formed by the Emperor Constantine in the 4th century CE after the collapse of the Roman Empire, idolatry continued to be a contentious issue. When the image of the Emperor went round the provinces, he was believed to be there too, the image being identical to the thing represented. Athanasius of Alexandria (328-373 CE) thought such a position clarified the nature of the Godhead: Father and Son were one, the Son being the image of the Father (Freedberg, 1991, p. 392).

Iconoclasts, though, inspired by eastern sects and the spread of Islam, vigorously opposed the identification of an image with that which it represented, claiming that this amounted to idolatry and in 725 and 726 CE the Emperor Leo III first prohibited the worship of images, then ordered their destruction. This decision was condemned by the pope but in the First Iconoclastic Council of 754, Leo's son, the Emperor Constantine V, banned all religious art in the Eastern Church and in the following years possessors of images were tortured, blinded, mutilated and executed. Mosaics were destroyed in the interior of the Hagia Sophia in Constantinople, and all the great art of the age of Justinian was destroyed, except in Byzantine Italy and the Sinai.

In 787 the Second Council of Nicaea, held under the auspices of the Empress Irene, brought to an end the first great phase of Byzantine iconoclasm. One of the major figures in the rehabilitation of icons was the Syrian theologian and Church Father, John of Damascus (675 CE-749 CE) who reasserted the doctrine that Christ was the image of God. He refuted the early Christian and Byzantine arguments that God, being divine, could not be represented in a material and circumscribed form by pointing out that Christ's birth in human form proves that he can be so depicted. Just as Christ was the image of God and must be worshipped, so images of Christ participate in his divinity and must be venerated and will, in their turn, pass this on to their prototype. To deny the power of images is to reject the fundamental Christian doctrine of Incarnation. Moreover, rather than dragging down the soul from heaven to earth, icons, by arousing the senses, take people to God. Painting itself is no tool of the devil, but is inspired by God himself who "paints" the virtues in man (Freedberg, 1991, p. 394, 401-405). Theodore the Studite (759-826) also defended images as divine representations, but what swayed the Council of Nicaea more than these theological disputations was pure pragmatism: monks and bishops came to the meeting replete with tales of wonders and miraculous cures effected by the icons and they realised the power of these images for the devotion of the masses.

A second wave of Byzantine iconoclasm was inaugurated in 815 CE and ended in the condemnation of iconoclasm at the Council of Orthodoxy, held in 843, when Empress Theodora the Second, widow of the iconoclast Emperor Theophilus, arranged for the election of the monk, Methodius, as patriarch. The restoration of icon veneration is known as the Triumph of Orthodoxy and is celebrated annually in the Eastern Church.

Apart from destroying so much Byzantine art, the iconoclasm worsened relations with Rome which began to seek allegiance with the Germanic tribes to the north. Within the Latin church, the debate on images continued throughout the Middle Ages. St. Thomas Aquinas (1225-74) justified paintings as a mean of instruction but was aware of the dangers of emotional involvement. St. Bernard was more critical, believing that the money spent on images could be more appropriately used to alleviate poverty.

After several centuries of comparative peace, European iconoclasm flared up again in the 16th century as a result of the Protestant Reformation. Beginning with sporadic attacks in Zurich in 1523, inspired by the preachings of Ulrich Zwingli (1484-1531), and in France and other European countries, it culminated in the violent Calvinist demonstrations in the Netherlands during August, September and October of 1566. Riots in Antwerp erupted during the annual procession of the Virgin on 18 August 1566, and contemporary accounts testify to the emotional frenzy. Not only was every statue and painting in the Cathedral torn down, but as they lay on the ground they "were broken with sledge hammers, hewn with axes, trampled, torn and beaten into shreds" (Freedberg, 1988, p. 10). Shocked at this desecration, Catholic writers such as Johannes Molanus, King Philip II of Spain's censor in the Netherlands, sought to justify the use of certain types of imagery.

However not all the destruction during this period was inspired by religious fanaticism: Henry VIII's dissolution of the monasteries, and appropriation of their wealth, between 1536 and 1540 was prompted by purely pecuniary concerns.

The Catholic Counter-Reformation tried to clarify the Church's position on religious art and in France, in December 1563, the Council of Trent passed a decree on images which reiterated the conclusions of the Second Council of Nicaea, namely that paintings on the walls of churches could educate the illiterate and that any honour shown to statues would be transmitted to the prototype. But it stipulated that no heretical ideas should be depicted, no profit should be made from the veneration and sale of religious relics, and all lasciviousness was to be avoided.

The 16th century witnessed the last major attack on religious art in Europe although in England in the 17th century the Puritans reacted against the excesses of King Charles II, who devoted a vast amount of time and money to art, and during the French Revolution the rejection of the Church resulted in statues of the Virgin Mary being thrown out.

Islam

Within Islam, which dates from 622 CE when the prophet Mohammed emigrated from Mecca to Yathrib (the future Medina), there is condemnation of image-making, although the proscriptions against figurative art are not codified in the *Qur'an* (Preaching), revealed to Mohammed by Allah, but in the *Hadith* (Traditions) of the 9th century. The reasons cited in the *Hadith* for the ban echo those of the iconoclasts of the Byzantine Empire, namely that the adoration of replicas of prophets and saints materialises worship while the creation of representational images is sacrilege as creation belongs to God alone.

Although the *Qur'an* contains no injunctions against idolatry it does place idolaters on a level with apes and swine and a major event in the life of Mohammed was the destruction of the idols in the *Ka'ba* sanctuary in Mecca in 629 CE. According to tradition, the prophet approached with 10,000 men and initially attempted to strike out the eyes of the figures with his bow (Eliade, 1985, p. 75).

Generally the rule against images was strictly observed in religious contexts – there are no figures in the Dome of the Rock in Jerusalem or in the mosque in Damascus or in decorations within the *Qur'an*, but secular palaces, such as the early 8th-century Mshatta, in the Syrian Desert, contain stone reliefs of real and fantastic animals. When human or animal figures were depicted they were placed within a decorative framework which resulted in Muslim artists, denied the opportunity for realistic representation, becoming masters of decorative patterns based on geometric and foliate forms and calligraphic ornamentation.

One area where figurative painting did survive was in book illustrations, most notably in the Persian manuscript paintings of the 14th and 15th centuries whose anthropomorphic figures had blank faces, a single concession to the law against idolatry.

Politically inspired iconoclasm

Religion and politics, though ostensibly opposed, are all too often intertwined. To destroy one set of idols and replace them with another is usually a political, rather than a religious, act. In Egypt during the Old Kingdom, statues of Queen Hatshepsut and her followers were destroyed by Thutmosis III; Akhenaten smashed images of Amun and replaced them with those of Aten; Amun in turn was reinstated by Tutankhamun. In China, attempts to suppress Buddhism from the 5th to the 9th centuries included the destruction of Buddhist statues and temples and peaked in the Hui-Chang suppression of 845 CE. Statues of secular leaders are regularly removed during revolutions: in 1917 the Russian Revolution saw the removal of the portraits and statues of the czars; in 1989 it was the turn of the Communist leaders; and during the Iranian Revolution of 1979 the equestrian statue of the Shah's father was torn down. Individual acts of violence are also often politically motivated and commonly directed at paintings. Bryan Organ's 1981 painting of Diana, the Princess of Wales was daubed with the letters IRA, the initials of the Irish Republican Army, and in 1914 the suffragette, Mary Richardson, slashed Velasquez' *Rokeby Venus* to protest against the British Government's imprisonment of Mrs Pankhurst, leader of the feminist movement. As the *Rokeby Venus* portrays a nude woman, the gesture was also a decrial of the portrayal of woman as the object of the male gaze.

Other attacks on individual works of art have been prompted by neurotic delusions and a desire for attention (the man who slashed Rembrandt's painting *The Nightwatch* in 1975 claimed that he was the Messiah and that he wanted his message to the world to appear on television [Freedberg, 1985, p. 11-13]); a disgust with the money spent on "undeserving" works (hence the attack by a Hungarian artist on a prize-winning model for a Reg Butler sculpture [Freedberg, 1985, 48 n. 72]); or a belief in the immorality of the image. David Freedberg, in his study *Iconoclasts and their motives*, seeks the underlying causes of contemporary iconoclasm. He believes that certain individuals manifest a neurotic desire to destroy precisely that which is valued and cherished by others. Moreover, he thinks that it is not the image alone but the tension between the image and that which it represents that prompts the violence. Essentially: "… iconoclasm represents the most heightened form of making plain one's superiority over the powers of both image and prototype, of our liberation from their unearthly thrall" (Freedberg, 1985, p. 35).

References

Bryar, A. & J Herrin. ed. 1975. *Iconoclasm*. Birmingham: Birmingham University Press.

Eliade, Mircea. 1985. *A History of Religious Ideas*. vol. 3. Chicago, Illinois: University of Chicago Press.

Freedberg, David. [1989] 1991. *The Power of Images: Studies in the History and Theory of Response*. Chicago, Illinois: University of Chicago Press.

Freedberg, David. 1985. *Iconoclasts and their motives*. Maarssen, the Netherlands: Gary Schwartz.

Freedberg, David. 1988. *Iconoclasm and Painting in the Revolt of the Netherlands 1566-1609*. New York: Garland Publishing.

Grabar, O. 1987. *The Formation of Islamic Art*. New Haven, Connecticut; London: Yale University Press.

Incest

Incest is defined in the dictionary as the sexual relations between persons who are so closely related that their marriage is illegal or forbidden by custom and as the statutory crime of sexual relations with such a near relative. Despite its tabooed status in society, it is often found in creation myths. At the beginning of time, if the myths are to be believed, everything was different from the way it is today: the earth did not yet exist and the earliest ancestors, when they appeared, often indulged in acts reprehensible to succeeding generations, such as patricide, fratricide and incest. Incest was sometimes unavoidable; like the biblical Lot seduced by his daughters, it was often the only way to produce heirs. (For an analysis of incest in the Bible see Leach and Aycock, *Structuralist Interpretations of Biblical Myth*.) An Australian myth from north-eastern Arnhem Land recounts how, during the "Dreamtime", Djanggawul and his two sisters wandered over the earth creating plants, animals and, finally, the ancestors of the Aborigines. They were endlessly fertile with huge genitalia so that:

> … when the Djanggawul brother had coitus with his sisters, he lifted aside their clitorises, entering them in the usual way. He was able to have incestuous relations with his sisters because at that time there were no marriage rules, no moities and no prohibition (Berndt in Sproul, p. 316).

With the establishment of marriage rules and all the trappings of 'culture', incest was no longer allowed. It is possibly because of creation myths such as this (and there are many tales of incest) that anthropologists, psychologists, sociologists and others have spent a lot of time speculating on the origin of the incest taboo.

During the 19th century scholars, perhaps wistfully, postulated a time of unbridled sexuality before human society evolved and imposed restraints. Looking at traditional cultures, which were believed to be at an earlier stage of development, would therefore reveal evidence of incestuous behaviour. In 1877 the American lawyer and ethnographer, Lewis Henry Morgan, published *Ancient Society* in which he charted the evolution of the family as a social institution. Morgan argued that although he found no consanguineous marriages among the Polynesian groups he studied, the fact that a child would refer to his father's sister by the same term he used for his mother suggested that a child's parents would once have been brother and sister while all that now remained of the custom was this linguistic fossil. Inspired by Charles Darwin's *On the Origin of Species by Means of Natural Selection*, which appeared in 1859, he surmised that the incest taboo was established when the biological consequences of inbreeding became apparent.

The British anthropologist, Edward Tylor, was less concerned with the deleterious biological results of conjugal relations with close kin than with the positive social advantages of marriage outside the immediate family. He coined the phrase "Marry out or be killed out", by which he meant that human societies could choose between offering their women in marriages that would create new political allegiances or remaining in small groups that could easily be wiped out by their numerous enemies. Marriage to strangers meant that a whole social framework based on co-operation and interdependence could be established. In 1865 the Scottish lawyer, John McLennan, introduced the concepts of exogamy (marrying outside one's group or clan) and endogamy (marriage within the clan). Exogamy is not exactly the same as an incest taboo as the clan is much wider than the immediate nuclear family (and in fact the term 'incest' is itself quite fluid as relationships that are forbidden as incestuous in one society – such as between first cousins – may be allowed elsewhere). McLennan was not as confident as Tylor that a group would willingly offer its wives in marriage. With his knowledge of classical texts, where success in battle was followed by the seizure and rape of the women of the defeated army, he imagined a time when, having depleted their own supply of women through the practice of female infanticide, men took wives from captured enemies.

The custom of exogamy then became the norm, even when the women no longer had to be taken by force, though remnants of the origin can be seen in the behaviour at wedding ceremonies of traditional societies where a symbolic capture of the bride is enacted. It is interesting to note that, while it is impossible to verify McLennan's hypothesis, recent reports from countries of the former Soviet Union describe the capture of women by foreign tribes, and the distress of these women who, having spent the night in a stranger's dwelling, are no longer welcome in their own villages.

A different approach, and one more directly linked to the origin of the incest taboo itself, is suggested by the psychoanalyst, Sigmund Freud. Examining infantile sexuality, he thought that a major part of a child's development consisted in overcoming his Oedipal desires: like the mythical figure who unwittingly killed his father and married his mother, the child was thought to harbour an unconscious sexual desire for his mother while his father aroused his repressed homicidal longings. The childhood desires of an individual, Freud believed, merely mirrored the "childhood" of a society, a concept that is developed in a series of four essays published under the title *Totem and Taboo* in 1913. Having accepted the evolutionary theories of the British anthropologist, James Frazer, and Charles Darwin, Freud studied the complex totemic kinship and marriage systems of the Australian Aborigines whom he believed to be at an earlier stage of development. He found a horror of the idea of incest which was averted by the prohibition on marriage to members of one's own totemic group (the totem is the animal that is linked to each group). Freud thought that originally humans lived in small groups consisting of a single father, his wives – whom in tyrannical fashion he kept for himself – and his children. At maturity, the sons were forced to leave home to prevent inbreeding. One day the sons rebelled, killed their father and ate his body (the idea of a cannibalistic feast derives from the work of W. Robertson-Smith) but were immediately consumed by guilt. They identified themselves with him and he became their totem and, by extension, their god. Then they forbade marriage to members of one's own totemic clan and the incest taboo was established, which thus lies at the root of both religion and human culture.

Some revisions and objections to Freud's theories have been summarised by W. Arens in his book, *The Original Sin. Incest and Its Meaning* (Arens, p. 39-43). Bronislaw Malinowski, an anthropologist, had studied the sexual life of the Trobriand Islanders and observed that, as they were a matrilineal society (tracing their descent through the female members), authority was vested in the mother's brother so that he, rather than the father, became the focus of the child's unconscious hatred (which occurred later in his development than Freud thought) while his forbidden sister became the object of his desire. With these reservations, Malinowski accepted Freud's findings on the dynamics, if not the origin, of incest. More recent criticism has been levied at Freud for denying the evidence of father-daughter incest (in which the father is the instigator), presented to him in his clinical capacity but dismissed as fantasy, or female "hysteria". The evidence for a "primal horde", in which the father is killed, eaten and deified is non-existent and the conjecture, though imaginative, is a testimony to the scholars' somewhat desperate search for the origins of human society.

Another person who believes the incest taboo signals the foundation of human culture is the French anthropologist, Claude Lévi-Strauss. In *The Elementary Structures of Kinship*, which first appeared in 1949 and was published in a revised English edition in 1969, he states dramatically that with the incest taboo:

> ... the whole situation is completely changed ... before it, culture is still non-existent; with it, nature's sovereignty over man is ended. The prohibition of incest is where nature transcends itself ... it brings about and is in itself the advent of a new order (Lévi-Strauss, p. 25).

Although Claude Lévi-Strauss is a structuralist, concerned with the numerous interlocking patterns that could be deciphered within the kinship systems that he studied, he nevertheless posits an origin for the taboo. Originally, the story runs, all the males selfishly kept their wives, sisters and daughters for themselves, enjoying free sexual relationships but not benefiting from any of the social advantages that gift-giving and sharing with other males can confer. The breakthrough came when a group of males, in a spirit of generosity, decided to offer their women to another group in the expectation that it would reciprocate in kind. As women were so valuable, this was the ultimate gift that could be offered. Henceforth daughters and sisters were reared for exchange so that social relationships with other groups of men could be established.

Like Tylor, Lévi-Strauss believed that the advantages of such social and political allegiances were important for survival. A necessary prerequisite for the exchange was the ability to distinguish between sister and wife. For the incestuous male, a sister could also be a wife and there would be no need for exchange. This is why the incest prohibition was necessary: as the brother gave his sister away in marriage, he had to refrain from selfish incestuous desires. Lévi-Strauss saw the binary opposition, sister-wife, as immensely symbolic in all human cultures and he believed that it demonstrated a natural propensity of the human mind: to think in terms of dynamic oppositions, whether between nature and culture, raw and cooked food or life and death. The incest taboo itself he considered both "social and pre-social" a composite of nature and culture — and this ambiguity accounts for its "sacredness" (Lévi-Strauss, p. 12). Lévi-Strauss was typical of many anthropologists writing in the mid-20th century in that he refused to concede that the genetic effects of inbreeding could have played a role in the prohibition.

Not all researchers have been looking for the origin of the taboo. Increasingly, the concern has been with the function of the ban within both the immediate family and the wider community (although obviously a search for origins does not preclude a concern with function). Bronislaw Malinowski thought that incest between parents and children would be a disruptive force within the family. Unlike animal groupings, the human family is characterised by an extended period of child dependency during which the social, educational and moral values of the community are inculcated. It is therefore the foundation of culture and social organisation. Incest would disrupt relationships and lead to "... the upsetting of age distinctions, the mixing up of generations, the disorganisation of sentiments, and a violent exchange of roles ..." (Malinowski in Arens, p. 50). A prohibition is therefore essential if a society is to function.

Subsequent anthropologists and sociologists reiterated Malinowski's suppositions. Talcott Parsons viewed incest as a regressive phenomenon while Kingsley Davies envisaged a taxonomist's nightmare. The male child of a father-daughter incest " ... would be brother of his own mother, i.e. the son of his own sister; a step-son of his own grandmother, possibly a brother of his own uncle; and certainly a grandson of his own father" (Davies in Arens, p. 52). While it is generally the case that incest, at least between father and daughter, causes intolerable social and psychological tensions within the family, Arens cites research by Christopher Bagley which demonstrates that it need not necessarily be harmful. In certain circumstances, for instance, where the mother has been unable to fulfil her role, her function has been assumed by the daughter with no ill effects (Arens, p. 58).

Another reason posited for the incest taboo is that consanguineous unions increase the risk of recessive (as opposed to dominant) genes

being transmitted in successive generations. This can result in a higher incidence of infant mortality, mental incapacity including severe retardation and seizures, bone deformity and cleft lip. As mentioned earlier, biological factors have been rejected as an explanation for incest taboos by many anthropologists who argue that, as incest is so rare, there is insufficient data for conclusive studies, but the evidence of an increased risk to offspring is now incontrovertible. One recent study has focused on the Amish of eastern Pennsylvania. Members of this religious sect, founded in Switzerland in the 17th century, rarely marry outsiders or accept new members. This has led to "genetic isolates" being formed which can be traced back to European founders. Of the 1,850 married couples observed, all but three had a relationship that was closer than second cousins:

> In this genetic setting, five congenital disorders were isolated, including some previously undetected ones. This condition was deduced to be a consequence of an inbreeding pattern which allows for the recognisable appearance of abnormal physical features. This included Ellis-van Creveld Syndrome, manifested by dwarfism, polydactyly (extra digits), dystrophy of the fingernails, and partial hairlip (McKusick in Arens, p. 20).

An argument has been advanced that while the effects of inbreeding on individual offspring would be deleterious, in the long term, the high mortality rate among those children might result in the recessive genes being eradicated. However, this is entirely speculative and a more pertinent inquiry would ask whether the genetic consequences, only scientifically verifiable in the 19th century, were the reason for the taboo on incest. Unfortunately, none of the preceding theories is able to apply empirical research to the actual origins of the prohibition. Similarly the sociological arguments, namely that stable family relationships, and by extension society itself, is threatened by consanguineous relationships explain the function, but not the origin, of the ban.

A different approach has been to question whether incest is tabooed because we naturally want to commit it but shouldn't or because, paradoxically, we have no desire to commit it anyway. The first person to suggest a possible human aversion to incest was Edward Westermarck who expounded his ideas in his three-volume work *The History of Human Marriage*. He was impressed by the evolutionary biological theory of Charles Darwin, which suggested that inbreeding was directly harmful and therefore naturally avoided, and adopted a functional approach in his own research which was conducted in Morocco and appeared in publications in the early decades of the 20th century. Westermarck found that:

> Generally speaking, there is a remarkable absence of erotic feelings between persons living very closely together from childhood. Nay more, in this, as in many other cases, sexual indifference is combined with the positive feeling of aversion when the act is thought of. This I take to be the fundamental cause of the exogamous prohibitions. Hence their aversion to sexual relations with one another displays itself in custom and law as a prohibition of intercourse between near kin (Westermarck, p. 80).

The important factor here is that it is the physical closeness in childhood, rather than the genetic link, that acts as a deterrent. Siblings raised apart could well find each other sexually attractive at maturity. The idea that it is natural not to desire those who are close to oneself was initially contested by James Frazer who, in his *Totemism and Exogamy* in 1910, raised the question as to why there should be a taboo against incest if it was never craved. He considered the inclination towards incest to be natural which was the reason it had to be

controlled. Another anthropologist, Émile Durkheim, thought the theory flawed in that if close relatives had no sexual feelings for one another, the same might apply to a husband and wife. Westermarck agreed that this might indeed be the case if they lived together long enough, although he also distinguished between those raised together from childhood and those who married as adults. Émile Durkheim's own theory of incest avoidance appeared in his book of 1898, *Incest: The Nature and Origin of the Taboo*, in which he claimed that members of the same totemic clan feared that they would be polluted by the blood of the totemic spirit if they indulged in sexual intercourse.

Sigmund Freud, with his theory of unconscious Oedipal desires, also vehemently opposed Westermarck who defended himself by saying that he had yet to be convinced of the "evidence" for the repressed desires. Westermarck maintained that specific acts, such as sodomy and bestiality, are prohibited not because they are natural but because certain individuals have aberrant desires and the rules are for them. This is also the case with the incest taboo.

In the 1930s and 1940s, biological reductionism was very unpopular in anthropological circles and Edward Westermarck was largely ignored but in the 1950s new evidence was found in support of his theory. In 1958 the ethnographer, Melford Spiro, published *Children of the Kibbutz* which was a study of a social experiment in Israel in which children of the same age-group were raised together in communal houses rather than living at home. Although the children indulged in typical childhood sexual experimentation, at puberty they drew apart and showed no sexual interest in one another. This would seem to be natural aversion and although Spiro did not draw this conclusion, an Israeli sociologist, Yonia Talman, did. Talman published an article in 1964 on the sexual and marriage patterns of kibbutz members of the same age. She found that out of 492 adults raised together from childhood there was not a single marriage; this was confirmation, she believed, of an avoidance syndrome, as there was no rule forbidding such unions.

In 1962, the anthropologist Robin Fox adopted a position that went some way towards reconciling the opposing views of Westermarck and Freud. While the findings of Spiro and research from the Trobriand Islands supported Westermarck's theory that children raised in close proximity demonstrate no sexual interest after puberty, the fact that Freud's patients, although siblings, were generally not raised with such intimacy, meant that they retained their innate incestuous inclinations (Fox, 1962, 13, p. 128-150). Fox attributed the lack of erotic interest among childhood companions to an internal biological mechanism leading to natural avoidance, a mechanism which he thought had developed in the process of man's evolution (Fox, 1980, p. 216). This superseded an earlier idea of his that favoured psychological conditioning – early sexual experimentation in childhood being frustrated due to immaturity – as an explanation.

Support for Westermarck's hypothesis can be found in a study of certain types of pre-arranged marriages (called *sim-pua* marriages) in China. In these marriages a female child was taken at very early age into the house of her future husband and in-laws. The researchers, initially Arthur Wolf who later worked together with C. S. Huang, looked at the effect of this early intimacy on the two children who were raised as siblings. Wolf discovered that marriages between such couples were about thirty per cent less fertile than marriages between strangers, with a higher rate of sexual infidelity and divorce. The age of adoption was particularly important: marriages between children who had been brought together before the age of four were twice as likely to end in divorce as those who were aged eight or over.

Another survey of the Israeli kibbutzim, this time conducted by a native, Joseph Shepher,

confirmed earlier findings of the lack of sexual attraction between children raised together. Of 2,769 couples from 211 kibbutzim, none involved a real union between peers who had spent the first six years of their lives together. Shepher thought this might be the result of "negative imprinting" (Shepher, 1971, p. 293), a basic learning process known to exist in the animal world. With humans, Shepher estimated that this took about four years and was complete by the age of six. He considered this imprinting to be a phylogenetic (a characteristic of the evolution of the race) adaptation designed to reduce the harmful effects of inbreeding. While Shepher looked at the effect of imprinting on peer groups, Hilda and Seymour Parker turned their attention to its influence on father-daughter incest, commonly regarded as sexual abuse. They found that fathers who abused their daughters had been much less involved in child-rearing activities during the first three years of their daughters' life than had non-abusers (Parker, p. 540-541). This had resulted in a lack of bonding or imprinting. Because adoptive or step-fathers were more likely to have been absent during the crucial early years than biological fathers, the incidence of abuse could be expected to be significantly higher, which in fact it was. If, however, levels of child-care were identical, there were no significant differences in the levels of abuse by natural and adoptive or step-fathers.

In 1983 Justine McCabe published an article that offered further evidence in support of Westermarck's hypothesis. Her fieldwork was conducted in an Arab village in Lebanon where she examined the marriage of first cousins, a custom that, while relatively uncommon, is more frequent in the Middle East than in other parts of the world. The patrilinear cousins were in close contact from birth and their relationships were characterised by "informality, candor, teasing, tattling, quarreling, laughing, joking" (McCabe, p. 59). Marriage between them was encouraged by the parents but resulted in fewer children and were four times more likely to end in divorce than unions between non-relatives.

That incest avoidance is natural, rather than, as Tylor, Freud, Lévi-Strauss and the British anthropologist, Edmund Leach, have proposed, the defining characteristic of human culture, is corroborated by evidence from the animal realm. Empirical studies of non-human primates, including gorillas, baboons and chimpanzees, have found an avoidance of inbreeding between mother and sons and siblings. This is accomplished by the transference of the sexually mature male or female to another troop or, in the case of gorillas in Central Africa, an inherent lack of sexual interest between parents and their offspring (see Bischof, 1975). Similar patterns of incest avoidance have also been found among such diverse non-primates as African elephants, lions, quails and the prairie vole. Moreover, the behavioural pattern of choosing a partner from outside the immediate family is considered to have been a characteristic of our last common primate ancestor, twenty million years ago (Maryanski and Turner, 1992). It is therefore highly unlikely that the human species, *Homo sapiens*, developed without this natural proclivity for outbreeding; rather, as W. Arens argues convincingly in *The Original Sin, Incest and its Meaning*, it would seem that the social rules merely reinforce a natural inclination.

The question as to why any cultural reinforcement is necessary if the incest avoidance is innate has already been answered in part by Westermarck in his reply to Freud, namely that certain individuals transgress the bounds of normal behaviour. Arens contends that this is because humans are able to overcome their biological inclinations – it is the incest rather than the taboo that is cultural (Arens, p. 94-101).

However, despite all the obvious biological and social advantages of incest avoidance, the prohibition is not, as is commonly thought, universal. In some societies there is no need for the taboo as the behaviour is considered so abhorrent as not to be practised. In other places there is evidence that incest between brothers and sisters was actually condoned. Material collected by Keith Hopkins provides proof that such marriages occurred in Egypt from about 300 BCE although the custom no doubt originated at a much earlier date. At this time there are records of marriages between Greek kings of Egypt and their full sisters as the Greek administrators adopted the Egyptian tradition. From 19-20 CE till 257-58 CE, the Romans conducted censuses of the Egyptian population and reported that out of 113 marriages, seventeen were definitely between brother and sister and another six possibly were. The unions appear to have been fertile and willingly engaged in. It is a practice validated by Egyptian myth: the Roman author, Plutarch, tells how the Egyptian god of vegetation and of the dead, Osiris, married his sister, Isis, a faithful woman who recovered his body after it had been dismembered by their jealous brother, Set. In 212-13 CE the Egyptians were made Roman citizens and such marriages were banned in accordance with Roman law.

Criticisms of Hopkin's work focus on the scantiness of the data and Arens (Arens, p. 11-112) suggests that the Egyptian term "sister" might be a euphemism for mistress or a sign of affection, not denoting any biological link. In other societies, such as in Hawaii, Peru and Thailand, incestuous unions have been permitted among the royalty. Ray H. Bixler draws the important distinction between sex and marriage. Marriages may have been necessary for political purposes but this does not mean that they were necessarily consummated. And in Egypt, a Pharoah may have taken many wives so that the offspring were not necessarily from his sister.

Other areas of the world where royalty has been exempt from the general incest prohibition include Central Africa, studied in detail by the anthropologist, Luc de Heusch, possibly in southeastern Africa where the Lovedu employ a complex matrimonial system involving divine queenship, and among the Shilluk of the southern Sudan. Explanations for the custom vary, but it is believed that royalty, in so far as it aspires to divinity, transcends mundane morality and emulates the primordial incestuous unions of so many origin myths.

At the end of the 20th century, many of the discussions of incest focused on the topic of child abuse (Willner, 1983 and La Fontaine, 1988). It is unclear whether father-daughter incest is more common than that between siblings; certainly the former is more likely to be reported as it often involves an abuse of power that cannot be resolved within the nuclear family. In other forms, such as that between mother and son, the issue is confused as to who is the aggressor and who the victim.

The taboo retains its strength, and while there is no conclusive evidence as to the validity of Westermarck's hypothesis or Shepher's theory of imprinting (avoidance of sex by peer group members may have been due to adult pressures to refrain during adolescence or a result of the small size of the groups making external marriages more likely), it is probably a mixture of the recognition of the deleterious genetic effects of inbreeding and the social and psychological advantages of exogamy that guarantees its survival.

References

Arens, William. 1986. *The Original Sin. Incest and Its Meaning*. New York; Oxford: Oxford University Press.

Berndt, Ronald M. in Sproul, Barbara. [1979] 1980 *Primal Myths*. London: Rider.

Bischof, Norbert. 1975. "Comparative Ethnology of Incest Avoidance". In *Biosocial Anthropology*. ed. Robin Fox. London: Malaby Press.

Bixler, Ray H. 1982. "Sibling Incest in the Royal Families of Egypt, Peru, and Hawaii". *The Journal of Sex Research*, no. 18, p. 264-281.

Dawkins, Richard. [1976] 1989. *The Selfish Gene*. Oxford: Oxford University Press.

de Heusch, Luc. 1972. *Le roi ivre*. Paris: Gallimard.

Fox, J. Robin. 1962. "Sibling Incest". *British Journal of Sociology*, no. 13, p. 128-150.

Fox, J. Robin. 1975. ed. *Biosocial Anthropology*. London: Malaby Press.

Fox, J. Robin. 1980. *The Red Lamp of Incest*. New York: E. P. Dutton.

Hopkins, Keith. 1980. "Brother-Sister Marriage in Ancient Egypt". *Comparative Studies in Society and History*, no. 22, p. 303-354, cited in Brown, Donald E. 1991. "Incest Avoidance". In *Human Universals*, p. 125-127. New York: McGraw-Hill.

La Fontaine, J. S. 1988. "Child Sexual Abuse and the Incest Taboo: Practical Problems and Theoretical Issues". *Man*, no. 23, p. 1-18.

Leach, Edmund, and Alan Aycock. 1983. *Structuralist Interpretations of Biblical Myth* Cambridge: Cambridge University Press.

Lévi-Strauss, Claude. [1949] 1969. *The Elementary Structures of Kinship*. London: Eyre and Spottiswoode.

Maryanski, Alexandra and Jonathan Turner. 1992. *The Social Cage*. Stanford, California: Stanford University Press.

McCabe, Justine. 1983. "FDB Marriage: Further Support for the Westermarck Hypothesis of the Incest Taboo?" *American Anthropologist*, no. 85, p. 50-69.

Parker, Hilda and Seymour. 1986. "Father-Daughter Sexual Abuse: An Emerging Perspective". *American Journal of Orthopsychiatry*, no. 56, p. 531-549.

Shepher, Joseph. 1971. "Mate Selection Among Second Generation Kibbutz Adolescents and Adults". *Archives of Sexual Behaviour*, no. 1, p. 293-307.

Shepher, Joseph. 1983. *Incest*. New York: Academic Press.

Westermarck, Edward. 1926. *Ritual and Belief in Morocco*. vols. 1 and 2. London: Macmillan.

Willner, Dorothy. 1983. "Definition and Violation: Incest and the Incest Taboos". *Man*, no. 18, p. 134-159.

Wolf, Arthur and C. S. Huang. 1980. *Marriage and Adoption in China. 1845-1945*. Stanford, California: Stanford University Press.

Initiation

Initiations, like all rites of passage, are suffused in taboos; neophytes may be denied food, clothes, comfort, companionship or speech.

Explanations and reasons for the prohibitions may at times seem obvious, at times impenetrable, to the outside observer. Sometimes, however, they are imbued with a persuasive logic, such as that evinced by the Luvale of Zimbabwe:

> A Luvale boy may urinate only against the following trees during the time of his initiation: *Pseudo achnostylus deckendti, Hymenocardia mollis, Afrormosia angolensis, Vangueriopsis lanciflora, Swartzia madagascarinensis*. These are hard woods symbolising the penis in erection, their fruits being associated with fertility and life. He is also forbidden to eat the flesh of various animals: *Tilapia melanopleura*, a fish with a red belly, the colour of blood; *Sarcodaces* sp. and *Hydrocyon* sp., which have sharp teeth symbolising the painful after-effects of circumcision; *Clarias* sp., whose slimy skin symbolises difficulty in the healing of the scar; the genet whose spotted skin symbolises leprosy; the hare with his sharp teeth and "hot" chillies which symbolise painful healing ... Female initiates are subject to analogous prohibitions (White, p. 97-98).

See also

Food Taboos; van Gennep, Arnold

References

Eliade, Mircea. [1955] 1959. *The Sacred and the Profane*. New York: Harcourt Brace.

La Fontaine, Jean S. 1985. *Initiation*. Harmondsworth, Middlesex: Penguin.

White, C. M. N. quoted in Lévi-Strauss, Claude. [1962] 1976. *The Savage Mind*. London: Weidenfeld and Nicolson.

J

Japanese Menstrual Huts

Japanese women, like women from many traditional societies, were subject to taboos during menstruation and required to retire to special huts where they wore old, ragged clothes and ate only raw food. The practice continued in the Japanese district of Aichi-ken, until the end of the 19th century. The abstention from cooked food was due to a belief that cooked food, brought to the hut, could cause the fire of the main house to become polluted. Menstruating women were also deemed capable of contaminating water and were not allowed near the well. Seclusion in the huts could be for as long as eleven days, after which the women ritually purified themselves by washing, cleaning their clothes and eating either in the village temple, at some other foreign hearth, or in front of their own houses, sharing tea with some children. After this rite of integration, known as *ai-bi* (sharing the fire), they could resume normal life.

At the end of the 19th century, women were no longer required to visit menstrual huts but they were still subject to taboos, and were made to eat leftovers in a corner of the house at a different hearth. Moreover, because of the perceived dangers, all the fires in the house were extinguished and re-lit during this period, while the pots and pans were thoroughly cleaned. Fortunately, by the beginning of the 20th century, although the women were still considered "unclean", purifying charms, known as *o-fuda* were available from Koyasan, the head temple of the Tendai sect of Buddhism in Wakayama-ken, so that the isolating taboos were no longer necessary.

Despite all the precautions, the onset of menarche, known as "the first blossom" in many parts of Japan, was a joyous occasion, celebrated by the eating of *sekihan*, rice boiled with red beans (a practice that continues to the present day). In some areas, such as Toba-shi in Mie-ken, the red dish was placed upon the altar. After the ceremonies, which could last several days, the girls were eligible for marriage.

See also
Menstruation

Reference
Segawa, Kiyoko. 1963. "Menstrual Taboos Imposed upon Women". In *Studies in Japanese Folklore.* ed. Richard M. Dorson, p. 239-250. Bloomington: Indiana University Press.

Jewish Dietary Laws

Jewish dietary laws are based on passages in *Leviticus* and *Deuteronomy* which describe in great detail not only those foods which are permitted or forbidden for consumption, but also the correct manner of killing the animals and serving the viands. The Hebrew term for the dietary laws is *kashrut* derived from a root meaning "proper", "right", "pleasing"; those animals which are taboo are *tame* ("unclean") while those allowed are *tahor* ("clean").

Contemporary anthropologists, investigating the forbidden animals, have noticed how the tabooed creatures are often those anomalies that defy classification as though some fanatical taxonomist excluded all that did not fit (Douglas, p. 41-57. But see also Food Taboos for a comprehensive discussion of the theories of Douglas and others, as well as later revisions by Douglas). Certainly the actual laws provide some support for this theory. *Deuteronomy* 14, 4-19 and *Leviticus* 11, 3-8 list as unclean those animals that are ruminant but with no cloven hoof, (the camel, hare, and hyrax, although the latter are not even ruminants) and those, such as the pig, which has a cloven hoof but is not ruminant; all of these fail to fit under the cloven-hoofed ruminant rubric.

Similarly taboo are 'counterfeit' fish, those creatures like eels and shellfish that live in water but do not have both fins and scales (*Leviticus* 11, 9-12; *Deuteronomy* 14, 9-10), and, amazingly, winged insects with four feet that do not leap over the ground (*Leviticus* 11, 20-23), which are neither birds (too many feet), nor insects (which leap). The problems arise when birds are considered – why are the vulture, griffon, osprey, kite, buzzard, hawk, raven, ostrich, owl, ibis, pelican, vulture, cormorant, stork, heron, seagull, hoopoe and bat (*Leviticus* 11, 13-19; *Deuteronomy* 14, 11-18) forbidden? The bat is a mammal and so no true bird but the others are birds, many of which fit into the Falconidae (carnivorous) or Vulturidae (carrion-eaters) classes. The Mishnah (a collection of the rabbinic law developed by scholars and compiled by Rabbi Jehuda Hanasi in Palestine around 200 CE) lists as unclean "a bird that seizes food in its claws" while one which has "an extra talon, a craw (crop), and the skin of whose stomach can be peeled (possessing a gizzard that can be easily peeled)" is clean (*Hullin* 3, 6). This is not a very comprehensive guide and in practice it is often tradition that determines which birds may be eaten and which not.

In the same way, while it could be argued that the Jewish proscription on mixing meat with milk-based substances (*Deuteronomy*, 14, 21) arises from a need to separate categories of food, a similar explanation cannot be affixed to the prohibition on eating the sciatic nerve or consuming the blood of the animal (*Leviticus* 7, 26-27; 17, 10-14), the latter being the reason all the blood must be drained from an animal before slaughter.

The Pentateuch itself gives no reason for the dietary laws – which, being divinely ordained, need no further justification – but *Ezekiel* 33, 25 equates the eating of blood with the shedding of blood, and the verse has been interpreted to mean that the consumption of blood induces violence. It is the same moral concern that forbids the eating of birds of prey: the injunction against eating them is a lesson to humans not to "prey" on their fellows (Rabinowicz, p. 42). Philo Judaeus of Alexandria, a Jewish philosopher of the 1st century CE, employed a similar use of allegory to explain the laws:

> Fish with fins and scales, admitted by the law, symbolise endurance and self-control, whilst the forbidden ones are swept away by the current, unable to resist the force of the stream. Reptiles, wriggling along by trailing their belly, signify persons who devote themselves to their ever greedy desires and passions. Creeping things, however, which have legs above their feet, so that they can leap, are clean because they symbolise the success of moral efforts (Philo of Alexandria in Douglas, p. 47).

Jewish mystics, with spiritual rather than ethical concerns, thought that the foods which were banned would pollute the soul and blunt the intellectual faculties and, like the followers of Pythagoras, held vegetarianism in high esteem. However, one of the most tenacious arguments for keeping *kashrut* is that it is hygienic. Maimonides, a 12th-century Jewish philosopher and physician, took this view in his *Guide for the Perplexed*. Swine's flesh was unwholesome because the animal had dirty habits; the fat of the intestines (the proscribed sacrificial fat) "… because it fattens and destroys the abdomen and creates cold and clammy blood" (Maimonides quoted in Rabinowicz, p. 43), and meat boiled in milk because it was too rich. However, Maimonides gave a second reason for not mixing milk and meat: the custom was supposedly connected with idolatry (Maimonides quoted in Rabinowicz, p. 44). Canaanite texts discovered in the 1920s at Ras Shamra, on the Syrian coast, and dating back to the 15th century BCE, tend to confirm the existence of a fertility rite in which a kid was boiled in its mother's milk, but the Israelites happily adopted many customs from their neighbours without worrying about idolatry.

The explanations based on hygiene have been widely supported; the existence of parasites and, in the 12th century, the discovery of bacteria and the spores of infectious diseases that circulate through the blood, have lent them some credence, and they appeal to those who desire a "scientific" basis for religious practices. When it comes to dietary laws, it is also true to say that scientific discoveries can lead to new problems. Van Leeuwenhoek invented the microscope in the 17th century and for the first time protozoa could be seen. The question arose as to whether or not protozoa were taboo. The general consensus is that, as they are invisible, it is difficult to prohibit food containing them but if a dish is known to contain the micro-organisms it should be avoided. On the other hand, they, like insects, were originally thought to arise through spontaneous generation from non-living matter, which would render them edible.

Some parties within Judaism have questioned the relevance of dietary laws, ordained so long ago, to modern life. At the Pittsburgh Conference in 1885 the Reform Movement resolved. "… such Mosaic rabbinical laws as regarding diet … originated in ages entirely foreign to our present mental and spiritual state" (Rabinowicz, p. 44) and the movement does not insist on the observance of *kashrut*. Liberal Judaism also leaves the question of diet up to the individual and it is only the Conservative or Orthodox Jews that insist on the holiness of the laws. The author, Chaim Bermant, has remarked on the vagaries of Jewish cuisine and the dietary laws:

> Wine … can be rendered non-kosher if touched by a non-Jew … but if it is … boiled, it becomes inviolate (the principle, I hasten to add, does not extend to pork, scampi, shrimps or oysters, but as lobsters have a cloven hoof, they might be half-kosher. If anyone could train lobsters to chew the cud he would be a rich man) (Bermant, p. 240).

See also

Douglas, Mary; Food Taboos; Halal; Pigs

References

Bermant, Chaim. 2000. *On the Other Hand*. London: Robson Books.

Carroll, M. P. 1978. "One more time: Leviticus revisited". *Archives européennes de sociologie*, no. 19, p. 339-346.

Douglas, Mary. [1966] 1984. *Purity and Danger: An Analysis of the Concepts of Pollution and Taboo*. London: Ark-Routledge and Kegan Paul.

Douglas, Mary. [1975] 1979. "Deciphering a Meal". In *Implicit Meanings: Essays in Anthropology by Mary Douglas*, p. 249-275. London: Routledge and Kegan Paul.

Harris, Marvin. 1974. *Cows, Pigs, Wars and Witches: the Riddle of Culture*. New York: Random

Maimonides. 1974. *The Guide of the Perplexed*. trans. Shlomo Pines. Introductory essay by Leo Strauss. Chicago, Illinois; London: Chicago University Press.

Rabinowicz, Harry. "Dietary Laws". In *Encyclopaedia Judaica*, vol. 6, p. 26-46. Jerusalem: Keter Publishing House Ltd.

K

Keesing, Roger M. (1935-93)

Roger Keesing was a linguistic anthropologist of American origin keen to show how ethnographers have misinterpreted cultural phenomena because of a tendency to supplement given information, often erroneously, in an effort to unify disparate, or fragmentary, elements. Such over-interpretation has led to a confusion over the precise meaning of the term *taboo*. As Keesing points out, the Oceanic Austronesian word *tapu/tabu* and cognates are canonically stative verbs but the word has also been treated by anthropologists as though it were a noun (for instance, one speaks of "the incest taboo"). The basic meaning in both Melanesian and Polynesian languages of *tapu* is "off limits". What is "off-limits" may be sacred or polluting, or neither:

> Something is off-limits, tapu, only if some (human or nonhuman) agent defines it as such. This agent may be a god, the ancestors, or a (god-like) chief. In many Oceanic languages, however, it may also be a parent telling a child not to do something. Something is off limits, tapu, only given a perspective. What is off limits to one person or category of persons may be permissible ... or even enjoined for another ... A menstrual hut may be tapu from the vantage point of men; from the vantage point of a menstruating woman, it would be tapu to be anywhere else ... Something that is off limits, tapu, is always off limits *to someone*, not in and of itself. Finally, being tapu, off limits, implies a context. A place, act or thing that is tapu this afternoon, from the perspective of some people and in the context of a particular ritual or circumstance, may be noa (or tapu) for *different* people tomorrow.

This underlies why translations of tapu as either "sacred" or "forbidden" are misleading (Keesing, p. 204-205).

This is a clear and comprehensive exposition of a term that has caused ethnologists considerable confusion since the time it was first mentioned by Captain James Cook.

See also
Cook, Captain James

Reference
Keesing, Roger M. 1985. "Conventional Metaphors and Anthropological Metaphysics: The Problematic of Cultural Translation". *Journal of Anthropological Research*, no. 41, p. 201-217.

Keesing, Roger M. and J. Fifi'i. 1969. "Kwaio Word Tabooing in its Cultural Context". *Journal of the Polynesian Society*, 78, p. 154-177.

Knots

A comprehensive, if dated, analysis of the magical and taboo use of knots has been conducted by anthropologist, James George Frazer in his book *Taboo and the Perils of the Soul* (Frazer, p. 293-317). Like most potent devices, knots could be used for both beneficial and malevolent ends. Knots were efficacious because they were credited with the magical power of binding. In the wrong hands, they could create invisible bonds that prevented such natural events as childbirth or the consummation of a marriage. They could pin the soul to the body so that it was unable to escape at death. A knot hidden in a ship could cause it to capsize. Moreover, sorcerers could magically tie up their enemies and then inflict harm, provoking attack by wild beasts, or causing sickness or death. On the other hand, knots could be tied as a protection against wild animals, witchcraft, demons and death. By tying a knot one could cure disease, win a lover or ensnare anything from an escaped slave to a besieging army.

To counter the magic it was necessary to undo or cut the knot. As a precaution, during childbirth, all knots were undone, a practice that has been recorded from Scotland to Indonesia. Frazer explains the mechanics:

> On the principles of homeopathic or imitative magic the physical obstacle or impediment of a knot on a cord would create a corresponding obstacle or impediment in the body of the woman (Frazer, p. 295).

Because of their association with the idea that there is such a thing as "primitive thought", Frazer's ideas on homeopathic or sympathetic magic have been widely criticised by scholars who have tended to prefer a psychological, sociological or linguistic interpretation of magical behaviour. For a recent discussion on Frazer's ideas on magic, see for example Stanley Jeyaraja Tambiah's *Magic, Science, and Religion, and the Scope of Rationality* and Fritz Graf's *Magic in the Ancient World*.

James Frazer is interested in the magical use of knots but the power of binding is also recorded in a religious context. Mircea Eliade has recognised how important the act of bind-

ing is in the Hindu Vedic texts that date back to before the 12th century BCE:

> Varuna, "all-enveloping", the great Vedic god, (guardian of the sacred law and cosmic Order) magically binds culprits, and one prays to him either to magically bind, or else to unbind them. Vritra, "restrainer", (a demon) imprisons the waters … (He is killed by Indra, king and warrior of the gods, who releases the waters). Indra, like Agni "fire" and Soma (both god and ambrosial drink of the gods), liberates men from the bonds of Varuna and from the chains of the funerary divinities; he "cuts" or "breaks" these bonds exactly as, in the myth, he cuts, dismembers and so on, the body of Vritra. Together with the warlike means which are proper and indeed exclusive to him, he does also employ "magical" means to triumph over the magician Vritra; but it remains true that "binding" is not one of his fundamental methods … On the contrary, bonds, cords and knots characterise the divinities of death (Yama, Nirrti) and the demons of the various maladies. And lastly, in the popular parts of the Vedic books, the charms against the bonds of these demons are no less numerous than the spell-binding sorceries aimed at human enemies (Eliade, p. 102).

A typical incantation in the *Rig Veda* appeals to healing plants to "free me from … what comes from Varuna, and from the fetter sent by Yama and from every offence of the gods" (*RV.* 10.97). What Varuna sends is a noose that consists in the disease of dropsy and other maladies.

The Iranian *Yasna* alludes to the demon, Astovidhotush, who ties the dying with "bonds of death" (*Yasna* 53,8), while the god, Tistrya secures the Pairika sorceresses with several ropes (*Yast*, 8,55). In the ancient Mesopotamian epic of creation, *Enûma elish,* composed towards the end of the 2nd millennium BCE, Ea, the god of the fresh waters and of wisdom, holds the primordial Apsû and Mummu with spells, passing a string through Mummu's nose, before killing them. In the same work, Marduk kills the seamonster, Tiamat, by encompassing her with his net, then tears her apart to create the cosmos. In the Bible, too, reference is made to magical binding. The prophet Ezekiel rails against women who sew frills around wrists, "the better to ensnare lives", presumably a familiar magical practice (*Ezekiel*, 13: 18). It is also noteworthy that knots were taboo in certain ancient Greek rituals, including the Eleusinian mysteries and the *flamen dialis*, the Roman priest, was allowed no knots in his hat, belt or anywhere else.

Eliade is convinced that the magical taboos on knots are symptomatic of a wider religious sensibility. Furthermore, he sees the knot as an archetype belonging to a whole cluster of archetypes including the thread of human destiny, the weaving of the Cosmos, the labyrinth and the chain of existence. The thread of life is familiar in many cultures: one thread is allocated to each individual and the cutting of the thread signals death. Greek myths portray the three Fates – Clotho, Lachesis and Atropos – weaving human destiny on a loom. In the Sanskrit Upanishads, the Universe is linked by the air (*vayu*) which unites this world and the next in an invisible web and the powers of Yoga are at times understood as an enchantment through binding (Eliade, p. 114-115). The labyrinth has been likened to a "knot" that must be "un-tied". It is a symbol of mystical initiation in which the neophyte must learn to undo the labyrinthine knot as a preparation for the soul's encounter with it after death.

In an existential sense, knots and binding symbolise the human condition. One is born bound and freedom is only to be found through a disavowal of the material world, whether in the form of stoical resignation or religious transcendence. Paradoxically, religion, often cited as a means of liberation, is full of

deities who bind or imprison mortals. Sorcery and knot-making, Eliade concludes, is not dissimilar from the binding practised by the gods:

as the "terrible sovereign", either historically or historicised, is striving to imitate his divine prototype, the "binding" god, so every sorcerer, too, is imitating the terrible sovereign and his divine prototype. Morphologically, too, there is no break in continuity between Vritra who "chains up" the Waters, Varuna who "binds" the guilty, the demons who catch the dead in their "net" and the sorcerers who bind the enemy by magic, or unbind the victims of other sorcerers (Eliade, p. 118).

In contemporary Taoist belief, the soul, at death, is still caught up in a web of darkness, sin, debt and despondency. It is necessary for a ceremony known as Untying the Knots and Dissolving Sins to be performed to liberate the entangled soul of the deceased and render it healed, cleansed, enlightened, and absolved from sin, debt and unfulfilled longings. This is described in detail by John Lagerwey:

The ritual is composed basically of seven identical segments. Holding a knotted skein of string in his hand, the officiant invokes the Heavenly Worthy of General Passage by the Bridge of the Law and then, facing the statuettes, sings a song describing a category of sins to be "dissolved" as he makes a rolling motion with the skein of string. Returning to the Cave-table, he invokes the Heavenly Worthy Who Undoes Resentments and Loosens Knots and reads a brief document summarising the purpose of the ritual. He comes back before the statuettes to recite a series of seven wishes and then, while a summary song is being sung, lights a cone of "old money", writes with it, and throws it in a basin on the south side of the altar. He goes through this entire sequence seven times, expressing in all 7 x 7 = 49 wishes, one for each day of the main mourning period after the death of a parent. At last he undoes the knot altogether and gives it to another priest to be burned. He receives a large bunch of newly lit sticks of incense and bows with them as he sings the names of four heavenly worthies of "great compassion and mercy". Sticks of incense are passed to the mourners, who bow with them and then return them to be planted in the burner. The ritual ends with a procession to the house and an offering of song (Lagerwey, p. 187-188).

The untying of knots is not just a problem for priests and magicians; mathematicians are also determined to unravel their mysteries. Primarily mathematicians are interested in the topological properties of knots – features that do not change despite continuous deformations.

Though principally important for mathematicians, exploring multidimensional spaces and other intricate questions, the subject of morphology also has a relevance in the fields of molecular biology and particle physics. Knots may be ancient magical devices but their importance has not diminished with time.

References

Eliade, Mircea. [1952] 1961. *Images and Symbols: Studies in Religious Symbolism.* trans. Philip Mairet. London: Harvill Press.

Frazer, James George. [1911] 1935. *Taboo and the Perils of the Soul. The Golden Bough.* New York: Macmillan.

Graf, Fritz. [1994] 1999. *Magic in the Ancient World.* trans. Franklin Philip. Cambridge, Massachusetts: Harvard University Press.

Kramer Heinrich and James Sprenger. [1486] 1971. *The Malleus Maleficarum.* trans. Montague Summers. New York: Dover Publications.

Lagerwey, John. 1987. *Taoist Ritual in Chinese Society and History.* New York: Macmillan Publishing Company.

The Rig Veda. [1981] 1983. trans. Wendy Doniger O'Flaherty. Harmondsworth, Middlesex: Penguin.

Stewart, Ian. [1987] 1996. *From Here to Infinity: A Guide to Today's Mathematics.* Oxford: Oxford University Press.

Tambiah, Stanley Jeyaraja. 1990. *Magic, Science, Religion, and the Scope of Rationality.* Cambridge: Cambridge University Press.

L

Laws of Manu

The Hindu compilation known as *The Laws of Manu* (in Sanskrit the *Manusmrti* or *Manavadharmasastra*) consists of 2,685 verses in which the rights and duties of the various Hindu castes are delineated, as well as ethical questions, social and legal issues, ritual practices, and cosmogony. Composed by Brahmins, or priests, probably around the 1st century CE, it is ascribed to Manu (literally "wise"), a mythical king and ancestor. Many of the laws (which are both descriptive, prescriptive and proscriptive) are concerned with ritual purity, and pollution avoidance, and list taboos on food and animals, sexual and marriage partners, menstruating women, people whose food one should not eat, castes with whom one should not mix, places one should not urinate, as well as bodily orifices, discharges and detritus that are considered unclean. Acts that incur a ritual state of pollution can sometimes be offset if particular procedures (such as ablutions) are followed but certain crimes, such as failing in one's prescribed duty, can lead to terrible transmigrations:

A priest who has slipped from his duty becomes a "comet mouth" ghost who eats vomit; a ruler becomes a "false stinking ghost" who eats impure things and corpses. A commoner who has slipped from his own duty becomes a

ghost "who sees by an eye in his anus", eating pus; a servant becomes a "moth-eater" (ghost) (*The Laws of Manu.* 12, p. 71-72).

Written by priests, a large proportion of the laws are directed towards the Brahmins, who are eager to protect their own interests and maintain the status quo. Thus, it is declared, there is no greater sin than the killing of a priest, no matter what his transgression (*Manu* 8, p. 380). Brahmins are subject to stricter rules of purity than other castes and, although they may eat sacrificial meat, vegetarianism is the ideal (in stark contrast to the earlier *Vedic* esteem for meat).

Naturally, many texts have a political dimension and, as the Sanskrit scholars, Wendy Doniger and Brian K. Smith point out, the *Manavadharmasastra*, which endorsed, and came to symbolise, the repressive Hindu caste system, was the text most often burned by the Untouchables in their protests (Doniger and Smith: lxi). Moreover, it was the code used by the British in colonial times as they set up a complex system of jurisprudence in India with a "personal" law, based on individual religious affiliation, complementing the "general law". It was the British, indeed, who translated *dharmasastra* as laws, (the term *dharma* can mean "religion", "duty", "law", "right", "justice", "practice" and "principle") so that it could be used for legal purposes, and who chose to privilege this text despite the availability of alternatives (Doniger and Smith: lx-lxi).

See also

Foods Forbidden to Brahmins

References

Doniger, Wendy and Brian K. Smith. 1991. "Introduction". In *The Laws of Manu*. trans. Doniger and Smith, p. xvi-lxxviii. London: Penguin.

The Laws of Manu. 1991. trans. Wendy Doniger and Brian K. Smith. London: Penguin.

Leach, Edmund R. (1910-88)

After studying mathematics and engineering at Cambridge University, Edmund Leach worked in China and the Philippines where he became interested in anthropology. His first fieldwork was carried out among the Kurds of Iraq. During the Second World War he stayed in Burma with the Kachin hill people whom he later organised into resistance groups after the Japanese conquered the country in 1942. Leach's later fieldwork took him to Sri Lanka. His work was influenced by the economic anthropology of Raymond Firth, the structural functionalism of Bronislaw Malinowski and the structuralism of Claude Lévi-Strauss. His most significant contribution to the study of taboo is the article, "Anthropological Aspects of Language: Animal Categories and Verbal Abuse", published in 1964.

Leach sees taboo as a means of creating discrete categories, whether the purpose is to distinguish "self" from "other", farm from field, field from wilderness, edible from inedible, eligible from incestuous. Where there is a danger of the categories becoming confused, the intermediate forms are banned or rendered sacred. Because they can blur at the boundaries of the body, excretions such as faeces, urine, semen, menstrual blood and hair and nail clippings are considered polluting and taboo in many cultures. In the same way, language, which, as Leach points out, provides names which allow classification, can also provide tabooed words to inhibit "the recognition of those parts of the continuum which separate the things" (Leach. 1964, p. 35). (For a full exposition of Leach's theories on taboo, see Food Taboos.)

In an article entitled "Magical Hair", Edmund Leach considers the differences between a psychoanalytical approach to the study of taboos (exemplified by the work of Sigmund Freud) and that of an anthropologist:

The psychoanalyst's thesis implies a causal nexus – sacred things are sacred *because* they are secret and taboo. The anthropologist argues the other way about: sacred objects are taboo because they are sacred – that is because they are full of dangerous potency, including sexual potency. The hidden element, the secrecy, is not, for the anthropologist, a crucial part of the pattern ... ritually powerful human hair is full of magical potency not because it is hair but because of the ritual context of its source, e.g., murder, incest, mourning etc. It is the ritual situation which makes the hair "powerful", not the hair which makes the ritual powerful (Leach. 1958, p. 159).

Thus, in Leach's view, it is not the repressed desires or a "sublimated libido" that cause one to project a taboo status onto a person or object, but the social value of an object in a ritual context.

See also

Food Taboos; Hair

References

Leach, Edmund, R. 1954. *Political Systems of Highland Burma: A Study of Kachin Social Structure*. London: London School of Economics and Political Science.

Leach, Edmund, R. 1958. "Magical Hair". *Journal of the Royal Anthropological Institute*, no. 88/2, p. 147-164.

Leach, Edmund, R. 1961. *Rethinking Anthropology*. London: Athlone.

Leach, Edmund, R. 1964. "Anthropological Aspects of Language: Animal Categories and Verbal Abuse". In *New Directions in the Study of Language*.

ed. Eric H. Lenneberg, p. 23-63. Cambridge, Massachusetts: MIT Press.

Leach, Edmund, R. 1968. "Ritual". *International Encyclopedia of Social Sciences*, no. 13, p. 520-526.

Leach, Edmund, R. 1973. "Levels of Communication and Problems of Taboo in Appreciation of Primitive Art". In *Primitive Art and Society*. ed. J. A. Forge, p. 221-234. London: Oxford University Press.

Left Hand, The

The left hand, the sinister hand (Latin, *sinister* = left), has long been the hand associated with sorcery and evil; it is the hand of treachery and fraud; the weaker, inferior, impure hand; the hand that women of the tribes of the lower Niger are forbidden to use for cooking if they wish to avoid accusations of poisoning and sorcery; the hand with which devout Muslims clean those polluting orifices of the body below the navel while the right hand is reserved for eating.

Robert Hertz, in 1909, was the first person to conduct a serious study of the predominance of the right hand. He found that arguments for an innate physiological predisposition towards use of the right hand (governed as it is by the left cerebral hemisphere) were insufficient to explain its extraordinary dominance. Instead, he thought that the organic asymmetry and polarisation resulted from a human need to differentiate between the sacred and the profane, and that any contact or confusion between the categories would be detrimental to both. Prohibitions and taboos were necessary to protect the sacred from pollution by the profane. In this way Hertz explained the taboos against the left hand in religious ceremonies:

> In religious ceremonies man seeks above all to communicate with sacred powers, in order to maintain and increase them, and to draw to himself the benefits of their action. Only the right hand is fit for these beneficial

relations, since it participates in the nature of the things and beings on which the rites are to act. The gods are on our right, so we turn towards the right to pray. A holy place must be entered right foot first. Sacred offerings are presented to the gods with the right hand. It is the right hand that receives favours from heaven and which transmits them in the benediction (Hertz, p. 104).

Hertz was a great inspiration to other scholars, who tested the veracity of his theories. In 1934 Ira S. Wile collected an overwhelming amount of evidence, from every part of the world, on the preference for the right. This preference could be found, as Rodney Needham recalls:

> in such varied fields as the Homeric poems, alchemy, and thirteenth century religious art, in Hindu iconography, classical Chinese state ceremonies, emblem books and bestiaries, as well as in Maori ritual, Bornean divination and the myths of the most disparate cultures (Needham, p. 110).

E. E. Evans-Pritchard, researching Nuer spear symbolism, confirmed the association of the right with strength, masculinity and goodness while the left signified weakness, femininity and evil (Evans-Pritchard, p. 92-108). He observed that only the right half of an animal or fruit offered in sacrifice could be eaten, that a young man was warned not to enter the hut of his bride on the left side, and that the Nuer youths would immobilise their left arms for months, or even years, by pressing metal rings into the arms so tightly that sores appeared and the arm was useless. If a man was left-handed, this hand was referred to as his right hand, proving that the symbolic significance of the left was of more importance than the actual physiognomy.

In Central Celebes the Toradja identify the left hand with death, the right with life. When they make gardens for the dead or set aside food

for the dead they must use the left hand. For the same reason, when the first new rice is cooked, care must be taken only to use the right hand. Omens are similarly determined: if a bird of good fortune flies across the path from left to right, it augurs well because adversity, in being transferred from the bad side to the good, is transformed into prosperity (Kruyt, p. 74-91).

Greek philosophers of the 6th and 5th centuries BCE, including Parmenides, Anaxagoras, Aristotle and Pythagoras, similarly favoured the right side. Aristotle argues, somewhat disingenuously, that the curious anomaly of such an important organ as the heart residing on the left side of the body is due to the necessity of heating this cold side (Lloyd, p. 167-186).

While Hertz has drawn attention to an important phenomenon, there are, of course exceptions. The left hand or side is not always inauspicious: in China it is the left hand that represents Yang, the male, the sky and summer while the female, the earth, winter and the right hand are Yin (although China favours a system of alternations in which each side is of equal importance) (Granet, p. 43-58). And Rodney Needham is puzzled by the taboos surrounding the left hand of the Mugwe, a religious person among the Meru of Kenya with a left hand so sacred that it must always be covered as the sight of it would cause instant death (Needham, p. 109-127). One must bear in mind, however, that when dealing with such elementary and apparently universal symbolism researchers may unwittingly misinterpret, simplify or modify the ethnological data.

References

Evans-Pritchard, E. E. [1973] 1978. "Nuer Spear Symbolism". In *Right and Left: Essays in Dual Symbolic Classification*. ed. Rodney Needham, p. 92-108. Chicago, Illinois: University of Chicago Press.

Granet, Marcel. [1973] 1978. "Right and Left in China". In *Right and Left: Essays in Dual Symbolic Classification*. ed. Rodney Needham, p. 43-58. Chicago, Illinois: University of Chicago Press.

Hertz, Robert. [1909] 1960. "Death and the Right Hand". In *The Pre-Eminence of the Right Hand:*

A Study in Religious Polarity. trans. Rodney and Claudia Needham, p. 89-160. London: Cohen and West.

Kruyt, Alb. C. [1973] 1978. "Right and Left in Central Celebes". In *Right and Left: Essays in Dual Symbolic Classification*. ed. Rodney Needham, p. 74-91. Chicago, Illinois: University of Chicago Press.

Lloyd, Geoffrey. [1973] 1978. "Right and Left in Greek Philosophy". In *Right and Left: Essays in Dual Symbolic Classification*. ed. Rodney Needham, p. 167-186. Chicago, Illinois: University of Chicago Press.

Needham, Rodney. [1973] 1978. "The Left Hand of the Mugwe". In *Right and Left: Essays in Dual Symbolic Classification*. ed. Rodney Needham, p. 109-127. Chicago, Illinois: University of Chicago Press.

Wile, Ira S. 1934. *Handedness: Right and Left*. Boston, Massachusetts: Lothrop, Lee, Shepard Co.

Liminality

The liminal (from the Latin *limen*, threshold), or transitional, phase of a "right of passage" that an individual traverses in the course of his life, whether birth, initiation, marriage or death, is often a time when normal social roles and restrictions are in abeyance and taboos are violated. In his classic study of the rites, Arnold van Gennep identifies three distinct stages: the first stage is that of separation, when a person symbolically "dies" to his old social role and the final stage is integration into the new role. During the transitional, or liminal, phase there is a suspension of ordinary secular life. Initiation ceremonies are often marked by the neophyte being separated from secular society, bound to a rule of silence, fasting, and wearing distinctive clothing, often fur, feathers and masks, that represent feral ferocity. Victor Turner, an anthropologist who has examined liminality in detail, explains:

> The initiand is in a sense freed from cultural restraints and receptive to the forces of nature and the cosmos. Hence the symbolic reference to beasts, birds and vegetation. Symbolically, the

structural life is obliterated by animality and nature, but it is also regenerated from these same forces (Turner, 1974, p. 253).

The freedom from cultural restraints means that myths told during the liminal period are full of tabooed acts such as murder, cannibalism, adultery or incest, all stressing transgressions of the moral code. Harnessing the vital and sacred, if amoral, regenerative forces may also involve orgiastic behaviour and, as a participant temporarily transcends not only his own social persona but also temporal laws, rites of reversal are common. These may take the form of transvestism or status reversals. Essentially, the initiand is returning to the beginning of time when all was chaos and social mores did not yet exist. Masked dancers represent the dangers and powers of the primordial monsters and spirits. At the same time, the sacred mysteries of the tribe may be revealed: marvels and sacred objects.

Turner recognises the manifestation of liminality in seasonal rituals and carnivals as well as in aspects of contemporary industrialised life and artistic activity. He dwells on the sense of what he terms *communitas,* that exists at this time, when the hierarchical social structure is suspended and all are equal, enjoying a kind of primordial paradise that was believed to exist before the inequities of social distinctions. This creates a sense of well-being and unity among the participants. There may also be a cosmic dimension: seasonal rituals often need to correct the "bad ritual state" created by the self-interest of the "social superiors", a situation that can have repercussions on the fertility of the soil or fecundity of the animals. To counter the catastrophe, the "social inferiors", frequently women (representing *communitas*) act out the roles of their superiors and create a social reversal that purges society of its selfishness and reverses the ritual state.

The liminality of more secular occasions such as carnivals, is similarly marked by a kind of "antistructure" which replaces the conventional social structure. Role and status reversals, transvestism, masked dances, grotesque costumes, inebriation, sexual license, scatological humour, social and religious parody and political dissent all appear here. With a temporary relaxation of social life, it is possible to explore existing patterns and imagine new ones:

> The liminal areas of time and space … are open to the play of thought, feeling, and will; in them are generated new models, often fantastic, some of which may have sufficient power and plausibility to replace eventually the force-backed political and jural models that control the centres of a society's ongoing life.

> The antistructure liminality provided in the cores of ritual and aesthetic forms represents the reflexivity of the social process wherein society becomes at once subject and direct object; it represents also its subjunctive mood, where supposition, desires, hypotheses, possibilities, and so forth, all become legitimate (Turner, 1977: vii).

After the period of transgression, during which breaches in the moral and social order only serve to highlight the existing hierarchies, there is, ideally, a return to traditional social structures. But the dissent expressed during this period may spill out and disrupt the community.

In industrial societies, liminality is often a characteristic of an individual who lives, for whatever reasons, on the margins of society. Turner uses the word *liminoid* to describe the creations, for instance, of a solitary artist. Certain religious sects may also exist outside the mainstream, claiming to be divinely inspired and characterised by ecstatic behaviour, spirit possession and divine revelation.

Folklore provides another arena in which to observe the chaos, danger and revelation of liminality. The time that is "betwixt and between", the thresholds of day and night or the "junctures" of the year – midnight, twilight, New

Year, solstice, equinox, Hallowe'en and Mayday Eve – are all auspicious, haunted by demons and deities. This is the time for divination, the time when the souls of the dead return to haunt the living, and when the living commonly abandon themselves to wild revelry. Thresholds exist on a spatial plane too. Rivers and lakes divide the lands of the living and the dead, as do caves, gateways, bridges and dark forests, while crossroads are dangerous in European, and more distant, traditions: these are places to bury the suicides and summon the spirits, often not to be traversed before the residing deity is appeased.

See also

Carnivals; Cross-roads; Douglas, Mary; Transvestism

References

Pentikäinen, Juha Y. 1986. "Transition Rites". In *Transition Rites*. ed. Ugo Bianchi. Rome: "L'Erma" di Bretschneider.

Turner, Victor W. 1967. *The Forest of Symbols: Aspects of Ndembu Ritual*. Ithaca, New York: Cornell University Press.

Turner, Victor W. 1974. *Dramas, Fields and Metaphors*. Ithaca, New York; London: Cornell University Press.

Turner, Victor W. 1977. *The Ritual Process: Structure and Anti-Structure*. Ithaca, New York: Cornell University Press.

Looking or Seeing

The fear of the hostile gaze, the evil eye, is extremely widespread as is the taboo upon looking at, or even inadvertently seeing, that which is forbidden. This terror of the eye, and of the voyeur, is told in tales and is manifest in myths in virtually every country in the world.

Sometimes it is a sight too terrible to be witnessed that is taboo. The wife of Lot cannot refrain from turning around to watch as fire and brimstone rain down on the towns of Sodom and Gomorrah, and the whole plain around (*Genesis* 19, 25-6). The pillar of salt

into which she is transformed would resemble similar saline structures at the southern end of the Dead, or Salt, Sea, and this is therefore an etiological tale, explaining the origin of the crystalline shapes. But it is also a stern warning of the price to be paid for disobedience.

Sometimes no warning is given but the sight is simply too holy, or too wonderful, to be witnessed. A Greek legend tells how Actaeon, son of Aristaeus, was leaning against a rock near Orchomenus when he happened to see the chaste Artemis (the Roman Diana) bathing in a stream nearby. He stayed to watch and she, worried that he might boast about seeing her naked, changed him into a stag and then set his own hounds upon him to tear him to pieces. Tearing the voyeur limb from limb is not uncommon in Greek texts. In Euripides' play, *The Bacchae* (5th century BCE), Pentheus, the king of Thebes, disguises himself as a Bacchic devotee to spy upon the frenzied Dionysian rituals in which his own mother, Agauë, participates. Alerted to his presence, they set upon him. He appeals to his mother:

"Mother!", he cried, touching her cheek, "it is I, your son, Pentheus, whom you bore to Echion. O mother, have mercy on me; I have sinned, but I am your son: do not kill me!"

Agauë was foaming at the mouth, her eyes were rolling wildly. She was not in her right mind; she was under the power of Dionysus; and she would not listen to him. She gripped his right arm between wrist and elbow; she set her foot against his ribs; and she tore his arm off by the shoulder. It was no strength of hers that did it; the god was in her fingers and made it easy. Ino was at him on the other side, tearing at his flesh; and now Autonoe joined them, and the whole pack of raving women. There was a single continuous yell – Pentheus shrieking as long as life was left in him, the women howling in triumph. One of them was carrying an arm, another had a foot with the shoe still on it; the ribs were stripped – clawed clean. Every hand was thick red with blood; and they were tossing and catching, to and fro, like a ball, the flesh of Pentheus (Euripides, p. 216-217).

Although another Greek character, Orpheus, was torn apart by the Maenads, this was not for disobeying an injunction on looking. His punishment for breaking that particular taboo – turning round to make sure that his beloved Eurydice was following him as he ascended the dark passage from the Underworld – was to lose her forever.

Gods and goddesses were often too fearful (rather than, like Artemis, too chaste) to be seen by mortals. In the biblical book of *Exodus* (33, 22), Yahweh refuses to reveal his face to Moses, declaring that no man may see his face and live, and a Greek myth tells how the insistence of the maiden, Semele, to discover the identity of her secret lover causes Zeus (for he it was) to reveal himself as thunder and lightning and to destroy her.

Sometimes it is a magical act that must not be witnessed. Yü the Great, the Chinese culture hero, controlled the floods that were inundating his land by cutting dykes through which the water could flow, although he was not above resorting to magical means. To pierce the pass of Houan-yuan, he metamorphosed into a bear and performed a strange dance upon the stones which his wife, Tou chan, was forbidden to see. He told his wife that when he wanted food brought to him he would sound his drum. One day he accidentally struck the drum and she, seeing Yü perform the magical dance, was turned to stone (Granet, p. 563-564).

Sex, even when it involves animals, is surrounded by taboos. In a Greek legend, Teiresias sees two serpents coupling and strikes them. He immediately changes sex and only when he later comes across another amorous pair of snakes, and repeats the gesture, does he regain his old form. Unfortunately, when asked by a curious Hera who derives the most pleasure from sex, men or women, he replies that it is the woman and is immediately blinded. The only compensation for his honesty is that – like numerous blind characters in myth – he attains "second sight" and becomes a seer. The Irish hero, CúChulainn, was forbidden to see a woman naked. To calm his battle fury after he returned to Emain and demanded fights with his fellow Ulstermen, women bared their breasts to him and claimed "These are the warriors who will meet thee today" (Reinhard, p. 160-161). Shamed, he hid his face.

Sometimes a terrible secret lies concealed. The hidden chamber in the subterranean castle of Bluebeard, containing the decaying corpses of his victims, must not be entered. The keys to all the rooms of his castle are entrusted to each new bride with the injunction not to look into that particular room. Disobedience causes the key to the room to redden with blood, an indication of the fate of the bride. In other tales the taboo upon looking is merely a test of obedience and what is seen is not so important as the fact that an order has been disobeyed.

Finally, there is the symbolic blinding which denotes impartiality: blind Fortuna casts her luck indiscriminately while the figure of Justice is blindfolded so that she is not seduced by an innocent eye or seductive smile as she pronounces her judgement.

See also

Evil Eye

References

Deonna, Waldemar. 1965. *Le symbolisme de L'oeil.* Paris: Éditions E. de Boccard. École Français d'Athènes Fasc.

Euripides. *The Bacchae and Other Plays.* trans. Philip Vellacott. [1954] 1967. Harmondsworth, Middlesex: Penguin.

Granet, Marcel. 1959 (1926). *Danses et légendes de la Chine ancienne. vol. two.* Paris: Presses Universitaires de France.

Reinhard, John Revell. 1933. *Táin Bó Cúalnge.* quoted in *The Survival of Geis in Mediaeval Romance.* Halle, Germany: Max Niemeyer.

Lysergic Acid Diethlyamide (LSD)

The psychotropic drug, LSD, was first produced in 1938 by Dr Albert Hofmann, a Swiss chemist, while he was seeking a formula for the relief of headaches. He began with lysergic acid which he obtained from the ergot fungus (claviceps pur-purea), a parasite that grows on the rye plant.

Ergot may already have featured in the Greek Eleusinian Mysteries which date back to pre-Hellenic times and celebrate the agrarian goddesses, Demeter and Persephone. Aristides, speaking of Eleusis in the 2nd century CE, mentions "ineffable visions" and it is possible that the *kykeon*, a kind of barley soup drunk at Eleusis during the Mysteries, contained the water-soluble ergonovine and traces of LSD.

Ergot was also familiar during the Middle Ages when it was sometimes inadvertently baked into bread and induced an experience known as "St. Antony's fire", Saint Antony being the patron saint of ergotism victims.

From the lysergic acid, Albert Hofmann synthesised the compound lysergic acid diethlyamide (LSD). Initially, Dr Hoffman was unaware that he had produced such a potent psychotropic drug. He tested the preparation on laboratory animals for its analgesic (pain-killing) properties, but as it appeared to have no positive results, he placed the bottle to one side. On 16 April 1943, he decided to do some further testing on LSD, and inadvertently swallowed some of the liquid. The effects were striking, as his diary entry confirms:

> Last Friday, April 16th, 1943, I was forced to stop my work in the labora-tory in the middle of the afternoon and to go home, as I was seized by a pecu-liar restlessness associated with a sensa-tion of mild dizziness. Having reached home, I lay down and sank into a kind of drunkenness which was not unpleasant and which was charac-terised by extreme activity of imagina-tion. As I lay in a dazed condition with my eyes closed (I experienced daylight as disagreeably bright) there surged upon me an uninterrupted stream of fantastic images of extraordinary plas-ticity and vividness and accompanied by an intense, kaleidoscopic-like play of colours (Trulson, p. 17).

Three days later, he returned to his labora-tory to confirm that the experience was indeed caused by the LSD. Taking what he imagined to be a small dose, 252 micrograms, he waited for the reaction. In fact this is five times the quantity necessary to induce intense hallucina-tions, and the results were electrifying. In addi-tion to feeling dizzy and observing that his limbs alternated between strong motor unrest and paralysis, he experienced synaesthesia – a state in which one sense is stimulated but is experienced as another:

> Colourful, very plastic and fantastic images passed before my closed eyes. It was especially noteworthy that all acoustical perceptions, such as the noise of a passing car, were translated into optical sensations, so that through each tone and noise, a corresponding coloured picture, kaleidoscopically changing in form and colour, was elicited (Trulson, p. 18-19).

Obviously, LSD was a powerful hallucino-genic, but its pharmaceutical use had yet to be determined. In 1949 it was sent to the United States and tested on a medley of creatures including spiders, fish, rats, cats, dogs, goats and elephants. The resulting anomalies in behaviour were dramatic. Under the influence of LSD, dogs and cats chased non-existent prey and adopted strange postures; the hair of rats and mice stood on end, they became more aggressive and scratched their ears more, as well as responding abnormally to sounds; and spi-ders constructed fewer webs (but tidier, more regular webs than after ingesting mescaline). Subsequent tests on apes showed them jumping about their cages as though trying to escape from hallucinations, grasping at empty air, screaming, running backwards, and covering their eyes.

Curiously, these results prompted experimentation on humans. Because Hofmann had described a feeling of depersonalisation, it was thought the drug could be instrumental in the treatment of psychiatric disorders, allowing the patient to look at the illness objectively. Throughout the 1950s and 1960s, it was tested on alcoholics, schizophrenics, narcotic addicts and those considered to have behavioural problems. LSD did not prove to be a miraculous cure, and, as the patients were often unaware that the drug was being administered, the experience must have been terrifying. One woman unsuspectingly received fourteen heavy doses of LSD during two months of psychotherapy. She suffered terrible nightmares in which she imagined she had shrunk and was now so tiny she could not get off her bed. However, the Czechoslovakian psychoanalyst, Stanislav Grof, conducted experiments at the Psychiatric Research Centre in Prague from 1960 to 1967 and came up with some interesting observations. His patients reported religious experiences and phenomena that, according to Grof, accorded with the basic tenets of the major world religions: sacrifice, suffering, agony and death followed by reincarnation and cosmic union. Grof's experimental drug therapy involved mature patients and was rigorously controlled. Other clinicians were not so scrupulous.

Predictably, others who became interested in research into lysergic acid diethylamide included the American Central Intelligence Agency (CIA) and military agencies. During the 1950s they thought LSD might be influential in mind or thought control. Both the aims of the tests and the experiments themselves demonstrate a callous lack of regard for the, often unwitting, subjects. The drug was given to a group of army scientists prior to attempting to alter their basic beliefs. The beliefs

remained unchanged but one specialist in chemical weapons who was secretly given the drug, Dr Frank Olson, became psychotic and, mistakenly believing that he had revealed important secrets while under its influence, jumped to his death from a tenth-floor window. Undeterred, these agencies continued to test the hallucinogen on unsuspecting drug addicts and prostitutes whose beliefs remained firm, despite such brutal tactics.

Given such official irresponsibility, it is surprising how fearful and repressive the establishment turned out to be when, in the 1960s, LSD became an intrinsic part of the youth culture. A major figure in the promotion of the drug was the clinical psychologist, and assistant professor of psychology at Harvard University, Timothy Leary. The taking of LSD, for Leary, constituted a religious experience. His personal conversion to hallucinogens came on a trip to Mexico when he ate sacred *Psilocybe* mushrooms. Together with another Harvard professor of psychology, Richard Alpert, he began promoting the use of psilocybin (a synthetic derivative of *Psilocybe*) and LSD as a means of expanding consciousness or the state of *ecstasis*. In 1963, he set up the International Federation for Internal Freedom (IFIF), in 1963-66 the Castalia Foundation and in 1966 the League for Spiritual Discovery.

Needless to say, the authorities at Harvard were not well-disposed to such aspirations. In 1963, Timothy Leary and Richard Alpert were dismissed from Harvard University on charges that they had, against university policy, involved undergraduates in drug experiments. Before being forced to resign, the pair had given psychedelics to priests, students, psychologists and criminals. They believed that with the correct preparation and with an appropriate guide, an initiate could have a profound spiritual experience. After leaving Harvard, Leary and Alpert continued their work in Mexico until they were asked to leave the country by the Mexican authorities. While in Mexico they encouraged prepared volunteers to plan their

157

own sessions, choosing a particular piece of music, or literature, or object to focus on. Particular use was made of the Tibetan *Book of the Dead*, a manual designed to guide and instruct the deceased through the act of dying and the intermediate period between death and reincarnation. The journey involves encounters with both peaceful *Devatas*, or gods, and terrifying, wrathful *Devatas* who drink blood from skulls. Timothy Leary believed the text could be useful in any state of altered consciousness, and could help to ensure that the experience was a trip to heaven rather than a descent to hell.

Leary defined the true religious experience as "… the ecstatic, uncontrovertibly certain, subjective discovery of answers to seven basic spiritual questions" (Leary, 1968). The seven questions being the Power Question, the Life Question, the Human Being Question, The Awareness Question, the Ego Question, the Emotional Question and the Escape Question. The list covered topics ranging from nuclear physics to psychology. Science, according to Leary, objectively concerned itself with the measurement of energy processes and sequences of energy transformations while religion attempted to answer the same questions subjectively, through direct personal experience.

Through his expulsions from Harvard and Mexico, and also because of his intense proselytising activities and his exhortation to "Turn On, Tune In, and Drop Out" (14 January 1967), Leary received considerable attention in the media. President Richard Nixon thought that he was a corrosive influence on society, and described him dramatically as "the most dangerous man in America". Nevertheless, throughout the 1960s, LSD and related drugs became increasingly popular, influencing a generation that had become disenchanted with the emptiness of materialism and opposed to the politics that had resulted in the Vietnam War.

Richard Alpert finally rejected hallucinogens in favour of a serious study of yoga. His enlightenment came when he found a guru in the foothills of the Himalayas, who swallowed an enormous dose of his "White Lightning" LSD and was not affected by it. Returning to America, as Baba Ram Dass, he wrote a book about his experiences entitled *Remember: Be Here Now*.

Probably because of the marked increase in its use, LSD became a proscribed drug in the mid-1960s, although it was for possession of marijuana, not LSD, that Timothy Leary was arrested in 1965 and 1968. He was imprisoned in 1970 but managed to escape and lived outside the United States for more than two years until he was recaptured in Afghanistan. Released in 1976, he continued to lecture during the 1980s and 1990s but never regained his earlier stature. He died in 1996, having requested that his ashes be sent up into space.

LSD declined in popularity during the 1970s, partly because of a report (subsequently questioned) claiming that it damaged chromosomes, and partly because of a preference for other substances, but it regained some of its popularity during the 1980s and 1990s. In 1971, the United Nations established the Convention on Psychotropic Substances, a set of regulations restricting the use of LSD along with other hallucinogens such as mescaline and psilocybine. Conforming with United Nations requirements, the United Kingdom considers production or possession of LSD an indictable offence. In 1967 A. Hoffer and H. Osmond spoke of the importance of hallucinogens with a revolutionary zeal:

> The use of hallucinogens has been described as one of the major advances of this century … they have had a massive impact upon psychiatry, and may produce marked changes in our society. The violent reaction for and against the hallucinogens suggests that even if these compounds are not universally understood and approved of, they will neither be forgotten nor neglected (Schultes, p. 3).

At the start of the 21st century it is clear that, though psychotropic substances can easily be produced synthetically, they have not radically altered either the social structure or ethical values of technological societies.

See also

Cannabis Sativa L.; Mescaline, Peyote and the San Pedro Cactus

References

Alpert, Richard. 1971. *Remember: Be Here Now.* San Cristobal, New Mexico.

de Ropp, Robert S. ed. 1976. *Drugs and the Mind.* New York: Delacorte Press.

Goodman, Jordan, Paul E. Lovejoy, and Andrew Sherrat (eds). 1995. *Consuming Habits: Drugs in History and Anthropology.* London and New York: Routledge.

Leary, Timothy. 1968. *The Politics of Ecstasy.* New York: Putnam.

Masters, Robert Edward Lee and Jean Houston. 1973. *The Varieties of Psychedelic Experience.* London: Turnstone Books.

Schultes, Richard Evans. 1972. "An Overview of Hallucinogens in the Western Hemisphere". In *Flesh of the Gods: The Ritual Use of Hallucinogens.* ed. Peter T. Furst, p. 3-54. London: George Allen & Unwin Ltd.

Trulson, Michael, E. 1985. *LSD: Visions or Nightmares. The Encyclopedia of Psychoactive Drugs.* ed. Solomon H. Snyder. London: Burke Publishing Company Limited.

Wasson, G. R., A. Hofmann, and C. A. P. Ruck. 1978. *The Road to Eleusis: Unveiling the Secret of the Mysteries.* New York: Harcourt, Brace, Jovanovich.

Marett, Robert R. (1866-1943)

The anthropologist, Robert Marett, published several essays on the topic of taboo. In 1907 he wrote "Is Taboo a Negative Magic" which was reprinted in 1914 in his book *Threshold of Religion* and in 1921 he wrote the entry "Tabu" in the *Encyclopaedia of Religion and Ethics*. Marett's main contention is that taboo is not, as James Frazer proposes, a negative magic but is, instead, a negative *mana*.

Frazer argues that sympathetic magic underlies taboos: the notion that there is a direct correspondence between things which can magically affect one another. For instance, a taboo on a drum is due to its use in simulating the sound of thunder to produce rain, and the tying of a knot is thought capable of similarly "binding" people even if they are far away, or of "tying" the entrance to the womb and in this way preventing childbirth. Marett, while not denying that the theory of sympathetic correspondences may explain certain taboos, finds it cannot have universal application. For instance, among the Arunta a certain danger, such as premature old age, may attend the violation of many different taboos and the forbidding of particular foods to boys before their initiation ceremonies has the social function of reminding them of their lowly social status.

Marett is well aware of the social and political application of taboos – they are used to regulate food consumption and maintain social hierarchies. Taboo itself can be defined as (in the words of R. Taylor) "a religious observance established for political purposes" (Marett, 1921, p. 182). The religious observance concerns the belief in *mana*, a supernatural force that pervades the world and is immanent in sacred objects and divinities. In the Polynesian islands the social influence of a class of priests is proportionate to their *mana*. People or things imbued with *mana* are dangerous to approach because the *mana* can exert a destructive force. They inspire fear. Taboo, says Marett, "stands for the whole mass of such fear-inspired inhibitions in so far as they proceed directly from the religious emotion, as it regulates the social tradition in the relative abeyance of reasoned direction" (Marett, 1921, p. 183). *Mana*, he continues, has both a positive and a negative aspect but from the standpoint of taboo only the negative side is apparent.

Finally, Marett defines two types of society, the modern scientific one that is based on reason and the "primitive" one believing in taboos and driven by emotion.

References

Marett, R.R. 1914. *The Threshold of Religion*. London: Methuen and Co., Ltd.

Marett, R.R. 1921. "Tabu". In *Encyclopaedia of Religion and Ethics*. vol. 12, p. 181-185. London.

Steiner, Franz. 1956. *Taboo*. London: Cohen and West.

Mead, Margaret (1901-78)

The American anthropologist, Margaret Mead, is best known for her books, *Coming of Age in Samoa: A Psychological Study of Primitive Youth for Western Civilisation* (1928), *Growing up in New Guinea* (1930), *Sex and Temperament in Three Primitive Societies* (1935) and *Male and Female: A Study of the Sexes in a Changing World* (1949). Based on her fieldwork, they propose that human nature is determined by culture, not by biology. In 1937 she wrote an article "Tabu" for *The Encyclopaedia of the Social Sciences* (502-505). In it she summarises the essential elements of Polynesian taboo:

a) any prohibitions enforced automatically, that is the punishment followed inevitably without external mediation; b) or the edicts of chiefs and priests, which are supported either by the superior mana of these individuals or by the temporal or spiritual forces which they have under their control; c) prohibitions against theft or trespass for which the sanctions are specific magic formulae; d) religious prohibitions which are referred in native theology to the decree of some deity or spirit; e) any prohibitions which carry no penalties beyond the anxiety and embarrassment arising from a breach of strongly entrenched custom (Steiner, p. 143).

Mead argues that only the first clause, namely that a transgression incurs automatic penalty without outside intervention, defines taboo in the strict sense of the word. By her reasoning, the Maori belief that the accidental eating of the chief's food will cause death is a true taboo while the Hawaiian enforcement of taboos by external forces (including capital punishment) evinces a degradation.

Franz Steiner, in his book, *Taboo*, shows that the divergences of the Maori and Hawaiian concepts were due to differing political structures. Among the Maori, the chief represented both secular and religious authority, and was sacrosanct. In Hawaii, kingship and priesthood were separated and the power of taboo was a source of contention between the followers of each party. Steiner also points out the limitations and inconsistencies in Mead's narrow definition of the term "taboo". Such discrete categories as she proposes rarely exist and taboos often combine many elements.

References

Mead, Margaret. 1928. *Coming of Age in Samoa: A Psychological Study of Primitive Youth for Western Civilisation*. New York: Morrow.

Mead, Margaret. 1930. *Growing up in New Guinea*. New York: Morrow.

Mead, Margaret. 1935. *Sex and Temperament in Three Primitive Societies*. London: Routledge.

Mead, Margaret. 1937. "Tabu". In *The Encyclopaedia of the Social Sciences*, p. 502-505. London: Macmillan.

Mead, Margaret. 1949. *Male and Female: A Study of the Sexes in a Changing World*. New York: Morrow.

Steiner, Franz. 1956. *Taboo*. London: Cohen and West.

Menstruation

Menstrual taboos, or, to be precise, rules governing conduct while a woman is menstruating, are extremely widespread although not, as is sometimes suggested, universal. The Rungus of Borneo, for instance, have no menstrual taboos (Appell, p. 110-111) and different societies implement different measures. The most common taboos include the avoidance of the menstrual blood itself, perceived to be dangerous and polluting, the isolation of menstruating women in "menstrual huts", the prohibition of sexual relations with a woman during this period, the banning of women from the hearth and food preparation, and general restrictions on the movement of women and the work that they are permitted to do.

While these rules have often been interpreted as a denial of women's equality, more recent research has shown that, far from oppressing women, in certain societies the taboos may actually serve female interests.

The dangers perceived to adhere to menstrual blood have been cited by Pliny the Elder in his *Historia Naturalis* (77 CE).

> A menstruating woman, if she approached a vessel of wine, would turn it sour; she would cause corn to wither, buds to shrivel, fruit to fall from trees, mirrors to dim, bees to die in the hive, and iron and steel to rust.

Even more lethal are the powers attached to menstrual blood by the Mae Enga of the Central Highlands of New Guinea:

> They believe that contact with it or with a menstruating woman will, in the absence of appropriate counter-magic, sicken a man and cause persistent vomiting, "kill" his blood so that it turns black, corrupt his vital juices so that his skin darkens and hangs in folds as his flesh wastes, permanently dull his wits, and eventually lead to a slow decline and death (Meggitt M., in Douglas. [1966] 1984, p. 147).

The prevalence of such beliefs have led physicians and anthropologists to posit the existence of a toxicity in menstrual blood; this would provide a "practical" explanation for its avoidance. The theory that bacterial "menotoxins" reside in the blood was proposed in 1920 by the physician, Bela Schick, and introduced into anthropological thought by the anthropologist, Ashley Montague. Montague, in an article written in 1940, argued that the chemical components of menstrual blood might indeed cause wine to sour, plants to wither and bread to fall (Buckley and Gottlieb, p. 19). It has also been suggested that the common taboo against menstrual sex may be a measure to protect men from adverse medical consequences. There are problems with this hypothesis. Firstly, it fails to account for many common restrictions placed upon women, such as the injunction against touching tools or weapons, or approaching sacred places. More pertinently, there is no proof that menotoxins exist: menstrual blood is different from venal blood in that it does not clot but there is no conclusive evidence of its toxicity. Moreover, many accounts that describe its pernicious nature also mention the blood's positive qualities. Pliny notes its medical use to treat gout, goitre, haemorrhages, inflammations of the salivary glands, hydrophobia, worms and headache and in Morocco it has been used in dressings for open sores and infants' eye diseases (Buckley and Gottlieb, p. 21).

Another hypothesis that is difficult to substantiate proposes an olfactory reason for the taboo; namely, that the scent of menstrual blood on humans will cause certain animals to attack, while others will be repelled by it (Buckley and Gottlieb, p. 22). Whilst this theory would explain the injunction against women handling weapons and hunting implements, and even their avoidance of men lest they impart lingering odours, it does not explain why they should refrain from cooking the meat, once caught, nor why, in many societies, they must avoid altars, or in the Greek Orthodox Church, be denied the Eucharist, if they are menstruating.

Rather than seeking an explanation for the taboos in some intrinsic quality of the menstrual blood itself, it is more fruitful to examine the symbolic, religious, social and psychological foundations for the ritual restrictions. Certainly, magical or potent qualities have been attributed to the blood but these are culturally variable and even within a single society the blood may be judged both pernicious and beneficial. For instance, the anthropologist, R. S. Rattray, observes that among the Asante of Ghana, the blood is considered to be a dangerous pollutant, and the breaking of certain menstrual taboos by the women can incur instant death, but the Asante priests can create fetishes (*kunkuma*) from brooms defiled with menstrual blood which serve as powerful, protective charms (Buckley and Gottlieb, p. 37). Moreover, menarche (the onset of menstruation) is celebrated with a public ritual in which the menarcheal girl is honoured with gifts, singing and dancing.

Traditionally, sociological and anthropological studies have focused on the negative qualities of female sexuality implied by taboos which appear to restrict women's activities. Psychoanalysts have tended to approach the subject from a similar anthropocentric viewpoint. Sigmund Freud, in a footnote in *Civilization and Its Discontents* (1930), proposes that the taboos originate in an "organic repression" of the natural male attraction which men feel for women while they are menstruating. Once man began to walk on two legs, his genitals became exposed, and therefore a source of shame, and any olfactory pleasure he had previously derived from intercourse, such as menstrual odour, was proscribed (Delaney, Lupton, Toth, p. 73). William Stephens adopts a different theory of Freud: that of male castration anxiety. In *The Oedipus complex: Cross-cultural evidence*, Stephens suggests that the sight of blood issuing from female genitals can cause a susceptible male to imagine that the woman has been castrated and to fear a similar fate. As the mutilation of the male is an intrinsic component of the "Oedipus complex", one would expect stringent menstrual taboos to coincide with strict paternal authority (Buckley and Gottlieb, p. 16). However, there is no consensus that the "Oedipus complex" actually exists in non-western societies and Stephens' correlations are far from conclusive. Another psychoanalyst, Bruno Bettelheim, sees male envy of female reproductive powers as the motivation for the menstrual taboos that protect the male from a perceived menstrual threat. To alleviate this progenitive deficiency, male circumcision rites are inaugurated which, by shedding genital blood, imitate the bleeding of women at menstruation and childbirth and thereby simulate female fertility. The connection is implicit in an Australian creation myth which tells of a semi-human bird, *Jurijurilia*, that throws a boomerang. On its return, the boomerang both circumcises the bird and cuts the vulvas of its wives, causing the first menstruation. Just as the women hide their menstrual rags from men, so Australian rites of circumcision, and the more bloody subincision, are hidden from women.

Bettelheim's hypothesis substitutes male envy for the male fear propounded by Freudians, but in neither case is the female, the one who actually menstruates, considered instrumental in the formation of taboos. Anthropologists and sociologists have similarly tended to view women as passive – the victims of male oppression. Frank W. Young thinks that the restrictions are calculated to reduce the status of women. In a work with Albert Bacdayan, he suggests that a weak solidarity among men combined with a fear of females leads to the imposition of rules that assure male dominance. This is often, no doubt, the case. Carol Delaney has observed how, in Turkish village society, women's bodies are seen as not only the source of reproduction but also the object of male fear and disgust. Menstrual blood epitomises the physical nature of woman which must be circumscribed by taboos so that men, aligned with the immutable spirituality of Islamic salvation, can feel secure (Delaney, p. 75-93). However, the ideas of Young and Bacdayan are not universally applicable. In the first place, the same dynamics are not operative in every society and not all taboos are of the same class. Moreover, menstrual taboos must be seen in the context of other restrictions placed on both women and men within a particular community. And, as the British anthropologist, James G. Frazer, already pointed out in *The Golden Bough* in 1890, the taboos can exist not merely to protect men from the menstruating woman but to protect the woman herself who is particularly vulnerable at this time:

> Whether enveloped in her hammock
> and slung up to the roof, as in South

America, or raised above the ground in a dark and narrow cage, as in new Ireland ... being cut off from both the earth and from the sun, she can poison neither of these great sources of life by her deadly contagion ... But the precautions thus taken to isolate or insulate the girl are dictated by a regard for her own safety as well as for the safety of others. For it is thought that she herself would suffer if she were to neglect the prescribed regimen ... In short, the girl is viewed as charged with a powerful force which, if not kept within bounds, may prove destructive both to herself and to all with whom she comes in contact (Frazer, p. 794-795).

More recently, in 1980, Deborah Winslow observed menstrual taboos among Catholics and Buddhists in Sri Lanka and found that although Buddhists viewed women as a threat to cosmos and society, Catholics saw women as vulnerable; threatened by cosmos and society (Buckley and Gottlieb, p. 10). Even the seclusion of women in "menstrual huts", often cited as a prime example of the subjugation of women, has been reassessed. Such huts can offer sanctuary, a respite from hard physical labour and the chance to establish female solidarity. More subversively, studies of the Djuka of Suriname, the Warao of Venezuela and the Kaska of western Canada have revealed how menstrual seclusion can give women an opportunity for sexual freedom and illicit love affairs (showing a scant regard not only for marital fidelity but also for the menstrual taboos themselves). In rural Portugal, also, women have manipulated stringent menstrual taboos for their own ends – in this case to maintain their positions of power within the household and to establish and control exchange networks between households, as they vie against each other for ascendancy (Lawrence, 1988, p. 117-136).

The common injunction against sexual relations at this time, so emphatically condemned in *Leviticus* 15: 19-33, is still observed by Orthodox Jewish women (who must be purified from the blood pollution by a ritual *mikvah* bath) although the view of menstruating women as polluted and evil has been challenged by some American Jewish women (Kaufman, 1991), and the temporary freedom during this time has been welcomed.

A more subtle analysis of menstrual taboos is achieved with the sociosymbolic approach of anthropologist, Mary Douglas. In *Purity and Danger* (1966), she argues that what is considered dirty, or polluting, is matter that is in the "wrong" place: a hair in the bath or shoes on the table. Things which are "out of place" defy classification and upset the symbolic system we erect to order existence. Moreover, as the physical body is a symbol of human society, the dangers of breaching the body's borders (through excreta such as faeces, spittle or menstrual blood) reflect the dangers of transgressing social and moral norms. Menstrual blood is a particular anomaly in that it flows even though there is no physical injury, and it issues from women whereas most forms of bloodletting, whether through hunting or warfare, are the preserve of the male. Mary Douglas later modified her views, concluding that things that cross boundaries are powerful but not necessarily polluting.

Just as anomalies are not always polluting, so menstrual taboos are not always enforced with equal vigour: if there is tension between the sexes, for instance because of intense competition, the women are seen as polluting and the taboos are rigorously applied as a means of differentiating male and female realms and establishing male dominance. If, on the other hand, there is no evident source of friction, there is no need for these markers. The Mae Enga of the Central Highlands of New Guinea, studied by Mervyn J. Meggitt, are exogamous and take wives from rival clans with whom they compete and fight. The wives thus represent an alien clan and are perceived as threatening (Douglas, [1966] 1984, p. 146-148). Among the Hadza hunters in Tanzania hostility between the sexes is intense, and there is a low level of labour division between the sexes, both of which contribute to male insecurity (Douglas, [1970] 1978, p. 132-134). This male fear of females explains, says Douglas, the stringent sexual abstinence enforced on the Mae Enga and Hazda women during menstruation (although in the case of the Hazda the husband, too, refrains from his usual tasks and is segregated – a means of affirming the marital role in a society in which the sexes lead independent existences). By contrast, Colin Turnbull found that the Mbuti pygmies of the Ituri forest in Africa manifest no obvious sexual antagonism. Many tasks, such as the erection of huts and hunting, are shared and the men consequently do not see the women as polluting and impose no sanctions (Douglas, [1970] 1978, p. 132-133).

The pollution theory of Mary Douglas has attracted considerable support. Laura Appell applies the term "gender symmetry" to the equable relationship and equal status between the sexes among the Rungus of Borneo, a people with no form of social separation of menstruating women (Appel, p. 94-112). However, she modifies the theory, arguing that the Rungus view menstruation as neither pure nor impure, merely as a manifestation of sexuality. As sexuality is seen as private and embarrassing, attention is not directed towards it and menstruation and menstrual blood are socially ignored. Another researcher to adopt Douglas' theory is Marjorie Mandelstam Balzer. Balzer sees evidence of the employment of menstrual taboos to subjugate women among the Siberian Khanty. Interestingly, although the Khanty men regard women as polluting they also acknowledge an increase in women's ritual and spiritual power with age (Buckley and Gottlieb, p. 29). Others have argued that women are seen as polluting in societies in which men are dependent on them, whether for social, economic or political prestige, and among people who view their environment as threatening and who project this fear onto women's bodies.

Influential though they remain, the theories of Mary Douglas have been criticised by other ethnographers. Thomas Buckley and Alma Gottlieb draw particular attention to the male bias of many studies: often it is the men who are interviewed and who define women as polluting and the views of women themselves are ignored. This has been aggravated by the emphasis on areas of male domination such as politics, economics and religion when defining social structures whilst the (often more informal) female spheres of control are ignored. As mentioned earlier, women's attitudes often differ considerably from those of their menfolk. A study conducted recently in Taiwan shows that some Taiwanese women see their periods as a source of health, not pollution as the men maintain (Furth and Ch'en, p. 27-48) and Yurok women in California have described how, far from being polluting, they are at the height of their spiritual powers at this time (Gottlieb, p. 187-209).

Besides, often the primary aim of the prohibitions is not the separation of male and female but something else altogether. The curiosity of anthropologist, Alma Gottlieb, was aroused by the taboos of the Beng of Ivory Coast. Though sex is not prohibited during menstruation, it is absolutely forbidden for a woman to enter the forest, other than to defecate, at this time (Gottlieb, p. 55-74). A woman who violated this injunction, and worked in her husband's yam field in the forest, saw all the yam plants in that field die and she herself developed stomach cramps. She consulted a diviner who accused her of having been in the forest while menstruating and having thereby polluted the Earth. But it is not only the woman's blood that spoils the crops and taints the forest; sexual intercourse is also forbidden in the woods and can lead to death and misfortune. The immediate punishment for such an act is drastic:

> [The couple] must return to the spot where they copulated. There they repeat the act in front of a large,

jeering audience of middle-aged and old men who brandish sticks and fire-brands with which, respectively, they beat and burn the couple during the act of sex. This over, a cow is sacrificed by the Master of the Earth. The couple's clothes are then taken from them and later given to the king of their region, and they are given new clothes to wear back to the village (Gottlieb, p. 63).

Gottlieb concludes that the aim of the restrictions is to separate human fertility, of which menstrual blood is a symbol, from the natural fertility of the forest and fields and the supernatural fertility of the spirit realm.

Among the Kel Ewey Tuareg in the Aïr Mountain region of north-eastern Niger, Susan J. Rasmussen has revealed another motivation for the menstrual taboos on women; namely, the preservation of class distinctions between nobility and peasants (Rasmussen, p. 751-769). Although the Tuareg are Muslims, Rasmussen argues, it is not primarily Islamic obligations that demand adherence to ritual restrictions. For certain injunctions that are placed on women in Muslim societies are here transferred to men. For instance, men, in this society, are the ones who wear the face-veils. These veils are most common among the pastoral nobility who are vulnerable to social pollution, the "evil eye" and "evil mouth" of the smiths and the former servile gardeners, who are motivated by jealously and inequality. Veils are "distancing devices" just as the menstrual taboos, most stringently observed by women of the nobility, allow these women to maintain a safe "social distance" from those of other classes. The nobles are traditionally pastoral nomads and they still retain certain privileges: they own most of the camels, control the caravan trade, collect a tithe of the harvest from the oasis gardens of former slaves and claim hospitality rights. By examining an entire range of Tuareg customs and beliefs, from marital practices to spirit possession, Rasmussen reveals

how ritual restrictions, including both the face-veil and the injunctions during menstruation, protect the interests of nobles by creating a symbolic distance between themselves and non-nobles while also strengthening bonds which favour nomadism, such as matrilocal relationships, to counterbalance the influences of patriliny and a sedentary lifestyle.

While most researchers in recent decades have focused their attention on individual societies, a broader and more hypothetical approach is that of anthropologist Chris Knight in *Blood Relations*. He sees menstrual taboos as crucial to the development of human culture and initiated by women to ensure access to the meat hunted by men. Drawing on such disciplines as sociobiology and archaeology, he approaches the question as to why, when a non-human female primate is in oestrus obvious signals are given to the male, such as a certain scent, to indicate fertility and availability, and there is little bleeding during menstruation, in humans the pattern is reversed: no overt sign is given at ovulation but menstruation is pronounced. In Knight's terms, the woman is indicating "no, I am not available" instead of "yes, I am". This, he thinks, goes back to a revolution among humans in the Upper Paleolithic in the Rift Valley in East Africa which, by about 43,000 BCE, had spread from there around the world. Initially, Knight speculates, a group of women inaugurated a sex-strike, denying their men conjugal relations unless they provided them with meat. This was integrated into the menstrual and lunar cycles. Synchronising their menstrual patterns, all the women bled during the dark phase of the moon and stayed at this time, and during the period of the waxing moon, with their kinship group. The men were denied access: sex with a menstruating woman became taboo. During the waxing moon, the males hunted, secure in the knowledge that their women could remain in the base camp, unmolested by other men – the women's own relatives being subject to the blood ban. At full moon, the hunters would return to camp with the meat; unable to eat it raw (again forbidden by the blood signal), they passed it to the women, who cooked it and, now ovulating, conferred their sexual favours.

With his theory, Chris Knight eloquently explains the taboos on menstrual sex, incest and the "own kill" injunction, according to which a hunter must not eat his own kill but must give it away, often to his in-laws. For evidence he draws on myths and cave-art: the rainbow snake extends back as a rock-art motif in northern Australia for 7,000 to 9,000 years and appears in many extant Aboriginal myths. When analysed, the myths show the snake to be a metaphor for menstrual solidarity, culminating in the monthly sex-strike, on the basis of which, says Knight, human symbolic culture emerged. Theories of menstrual synchrony and suppression are based on the scientific findings of Martha McClintock in 1971 and include the ideas of Thomas Buckley, who proposes that synchronised menstruation among the Yurok Indian women of California allows them to dictate the temporal structure of communal life, and Frederick Lamp, who sees menstrual and ovulatory synchrony among the Temne of Sierra Leone as a useful means of ensuring that ritual adultery does not produce illegitimate children (the rhythm method of contraception) (Lamp, p. 210-231). But, as Lamp himself acknowledges, amenorrhoea (the absence of periods) is widespread in non-industrial societies due to a combination of late menarche, early menopause, frequent pregnancies with extended nursing periods, vigorous exercise, malnourishment and disease. It therefore becomes extremely difficult to find evidence of this communal bleeding in non-western societies, however elegant the theory.

In modern Western society, menstruation remains a controversial topic, with feminists undecided as to whether it is indeed the curse bestowed upon Eve for desiring forbidden fruit or the magic elixir conferring power on the female sex (or neither). An American artist,

Judy Chicago, has attempted to break the taboos still surrounding menstruation by graphically depicting a woman removing a tampon and creating a "Menstruation Bathroom", a room described in her autobiography, *Through the Flower: My Struggle as a Woman Artist*: "under a shelf full of all the paraphernalia with which a culture 'cleans up' menstruation, was a garbage can filled with the unmistakable marks of our animality". Stated like this, the room seems to be an assault on our sanitised culture, rather than on blood pollution per se, but Judy Chicago does mention the fascination this presentation held for men: a glimpse into forbidden realms. The writer, Erica Jong, ever desiring to shock, introduces the theme of eating menstrual blood in her book *Parachutes and Kisses*. The Tampon Taster is a bizarre, comic figure, but the practice of imbibing menstrual blood is not so new: among the Mae Enga menstrual blood introduced into a man's food quickly kills him – a sure revenge for infidelity – while others, including the Beng of Ivory Coast, the Roman writer, Pliny the Elder, medieval farmers in south-west France and whites in the United States have considered it a potent love potion – one taste is sufficient for eternal fidelity.

See also

Douglas, Mary; Pollution

References

Appell, Laura W. R., 1988. "Menstruation among the Rungus of Borneo: An Unmarked Category". In *Blood Magic: The Anthropology of Menstruation*. ed. Thomas Buckley and Alma Gottlieb, p. 94-112. Berkeley; Los Angeles: University of California Press.

Bettelheim, Bruno. 1954. *Symbolic wounds: Puberty rites and the envious male*. New York: Free Press.

Buckley, Thomas and Alma Gottlieb. 1988. "A Critical Appraisal of Theories of Menstrual Symbolism". In *Blood Magic: The Anthropology of Menstruation*. ed. Thomas Buckley and Alma Gottlieb, p. 3-50. Berkeley; Los Angeles: University of California Press.

Buckley, Thomas. 1988. "Menstruation and the Power of Yurok Women". In *Blood Magic: The*

Anthropology of Menstruation. ed. Thomas Buckley and Alma Gottlieb, p. 187-209. Berkeley; Los Angeles: University of California Press.

Carol Delaney. 1988. "Mortal Flow: Menstruation in Turkish Village Society". In *Blood Magic: The Anthropology of Menstruation.* ed. Thomas Buckley and Alma Gottlieb, p. 75-93. Berkeley; Los Angeles: University of California Press.

Chicago, Judy. 1982. *Through the Flower: My Struggle as a Woman Artist.* London; New York: Women's Press.

Delaney, Janice, Mary Jane Lupton and Emily Toth. [1976] 1988. *The Curse: A Cultural History of Menstruation.* Urbana, Illinois; Chicago, Illinois: University of Illinois Press.

Douglas, Mary. [1975] 1979. "Couvade and Menstruation". In *Implicit Meanings: Essays in Anthropology,* p. 60-72. London: Routledge and Kegan Paul.

Douglas, Mary. [1966] 1984. *Purity and Danger: An Analysis of the Concepts of Pollution and Taboo.* London: Ark, Routledge and Kegan Paul.

Douglas, Mary. [1970] 1978. *Natural Symbols: Explorations in Cosmology.* Harmondsworth, Middlesex: Penguin Educational.

Frazer, James Georges. [1922] 1971. 794-795. *The Golden Bough: A Study in Magic and Religion.* London: The Macmillan Press. Abridged Edition.

Furth, Charlotte and Shu-yueh Ch'en. 1992. "Chinese medicine and the anthropology of menstruation in contemporary Taiwan". *Medical Anthropology Quarterly,* no. 6(1), p. 27-48.

Gottlieb, Alma. 1988. "Menstrual Cosmology among the Beng of Ivory Coast". In *Blood Magic. The Anthropology of Menstruation.* ed. Thomas Buckley and Alma Gottlieb, p. 55-74. Berkeley; Los Angeles: University of California Press.

Kaufman, Debra R. 1991. *Rachel's Daughters: newly Orthodox Jewish women.* New Brunswick, New Jersey: Rutgers University Press.

Knight, Chris. 1991. *Blood Relations: Menstruation and the Origins of Culture.* New Haven, Connecticut; London: Yale University Press.

Lamp, Frederick. 1988. "Heavenly Bodies: Menses, Moon, and Rituals of License among the Temne of Sierra Leone". In *Blood Magic: The Anthropology of Menstruation.* ed. Thomas Buckley and Alma Gottlieb, p. 210-231. Berkeley; Los Angeles: University of California Press.

Lawrence, Denise L. 1988. "Menstrual Politics: Woman and Pigs in Rural Portugal". In *Blood Magic. The Anthropology of Menstruation.* ed. Thomas

Buckley and Alma Gottlieb, p. 117-136. Berkeley; Los Angeles: University of California Press.

Laws, Katherine Sophie. 1990. *Issues of Blood: The Politics of Menstruation.* Basingstoke; London: The Macmillan Press Ltd.

Rasmussen, Susan J. 1991. "Lack of prayer: ritual restrictions, social experience, and the anthropology of menstruation among the Tuareg". *American Anthropologist,* no. 18, p. 751-769.

William Stephens. 1962. *The Oedipus complex: Cross-cultural evidence.* New York: Free Press.

Young, Frank W. and Albert Bacdayan. 1965. "Menstrual taboos and social rigidity". *Ethnology,* no. 4, p. 225-240.

Mescaline, Peyote and the San Pedro Cactus

Mescaline is the principal alkaloid of the peyote cactus, *Lophophora Williamsii,* of Mexico, which contains around thirty alkaloids. It is also found in the *Trichocereus Pachanoi* or San Pedro cactus of the Andes in South America. In 1971, along with other hallucinogens including LSD and psilocybine, mescaline became a controlled substance under legislation passed during the United Nations Convention on Psychotropic Substances. The reason for the legislation at that particular time was the increased use of hallucinogens by the younger generation.

A famous account of the effects of mescaline is given by the British writer Aldous Huxley in *The Doors of Perception,* a book that was to prove immensely popular with the underground movements of the 1950s and 1960s. It was published in 1954, one year after Huxley swallowed four-tenths of a gram dissolved in water and sat down to await the results. After one-and-a-half hours he found himself staring at a glass vase:

> The vase contained only three flowers – a full-blown Belle of Portugal rose, shell pink with a hint at every petal's base of a hotter, flamier hue; a large magenta and cream-coloured carnation; and,

pale purple at the end of its broken stalk, the bold, heraldic blossom of an iris (Huxley, p. 7).

For Huxley the visual transmutation of the flowers that followed was less important than his personal sense of revelation; he had opened the doors of perception, and was capable now of apprehending those truths which the conscious mind, in its struggle for survival, filtered from view:

> I was seeing what Adam had seen on the morning of his creation ... *Istigkeit* – the Being of Platonic philosophy ... a bunch of flowers shining with their own inner light and all but quivering under the pressure of the significance with which they were charged ... what rose and iris and carnation so intensely signified was nothing more, and nothing less, than what they were – a transience that was yet eternal life, a perpetual perishing that was at the same time pure Being, a bundle of minute, unique particulars in which, by some unspeakable and yet self-evident paradox, was to be seen the divine source of all existence (Huxley, p. 7).

The experience is akin to that of the poet and mystic, William Blake, who saw "a World in a Grain of Sand" (*Auguries of Innocence*). In fact, the title of Aldous Huxley's book is taken from Blake's *Marriage of Heaven and Hell*: "If the Doors of Perception were cleansed, everything would appear to man as it really is, infinite. For man has closed himself up, till he sees all things through narrow chinks of his cavern".

Despite the mystical revelations, which call to mind Taoist, Zen Buddhist and Hindu teachings, Huxley did not consider mescaline to be suitable for everyone. If taken by someone who had recently suffered from jaundice or who suffered from periodic depressions or anxiety, it could induce nightmares, or a state of schizophrenia. A schizophrenic, he thought, was like a person permanently under the influence of mescaline, unable to distance himself

from a world of burning intensity, which, because he was not holy enough to comprehend, he interpreted as a sign of human or cosmic malevolence. His fear would provoke drastic reactions ranging from murderous violence to catatonia or psychological suicide.

Aldous also speaks of peyote, taken communally among tribes of the Native American Church in areas ranging from Texas to Wisconsin. The Native American Church is a synthesis of Christianity and traditional indigenous beliefs and practices. In the rituals, which resemble the Early Christian Agape, or Love-Feast, peyote replaces the sacramental bread and wine. Peyotism among the Menomini Native Americans of Wisconsin was studied by the anthropologist and convert to the peyote church, J. S. Slotkin. He marked how Divinity, for the Menomini, is in the form of a Great Spirit who created the Universe and controls destiny. To help mankind, the Great Spirit invested peyote with some of his supernatural power so that, by eating the cactus in a ritually prescribed manner, the Menomini can partake of the Divine, just as the traditional Christian ingests the body of Christ at Holy Communion. In 1972, there were an estimated 250,000 Native Americans practising this religion which advocates abstention from alcohol and brotherly love.

The earliest recorded use of peyote in the United States dates from 1760 in Texas. Around 1880 the Kiowa and Comanche tribes began to observe a peyote ceremony that differed essentially from the original peyote rituals of north-western Mexico. By the late 1920s, strong hostility from Christian missionary groups forced the cult to integrate with the legally constituted Native American Church. Peyotism edged out other Native American movements such as the Ghost Dance religion which arose in 1870 and ended tragically with the massacre of 300 unarmed Sioux at Wounded Knee Creek in 1890.

In Mexico, peyote was first described by the Spaniard, Francisco Hernández, in 1651. He called it *Peyotl zacatecensis*:

The root is nearly medium size, sending forth no branches or leaves above the ground … This root … causes those devouring it to foresee and predict things … or to discern who has stolen from them some utensil or anything else; and other things of like nature … On which account, this root scarcely issues forth, as if it did not wish to harm those who discover it and eat it (Schultes, p. 11).

This considerate, spineless, psychotropic cactus was more seriously discussed by the Spanish chronicler, Fr. Bernardino de Sahagún, in the mid-16th century in his *History of the Things of New Spain* (*Florentine Codex*). Sahagún suggested that peyote, known to the Aztecs as *peyotl* and to the Huichol as *híkuri*, had been known to the Toltecas and Chichimecas for many hundreds of years. The Chichimecas used it to gain fortitude for fighting, to enable themselves to transcend hunger and thirst, to protect themselves from danger and to confer visions. The description given by Sahagún of the peyote ritual of the northern desert hunters recalls the present-day peyote hunt in which bands of Huichol gather in the desert, 300 miles north-east of their homeland in the Sierra Madre mountains of western Mexico, to collect the cactus

The indigenous population of the Sierra Madre Occidental used peyote ritually in various contexts and although it was not native to the region, Jesuit and Franciscan clergy of the 17th and 18th centuries attest to its importance in western Mexico. P. José Ortega denounced it as a "diabolical root" and the Jesuit writer, Fr. Antonio Arias de Saavedra, reported that the Cora of the Sierra of Nayarit sealed their pacts with their spirits by drinking infusions of peyote. P. Andrés Estrada Flores described the ceremonial drinking of peyote for medicinal reasons and spoke of the "horrible visions" they saw when intoxicated and Andrés Pérez de Ribas, writing at the beginning of the 17th century, said that despite its medicinal

applications, peyote was banned because it was so inextricably linked to "heathen rituals and superstitions" and used for diabolical invocations. Peyote was in fact prohibited throughout Mexico in 1720 and the rituals had to be conducted in secret, but today it is freely available in the marketplace (Furst, p. 142-145). Despite sustained efforts, conversion of the Huichol to Christianity proved difficult and even today many of their rituals remain intact.

The most important ritual events are the peyote pilgrimages, or hunts, in which the *híkuri*, as it is called by the Huichol, is envisaged in the form of a deer (Deer-Peyote) and hunted with bow (bow drum) and arrows. The pilgrimages take place between the end of the rainy season in October to November and the beginning of spring. They commemorate the primordial quest of the gods for peyote. In the beginning, relates the myth, the gods gathered together in the first *túki*, the Huichol sanctuary constructed by *Tatewarí* (literally, "our Grandfather", the deified fire, often referred to as *Mará'akáme*, the First Shaman), the first of the Huichol shamans. The gods were in a sorry state: diseased, with the rain-givers unable to bestow rain and the masters of animals unable to find prey. They were called there by the *Mará'akáme* (singing shaman of the *túki*), *Tatewarí. Tatewarí* told them they were ill because they had failed to visit *Wirikúta*, sacred home of the peyote or *hikurí* and the place where the sun was born. They must make this journey but there were many taboos that they must not break on the way. They must not eat salt or chilli and they must fast, only nibbling dried tortillas and drinking the odd drop of water.

The present-day peyote hunt of the Huichol repeats the mythical journey and involves similar prohibitions. Besides, because the journey is such a sacred event, each participant must be given a new name and the names of things are reversed. The anthropologists, Barbara Myerhoff and Peter Furst, have participated in peyote pilgrimages. Myerhoff recalls how

Ramón, the *mará'akáme* of the trip, explains the naming and reversals:

> On the peyote hunt, we change the names of things because when we cross over there, into *Wirikúta*, things are so sacred that all is reversed … the peyote is very sacred, very sacred. And the journey … is very sacred. That is why it is reversed. Therefore, when we see a dog, it is a cat, or it is a coyote … To say, "Let us stay here," means to go, "Let us go" … "I am going to urinate" means "I am going to drink water", … the testicles, they are called avocados. And the penis, that is his nose" (Myerhoff, p. 148, 186-188).

Moreover, the camper is a "burro" which will stop if it runs out of "tequila". Ramón claimed that he dreamed new names for things each year, which would serve to disguise the sacred places, or preserve the common taboo against naming the sacred. Reversal is also a logical means of transition from the secular to the sacred, or from the commonplace to the fantastic; in Lewis Carroll's story, Alice notices that not just writing, but everything, is reversed in the Land of the Looking Glass. It may also indicate the change of status of each participant upon entering the hallowed land.

As the journey is a return to innocence, to the purity that existed at the beginning of time, all the peyote pilgrims must be cleansed of their sexual transgressions. Seated around a ceremonial fire, one by one, they must reveal the names of their illicit lovers; each name is knotted into a cord of sisal fibre. If anyone fails to disclose a name, the sacred quest will fail, or the person will fall a prey to sorcery, or suffer terrible hallucinations or die. However, sometimes, if a Huichol has had a long life with numerous lovers, one large knot will suffice for many names. After they have disclosed the names, Ramón brushes the pilgrim down with his plumed arrow and motions as if to shake the trespasses into the purifying fire. The peyote seekers must also cleanse themselves at the side

of the fire and as a final precaution, the entire rope is thrown into the flames and burned. From this moment on, the pilgrims are no longer mortal, and become known to each other as the Ancient Ones.

Later, another cord is passed round and knotted; this unites the company – at the end of the trip it will be untied. At each stage in the hunt, there are prescriptions and prohibitions. New initiates to the journey must be blindfolded before passing through the perilous Gateway of Clashing Clouds into the sacred territory, because, as Peter Furst reports, they could be:

> easily blinded by the glare emanating from the sacred country on the other side of the clouds and especially vulnerable to whirlwinds and other dangers which malevolent sorcerers cast in the way of híkuru seekers. Blindfolded they would be safe, but they would have to proceed with caution (Furst, p. 163).

Their blindfolds are removed when they reach *Tatéi Matiniéri*, Where Our Mother Dwells. First, though, they must be ritually washed with the fertilising water drawn from water-holes at this spot. This enables them to observe the mountains on the eastern horizon where the peyote is to be found.

The cactus grows in the Colonial Spanish mining district of Real de Catorce, in the high desert of north-western San Luis Potosí, known to the Huichol as *Wirikúta*, the "Patio of the Grandfathers". The deer-peyote, also known as maize, is carefully stalked. Furst describes how Ramón suddenly stops and points, "There, there, the Deer". He is pointing to a cluster of flat-topped *Lophophora Williamsii*, barely visible above the ground. Ramón carefully creeps up on tip-toe so as not to frighten it away, then shoots an arrow which lands just to the east of the nearest plant. Two more arrows are fired, and finally Ramón "kills" the *híkuri*, sticking a ceremonial arrow with hawk feathers into the ground so that the plant is hemmed in by an arrow in each of the world quarters. The pilgrims cry for the "dying" Elder Brother. Before they leave, having filled their baskets with peyote and savoured its delights, they propitiate the plants, leaving sacred offerings of tobacco in the empty holes from which the peyote has been taken. Though it is a paradise, the peyote hunters must leave as soon as they have gathered sufficient *híkuri* for the year ahead. If they stay, they are in great peril – it is possible to lose one's soul, especially if this is the first visit. The communal bliss that they have enjoyed on the pilgrimage must be followed by a return to secular, social life.

While north of Mexico, in the United States, it is normally the dried top, or crown – the "mescal button" – that is swallowed, in Mexico the plants are collected where they grow and may be eaten fresh. The *Trichocereus pachanoi*, or San Pedro cactus of northern Peru, used today for folk-healing, is sliced, placed in water, and boiled for seven hours. It is a relatively thin, columnar cactus of the *Cereus* family and has been depicted together with the sacred jaguar and spirit beings on ceremonial pottery of the Chavín period (1200-600 BCE). The cactus is a diuretic, and is also used as an antiseptic and for healing and witchcraft. The folk healer, the *curandero*, or *brujo* (sorcerer), invokes the power of his hallucinogenic plants, supplemented by liquid tobacco and Christian symbols such as images of saints. Each *curandero* has a mesa, a kind of altar, with artifacts connected with the forces of evil and sorcery on one side (such as fragments of ancient ceramics, a deer foot, a triton shell) and those connected with good (religious icons, a glass, a dagger, shells, tobacco and a five-gallon can of San Pedro infusion) on the other. In between is a neutral zone containing a stone symbolising the sea and winds and a crystal "mirror".

Curing sessions begin with prayers, invocations and chants, accompanied by a shamanic rattle. Each participant must imbibe *tabaco* – a mixture of dried tobacco leaves, the hallucinogenic San Pedro, sugar candy and lime juice – through the nostrils. At midnight, everyone must drink one cup of a pure San Pedro infusion. One by one, they approach the mesa and everyone concentrates on the staffs, positioned in the good, evil and neutral zones around the mesa. One of the staffs is supposed to vibrate and this represents the focal point of the patient's ailment. The *curandero* hands the staff to the patient to hold in his left hand and begins to recall events and people from the patient's life. He then divines the cause of the patient's sickness, whether the trouble is due to *daño* (witchcraft), *enredo* (love magic) or *suerto* (fate, or bad luck). Once the evil is exorcised, the *curandero*'s two assistants imbibe through the nostrils ingredients of the *tabaco* mixture, as does the patient, and an assistant "cleanses" the patient, by rubbing the staff all over his body.

The San Pedro cactus acts as a catalyst, throughout the healing session, activating the visionary and divinatory powers of the *curandero* and rendering the patient receptive to treatment. The subconscious of the patient "opens" and makes the forces that cause him to be sick visible and susceptible to the curer's powers. Occasionally, the illness-causing forces are powerful enough to attack a patient during a curing session. In such cases, the *curandero* seizes a sword and battles furiously with the attacking spirits, then performs seven somersaults in the form of a cross, grasping the sword in both hands. Though extremely potent, the San Pedro is one of a number of "magic" plants, both medicinal and magical, that can be purchased at the herb stands in the markets of the coastal towns and cities of Peru (Sharon, p. 114-135).

See also

Cannabis Sativa L.; Lysergic acid diethlyamide (LSD)

References

Anderson, Edward. 1980. *Peyote, the Divine Cactus*. Tucson, Arizona: University of Arizona Press.

Furst, Peter, T. 1972. "To Find Our Life: Peyote Among the Huichol Indians of Mexico". In *Flesh of* the Gods: The Ritual Use of Hallucinogens. ed. Peter T. Furst, p. 136-184. London: George Allen and Unwin.

Huxley, Aldous. [1954] 1994. *The Doors of Perception*. London: Flamingo-HarperCollins.

La Barre, Weston. 1938. *The Peyote Cult*. New Haven, Connecticut: Yale University Press.

Myerhoff, Barbara G. [1974] 1986. *Peyote Hunt: The Sacred Journey of the Huichol Indians*. Ithaca, New York; London: Cornell University Press.

Schultes, Richard Evans. 1972. "An Overview of Hallucinogens in the Western Hemisphere". In *Flesh of the Gods: The Ritual Use of Hallucinogens*. ed. Peter T. Furst, p. 3-44. London: George Allen and Unwin.

Sharon, Douglas. 1972. "The San Pedro Cactus in Peruvian Folk Healing". In *Flesh of the Gods: The Ritual Use of Hallucinogens*. ed. Peter T. Furst, p. 114-135. London: George Allen and Unwin.

Miasma

Miasma is a Greek word meaning defilement or pollution. Its opposite, cleansing of pollution, is rendered by the term *katharmos*. The subject has been discussed at length in a monograph by Robert Parker, *Miasma: Pollution and Purification in Early Greek Religion*. In classical times, *miasma* referred to a certain proscribed act that offended the gods and disturbed the ritual purity of the individual and the state. The consequences of transgression initially affected the offender, who was rendered unfit to enter the temple, and spread, through contagion, to endanger the entire community. Greek tragedies are replete with examples: the unwitting patricide and incest of Oedipus are responsible for the plague in Sophocles' *Oedipus Tyrannus*; in his *Antigone*, the refusal of Creon to allow Antigone to bury her brother, Polyneices, results in birds of prey carrying scraps of the corpse to the altars, polluting the sanctuary and making impossible all contact between man and god; in Aeschylus' *Oresteia*, Orestes, fearing the pollution that would result if he failed to avenge the murder of his father, Agamemnon, kills both Aegisthus and his own mother, Clytaemnestra, even though this matricide incurs a further pollution.

Death, killing, contact with a corpse, and, at the opposite end of the lifespan, birth, are amongst the most frequently cited sources of pollution in Greek texts. Birth or death within a temple were sacrilege, and the sacred island of Delos had to remain free from the taint of mortality. Birth taboos began at the onset of pregnancy, when a woman was required to remain secluded for forty days, and resumed after childbirth for three days during which time she would pollute anyone entering her abode. Similarly, at the moment of death, the entire house became polluted and rituals were necessary to alleviate the danger. A 5th-century law from Iulis, on Keos, describes the procedure following a death: a water vessel fetched from a neighbouring house which was not polluted was left outside the house to purify those leaving and the corpse itself was washed and anointed, crowned, dressed in clean robes and laid upon a bier so that, at the wake, it alone was pure in the midst of impurity. Early on the third day the body was carried outside the city, far from the temples; no priest attended the ceremony of disposal as proximity to the corpse would contaminate him.

An unnatural death is even more serious: the blood of a murder victim stains the murderer and in this case the pollution is augmented by the victim's anger which pursues the killer in the form of "avenging demons" (Parker, p. 104-107). In Aeschylus' play, *Eumenides*, the demons of destruction are the Erinyes which threaten to pollute the whole of Athens for failing to expel the murderer.

Another crime in ancient Greece that caused impurity was sacrilege; the defiling of an altar passed pollution on to the gods so strict rules of behaviour were enforced. The right of access to shrines and festivals was generally denied to slaves, foreigners, the ritually unpure, and, depending on the festival, women or men. Objects such as swords, knots, metal objects, pack animals and skins were taboo and certain rituals, such as the Eleusinian mysteries and the Thesmophoria, were protected by a rule of secrecy. To transgress the rules meant divine vengeance, in the form of madness, disease or death.

The restoration of ritual purity could be achieved in a number of ways. Cleansing with water removed the impurities contracted though contact with a corpse or other pollutant and was a necessary prelude to participation in rituals. Fire also eradicated impurities; after the Persians withdrew in 479 BCE, Greek leaders at Plataea were warned by the Delphic oracle "not to sacrifice before they had extinguished the fire in the country, since it had been polluted by the barbarians, and fetched pure fire from the common hearth at Delphi" (Plutarch *Arist.* 20.40) and at Argos, new fire was brought from the house next door to the deceased's at the conclusion of mourning. Cleansing by blood, paradoxically erasing the defilement contracted through shedding human blood by sprinkling the hands with a sacrificed animal's blood, is mentioned in Cyrene cathartic law in the 4th century BCE and had already been condemned by Heraclitus in the 6th century BCE. Similarly madness and epilepsy (known in ancient Greece as the 'sacred disease' because it was thought to be god-given) were punishments for violating taboos but were also, at least in myth, agents of purification. The maenads are freed from the madness caused by their rejection of Dionysus when they celebrate the Dionysic rites with wild abandon and Aristophanes mentions the frenzied Corybantic rites among the treatments for madness (Parker, p. 246, 288).

As pollution was contagious it was often necessary to purge the entire city and in this case a scapegoat, called in Greek a *pharmakos* (medicine) or *katharma* (offscouring), could be used to carry the impurities out of the area. According to legend, a character named Pharmakos was caught stealing Apollo's sacred cups and was stoned to death by the friends of Achilles. The *pharmakos* of the ritual was, like his namesake, attributed with a sin that brought drought or plague upon the community. In practice, a despised member of the community, a beggar or a criminal, was fed, paraded about the city to soak up the impurities and then chased out across the city boundaries with sticks or stones. Present evidence suggests that, miserable as his fate was, he was not actually killed (Burkert, p. 82-84). In Athens, in the late 5th century BCE, scapegoats were sent out during the Thargelia, a festival of Apollo and the first fruits of the year, and it is a characteristic of *pharmakos* rituals that they form part of the festival year.

Naturally it was more desirable to avoid pollution than to cleanse it, and besides the taboos already mentioned, numerous injunctions and prescriptions are attributed to Pythagoras relating to sexuality, washing, bodily functions, and diet: nails and hair were not to be cut at a festival; beans, eggs, animal flesh and fish were prohibited by the Pythagoreans; temples had to be entered barefoot and from the right; libations were to be poured from the edge of the cup so that men and gods would not drink from the same part; moreover, a danger existed in turning around at a boundary as this was where the Erinyes lay in wait. At the end of Hesiod's *Works and Days* (8th century BCE), similar rules can be found:

> Never omit to wash your hands before you pour to Zeus … Do not lie down beside the fire when you have just made love, and show your naked parts. Also, it is unwise to sow your seed when you have just come from a funeral … if you cross a river with your hands and crimes uncleansed, the gods will punish you … a pot unblessed by sacrifice brings harm … Don't let a boy of twelve years, or twelve months, sit upon a tomb or other sacred thing, it will unman the baby or the boy. Nor should a man use water for his bath with which a woman bathed herself before, the punishment is awful … Don't urinate in springs (Hesiod, p. 82-84).

Certain of the proscriptions are intended to avoid confusion between different categories:

between male and female, life and death, gods and men, the pure fire and the fire of lust. Others are concerned with serious crimes such as murder. Gradually, from the 5th and 4th centuries BCE onwards, legislation was introduced and homicide was dealt with in the courts, the murderer no longer a source of pollution but merely a criminal to be punished. The rules on ritual purity, however, did not disappear overnight and contact with Egyptian and oriental cults led to an increase, rather than a decline, in ritual abstinences.

See also

Death; Douglas, Mary; Food Taboos; Hair; Pollution; Van Gennep, Arnold

References

Burkert, Walter: [1977] 1985. *Greek Religion.* trans. John Raffan. Oxford: Basil Blackwell.

Hesiod. [1973] 1979. *Works and Days. Hesiod and Theognis*, p. 720-770. trans. Dorothea Wender. Harmondsworth, Middlesex: Penguin.

Parker, Robert. 1983. *Miasma: Pollution and Purification in Early Greek Religion.* Oxford: Clarendon Press.

Milk

Milk is avoided by vegans, who disdain to eat any animal produce either on religious or moral grounds, while within Judaism dairy produce must not be eaten together with meat, a prohibition which also applied to the Masai warriors of East Africa, who took a strong purgative to cleanse their stomachs of milk before eating meat (Simoons, p. 109). The Chinese dietician, Chia Ming, offers other advice on the dangers of mixing milk in his *Yin-shih hsü-chih* (Essential Knowledge for Eating and Drinking) of 1368:

> Milk [*ju lo*]: its flavour is sweet and acid; its character is cold. Persons suffering from diarrhoea must not consume it. Sheep [goat] milk taken together with preserved fish [season-

ing] will cause intestinal blockage. It does not go with vinegar. It should never be consumed along with perch (Mote, p. 233).

Chia Ming is guided by an ancient Chinese theory which states that all foods have certain qualities: they may be "hot" or "cold" and the flavour may be sweet, sour, bitter, pungent or salty. To be healthy, a person must have the right balance of hot and cold foods and be careful when mixing flavours.

Curiously, those societies that avoid milk and have taboos upon drinking it may do so precisely because it makes them unwell. This is the theory proposed by Peter Farb and George Armelagos. They observe how certain cultures have refrained from milking their animals or, if they do, they transform the raw milk into yoghurt, butter, cheese or ghee. Those countries that have traditionally eschewed milk include China (although during the T'ang dynasty, from the 7th to the 10th century CE, the upper classes enjoyed milk delicacies), Japan, Korea, Burma, Malaysia, Indonesia, and regions of Africa stretching from the Guinea coast and Congo River Basin in the west to Mozambique in the east and southwards into Angola. Native Americans do not drink milk and neither do Australian aborigines except where European habits have been adopted. When relief agencies sent powdered milk to the Kanuri of West Africa they threw it away, believing it to be the food of evil spirits, and the Navaho tribes similarly disposed of it (Farb and Armelagos, p. 187).

Farb and Armelagos are not fully convinced by the ecological argument that milk was not drunk in certain regions of Africa and Asia because the terrain is unsuitable for dairy cows; after all, immigrants from areas like India and Pakistan (where milk products form an important part of the diet) have successfully introduced dairying into parts of Southeast Asia. Instead, they think that taboos on milk have arisen where the indigenous population lacks the enzyme, lactase, which is needed to digest lactose, or milk sugar. Though present at birth, after weaning it may no longer be manufactured by the body. This is especially true of many hunter-gatherer societies, which are unable to drink untreated milk. But with the domestication of animals, around 10,000 years ago, non-human milk became available as an alternative source of food and gradually individuals evolved who were capable of producing the lactase enzyme. Research has shown that the areas in which milk is highly valued as a food, and in which dairying has a long history – northern Europe, the pastoral parts of the Near East, Africa, the Caucasus, Central Asia, Pakistan and certain provinces of India – coincide with inhabitants who are lactose-tolerant. This leads Farb and Armelagos to the natural conclusion:

> Everything that has been learned in recent years about lactose intolerance supports the conclusion that Asiatics do not avoid milk because they do not wish to deprive infant mammals of it, that Africans do not fear it because of evil spirits, and that the Chinese are not perverse in finding a thick milkshake repugnant. These attitudes were undoubtedly adopted as rationalisations to explain the already-existing intolerance of milk (Farb and Armelagos, p. 189).

They do concede that societies exist in which animals have been milked for a considerable time without all the individuals developing a tolerance of milk. Among the Greeks, Arabs and Near Eastern Jews, many individuals cannot digest raw milk. However, they are able to eat milk products such as cheese, yoghurt and butter which are low in lactose.

The idea that aversion to milk, and the taboos on drinking it, are due to an innate intolerance of lactose is supported by Marvin Harris (Harris, p. 130-153). He notices that the greatest tolerance of milk is to be found in northern Europe where over ninety five per cent of the Dutch, Danes, Swedes and

Norwegians can digest large quantities of lactose. This tolerance decreases towards the Mediterranean and the Middle East, and he records that in Asia fewer than five per cent of adult Chinese, Japanese and Koreans can absorb lactose. Harris surmises that the northerners needed the lactose in untreated milk to help the body absorb calcium. This was necessary in a region with insufficient sun for solar-activated vitamin D, which, like lactose, assists in the absorption of calcium. Neither did the diet of the Neolithic northern Europeans include sufficient quantities of the marine fish oils or dark-green vegetables which are such a rich source of vitamin D. Outside Europe, lactase sufficiency has developed among those populations that depend on milk: the Bedouin rely on camel's milk during their long treks across the desert and certain East African pastoral groups, who subsist almost entirely on milk, have similar levels of lactase sufficiency to the Scandinavians.

Though the "rational" explanation – that taboos on milk arise in populations that lack the lactase enzyme – is persuasive, it is wise to remember that milk may also have a religious or a symbolic significance. Buddhist belief in China has equated the treatment of milk with the purification of the soul: t'i-hu, resembling clarified butter or the Indian ghee, represents the perfection of the spirit. A less exalted stage is signified by lo or kumiss, made by heating animal milk and allowing it to ferment through the action of lactobacillus. During the T'ang era (618-907 CE) it was a Buddhist custom to offer milk and milk products to stellar deities and kumiss was offered to the spirit of the lunar station mao, known in the West as the Pleiades (Schafer, p. 106, 134). Extreme Buddhist sects have been known to abstain from milk and milk products, although asceticism has been the motivating factor rather than the sacred product itself. The Dyak tribes of Sarawak hold cows in such esteem that they will not drink their milk. On the other hand, the Shin, a nominally Muslim people of Dardistan in north-west India, view cattle with repugnance and avoid both milk and dairy products (Simoons, p. 48, 52, 120, 162).

See also

Chinese Food Taboos; Food Taboos; Jewish Dietary Laws

References

Farb, Peter and George Armelagos. 1980. *Consuming Passions: The Anthropology of Eating.* Boston, Massachusetts: Houghton Mifflin Company.

Harris, Marvin. 1986: *Good to Eat: Riddles of Food and Culture.* London: Allen and Unwin.

Mote, Frederick W. 1977. "Yüan and Ming". In *Food in Chinese Culture: Anthropological and Historical Perspectives*, ed. K. C. Chang, p. 193-257. New Haven, Connecticut; London: Yale University Press.

Schafer, Edward H. 1977. "T'ang". In *Food in Chinese Culture: Anthropological and Historical Perspectives*, ed. K. C. Chang, p. 85-140. New Haven, Connecticut; London: Yale University Press.

Simoons, Frederick J. [1961] 1967. *Eat Not This Flesh: Food Avoidances in the Old World.* Madison, Wisconsin: University of Wisconsin Press.

Mirrors

Mirrors are dangerous for the dead, the "undead" (vampires), demons and spirits, and for those who have not yet died. In Europe, North America, Madagascar, parts of the Crimea and India mirrors were not to be exposed in the presence of a corpse and were commonly turned to the wall or covered with drapery when a person died, a custom still preserved by Orthodox Jews. The explanation for this is that if the glass is not covered, the soul fleeing from the corpse will be trapped within the mirror and, unable to reach the other world, it will haunt the living. Though the soul can be caught in a mirror, very often the mirror itself is the doorway to the other world. This is a common theme in fiction: Lewis Carroll's tale, *Alice Through the Looking-Glass*, and Angela Carter's short story, "Reflections",

involve journeys through a mirror to strange regions where all is reversed and illogical, and in the French film *Orphée* by Jean Cocteau, Death enters and leaves through the mirror. In France and Germany it was believed that the dead could be be seen in mirrors at certain auspicious times, New Year's Eve or the eve of Epiphany, if certain rituals were enacted and in Mexico the Aztec god, Tezcatlipoca, employed a "smoking mirror" of obsidian glass to enter the world of the spirits. Pausanius records how a mirror was used for divination at the sanctuary of Demeter at Achaia. Suspended over a spring, it could reveal whether a sick man was alive or dead (Lloyd-Morgan, p. 99).

A study of the subject by Julius von Negelein concludes that mirrors are feared because the image in the mirror reflection (like the reflection in water or the shadow) is seen as a kind of soul or double, which must be protected from danger (Negelein, p. 1-37). James George Frazer says much the same thing in his comprehensive work, *Taboo and the Perils of the Soul,* and many of the traditional beliefs and superstitions surrounding mirror-gazing give credence to this view, as Otto Rank observes:

These ideas are associated with the prohibitions of gazing at oneself in the mirror at night. If this is done, one loses his own image – i.e. soul. As a result, death is a necessary consequence, an idea based in East Prussia upon the belief that in such cases the reflection of the devil appears behind one. If, in fact, anyone notices the reflection of another face beside his own, he will soon die. For similar reasons it is disastrous for ill ... persons to see their reflections. In all of Germany the falling down or breaking of a mirror is taken to be a sign of death, although along with that, and as a euphemistic compensation, seven years of trouble are in prospect. Also, whoever's last view of himself was in a broken mirror must die or suffer seven years of distress ... Precautions, too, are taken against allowing small children to gaze at themselves in a mirror. These precautions result from the fear of one's own reflection, which subjects one's double to all kinds of harm; and if the child is not protected, he will become proud and frivolous or else will become ill and die (Rank, p. 63-64).

Several South American tribes similarly identify the soul with the reflection mirrored in glass or water, or manifest in the shadow. The fear of seeing one's reflection in water, an omen of death according to the ancient Greeks, has led James Frazer to conclude that the classical myth of Narcissus, the beautiful youth who pined for his aqueous image, is a reinterpretation of an older tale of death by reflection (Frazer, p. 94). But in its extant form, the myth is also a warning against the vanity which the image inspires, commonly a source of misfortune. One of the early Church fathers, Tertullian, saw mirrors as an incitement to licentiousness (*de Cultu Feminarum* I.1.3) and a device of the devil. Late medieval and Renaissance prints depict a woman preening herself before a looking-glass while a devil or skeleton appears to stalk her – an allegory on the folly of earthly conceits in the face of death and eternity. Pride is also the downfall of the hero of Oscar Wilde's tale, *The Picture of Dorian Gray*, although in this case the soul does not reside in the mirror, which retains the exquisite form of the eternally juvenile youth, but in his portrait which ages horribly under the weight of all his sins.

If the soul is captured in a mirror, then those without a soul – ghosts, spirits and vampires – have no reflection. In this way their true identity is revealed, however convincing the outward disguise. This is also the case in China, where Taoists carry hand-mirrors into the mountains as a protection against diabolical influences, although here the glass shows the original form of the demon. An adept explains:

Know that all things, as they age, become capable of taking on human forms and manage thereby to deceive the human eye. In this guise they are continuously taking people in. It is only in mirrors that they reveal their true form. This is why, since ancient times, Taoists who go into the mountains always carry a nine-inch mirror (a solar number) on their backs; in this way, the ghosts of old things dare not go near them. If by chance they come to provoke the adepts, the latter will have only to turn around and look into the mirror: if they are Immortals or true mountain gods, they will keep their human aspect even in the mirror; but if they are perverse animals or ghosts of old things, then the mirror will reflect their true appearance (Schipper, p. 171).

In China hand-mirrors are emblems of truth; they have an allegorical function, revealing the essence of things, and serve as aids to conjugal happiness. They also accompany the dead: Li Xueqin describes in detail the many bronze mirrors that have been found in graves in China (Xueqin, p. 295 *passim*). Outside China, a copper mirror has been found in front of the face of an Egyptian mummy in Egypt and it is possible that the Bronze Age Cycladic pans found in graves may have served as elementary water-filled mirrors. Mirrors have also been found as grave offerings in Madagascar and in Serbo-Croatia they adorned the graves of those who had died prematurely. In these cases, it is possible that the mirrors, by ensnaring the reflection, kept the malicious soul from leaving the tomb.

Paul Barber thinks that the taboo on uncovered eyes on a corpse has a similar origin: open eyes may reflect and trap the souls of the living and it is to prevent this danger that the eyes are securely sealed with wax or pinned with needles and covered with a stone, coin or piece of cloth (Barber, p. 182). A further possibility is that the eyes are shut to forestall any threat from the envious evil eye of the cadaver. Barber also surmises that it is the mirrored reflection in water that prevents a spirit from crossing water, a common belief in European folklore. In eastern Prussia, for instance, the *Leichenwasser*, the water used for washing a corpse, was poured between the coffin and the house, once the funeral party had left, to provide a barrier to the soul's return (Barber, p. 181).

In psychoanalytic terms, taboos on mirrors are related to the concept of the ego. In 1914, in his study of the concept of the double, Otto Rank argued that the double was originally an insurance against the destruction of the ego, a means of denying the power of death. As a soul, the double could exist beyond the grave. The motivation for such a belief stemmed from an inordinate self-love or primitive narcissism which dominated the mind of both early mankind and early childhood. Once this stage had been surmounted, as Freud put it, "the double reverses its aspect. From having been an assurance of immortality, it becomes the uncanny harbinger of death" (Freud, p. 357).

Jacques Lacan similarly dwells on the mirror phase (*le stade du miroir*) of an individual's development (although no scholar would continue to identify this stage with a preliterate society). Looking in the mirror a person begins to shape the sense of self, realising that the mirrored image is both "self" and "other". Boundaries are formed and the ego, confronted with this "otherness" defines itself (Armitt, p. 46-47). But, as Freud perceives, the idea of the double need not disappear after the stage of primary narcissism has passed. It can be transformed into an independent observer that criticises and censors the ego in the form of a conscience, which, in the pathological condition involving delusions of observation, is totally dissociated from the ego (Freud, p. 357). In literature this paranoid state is often portrayed as the pursuit by the mirrored image or the double: Fedor Dostoyevsky's *The Double* (1846) and Guy de Maupassant's *The Horla* (1887) are just two well-known examples.

An interesting variation on the theme of the danger of the mirrored image appears in the writings of the 3rd-century Neoplatonist, Plotinus. For Plotinus, the human soul is divine but it allows itself to be seduced by its reflection in the mirror of matter and sensible form which is its own body. The captivation with the corporeal, with the beautiful flesh that it sees reflected, leads to the soul's fall from grace, "the souls of men seeing their images in the mirror of Dionysus as it were, have entered into that realm in a leap downward from the Supreme" (*Enneads* 4.3.12).

Gnosticism, another doctrine that disdains the sensible world, also considers an infatuation with the mirrored image to be the initial human error. A gnostic myth tells how Adam Kadmon, the first man, was tricked by the evil demiurge who created the world. The demiurge captured the image of primordial man, reflected in the ocean, and his shadow, reflected on the earth, and Adam, entranced by these forms, rushed after them and became sunk in the material world. Thereafter, his soul was trapped in the realm of the senses, subject to the disquieting passions which haunt mankind (Alliez and Feher, p. 59).

Whether rooted in psychology, religion or in folk belief, essentially the taboos on the mirrored reflection spring from the magic of the image which at one and the same time presents a true resemblance and a total illusion. As the poet, Koert Linde, puts it in his riddle of the mirror, "the measure of my truthfulness/is the depth of my deception" (Linde, p. 80).

References

Alliez, Eric and Michel Feher. [1989] 1990. "Reflections of a Soul". In *Fragments for a History of the Human Body*, Part Two. ed. Michel Feher, p. 46-84. New York: Zone.

Armitt, Lucie. 1996. *Theorising the Fantastic*. London: Arnold.

Barber, Paul. 1988. *Vampires, Burial and Death: Folklore and Reality*. New Haven, Connecticut; London: Yale University Press.

Frazer, James George. [1911] 1935. *Taboo and the Perils of the Soul. The Golden Bough*. New York: Macmillan.

Freud, Sigmund. [1919] 1990. "Das Unheimliche (The "Uncanny")". In *The Penguin Freud Library vol. 14 Art and Literature*. trans. James Strachey, p. 336-376. London: Penguin.

Linde, Koert. 1999. *Ananke*. Gifford, Scotland: Wolfstar Books.

Lloyd-Morgan, Glenys. 1989. "A Mirror for the Goddess: Dedications of Mirrors at some Graeco-Roman Sanctuaries". In *Polytheistic Systems. Cosmos*, vol. 5. ed. Glenys Davies, p. 92-104. Edinburgh: Edinburgh University Press.

Negelein, Julius von. 1902. "Bild, Spiegel und Schatten im Volksglauben". *Zeitschrift des Vereins für Volkskunde*, no. 5, p. 1-37.

Plotinus, *Enneads* 4.3.12. trans. Stephen MacKenna. 1991. London: Penguin.

Rank, Otto. [1914] 1971. *The Double: A Psychoanalytic Study*. trans. Harry Tucker, p. 63-64. Chapel Hill, North Carolina: The University of North Carolina Press.

Schipper, Kristofer. [1982] 1993. *The Taoist Body*. trans. Karen C. Duval, p. 171. Berkeley; Los Angeles: University of California Press.

Xueqin, Li. 1985. *Eastern Zhou and Qin Civilizations*. trans. K. C. Chang. New Haven, Connecticut; London: Yale University Press.

Mountains

Taboos surrounding mountains are not surprising given the awe which high peaks inspire and the dangers of their ascent. Appearing to reach to the heavens, the dwelling-place of the gods, mountains are sacred in many traditions. In Iran, mount Haraberazaiti (Harburz) is located at the centre of the earth and fastened to the sky; in Hindu mythology the holy mountain is mount Meru while biblical tradition includes the peaks of Sinai and Tabor; in Islamic thought the highest spot on earth is the summit of the Ka'aba and in Christian belief Golgotha is holy.

Sometimes, but not always, it is necessary to scale the peaks. To practise the Tao, says the Taoist master Ko Hung (also known as Pao-p'u tsu, "Master Who Embraces-Simplicity"), it is necessary to go to the mountains. This sage, who lived from 283-343 CE, judged that mountains were the ideal place to find the marvellous mushroom (*ling-chih*) that grows on rocks of cinnabar, to mix the elixirs of immortality and to escape distractions. The route to the mountains, though, could be perilous:

> … whoever does not know how to take on the mountain risks death. That is why a proverb says: "At the foot of Hua-shan [sacred mountain of the West], there are piles of white bones!" [of those who sought immortality]. These skeletons belong to those who knew only one method and were ignorant of the rest. If this is the case, even with the most excellent resolve, one will meet a cruel death … Those who do not know the right technique … will fall ill or injure themselves. They will be frightened constantly, will see lights, and hear strange sounds. Across their path, without there being any wind, tall trees will crash down; rocks will begin to roll for no reason at all and will strike and rush the passerby. Sometimes they [these unschooled adepts] will go mad and throw themselves into ravines; or still again they will meet tigers, wolves, venomous snakes. Never enter lightly into the mountains (*Pao p'u tsu nei p'ien* cited in Schipper, p. 171).

The "right technique" means, in the first instance, fasting for seven days. It is also important for the novice to know the days on which the mountains must not be visited, for the mountains are open or closed at certain periods of the year. One must be careful not to disturb a mountain by approaching it from the wrong direction: in spring one must not come from the east, in summer not from the south, in autumn not from the west and in winter not from the north. Another route to failure is ignorance of the Hidden Periods (*tun-chia*), a complex method of computing time by counting days; without this knowledge the mountain will remain forever sealed. Adhering to these prohibitions is yet not sufficient to ensure success. A nine-inch mirror must be carried on the back of the pilgrim so that the ghosts of old things dare not approach; this mirror reveals the *true form* of things so that demons and ghosts will be stripped of their disguises and appear in their true forms.

As well as this, the higher adepts who wish to climb the mountain must secure several talismans including the *Esoteric Signs of the Three Sovereigns* and the *Map of the True Form of the Five Sacred Mountains*. The talismans consist of signs, writings and figures that reveal the secret names of the first sovereigns and a map of the labyrinth of the mountain; they allow the adept to be recognised as an initiate by the gods and Immortals. With a further document, the *Register of Demons*, the adept can communicate with the Earth God and the guardian spirits of the sacred places; these will, provided of course he knows the *times* of the mountain, let him enter.

Upon entering the mountain one must not walk normally but must dance the Step of Yü, mirroring the limping dance practised by the culture-hero, Yü the Great, when he magically controlled the floods and led the water back to its banks:

> Thus, inside the labyrinth the adept progresses, dancing the Step of Yü, from the Palace of Light and the Star of Fire down to the depths of the dark regions of water ... The Master [Who-Embraces-Simplicity] teaches us how to dance this step: hop from the left foot to the right, one time *yin*, one time *yang*. The tracks left behind look like two Trigrams, *li* and *k'an*, the Powers of Heaven and Earth. With each step forward, one also has to hold one's breath (Schipper, p. 173-174).

Without the maps of the mountain, the knowledge of the secret names and the times and direction to approach the peak, as well as the mirror to unveil demons, it is impossible to gain egress. Without a knowledge of the Step of Yü and the correct breathing exercises, the adept cannot complete the passage from the outer *yang* world to the *yin* within. With these things, the mountain, if not exactly tamed, will at least lie still and reveal its treasures.

See also
Mirrors

References
Eliade, Mircea. *Patterns in Comparative Religion.* [1958] 1979. London: Sheed and Ward.

Schipper, Kristofer. [1982] 1993. *The Taoist Body*. trans. Karen C. Duval, p. 171. Berkeley; Los Angeles: University of California Press.

Mushrooms

Although many mushrooms are highly valued for their psychotropic properties and Gordon Wasson has argued that *soma*, the divine elixir of the Aryans that bestowed immortality, was none other than a preparation of the *Amanita muscaria* or fly agaric (Wasson, p. 201-213), mushrooms have often been proscribed for quite different reasons. The Hua people of the Eastern Highlands of Papua New Guinea have forbidden certain mushrooms to male initiates because they resemble the vagina, grow only during *a'di kuna* (women's time of menstruation, the new moon), smell of *be'ftu* (the smell of menstruation and rotting things), are red, grow on the ground which is associated with women and filth, are associated with possum (the most taboo animal in this society), and have an ashy, dry surface which can be passed on to the eater (Meigs, p. 142-146). While the taboos manifest a certain logic in that they are mostly connected in some way with women, the reasons for allowing other mushrooms to be eaten are more curious. According to one informant, the *tane* mushroom is edible because it is dry, hard, and crackles when eaten and the *harru* is permitted because it is slippery and slippery foods are important because eating them allows a person to slip away from those trying to bewitch him.

See also
Food Taboos; Possum

References
Meigs, Anna S. 1984. *Food, Sex, and Pollution: A New Guinea Religion.* New Brunswick, New Jersey: Rutgers University Press.

Wasson, R. Gordon. 1972. "The Divine Mushroom of Immortality". In *Flesh of the Gods: The Ritual Use of Hallucinogens.* ed. Peter T. Furst, p. 185-200. London: George Allen and Unwin.

Wasson, R. Gordon. 1972. "What Was the Soma of the Aryans?" In *Flesh of the Gods: The Ritual Use of Hallucinogens.* ed. Peter T. Furst, p. 201-213. London: George Allen and Unwin.

Musical Harmony

Like the Pythagoreans, the early Christian Church embraced an ideal of unity and harmony rather than duality and disharmony. In musical terms, this meant that it rejected all heterophony and polyphony, preferring the monophonic (unharmonised, single-part) vocal music, known as plainchant or plainsong. Just as all souls were to be united in the Christian liturgy, so all voices were to join in a single symphony. This is expressly stated by Clement of Alexandria, the 2nd-century church father, in his *Protrepticos:*

> We want to strive so that we, the many, may be brought together into one love, according to the union of the essential unity. As we do good may we similarly pursue unity … The union of many, which the divine harmony has called forth out of a medley of sounds and division, becomes one symphony, following the one leader of the choir and teacher, the Word, resting in that same truth and crying out, "Abba, Father" (*Protrepticos* 9. quoted in Quasten, p. 67).

The divine harmony is thus epitomised by the plainsong which consists of melodies composed in free rhythm, depending on the accentuation of the words, and sung in unison.

The patrons of this Christian singing are the biblical David, the "sweet psalmist", Miriam, the prophetess, and Deborah, as well as all the other performers of songs and dances of victory, whose role was to enhance the divine worship in the Jerusalem temple. The music Clement wishes to ban is chromatic music "with its colourful harmonies … Thracian music, which follows Jubal" (Quasten, p. 67) Jubal is named in *Genesis* as the father of all who play the lyre and flute and Clement is here referring to all the instrumental music which originated with the cithara. In a tone reminiscent of Plato, he remarks in the *Pedagogue,* his work on Christian education:

> But we shall choose temperate harmonies; we shall keep far away from our virile minds all liquid harmonies which by modulating tones lead to a dangerous art which trains to effeminacy and langour. Austere and temperate songs protect against wild drunkenness; therefore we shall leave chromatic harmonies to immoderate revels and to the music of courtesans (*Paidagogos.* 2, 4. quoted in Quasten, p. 68).

Curiously, Jubal was initially respected in the scriptures, but the alarm generated by David's frenzied dancing before the Ark of the Covenant suggests an ambivalent attitude towards music and dance among the Israelites and with the destruction of the Second Temple, in 70 CE, instrumental music was no longer a part of Jewish worship. The early Christians preserved the musical influences of the Jews and were also mindful of Plato's warnings in *The Republic* about the detrimental consequences of "lascivious" music. Text-dominated chanting in praise of God, propagated in the name of Pope Gregory I (who reigned from 590-604) and commonly known as Gregorian chants, became the ideal form of Christian worship.

There are, predictably, many textual references which support Clement of Alexander's argument for plainchant. The Prefaces of the Mass speak of all the angels singing in one voice, as does the *Ascension of Isaiah*, a Pseudepigraphal work dating from the 2nd to 4th century CE, in which the prophet gives an eye-witness account of his journey to the seven heavens.

As for the liquid harmonies which are thought to induce drunkenness, St. Augustine (354-430 CE) singles out the cithara for blame (curiously, an instrument that had escaped Plato's censorship). In his second discourse on Psalm 32 (33), he asks, "Has not the institution of those vigils in Christ's name caused the citharas to be banished from this place?" (*Enarratio II in Ps.* 32,5. Quoted in Quasten, p. 74). The place in question is the chapel of St. Cyprian and it is clear from the context that vigils had taken place there in which citheras had been played, probably at popular religious feasts, although it is unclear when the ban was introduced.

On other occasions ecclesiastical decrees forbade the use of all musical instruments. The *Quaestiones et responsiones ad orthodoxos* – one of the four Pseudo-Justinian tracts attributed to the Byzantine Emperor, but probably dating from no earlier than the 5th century – mentions another lewd act to which instruments give rise; namely, dancing:

> Singing of itself is not to be considered as fit only for the unclean, but rather singing to the accompaniment of soulless instruments and dancing and the noise of the krotala. Therefore the use of such instruments with singing in church must be shunned, as well as everything else that is proper only for fools. Simple singing alone remains … it is and remains God's word, whether it is contemplated, sung or listened to, a protection against the demons (Ps. Justine, *Quaestiones et responsiones ad orthodoxos* 107. Quoted in Quasten, p. 74-75).

If Plato's warnings concerning the pernicious moral effects of certain types of music was heeded by the early Christians, another aspect of his philosophy, namely his musical cosmology, was to influence the 6th-century Christian philosopher, Boethius. In his influential treatise on music, *De institutione musica*, Boethius identifies three types of music: the music of the universe, caused by the mechanism of the sky as it moves through the heavens; human music, which joins together the parts of the body and unites the soul; and instrumental music, shaped by the kithera, tibiae or other instruments, and creating the melody. Musical cosmology, especially its numerical dimension, "the proportioned dimensions of sound" (*Scholia enchiriadis*, 10th century), provided a partial scholastic justification, in the Middle Ages, for an elementary type of sacred polyphony known as *organum*.

Nevertheless there were those who still condemned polyphony. In the 12th century, John of Salisbury likened such singing to "a chorus of sirens" and Pope John XXII, in a bull issued at Avignon in 1324/5, sought to ban almost all polyphony, complaining that the modest plainsong was being obscured by voices:

> … incessantly running to and fro, intoxicating the ear, not soothing it, while the men themselves endeavor to convey by their gestures the sentiment of the music which they utter. As a consequence of all this, devotion, the true end of worship, is little thought of, and wantonness which ought to be eschewed, increases (Ringer, p. 210).

Despite their disapproval, they were unable to stem the tide of musical innovation. Gradually, from the 12th century, more elaborate forms of *organa* evolved and the 14th century saw the first integrated polyphonic setting of the mass. This led, in turn, to the polyphonic masses of the 15th-century Burgundian composer, Guillaume Dufay, which included instrumental parts. Although another 15th-century composer, Johannes Okeghem, rejected the intrusion of instrumental parts, and the Protestant leader, Martin Luther, condemned what he termed "popish" musical practices, instrumental music, including organs, and, in Italy in the 17th century, string instruments, became an acceptable part of church music.

The Eastern Orthodox church, with its base in Constantinople, was more conservative and its liturgy was dominated by monophonic hymns. After the sack of Constantinople in 1453, Russia became the principal defender of the Orthodox faith and, anxious to preserve its musical purity, Ivan the Terrible inaugurated the Russian Imperial Chapel to continue the propagation of the monophonic chant. Only with the reign of Peter the Great, from 1682 to 1725, was polyphony gradually accommodated within the liturgy, although it was still treated suspiciously, as a western "heresy", until the mid-18th century when the composer, Dmitrii Bortnianskii, visited Italy and returned to Russia to found the choral repertory that has characterised Russian Orthodox church music ever since.

The Jewish communities of Europe were also keen to preserve their monophonic musical tradition which was based on Hebrew biblical cantilation. Although Jews began to enjoy greater emancipation after the French Revolution and this was to have an effect upon the liturgical music, even leading to the introduction of choirs, instrumental music is not part of the tradition and usually the prayers are led by a musically-gifted, but otherwise unassuming, cantor.

Certain Protestant sects have tried to ban musical instruments in church. In The Netherlands, in the early 17th century, church organs were destroyed by zealous Calvinists and the New England Puritans also rejected instruments. It is fortunate that few members of the church have remained antithetical to musical instruments and to harmony in the liturgy. Some of the most moving and powerful sacred music, from the masses and passions of the baroque composer Johann Sebastian Bach to the 20th-century works of Olivier Messiaen, John Tavener and Arvo Pärt, could not exist without the musical forms condemned by the early Christian church.

See also

Diminished Fifth, The; Plato on Music

References

Cooke, Deryck. 1959. *The Language of Music*. London: Oxford University Press.

Quasten, Johannes. [1973] 1983. *Music and Worship in Pagan and Christian Antiquity*. Washington, DC: National Association of Pastoral Musicians, p. 67-68, p. 74-75. Originally *Musik und Gesang in den Kulten der heidnischen Antike und christlichen Frühzeit*.

Ralls-MacLeod, Karen. 2000. *Music and the Celtic Otherworld*. Edinburgh: Polygon.

Ringer, Alexander. 1987. "Music. Religious Music in the West". In *The Encyclopedia of Religion*, vol. 10. ed. Mircea Eliade, p. 209-216. New York: Macmillan.

Werner, Eric. 1959-1984. *The Sacred Bridge*. 2 vols. New York.

N

Naming

The taboo on naming, the secrecy of names, and the power conferred upon one who knows or discovers the secret name, is a topic that has long fascinated anthropologists, folklorists and religious historians. The tale of Rumpelstilzchen, collected by Jacob and Wilhelm Grimm in the 19th century and still told to children today, exemplifies the belief. In the story, a poor miller's daughter promises her first-born to a dwarf because he has spun straw into gold and thereby saved her life. After marrying the cruel king who had locked her in the room and compelled her to spin the straw, she becomes queen and, when her first child is born, the dwarf returns to collect his fee. Distraught, she begs him not to take the child, and he, more merciful than the king, agrees not to take the child if, within the next three days, she can guess his name. After two unsuccessful days, someone chances upon the dwarf at night, hopping round a fire and crying his name. His name discovered, he furiously drives his foot into the ground and tears himself in two.

Names are mysterious things; the name of a person, a deity, a spirit, or any other phenomenon is often thought to be linked to its very essence. Merely to pronounce a name is sufficient to raise a spirit or expel a demon. In Hinduism the recitation of divine names, and especially that of Krishna, helps to bring release

from the round of constant reincarnations. In Mahayana Buddhism it is Buddha's name that must be invoked while every Muslim whose name contains that of the prophet Mohammed will go to paradise. The Netsilik Inuit (Eskimo) are forbidden to practise female infanticide once the child has been named and conversely, in ancient Egypt and China, the removal of a name meant that the person (or god) ceased to exist (Denny, p. 300-307). According to Jewish tradition, the divine name of God, Yahweh, is too holy to be pronounced. It is not clear whether it is God, an angel or a man who fights Jacob as he crosses the ford of the Jabbok (*Genesis* 32, 26-9), but whoever it is, he refuses to tell Jacob his name.

It is because names are so powerful, and the knowledge of them so often dangerous if revealed, that they are surrounded by so many taboos. An attempt to classify name taboos has been made by George B. Foucart. He divides the prohibition on names into five categories:

a) taboos on mentioning the personal name of an individual, sometimes even by the person himself;

b) prohibitions on pronouncing the names of gods, genii, spirits and animistic powers;

c) the same taboos applied to those secret names conferred at initiations and consecrations upon those chosen to act as intermediaries between the human and spirit worlds;

d) taboos on naming the dead and;

e) the naming of certain animals, plants and topological features (Foucart, p. 130-136).

Because knowledge of a personal name allowed malevolent magic to be practised against its bearer, it was often kept secret, or known only to a select few, while a substitute was used in everyday life. Hutton Webster mentions the absolute secrecy surrounding private names among the Naga tribes of Manipur, and the danger of disclosure: "If it becomes known, the whole village is tabooed, or *genna*, for two days, and a feast must be provided at the expense of the offender" (Webster, p. 220-221). In Aboriginal Australia secret names associated with sacred and totemic beings were whispered in a ritual setting but never spoken outside the totemic group. The Tiwi of the Melville and Bathurst islands forbade the use of proper names during initiation and childbirth and a traditional Hindu wife never uttered her husband's name or called it out. The ancient Egyptians believed that the soul, or life-force, of a person was intimately bound to his name, and, like many other peoples, they believed in the dangers, including death, of the name being spoken by the wrong person. But the name could also be seized for beneficial purposes. The name of a dead man, declaimed and captured by a priest, could be placed upon his image or statue to animate it and give power to the bearer in the tomb, and one of the most important commands (mentioned in the *Book of the Dead*, the guide through the other world) for a dead person hoping to reach the further shores of death was to "Remember your name".

The gods and spirits could be as protective of their names as ordinary men. An Egyptian myth relates how the supreme god, Ra, had a secret name which symbolised his supremacy and which the goddess Isis tried her utmost, through trickery, to have revealed to her so that she could dominate not only him, but the entire world. Though the texts imply that she was successful, and was able to relate the name to her son, Horus, the papyrus was careful not to transcribe it as such power could not be sustained by mere mortals. At the other end of the world, in south-eastern Australia, the secret name of the supreme deity, who instituted laws and initiation rituals, was known only to initiated males of high status. It was revealed during initiation rites in the sound of the bull-roarer (Denny, p. 303).

New names, revealed by a shaman or bestowed at initiations, or at the inauguration of a new chief, were subject to similar prohibitions, as were the names of shamans themselves. But the names most carefully guarded by taboos, those most dangerous to pronounce, and with the direst consequences if spoken, were the names of the dead themselves. In Confucian ancestral rites, the deceased was never mentioned by name but a spirit tablet, or "soul silk" was inscribed with the taboo name and venerated. In Madagascar the Malagasy give another name to the deceased; among the Bara tribe this is "Master shining", an appellation shared with the moon, which, as a heavenly body, is regarded as a god and subject to a similar name taboo. Those with the same name as the deceased must immediately change their names (Ruud, p. 171-180). In Australia and America, even words with a phonetic resemblance to the names of the dead are considered contaminating. This is why the Tiwi ban not only the proper name *Mulankina* but also the word *mulikina* which means "filled, enough" and the Yurok of California, when *Tegis* died, would not use the word *tsis* (woodpecker scalps) in the presence of the man's relatives (Lévi-Strauss, [1962] 1976, p. 176-177).

Various explanations have been offered, by both anthropologists and practitioners, for the strong taboos on naming the dead. One explanation is that the survival of a man's name signifies his continued existence so that naming him is equivalent to necromancy. The dead can be malicious and are best not disturbed: "If you name the dead, their spirits answer us, and that's what makes us ill" as one Ilongot woman put it (Rosaldo, p. 14). Moreover, the name of the dead man is subject to the contagion of death and, like the handling of his corpse, can pollute the living. Sometimes the survivors change their names during the period of mourning as a disguise to confuse returning spirits or to escape the death pollution (Webster, p. 185). Lévi-Strauss, however, considers the fear of ghosts insufficient to explain the complexities of the name taboos on the dead which cannot be treated in isolation but form part of a highly symbolic system of classification that must be understood in its entirety. As an example, he takes the western Penan, nomads of the interior of Borneo. The Penan have three terms of designation: a personal name, a teknonym expressing family relationships ('brother' or 'father' of someone) and a necronym, which expresses the kinship relation with a dead relative ('father dead', 'niece dead'). These are not used simultaneously but alternate according to circumstance:

> ... a child is known by its proper name until one of his ascendants dies. If it is a grandfather who dies, the child is then called Tupou. If his father's brother dies he becomes Ilun and remains so until another relative dies. He then receives a new name. A Penan may thus pass through a series of six or seven more necronyms before he marries and has children.
>
> At the birth of their first child a father and mother adopt a teknonym expressing their relation to the child whose name forms part of it. Thus: Tinen Awing 'mother of Awing'. Should the child die, the teknonym is replaced by a necronym: 'Eldest child dead' (Lévi-Strauss, [1962] 1976, p. 191).

It is the structure of family relationships that is important – personal names are only used by default, as it were – and the names of the dead are never mentioned because they are incorporated into the world of the living through the use of teknonyms. In other words, the dead are not spoken of because they do not exist except in their relationship with living relatives. Furthermore, when parents procreate, they are not seen as adding to the population

but as substituting a new life for their own; they cannot use their own names as, symbolically, they are 'dead' and therefore only exist in their relationship with their offspring (Lévi-Strauss, p. 191-216). In some other societies, like the Yurok of California, taboos surrounding the name of the dead come to an end when a younger relative adopts the name – again a case of a name gaining validity through its connection with the living.

Besides the names of the dead, the living, and the divine, taboos are applied to the names of plants and animals – which may represent the totem of a particular clan, and be prohibited as food to clan members – and inanimate objects.

But not all prohibitions on naming are concerned with serious issues. The Ilongots of northern Luzon in the Philippines love making witty puns on names, inventing names and mocking people with their word-play. With knowledge of the name comes the opportunity for teasing, shaming and, if their wit is superior, commanding others. In-laws are therefore not immediately named as this would lay them open to abuse and shame. Only with time and familiarity does the naming and taunting begin (Rosaldo, p. 11-24).

See also
Death; Pollution

References

Denny, Frederick Mathewson. 1987. "Names and Naming". In *Encyclopedia of Religion*. ed. Mircea Eliade, p. 300-307. New York: Macmillan.

Foucart, George B. 1917. "Names (Primitive)". In *Encyclopaedia of Religion and Ethics*. ed. James Hastings. vol. 9, p. 130-36. Edinburgh.

Lévi-Strauss, Claude. [1962] 1976. *The Savage Mind*. London: Weidenfeld and Nicolson.

Rosaldo, Renato. 1984. "Ilongot Naming: The Play of Associations". In *Naming Systems*. ed. Elisabeth Tooker, p. 11-24. Washington, DC: Proceedings of the American Ethnological Society.

Ruud, Jørgen. 1960. *Taboo: A Study of Malagasy Customs and Beliefs*. Oslo: Oslo University Press.

Webster, Hutton. 1942. *Taboo: A Sociological Study*. Stanford, California: Stanford University Press.

Necrophagy and asceticism

Necrophagy, the eating of corpses, has been much reported but rarely witnessed, except in cases of extreme hunger – after a plane crash or in some other desperate situation. It is usually considered a nefarious act, an aberration of depraved murderers or a component of the dark, subversive imagination of gothic literature. Yet it is precisely because it is surrounded by such strong taboos that it is celebrated by certain ascetics in India, in particular the Aghori devotees of the Hindu god, Siva, in his aspect of Lord of the Cremation Ground and Conqueror of Death. Whether or not the Aghoris actually devour human flesh is perhaps less important than the fact that they themselves claim to do so, they are believed to do so by their followers and they were prosecuted in court for such acts during the British raj. One Aghori, tried in 1862 in Ghazipur, was allegedly:

> … found carrying the remains of a putrid corpse along a road. He was throwing the brains from the skull on to the ground and the stench of the corpse greatly distracted the people. Here and there he placed the corpse on shop boards and on the ground. Separating pieces of flesh from the bones he ate them and insisted on begging (Barrow, H. W. quoted in Parry, p. 90).

Necrophagy is not the only taboo flouted by the ascetics. They traditionally live in cremation grounds, eating out of scoured skulls, wandering naked or wearing a shroud pilfered from a corpse; they are not adverse to ingesting excrement, urine and ash from a cremation pyre, sleeping with prostitutes in *coitus reservatus*, and especially – given the ultimate profanity that it involves – mating with them while they are menstruating.

All this may seem at variance with the principles of Hinduism, with its fastidious rules of purity, its rigid caste system in which those that handle excrement have been designated "untouchable" and treated as social pariahs, while the higher castes are strict vegetarians, eschewing not only beef but all meat. Yet the Aghori are deemed holy, not polluting. They trace the foundation of their order to the 18th-century ascetic, Kina Ram, whom they avow to be an incarnation or *avatar* of Siva and whose tomb, in Benares, is one of their most important centres. Through their observances, Aghoris are believed to acquire *siddhis*, supernatural powers that enable them to cure the sick, bestow riches and fertility, raise the dead, and control ghosts. An Aghori *guru*, Baba Bhagvan Ram, has founded a hospice for lepers across the river from Benares, proving that they are not adverse to conventional medicine, but it is their magical power to determine the outcome of events that draws people to them at times of personal crisis. Conversely, the curse of an Aghori can turn food to excrement, inflict disease and cause infertility.

It is not merely the lifestyle of an Aghori that defies conventions. His death too, at least according to the reports of his followers, differs from the norm; indeed, he is credited with defying mere mortality. While it is necessary for a religious Hindu to be ritually cremated in order to be rejuvenated into the endless cycle of life, until he is finally absolved, reaching dissolution into Brahma, the body of an Aghori is not burned. The Aghori is said to avoid death by entering *samadhi* while still alive. *Samadhi* is a term referring both to the tomb into which the ascetic enters while still alive and his cataleptic condition within it. Arranged in the cross-legged meditational posture, the Aghori is lowered into a box which is buried in a sacred place and oriented towards the north. Through this burial, his body is thought to evade decay and his soul to elude transmigration, the latter able to be recalled to the body by the prayers of the devotee.

The defying of convention and flouting of taboos is not unique to the Aghoris – in many respects they resemble tantric mystics but their practices are more extreme. The justification for their acts is their desire to deny, or transcend, worldly existence; to conquer the limitations of the human condition and the restraints of society. This involves overcoming natural inclinations and tastes, and rejecting the distinction between good and evil, divine and human, pure and polluted, pleasant and unpleasant. Just as human excrement enriches a sterile soil, so the assimilation of all kinds of filth makes the mind capable of all forms of meditation. Aghoris similarly reject caste distinctions and family lineages.

The god, Siva, to whom the Aghoris of Benares owe allegiance, is credited with beheading Brahma and carrying Brahma's skull to the city, thereby inspiring the Kapalikas, or skull-bearers, who are mentioned in Sanskrit texts and are possibly precursors of the Aghori. Siva himself is described in the Sanskrit text, the *Brahmanda Purana* (300-500 CE):

> His body was pale with the ashes smeared on it; he was naked, and all his identifying marks were defaced; his hair was disordered and loose; he had enormous pointed teeth; his hands were busy with fire-brands and his eyes were red and tawny. His penis and testicles were like red chalk, the tip ornamented with red and white chalk. Sometimes he laughed horribly; sometimes he sang, smiling; sometimes he danced erotically; sometimes he yelled and yelled again (*Hindu Myths*, p. 142).

Later in the same text, the use of ashes is expounded by the god:

> ... one who has purified his soul by bathing in ashes, conquered his anger, and subdued his senses will come into my presence and never be reborn again. The vow of the ... yoga of the skull ... was created by me and has shame, delusion and fear as its soul ... Let a man smear his body

until it is pale with ashes and meditate upon Bhava ["existence", a form of Rudra, antecedent of Siva] in his heart, and then even if he does a thousand things that one ought not to do, by bathing in ashes he will cause all of that to be burnt to ashes as fire burns a forest with its energy (*Hindu Myths*, p. 148-149).

By imitating Siva and following his teachings, refusing to accept moral or social hierarchies, breaking taboos, uniting opposites and entering the tomb while still alive, the Aghori ascetic hopes to reach the time of non-differentiation, the eternal time of creation and unity with Brahma.

See also

Cannibalism; Death; Excrement; Menstruation

References

Barrow, H. W. 1893. "On Agoris and Aghoripanthis". *Journal of the Anthropological Society of Bombay*, no. 3, p. 197-251.

Hindu Myths. 1975. trans. Doniger O'Flaherty. London: Penguin.

Eliade, Mircea. [1954] 1973. *Yoga: Immortality and Freedom*. Princeton, New Jersey: Princeton University Press, Bollingen Foundation.

Parry, Jonathan. [1980] 1982. "Sacrificial death and the necrophagous ascetic". In *Death and the Regeneration of Life*, ed. Maurice Bloch and Jonathan Parry, p. 74-110. Cambridge: Cambridge University Press.

Siegel, Lee. 1995. *City of Dreadful Night*. London; Chicago, Illinois: University of Chicago Press.

Necrophilia

Necrophilia, the morbid love of corpses, appears to be more common in fiction than in real life, perhaps because of an innate fear of death and putrefaction, reinforced by cultural taboos that regard the corpse as a source of pollution, not to be touched by the holy (Brahmins in Hinduism, Cohens in Judaism).

Nevertheless, within the domains of literature, necrophilia thrives. An early example is the tale of Melissa and Periander mentioned by the Greek historian, Herodotus (*Histories* 5.92.) in the 5th century BCE. In this story, the Corinthian tyrant, Periander, requests the Oracle of the Dead on the river Acheron in Thesprotia to raise his wife's spirit so that she can help him find a missing object. When Melissa appears, however, she is too angry to answer her husband's question because he has cremated her without her clothes and she has suffered greatly from the cold. This distress is compounded by the fact that he himself is responsible for her death and has, moreover, "put his loaves into a cold oven", in other words, made love to her dead body (Felton, p. 78-79).

Necrophilia is especially common in that branch of literature known as Gothic, which emerged late in the 18th century as part of the Romantic movement. Gothic literature, so called because of the medieval castles, monasteries and ruins which feature in its novels, represents a reaction against the rationality of the Enlightenment and revels in the breaking of taboos. The famous Gothic novel, *Melmoth the Wanderer*, written in 1820 by Charles Robert Maturin mingles death and eroticism in a nightmarish way. In the book, a young man sells his blood so he can help his impoverished family. Unfortunately, the vein is severed in such a way that he almost bleeds to death. Though unconscious, the noble young man presents an exquisite body:

> he lay ... in a kind of corpse-like beauty, to which the light of the moon gave an effect that would have rendered the figure worthy of the pencil of a Murillo, a Rosa, or any of those painters, who, inspired by the genius of suffering, delight in representing the most exquisite of human forms in the extremity of human agony. A St Bartholomew flayed, with his skin hanging about him in graceful drapery

> – a St Lawrence, broiled on a gridiron, and exhibiting his finely-formed anatomy on its bars, while naked slaves are blowing the coals beneath it, – even these were inferior to the form half-veiled, – half-disclosed by the moonlight as it lay (Maturin, p. 551).

Not surprisingly, that master of sexual deviation, the marquis de Sade, also writes of the eroticism of death. His novel, *Juliette*, combines incest, orgy and intercourse with the dead: the father of a dead girl persuades the gravedigger to disinter his daughter and he takes the opportunity to undress and rape her. He is later joined in the vault, where the body and coffin have been replaced, by the novel's heroines, La Durand and Juliette, and an orgy ensues.

Despite the unlikely plots of de Sade, cadavers are known to have been stolen for anatomical research and, according to the procurator general of Paris in 1781, possibly served more nefarious ends:

> The bodies lowered into this common pit are every day exposed to the most infamous violations. On the pretext of study, certain persons, not content with the bodies that are given to the hospitals, also steal dead bodies from cemeteries and commit on them everything that impiety and debauchery might inspire (Ariès, p. 46).

Verification of alleged offences is difficult but that does not mean that they have never taken place. What is even more unlikely is the ravishing of the living by the dead which is strictly speaking fear, rather than love, of the dead although often the passion is portrayed as mutual. The theme of "Death and the Maiden" has appeared in paintings and etchings since the Middle-Ages. A print in Basle Museum by the artist, N. M. Deutsch, depicts a passionate skeleton trailing ribbons of flesh and embracing a female who seems to be guiding his hand. The maiden is more resistant in a 16th-century painting by Hans Baldung Grien; hands clasped in supplication, tearful, and dragged by the hair to the nether regions. The works are allegories of vanity but painted in such a way as to emphasise the highly erotic subject matter.

Also suffused with eroticism is the theme of the vampire, in fiction at least (in folklore the vampire is frightening but asexual). In 1818, John Polidori wrote "The Vampyre", a tale of an aristocrat, Lord Ruthven, a seducer and master of transgression, who is dead yet not dead, and who needs blood to sustain his immortality. But the most famous literary vampire appears in Bram Stoker's *Dracula*; written in Victorian England (1897), it features what was to become a classical theme – the handsome aristocrat who seeks out beautiful young women, sinking his teeth into their throats and sucking out their blood.

Attempts to explain the popularity of necrophilia as a theme in art, literature and, more recently, film, are frequently based on the psychological theories of Sigmund Freud. Ernest Jones, for instance, thinks that a fascination with corpses stems from a regressive personality that has not progressed beyond what Freud defined as the "anal" stage:

> Bearing in mind the anal-erotic origin of necrophilia … we are not surprised to observe what stress many writers on the subject lay on the horrible stink that invests the vampire (Ernest Jones, "On the Vampire" Quoted in Barber, p. 130).

Also Freudian-based (with borrowings from Jacques Lacan) is Rosemary Jackson's explanation of Dracula's popularity. She interprets the vampire's attacks as a symbolic *reversal* of the Oedipal stage of development. First Dracula penetrates the woman with his canine (phallic) teeth. This penetration by a father-figure is a reversal of the child's sexual desire to enter the mother. It allows Dracula to suck the blood, which he needs for sustenance, just as the infant sucks the breast. He has thus entered the pre-Oedipal condition, before separation from the mother, a time of bliss:

With each penetration and "return" to the unity of the imaginary, a new vampire is produced: further objects of desire are endlessly generated, creating an "other" order of beings, for whom desire never dies and whose desire prevents them from dying – hence the subversive power of the vampire myth (Jackson, p. 120).

Such happiness cannot be allowed to continue:

> … The sadistic piercing of the vampire with the stake re-asserts the rule of the father, re-enacting the original act of symbolic castration visited upon the subject for desiring union with the mother (Jackson, p. 121).

The logic is ingenious but psychological explanations are notoriously difficult to either confirm or deny. They are based upon the psychological premise that the repression of basic instincts marks an individual's maturity and socialisation and that the overt flouting of taboos must therefore be a sign of regression. Georges Bataille takes up the notion (also Freudian) of the tabooed object evoking both horror and desire. The realisation of desire involves overcoming an initial anguish, breaking an innate taboo, and the greater the original anguish the more satisfying the transgression. His starting point is de Sade's comment that the best way to know death is to link it with a licentious image and he goes on to explore the relationship between fear, revulsion and desire, eroticism and death.

Others have explained the popularity of necrophilia in literature as a reaction to periods of social turbulence. David Punter interprets the vampire figure as the representative of a vanishing aristocracy. Traumas such as the French Revolution have created a new, bourgeois class. The vampire, generally a lord or count, is cruel, cynical and dismissive of the values of the middle class; he is preoccupied with blood and lineage, not rationalism and conformism. Uneasy about their own identity, the bourgeoisie have created the vampire myth to encapsulate their own fears, projected onto their antecedents (Punter, p. 119). Rosemary Jackson similarly sees the vampire as an affront to conventional, and in particular Victorian, morality. Of *Dracula*, she is aware that:

> It blasphemes against Christian sacraments – Renfield, the count's disciple, chants "The blood is the life! The blood is the life!" It offends sexual taboos. Not only the count, but also his female converts, return ... to suck away life: the sexual undertones are barely concealed (Jackson, p. 119).

The subversive forces must be defeated. Yet the vampire myth is also a powerful vehicle for catharsis; it reveals, and provides an outlet for, repressed erotic desires.

At the beginning of the 21st century, when sexual taboos have been considerably relaxed, necrophilia still has the power to shock. In a recent French film, *J'aimerais pas crever un dimanche* (Don't let me die on a Sunday) by the writer-director Didier Le Pêcheur, two morgue attendants watch pornographic tapes between shifts to pass away the time. When the body of a girl who has died from excessive partying is brought in, one of the attendants makes love to the corpse and brings her back to life.

See Also

Necrophagy and Asceticism

References

Ariès, Philippe. [1977] 1981. *The Hour of Our Death*. trans. Helen Weaver. Harmondsworth, Middlesex: Penguin.

Barber, Paul. 1988. *Vampires, Burial, and Death: Folklore and Reality*. New Haven, Connecticut; London: Yale University Press.

Bataille, Georges. [1957] 1987. *Eroticism*. trans. Mary Dalwood. London: Marion Boyars.

Felton, D. 1999. *Haunted Greece and Rome: Ghost Stories from Classical Antiquity*. Austin, Texas: University of Texas Press.

Jackson, Rosemary. 1981. *Fantasy: The Literature of Subversion*. London: Methuen.

Maturin, Charles Robert. [1820] 1977. *Melmoth the Wanderer: A Tale*. Harmondsworth, Middlesex: Penguin.

Punter, David. 1980. *The Literature of Terror: A History of Gothic Fictions from 1765 to the Present Day*. London: Longman.

Noa

Noa is a Polynesian word applied to all that is free from the restriction of taboo. It means 'not tied to specific ends' and designates the unspecified, the neutral and free, including everything from which a taboo has been lifted. On certain occasions two conflicting taboos could result in a state of noa. While Maori women were forbidden to eat human flesh, and any transgression would incur disaster in future battles, it was the duty of the *wahine ariki*, the eldest and most senior woman of the tribe, to eat an ear from the first enemy killed. This rendered the returning warriors noa.

References

Hanson, F. Allan and Louise Hanson. 1983. *Counterpoint in Maori Culture*. London: Routledge and Kegan Paul.

Smith, Jean. 1974. *Tapu Removal in Maori Religion*. Wellington: Polynesian Society.

North-East

North-east is an inauspicious direction according to the laws of *feng-shui* (wind-water), a form of Chinese "geomancy" originally practised in the Far East to orient buildings and to divine where to site graves. Because it is so inauspicious, the bathroom or kitchen of a house should never be placed on the north-east side of a house.

Taoist texts of the 4th and 5th centuries place the hill Feng-tu, situated on the Yangtze river in the province of Szechuan, in the north-east. Feng-tu is the land of the dead, of "obstructed souls," and this, according to the sinologist, John Lagerwey, "is why the north-east is the Gate of Demons and the source of the energies of the dead" (Lagerwey. 1987, p. 35). Feng-tu is ruled by the Lord-emperor of the North and:

> According to *The Book of the Three Origins* (*San-yüan ching*) Feng-tu is also called Northern Feng, and it is where the names of those who do not fast attentively will be reported by the "divine soldiers of the Five Emperors". These people will lose their right to enter the Hall of the Fast (*chai-t'ang*) (Lagerwey, 1987, p. 35).

One of the tasks of the Taoist priests is to ritually seal the Gate of the Demons, trapping the demon, by taking a sword and inscribing the Chinese character for "demon" on rice (a purifying agent) that lies in a bucket (symbolising a "metal well") on the north-eastern corner of the altar.

Reference

Lagerwey, John. 1987. *Taoist Ritual in Chinese Society and History*. New York; London: Macmillan Publishing Company.

Ockam's Razor

The scientific principle known as Ockam's Razor is that "Entia non sunt multiplicanda sine necessitate", or "Entities are not to be multiplied beyond necessity". This statement is attributed to the Francisan monk, William of Ockam (also spelled Occam and Ockham) who lived from around 1285 to 1349 and was an influential medieval thinker, constantly involved in disputes with popes and antipopes. Whether or not he actually spoke the words, what Ockam meant was that one should not resort to new assumptions or hypotheses (entities) unless necessary. In other words, the simplest theory is preferable to the more complicated one. If, for instance, a footprint is found in the snow, it is simpler, and therefore preferable to assume it was made by a bear rather than by the abominable snowman or yeti. Similar doctrines to that of Ockam were proposed earlier by Duns Scotus and Odo Rigaldus.

Obviously, sometimes it is necessary to introduce a new hypothesis or "entity" to explain a phenomenon. Copernicus' theory of heliocentricity was a new hypothesis that replaced the conviction that the earth was the centre of the universe. In mathematical terms, of course, the theory of heliocentricity is much simpler than its predecessor. The application of the Ockam Razor principle can also lead to

mistakes. Scientists from the French Academy rejected, for a long time, the reality of meteorites, believing them to be terrestrial rocks to which credulous people had attributed a celestial origin. Their scepticism resulted in dozens of specimens being thrown out of European museums.

References

Poundstone, William. [1988] 1991. *Labyrinths of Reason: Paradox, Puzzles and the Frailty of Knowledge.* London: Penguin.

Webering, Damascene. 1953. *Theory of Demonstration according to William of Ockam.* St. Bonaventura, New York: Franciscan Institute.

Onanism

The sin of onanism, the wanton spilling of seed, is mentioned in the biblical book of *Genesis*. Onan, the son of Judah, is requested by his father to marry Tamar, the widow of his brother, Er, so that he may produce a surrogate child for his brother. However, aware that the child will not be his own, Onan deliberately allows his semen to fall on the ground every time he makes love to Tamar. For flouting his fraternal duties, Onan is punished with death (*Genesis* 38: 7-10). In Jewish folklore, any semen not used for procreation will be seized by the demoness, Lilith, the first wife of Adam. Denied human children because of her refusal to obey her husband, she comes to men at

197

night and causes them to spill their seed. For this reason, it is dangerous for men to sleep alone (Patai, p. 233-236).

The Christian denunciation of onanism or masturbation is based as much on the illicit pleasure the practice affords as on its adverse effect on childbirth. Saint Thomas Aquinas deemed it more dangerous than fornication. If the religious injunctions were insufficient to prevent masturbation, medical evidence was resorted to. This was especially the case from the end of the 18th century to the end of the 19th century when it was considered important that young males from a privileged background should not squander their vital fluids but preserve them in order to secure a healthy line of succession. Boarding schools introduced strict supervision to prevent boys congregating and indulging in what was seen as a pernicious habit (Foucault vol. 1, p. 121).

Reports of the adverse effects of masturbation continued into the 20th century. With frequent masturbation, according to one report published in the United States in 1926:

> The health soon becomes noticeably impaired; there will be general debility, a slowness of growth, weakness in the lower limbs, nervousness and unsteadiness of the hand, loss of memory, forgetfulness and inability to study or learn, a restless disposition, weak eyes and loss of sight, headache and inability to sleep, or wakefulness. Next come sore eyes, blindness, stupidity, consumption, spinal affection, emaciation, involuntary seminal emissions, loss of all energy or spirit, insanity or idiocy – the hopeless ruin of both body and mind (Ruddock, p. 863).

Such erroneous accounts of the harmful consequences of onanism are at odds with the views expressed by many of the people interviewed in the United States during the 1970s by the researcher, Shere Hite. Conducting surveys on the sexual habits of women and men, Hite found widespread support for the view of masturbation as a healthy and natural pursuit. Nonetheless, Philip Thody reports how, as recently as December 1994, the United States Surgeon-General, Jocelyn Elders, was forced by President Clinton to resign after the outcry following her remarks that masturbation helped limit the spread of AIDS and teenage pregnancy (Thody, p. 50-51).

It is not merely the Western tradition that has been wary of the wanton spilling of semen. In Taoist and Tantric yoga belief, sperm must be retained if life is to be prolonged. Even the erotic "bedroom manuals", which date back to the 2nd century BCE and were an important source of information for the sinologist, R. H. van Gulik, express a fear of losing one's semen. Guides like the *Su-nüching* specifically direct a man to "Save your semen so that your life will not end" (Schiffer, p. 148). If a man is able to make love to several women in succession without reaching orgasm, he is considered capable of nurturing the *yang* (male essence) with the *yin* (female). Women have a similar goal and are frequently portrayed as vampires: like the incubus Lilith, from Jewish folklore, the great goddess and Queen of the West is believed to have attained immortality through stealing men's seed and exhausting them, while growing ever more radiant herself (Schipper, p. 147).

See also

Cunnilingus

References

Ehrenreich, B. and D. English. 1979. *For Her Own Good: 150 Years of the Experts' Advice to Women.* London: Pluto Press.

Ellis, H. [1896-1928] 1942. *Studies in the Psychology of Sex.* New York: Random House.

Foucault, M. [1976] 1979. *The History of Sexuality.* 3 vols. trans. Robert Hurley. London: Penguin, Allen Lane.

Gulik, R. H. van. 1961. *Sexual Life in Ancient China.* Leiden, the Netherlands: Brill.

Hite, Shere. 1976. *The Hite Report: A Nationwide Study of Female Sexuality.* New York: Macmillan; London: Collier/Macmillan.

Hite, Shere. 1978. *The Hite Report on Male Sexuality*. New York: Macmillan.

Patai, Raphael. [1967] 1990. *The Hebrew Goddess*. Detroit, Michigan: Wayne State University Press.

Ruddock, Edward Harris. 1926. *Vitalogy. An Encyclopedia of Health and Home*. Chicago, Illinois: Vitalogy Association.

Schipper, Kristofer. [1982] 1993. *The Taoist Body*. trans. Karen C. Duval. Berkeley; Los Angeles; London: University of California Press.

Otters

One reason the otter is not eaten by the villagers of Phraan Muan in northeastern Thailand is because its name, *naag*, generally denotes the mythical water snake that inhabits rivers and swamps. The *naag* appears in Buddhist mythology as a guardian of the faith, and is viewed with ambivalence by the Thai; at times malevolent, at times propitious, it represents rain and fertility yet opposes humans in rain-making rites. The otter is also taboo because it resembles the dog which is much maligned by the villagers as a filthy, incestuous beast (Tambiah, p. 445).

See also
Dogs; Food Taboos

References
Tambiah, S. J. 1969. "Animals are Good to Think and Good to Prohibit". *Ethnology*, no. 8, p. 423-459.

Oysters

Oysters are forbidden in Judaism, along with all other shellfish, because, though they live in the water, they have neither fins nor scales (*Deuteronomy* 14: 9-19; *Leviticus* 11: 9-12). Scales and fins are not mentioned in a folk belief of the Anglo-Saxon world in which oysters are said to be poisonous during those months that (in English) do not contain the letter *r*. The prohibition from May to August gives the creatures a lucky reprieve during the spawning season (Farb and Armelagos, p. 236 n. 88). In the West oyster-eating is thought to enhance sexual prowess, maybe due to the oyster's resemblance to female genitalia. In China, where oysters are an important source of protein, their consumption has interesting side-effects, quite different from those imagined in Europe. The 7th-century pharmacologist, Meng Shen, describes how they inhibit nocturnal emissions, or, as he puts it, "copulation with ghosts and emission of sperm" (Schafer, p. 105).

See also
Chinese Food Taboos; Jewish Dietary Laws

References
Farb, Peter and George Armelagos. 1980. *Consuming Passions: The Anthropology of Eating*. Boston, Massachusetts: Houghton Mifflin Company.

Schafer, Edward H. 1977. "T'ang". In *Food in Chinese Culture: Anthropological and Historical Perspectives*. ed. K. C. Chang, p. 85-140. New Haven, Connecticut; London: Yale University Press.

P

Parents-in-Law

Certain cultures have very strict taboos surrounding the relationships with in-laws. The anthropologist Claude Lévi-Strauss records how, among the Algonquin-speaking Native Americans living on the Plains, to the west of James Bay (a group that includes the Blackfoot, the Ojibwa and the Cree), a man may not speak to his mother-in-law unless he has first presented her with a scalp. Among the Hidatsa (a tribe living on the banks of the Missouri river), the scalp, captured in battle, is presented to the mother-in-law as though it were a walking-stick, and she is entitled to carry it thereafter when she joins the victory dance (Levi-Strauss, 1979, p. 399).

Reference

Lévi-Strauss, Claude. [1968] 1979. *Introduction to a Science of Mythology* vol. 3; *The Origin of Table Manners*. trans. John and Doreen Weightman. New York: Harper and Row.

Perspective in Painting

The classical art of Greece and Rome introduced perspective in painting to create an illusion of depth and favoured three-dimensional sculptures which were more life-like than reliefs. But the move towards realism was not universally acclaimed. The 3rd-century CE Neoplatonist, Plotinus, condemned geometric perspective or depth (*bathos*) because it establishes the dimension of matter, and matter is anathema to someone who views the material world as a trap for the spirit. Besides, he argued that perspective creates only an illusion, or degradation, of reality, because things seen in the distance are distorted and colours are blurred. Instead, he advocated a form of painting that conveyed the luminous intensity of the spirit, conceived on a flat spatial plane and painted in bright, intense hues.

References

Alliez, Eric and Michel Feher: [1989] 1990. "Reflections of a Soul". In *Fragments for a History of the Human Body* Part Two. ed. Michel Feher, p. 46-84. New York: Zone Books.

Plotinus. 1991 *The Enneads*. trans. Stephen MacKenna. London: Penguin.

Pigs

The flesh of pigs is taboo to Muslims and Jews. Various explanations for the ban have been offered. The anthropologist Marvin Harris offers an economic explanation: after widespread deforestation, the arid conditions in the Middle East were not conducive to pig-rearing, as the animals like to forage for food. Unlike sheep and goats, they can not be milked and, as they do not eat grass, they compete with humans for grains. Maimonedes, a 12th-century Jewish philosopher, considered the animal unclean and unwholesome. Mary Douglas attributes its unpopularity among the Israelites to the fact that it defies classification: although it has cloven hoofs, it does not chew the cud and therefore does not fit into the category of herbivores. Things that confuse our taxonomies disturb our sense of order, they are considered dangerous and polluting. M. P. Carroll thinks that it is a question of confusing the natural and cultural realms: humans (representing culture) may eat meat while animals (nature) should be vegetarians. The pig eats carrion and vermin; while being part of the animal kingdom, it invades the realm of man. Edmund Leach considers the pig too close to man because it traditionally lives around the farmhouse, eating the remains of human food. To eat a pig would be tantamount to cannibalism, and taboos are placed upon it to protect human identity by marking the difference between man and beast. But according to Mary Douglas the taboo also serves to protect cultural identity: the Jews refrain from pork precisely because their neighbours eat it; in the same way Muslims do not eat pigs because Christians, and Hindus, do.

See also

Douglas, Mary; Food Taboos; Jewish Dietary Laws

References

Bulmer, R. 1967. "Why the Cassowary is Not a Bird: A Problem of Zoological Taxonomy among the Karam of the New Guinea Highlands". *Man*, no. 2, p. 5-25.

Carroll. 1978. "One More Time: Leviticus Revisited". *Archives européennes de sociologie*, no. 19, p. 339-346.

Douglas, Mary. [1966] 1984. *Purity and Danger: An Analysis of the Concepts of Pollution and Taboo*. London: Routledge and Kegan Paul.

Douglas, Mary. [1975] 1979. "Deciphering a Meal". In *Implicit Meanings: Essays in Anthropology by Mary Douglas*, p. 249-275. London: Routledge and Kegan Paul.

Douglas, Mary. 1990. "The pangolin revisited: a new approach to animal symbolism". In *Signifying Animals: Human Meaning in the Natural World*. ed. Roy G. Willis, p. 25-36. London: Unwin Hyman Ltd.

Leach, Edmund. 1964. "Animal Categories and Verbal Abuse". In *New Directions in the Study of Language*, p. 23-63. Cambridge, Massachusetts: Massachusetts Institute of Technology Press.

Maimonides *Guide for the Perplexed*, 3, 48. quoted in H. Ra. Dietary Laws.

Rappaport, Roy A. [1968] 1984. *Pigs for the Ancestors: Ritual in the Ecology of a New Guinea People*. New Haven: Yale University Press.

Tambiah, S. J. 1969. "Animals are Good to Think and Good to Prohibit". *Ethnology*, no. 8, p. 423-459.

Plato on Music

The Greek philosopher, Plato (c. 427-347 BCE) was repelled by the corruption and violence that he saw in Athenian political life. This prompted him to write *The Republic*, a work in which he applied philosophy to political affairs and, in the form of dialogues, put forward his proposals for an ideal state. While discussing education, he set out his proscriptions on certain types of music.

The Greeks recognised different types of musical style which they associated with different moods. Plato initially rejected the modes known as the Mixed Lydian and the Extreme Lydian, used for dirges and laments, and the Ionian and certain Lydian modes which tended to accompany drinking, relaxation and idleness. These styles were considered unsuitable for the education of the young; only that music which encouraged bravery and fortitude on the one hand and moderation and tolerance on the other were allowed, exemplified by the Dorian and Phrygian modes.

Harps, dulcimers and flutes were to be banned as the wide harmonic range of these instruments was superfluous; only the lyre and the cithara escaped this censorship. The music of Apollo, who played a cithara, was preferable to that of Marsyas, a Phrygian who had played the flute and lost a musical contest against the war god. For losing, Marsyas, a satyr, was flayed alive, a harsh punishment but not an unusual one: Thamyris, a singer, was blinded for challenging the Muses.

Plato believed that changing to a new kind of music involved far-reaching danger as the music of a country could not be altered without incurring major political and social changes. Between 1973 and 1976 the Dutch composer, Louis Andriessen, wrote *De Staat* (The Republic) as a contribution to the discussion of the place of music in politics. He expresses regret that Plato was wrong: "If only it were true that musical innovation represented a danger to the State!" Despite Andriessen's comment, many societies and governments have agreed with Plato's contention that certain types (or, in the case of extreme Protestant groups, all types) of music are corrupting and have forbidden their performance.

See also

Musical Harmony

References

Andriessen, Louis. 1978. *De Staat* (record sleeve). Amsterdam: Donemus.

Plato. *The Republic*. [1955] 1983. trans. Desmond Lee. London: Penguin.

Political Censorship – Jokes

There is no such thing as a totally "open" society and political censorship is one of the methods used by those in power to maintain control. While democracies are generally more tolerant of criticism than totalitarian states, and are not guilty of the excesses of political repression reported by Amnesty International and other humanitarian organisations, they are not adverse to censoring "politically sensitive" material and satirical magazines. In countries where political oppression is more overt and where freedom of speech is absent, the political joke becomes a form of protest, a channel for criticising political leaders, their policies and the government. Samer S. Shehata has observed the phenomenon in his arti-

cle "The Politics of Laughter: Nasser, Sadat and Mubarek in Egyptian Political Jokes". In a repressive regime, truth is banned or at least, totally disregarded; as this Egyptian joke demonstrates:

A fox in the Western Desert escaped to Libya and the Libyans asked, "Why do you come here?" The fox said, "Because in Egypt they arrest camels." The Libyans said, "But you are not a camel." The fox then said, "Of course not, but try telling that to the police!" (Shehata, p. 80).

This joke is very old; Shehata reports that a similar one has been found in 11th-century Arabic sources and versions have been documented in 12th- and 13th-century Iranian sources and in Czarist Russia, Nazi Germany and communist Eastern Europe.

Another joke from the region tells how an Egyptian dog runs all the way to the Libyan border to bark because he is forbidden to "open his mouth" in Egypt (Shehata, p. 80). Speaking is tabooed except when demanded by the authorities; humour may palliate, but does not hide, the grim reality:

A little ancient Egyptian statue was found, but no one could find out anything about it. They summoned experts from abroad, and still they couldn't find out a single thing about it. The secret police heard about the statue, and they said, "Give it to us for twenty-four hours."

"Twenty-four hours! What can you do in twenty-four hours?"

"None of your business. Just give it to us." They took it and before the day was over, they came back with it and said, "This is King So-and-so, son of So-and-so; he ruled at such and such a time and place, and ..., and ..., and!" They told them everything.

"How did you find all that out? Did you locate his tomb?"

"No sir! He confessed! (Shehata, p. 80).

Shehata remarks that the satire in this joke is directed at the régime of president Jamal

Abdel Nasser of Egypt, during the 1950s and 1960s, when the secret police regularly tortured members of the *Ikhwan Al-Muslimin* (The Muslim Brotherhood). Political jibes generally are of great importance in Egypt and Nasser was even rumoured to collect jokes about himself via the secret police. The humour, however, belies the seriousness of the situation. In intolerable circumstances, jokes provide a measure of relief. Moreover, because they are transmitted orally, they are difficult to censor and as folklorist Alan Dundes points out:

> Jokes are by definition impersonal and they provide a socially sanctioned frame which normally absolves individuals from any guilt which might otherwise result from conversational (= nontraditional) articulations of the same content (Dundes quoted in Shehata, p. 76).

Despite this proviso, it is not unknown for jokes and satire to lead to arrest and even, in some circumstances, to execution.

References

Douglas, Mary. [1975] 1979. "Jokes". In *Implicit Meanings: Essays in Anthropology by Mary Douglas*, p. 90-114. London: Routledge and Kegan Paul.

Dundes, Alan. 1971. "Laughter Behind the Iron Curtain: A Sample of Rumanian Political Jokes". *The Ukranian Quarterly*, no. 27, vol. 1, p. 51-59.

Popper, Karl. R. 1966. *The Open Society and Its Enemies*. London: Routledge and Kegan Paul.

Shehata, Samer S. 1992. "The Politics of Laughter: Nasser, Sadat, and Mubarek in Egyptian Political Jokes". *Folklore: The Journal of the Folklore Society*, no. 1, 1992, p. 75-91. (The footnotes to this article provide a comprehensive bibliography of political humour).

Pollution

Many cultures believe that the violation of a taboo leads to a state of ritual impurity or pollution; it may be the individual transgressor who is polluted or an entire community may be affected by the actions of a single person. The act may also lead to the contamination of a sacred site, whether temple, shrine, river, fire or city. The taboos themselves exist to protect individuals from the dangerous consequences of eating a "polluting" food, touching a "polluted" person, engaging in forbidden pursuits, or the myriad other events that can trigger the impurity such as a death, war, childbirth, initiation, profanation of a sacred precinct, the birth of twins or a woman's menses. In some societies an unfortunate person may be born into a class or caste that is considered "impure"; this was the case with the Hindus known as "untouchables" in India. Those deemed "polluted" are in danger themselves and may pollute others through contagion, either because other people are in the vicinity or because they are linked through kinship ties.

Because pollution is generally considered to be an "inner" state, like the state of sin in Catholicism, its effects may not be immediately visible although it may manifest itself in the form of disease, deformity, insanity, sterility or death. Pollution can also be responsible for plagues and pestilence, or some other natural catastrophe (just as, in the Oedipus myth, the hero's unwitting patricide and incest affects Thebes). Pollution may be ordained by a deity because of a sin, or violation of a religious or moral code, or may be caused by some other supernatural agency, whether witchcraft, demons or other invisible forces, or it may be intrinsic to the polluted object. In many cases, it can be cleansed by purification rituals which frequently include prayers, incantations, fasting, purgations, seclusion, lustrations (purifications by means of an offering) or rites involving sacrifice, blood or bloodletting, fire, fumigations, ashes, incense, wind, salt, urine, perfumes and aromatic herbs. The polluted person or object may be destroyed, exiled or killed or the impurity may be transferred to a scapegoat or effigy which is then expelled, burned or slain.

Sherry Ortner identifies four major categories of pollution, namely: 1) physiological processes; 2) violence and associated processes; 3) anomalies; and 4) social classes and castes (Ortner: Britannica CD2000). Physiological processes, which include birth, menstruation, sexuality, sickness and death as well as bodily excretions such as urine, excrement, blood, semen, sweat, saliva, mucus and exuviae like hair and fingernail cuttings, are deemed polluting in many societies (although, as Mary Douglas has emphasised, cultures vary tremendously in their tolerance of individual pollutants). Under this category she places food taboos because eating is a physiological process that results in excrement. The body below the waist (the site of the most pungent excretions) is deemed more polluting than the upper body, the left side more than the right, and women's bodies more than men's. The corpse, at least in a state of putrefaction, is the most polluting of all. The category "violence" includes murder, warfare and hunting as well as aggressive language, wild animals and things like alcohol that may induce aggression. "Anomalies" groups together unusual phenomena like earthquakes and eclipses, physiological peculiarities such as congenital malformations and unusual births, plants and animals that defy easy classification, sexual perversions and those individuals in a "liminal" or transitional state, either because they are strangers or because they are experiencing a "rite of passage". Ortner's fourth category concerns hierarchies of class or caste.

Theories of pollution

Anthropologists have tended to concentrate on the social dimensions of pollution beliefs. A society cannot function unless it is ordered. Pollution beliefs arise whenever there is a threat to the cultural classification. Mary Douglas is a proponent of this view:

> Pollution beliefs are cultural phenomena. They are institutions that can keep their forms only by bringing pressure to bear on deviant individuals ... The dangers and punishments attached to pollution act simply as means of

enforcing conformity ... Pollution beliefs ... derive ... from the process of classifying and ordering experience (Douglas, p. 58).

Those things that threaten the order – anomalies or people or things at the margins (during a "rite of passage" an individual is between two social roles and people from a low social class or foreign country exist at the edge of society) – are dangerous and polluting. Similarly those things that transgress the body's boundaries – secretions and hair and nail clippings – are hazardous as are natural, social and physiological anomalies.

Psychoanalytical theories are commonly inspired by Sigmund Freud. He proposed that humans are born with various instinctual drives, sexual and aggressive, which need to be overcome if the individual is to develop into a well-adjusted social being. The suppression of innate desires, and the fear of transgression, leads to the external projection of the repressed instincts in the form of pollution beliefs.

Sherry Ortner sees limitations in these theories which can be overcome if they are combined under a more general theory of denial. For instance, Freud speaks of a denial of basic instincts (which include an obsession with bodily functions and excretions and violent emotions). Freud's theory could therefore be applied to the first two categories listed by Ortner. The classificatory theories involve a denial of non-conformity – anomalies are pollutants – hence the suspicion of things in Ortner's third category. To explain the fourth category – the fear of lower castes – she draws on the "sociopolitical notion of oppression": a certain group is denied full social and political participation. Wherever there is repression or denial, there is a danger of eruption. The situation is volatile and this is why things seen as polluting are threatening (Ortner: Britannica CD2000). Sherry Ortner's theory is persuasive but does not explain, for example, why the left side of the body is disadvantaged. Pollution is an extremely complicated topic that arises in almost any discussion of taboo or the sacred.

Perhaps predictably, people and things regarded as polluting and dangerous are often accredited considerable power. Those at the margins – the stranger, the sorcerer, the old woman – are thought to have demonic powers, such as an evil eye that blights the crops, sours the milk or causes sickness and death. In India, bands of ascetics gain power through their ability to transcend impurity. One such sect, the Aghori of Benares, worship the Hindu god Siva in his role as "Lord of the Cremation Ground and Conqueror of Death". Living in cemeteries, eating out of human skulls, reputed to devour human flesh and excrement, the Aghori ascetics acquire *siddhis*, supernatural powers that enable them to heal the sick, grant riches, raise the dead and control ghosts.

Moreover, a substance that is generally seen as impure may be holy if it comes from a sacred source. In Mazdean Iran, the *gomez* or bull-urine remedy was used in purification rituals because of the religion's reverence for the bull. Medieval Japan offers another example. The Japanese established distinct categories: *hare* meaning bright, clear, pure, was applied to new rice, clear sunny days, festival days, sacred sites and waterfalls; *kegare* meaning polluted, defiled or filthy, included both red and black pollution. Both were powerful and dangerous. Red pollution (*akafuji*) generally referred to menstruation and childbirth as well as bloodletting and wounds. Black pollution (*kurofujo*) encompassed death, the corpse, the mourners and all acts of violence, murder and slaughter. In between these categories lay the impurity incurred by coming into contact with bodily excreta: blood, semen, mucus, pus, urine, faeces and vomit. Yet the bodily products of deities were creative. A myth tells how Izanami no Mikoto gives birth to a deity called Hi no Kaga Hiko no Kami. Because she bore this child:

her genitals were burned and she lay down sick. In her vomit, there came

into existence the deity Kana-yama hiko no kami; next Kana yama hime no kami. Next, in her faeces there came into existence the deity Pani yasu hiko no kami; next Pani yasu bime no kame. Next, in her urine there came into existence the deity Mitu-pa-no-me-no-kami (Law, p. 64).

Even the purification of Japanese deities produces miracles. After being polluted by the rotting corpse of his wife, Izanami purifies himself in a river:

Deities arise from his polluted articles of clothing and various parts of his body. Washing his left eye, he creates the sun goddess Amaterasa; washing his right eye, he creates the moon, Tsuku Yomi. From his nose comes the turbulent Susanoo (Law, p. 65).

See also

Freud, Sigmund; Miasma

References

Douglas, Mary. [1968] 1975. "Pollution". In *Implicit Meanings: Essays in Anthropology*. London: Routledge.

Freud, Sigmund. [1912-1913] 1985. "Totem and Taboo". In *The Origins of Religion. The Penguin Freud Library vol.13*. trans. Albert Dickson, p. 45-224. London: Penguin.

Law, Jane Marie. 1997. *Puppets and Nostalgia: The Life, Death and Rebirth of the Japanese Awaji Ningyo Tradition*. Princeton, New Jersey: Princeton University Press.

Ortner, Sherry B. 1994-1998. "Purification Rites and Customs". Britannica© CD2000: Encyclopædia Britannica, Inc.

Pornography

The word "pornography" is derived from the Greek *porni* (harlot) and *graphein* (to write) and was originally used to denote books or paintings that portrayed the lives of prostitutes. It is now applied to sexually explicit material, whether in the form of books, paintings, photographs, sculptures, films or videos, that intends to sexually excite the observer. However, what actually constitutes pornography remains a matter of debate: the distinctions between the erotic, the artistic and the pornographic are not always clear. Nor is it always possible to determine the motivation underlying a sexually explicit image or text.

Unambiguous depictions of the sexual act were already common among the Greeks of the archaic and early classical periods. The cult of Dionysus (the god of wine) inspired much erotic imagery. Cups and vases from around the 5th century BCE depict ithyphallic satyrs while bawdy songs accompanied the frenzied Dionysian festivals. Classical cups, medallions and vases which have no obvious cultic significance frequently portray heterosexual and homosexual combinations as well as acts of fellatio and bestiality. Satyrs and hermaphrodites are recurring participants in these revels. Greek art influenced that of the Etruscans who commonly painted erotic scenes in tombs. A typical example is a wall-painting from the Tomb of the Bull, Tarquinia, which shows a human-faced bull charging towards a copulating couple. The Romans also displayed a lively interest in the lascivious. The Roman poet Publius Ovidius Naso (known as Ovid, 19 BCE-18 CE) wrote a poem entitled *Ars amatoria* (the art of love), a treatise on the art of seduction and deceit. A more serious approach to the erotic is that evinced by the frescoes found in the Villa of Mysteries at Pompeii, from around the 1st century CE. These illustrate episodes from the Dionysiac rites such as a girl unveiling a symbolic phallus and semi-nude figures engaged in flagellation (although the significance of the acts is by no means clear).

In India, too, classical art readily embraced enticing images. The sculpted torso of a *yakshi* (a nature spirit concerned with fecundity) from the 1st century BCE has sensuous curves and is more voluptuous than her Greek counterparts. By the 10th century CE temples had espoused the full repertoire of the erotic. The carved facade of the Kandarya-Mahadeva Temple in Khajuraho (10th-11th century CE) is a mass of entwined divinities and seductive females as is the 13th-century temple at Konarak. India also produced the ancient sex manual, the *Kama Sutra*, a text that considers the spiritual aspects of sexuality and explores the many sexual positions and techniques that enhance lovemaking. Indian miniature paintings produced at Indian courts from the end of the 16th to the mid-19th centuries provided illustrations for the *Kama Sutra* as well as for the *ragas*, the modes of Indian music, many of which celebrate the erotic adventures of the god, Krishna.

Such open displays of sexuality were anathema to Christianity, a religion that distrusts sensuous pleasures and celebrates the purity of the soul. When the medieval stonemasons carved lewd figures on the cornices of European cathedrals they were creating allegories on the wages of sin: voluptuous nude females are shown writhing in hell, tormented by demons. In the doorway of Bourges Cathedral in France, human heads are depicted on the stomachs and genitalia of the devils, signifying the triumph of base desires. Yet prayer books dating from the 13th century, commissioned by wealthy patrons, sometimes contained tiny, explicit images in the margins. In an Italian *Book of Hours* from the 15th century a penitent kisses the buttocks of a monk and the *Bible moralisé*, prepared for Charles V of France, has a picture of a naked couple making love, encouraged by a devil. The image is justified as a didactic device – drunkenness leads to lust – but the effect on the viewer may be more ambiguous. From the 14th century onwards, carnivals provided an outlet for sexual repressions and inspired many bawdy and satirical songs, often at the expense of the repressive clergy. In the mid-14th century the Italian writer, Giovanni Boccaccio, wrote the *Decameron*, a collection of one hundred stories, sometimes of a licentious nature, supposedly narrated by survivors of the Florentine plague of 1348.

The invention and proliferation of printing presses in the 15th and 16th centuries meant that works that had previously been restricted to a very select audience could now be enjoyed by the masses (although written literature still required literacy). This posed a problem for the Church who were worried at the effect of salacious images on the uneducated. For instance, in 1524 a duke commissioned the Roman artist, Giulio Romano, a pupil of Raphael, to paint a series of frescos for his *Palazzo del Tè* in Mantua. The images were often explicit, such as the ravishing of Olympia by Jove disguised as a dragon, but because the pictures depicted mythical events and were for the perusal of the rich, the Church raised no objections. Yet when Romano's drawings were given to Marcantonio Raimondi and the latter printed sixteen sexual positions based on Romano's paintings (which were in turn inspired by erotic designs from Roman tombs), and offered them for sale, he was imprisoned in Rome. In 1527, the Italian writer Pietro Aretino, wished to write erotic sonnets to accompany the engravings. Aretino's writing was often political and he was forced to flee Rome when Pope Adrian VI was elected.

A direct censorship of literature came in 1559 when Pope Paul IV issued an index of forbidden books.

In the 18th century there was an explosion of openly pornographic material. Many tracts were written by philosophers of the Enlightenment who used erotic material to interest the proletariat in their ideas. Demanding freedom, they protested against the strictures imposed by the Church and State. In 1761 the German-born, French philosopher, Paul Heinrich Dietrich Holbach, wrote *Le Christianisme dévoilé* (Christianity unveiled), a vehemently anti-religious work, and other philosophers were not averse to ridiculing priests by propagating images of them with raised cassocks. French pornographic pamphlets ridiculed the ruling class, attacking the virility of Louis XVI and Marie Antoinette's alleged promiscuity. Read aloud, by street hawkers, to a gathered crowd, they helped prepare the proletariat for the Revolution of 1789. One French writer who supported the Revolution (although he denounced the brutality of the revolutionaries) was the Marquis de Sade. He was appointed secretary of the Revolutionary Section of Les Piques in 1792 but was later condemned to the guillotine and only narrowly escaped death. His work, much of which was written in prison, has had a profound influence on contemporary pornography although the philosophy underlying it has been largely neglected.

One British erotic work of the 18th century is *Fanny Hill,* or *Memoirs of a Woman of Pleasure,* a social satire written in 1749 by John Cleland. It was the social dimension that led to a United States Supreme Court ruling concerning the book in 1966. The court decided that a work was only to be considered pornographic if it had no redeeming social value.

The first British prosecution for a publication that was considered "indecent" came in 1727 but it was not until 1857 that the Obscene Publications Act (also known as Lord Campbell's Act after the chancellor who introduced it) came into being. In the United States, the Comstock Law of 1873 made it a criminal offence to send or receive "lewd" or "lascivious" publications through the postal service. Since that time, there has been considerable debate over what constitutes an "obscene publication". In 1857 the French novelist, Gustave Flaubert, was acquitted of a charge of offences against public morals for his book *Madame Bovary.* His lawyer argued that, far from encouraging adultery, the novel warns of the dangers (the heroine falls into debt and commits suicide when her creditors threaten to tell her husband) of extra-marital liaisons. Many other works of great literary merit have encountered difficulties because of their explicit contents. James Joyce's *Ulysses* faced difficulty with publication and in 1960 the British publishers, Penguin Books, were put on trial for publishing D. H. Lawrence's novel *Lady Chatterley's*

Lover. The trial of Penguin was an important test of the revised Obscene Publications Act of 1959 which stated that prosecution should not take place if the publication was "in the interests of science, literature, arts or learning", or of literary, artistic, scientific or other merits (Obscene Publications Act. Britannica CD2000). According to these criteria, the book was exonerated.

The debate over what constitutes pornography continues along with a massive increase in the number of visual representations of sex in the form of photographs, films and videos. Explicit photographs of homosexual sado-masochism by Robert Mapplethorpe are exhibited as art but viewed by some as pornography: in 1995 the incensed Republican Senator for North Carolina, Jesse Helms, destroyed a copy of a Mapplethorpe exhibition catalogue on the floor of the Senate. In 1977 the Obscene Publications Act was extended to include the distribution of pornographic films; more recently, concern has been raised over the control of the Internet which provides a fast, efficient and anonymous means of distributing illicit material.

Because pornography is generally produced for a male audience, some feminists have argued that it degrades the female, turning her into a mere object of male desire. It is true that female sexuality is largely ignored (even depictions of lesbians are designed to excite the male) although a Japanese print by Hokusai, *The Dream of the Fisherman's Wife* (1820) in which an octopus entwines a supine girl, attempts to capture the female experience. Feminists have also worried that the proliferation of pornographic images might encourage sexual assaults upon women. Two influential works on this theme, written in the 1980s, are Andrea Dworkin's *Pornography: Men Possessing Women* and Susan Griffin's *Pornography and Silence.* Susan Griffin argues that pornography (as opposed to erotic images) offers men control over women's bodies without a need for intimacy, silencing the portrayed image and deny-

ing emotional involvement. Pornography, she asserts, "shocks us away from feeling" (Griffin. 1981, p. 83). Nonetheless, other feminists, such as Ann Ferguson, have argued that there is no direct link between exposure to pornography and an increased incidence of rape or violence against women and that any consexual activity that brings pleasure is desirable (Ferguson, p. 107) and Susan Sontag, criticised by Griffin for never writing about her own experience, defends literary pornography. In her essay "The Pornographic Imagination", Sontag defends texts like Bataille's *The Story of the Eye* on the grounds that the transgression, which is not just thematic but also literary and linguistic, opposes the dominant realism so dear to totalitarian principles (Sontag, p. 104, 116-117). The sexual excess, fantasy, transgression and obscenity reveal the foundation of our vital energies; in this way sexuality can explore and transcend the boundaries of good and evil, love and sanity.

Many debates on pornography focus on the relationship between pornography and power. Susan Sontag, in her essay, was responding to George Steiner's "Night Words". Steiner thinks that pornography is intrinsically linked to totalitarianism. Both, he maintains, "set up power relations which dehumanise the individual, violate privacy, and create a concentration camp mentality" (Steiner, p. 95). While the power relations may suggest totalitarianism, there is no doubt that pornography, as a marketable commodity, thrives in a capitalist economy. As Stephen Heath comments, "there is a capitalism of the sexual and we live under it … a multi-million pound industry which spreads sexuality like butter on all its products" (Heath, p. 149). Whether a means of liberation or of repression, or merely a product to be traded in the market place, pornography is likely to remain controversial for some time to come.

See also

References

Caplan, Pat. [1987] 1996. ed. *The Cultural Construction of Sexuality*. London; New York: Routledge.

Dworkin, Andrea. 1981. *Pornography: Men Possessing Women*. London: The Women's Press.

Ferguson, A., I. Philipson, I. Diamond, L. Quinby, C. Vance and A. Snitow. 1984. "Forum: The Feminist Sexuality Debates". *Signs*, no. 10, vol. 1.

Griffin, Susan. 1981. *Pornography and Silence: Culture's Revenge against Nature*. London: The Women's Press.

Heath, Stephen. 1982. *The Sexual Fix*. London: Macmillan.

Hoyles, John. 1979. "Georges Bataille 1897-62: Jouissance and Revolution". In *The Sociology of Literature. Volume One – The Politics of Modernism*. ed. F. Barker, et. al. Colchester: The University of Essex.

Lucie-Smith, Edward. 1972. *Eroticism in Western Art*. London: Thames and Hudson.

Mâle, Emile. [1913] 1972. *The Gothic Image: Religious Art in France of the Thirteenth Century*. trans. Dora Nussey. New York; Evanston, Illinois; San Francisco; London: Harper and Row.

Obscene Publications Act. 1994-1998. Britannica CD2000: Encyclopædia Britannica, Inc.

Pornography: The Secret History of Civilisation. 1999. London: Channel 4.

Segal, Lynne and Mary McIntosh. eds. 1992. *Sex Exposed: Sexuality and the Pornography Debate*. London: Virago.

Sontag, Susan. [1967] 1979. "The Pornographic Imagination". In *Story of the Eye*. Georges Bataille. London: Marion Boyars.

Steiner, George. [1965] 1968. "Night Words". In *Language and Silence*. London: Penguin.

Strossen, Nadine. 1995. *Defending Pornography*. New York: Simon and Schuster.

Possum

Possom (or opossum) is the general name of the thick-furred marsupial mammals. For the Hua people of the Eastern Highlands of New Guinea, possum is the most heavily tabooed of all foods. It is considered the counterpart of women, and is symbolic of female reproductive power. Should a male eat it, he will become pregnant and, unless immediate countermeasures are taken, his body will be ruptured and die once the foetus has cut its two bottom teeth. Possums are considered so deadly that a male initiate may not even enter a forest for fear of encountering one and the flying fox cannot be eaten because it resembles possum and has its peculiar *be' ftu* smell. This smell is thought to be dangerous, repugnant, but also strangely attractive.

Curiously, but maybe not surprisingly, the anthropologist Anna S. Meigs discovered that the possum taboo is only a "public pose" and that males secretly eat possums during ceremonies in the *zga zu'* (possum house). Eating possum is believed to confer health and vitality but women may know nothing of this. In the past, it is said, a woman was killed if she discovered this male predilection and even today no woman admits to the knowledge (Meigs, p. 154-155).

The eating of possums is (at least publicly) also forbidden in many tribes of South America. For those males who cannot resist, the punishment is premature old age or death. Several myths treat this theme which seems to equate the eating of possums and loss of youth with the origin of cultivated plants. Lévi-Strauss cites a typical tale from the Ge Apinaye of central Brazil:

> A young widower, who was sleeping out in the open air, fell in love with a star. The star appeared to him first of all in the form of a frog, then in the form of a beautiful young woman, whom he married. At that time men knew nothing of gardening, and they ate rotten wood with their meat instead of vegetables. Star-woman brought her husband sweet potatoes and yams and taught him how to eat them ...
>
> One day, while Star-woman was bathing with her mother-in-law, she changed into an opossum and jumped on the old woman's shoulder until she drew the

latter's attention to a large tree laden with cobs of maize. She explained that "the Indians were to eat this maize instead of rotten wood". As an opossum, she climbed up and threw down quantities of cobs. Then she reassumed human shape and showed her mother-in-law how to make maize cakes. Delighted with this new food, men decided to chop down the maize tree with a stone axe. But when they stopped for breath, the notch they had cut closed up again. They sent two boys to the village for a better axe. On the way the two discovered a steppe opossum, which they killed and immediately roasted and consumed, though this animal is taboo to boys. Hardly had they finished their meal when they turned into senile, stooping old men (Lévi-Strauss, p. 165).

Death as the price for agriculture or for violating a taboo is a common motif of myth. Why the woman should need to change into an possum in order to bestow maize is a question deliberated by Lévi-Strauss in his "Opossum's Canata". The possum, he concludes is a putrid-smelling animal and can only be eaten by old men who no longer fear corruption. Corruption, or decay, is the antithesis of cultivation. The possum is also an animal and therefore it "personifies a kind of anti-agriculture which is at one and the same time pre- and pro-agriculture"; the marsupial brings cultivation yet, if eaten, causes corruption. Its ambiguous position makes it the perfect mediator between nature (eating rotten wood) and culture (or cultivation), growth and decay. Since Lévi-Strauss considers the primary function of myths to be the creation of a model in which contradictions are articulated and reconciled (thereby making acceptable new techniques such as cooking and agriculture), the role of the possum is clear.

References

Lévi-Strauss, Claude. [1964] 1973. *The Raw and the Cooked: Introduction to a Science of Mythology.*
Vol. 1. trans. John and Doreen Weightman. New York: Harper and Row.

Meigs, Anna S. 1984. *Food, Sex, and Pollution: A New Guinea Religion.* New Brunswick, New Jersey: Rutgers University Press.

Procreation

Though it is tempting to think of the problem of overpopulation as a recent phenomenon, there has been concern over this issue for a long time. In the Babylonian epic of Atrahasis, which dates back to 1700 BCE, the increase in population causes a mighty din that is anathema to the gods who call for remedial action. The tale relates how humans were originally created from clay to relieve the gods of their arduous tasks (which included digging out the beds of the Tigris and Euphrates rivers) but as mankind grew more numerous, noise levels increased until the gods, and Enlil in particular, could no longer sleep. To solve their problems the gods tried to reduce the population by means of a plague, famine and a drought but these were only temporary solutions: it was not long before numbers once more increased and the cacophony resumed. Eventually the gods decided to destroy mankind in a flood but the god Enki instructed a man named Atrahasis to build an ark so that he escaped drowning. With the other humans gone, the gods began to repent of their actions; this was not for any ethical concern but because there was no-one to offer sacrifices so they became hungry and thirsty. The wise Atrahasis brought a sacrifice for the gods to eat while Enki came up with a permanent solution. He instructed the birth goddess, Nintu, to create new creatures for the new world:

> In addition let there be one-third of
> the people,
> Among the people the woman who
> gives birth yet does
> Not give birth (successfully);
> Let there be the *pašittu*-demon among
> the people,

To snatch the baby from its mother's lap.

Establish *ugbabtu*, *entu*, *egisitu*-women:

They shall be taboo, and thus control childbirth (Atrahasis. Tablet III, Old Babylonian Version. In *Myths from Mesopotamia*, p. 9-38).

With infertility, difficult childbirth, infanticidal demons and, in particular, classes of female devotees like the *ugbabtu*, *entu* and *egisitu*, who were attached to the temples and not normally allowed to bear children, the problem of overpopulation appeared to have been solved.

References

Frymer-Kensky, Tikva. 1988. "The Atrahasis Epic and Its Significance for Our Understanding of Genesis 1-9". In *The Flood Myth*. ed. Alan Dundes, p. 61-73. Berkeley; Los Angeles: University of California Press.

Jacobson, Thorkild. 1976. *The Treasures of Darkness: A History of Mesopotamian Religion*. New Haven, Connecticut; London: Yale University Press.

Myths from Mesopotamia. 1991. trans. Stephanie Dalley. Oxford: Oxford University Press.

Propp, Vladímir Jácovlevic (1895-1970)

In 1928 the Russian folklorist, Vladímir Jácovlevic Propp, published *Morphology of the Folktale*, a work in which he applied structural analysis to a corpus of Russian wondertales (*märchen*) chosen from the collection of a fellow Russian, A. N. Afanás'ev. Propp argued that previous classifications of tales, which used the dramatis personae to define the type of tale, were misleading because it was the action, or function, of a character that remained constant, rather than the character itself, which could be substituted without any alteration to the plot. For example, Afanás'ev examined three tales in which a persecuted stepdaughter is sent into the woods, meets a dangerous figure (in one story Frost, in another a wood goblin, and in a third a bear), is tested, and rewarded, while a spoiled daughter fails the test and is punished. Afanás'ev thought that these were three different stories because they contained three different adversaries but for Propp they were merely three variants of the same tale because the plot was identical. In the same way it made no essential difference to the type of story who the character giving an interdiction, or prohibition, happened to be; what was important was the interdiction. Propp identified thirty-one functions whose sequential arrangement constituted the form of the wondertale. The second function, "An Interdiction is Addressed to the Hero", was paired with the third function he identified, "The Interdiction is Violated". If an interdiction was addressed to the hero or heroine ("Do not look into this closet", "Don't pick the apples", "Don't pick up the golden feather", "Don't open the chest", "Don't kiss your sister", "If Bába Jagá comes, don't say anything, be silent"), it was certain to be violated, usually with dire consequences. The use of this narrative device, which heightens the tension as the audience waits with baited breath for the hero's reaction, can be seen in contexts far beyond the Russian wondertale: In the Book of Genesis, Eve eats the forbidden fruit and is expelled from Paradise and in the story of Orpheus and Eurydice, Orpheus disobeys the injunction not to look back, and sees his wife disappearing forever.

A particular taboo that fascinated Propp was that of laughter and in 1939 he published the essay "Ritual Laughter in Folklore". The study begins with the tale of Nesmejana, a princess who will not laugh and who is offered in marriage by her father to the suitor who can make her merry. The task is solved in different ways: in one variant the hero is carefully cleaned by animals after falling in the mud, in another the hero brings a golden goose to which everyone sticks, in a third the hero makes the princess laugh by playing a magic pipe that causes three pigs to dance. Looking for the historical roots of this motif, Propp examines the interdiction on laughter in plots in which a living person must enter the realm of the dead. In an Inuit myth the consequences of laughing are particularly painful:

> The souls who go to the over-world have to pass the abode of a strange woman who dwells at the top of a high mountain. She is called Erdlaverissok (i.e. the disemboweller), and her properties are a trough and a bloody knife. She beats upon a drum, dances with her own shadow, and says nothing but 'My buttocks, etc.,' or else sings 'Ya, ha, ha, ha!' When she turns her back she displays huge hindquarters, from which dangles a huge sea-scorpion; and when she turns sideways her mouth is twisted utterly askew, so that her face becomes horizontally oblong. When she bends forwards she can lick her own hindquarters, and when she bends sideways she can strike her cheek, with a loud smack, against her thigh. If you can look at her without laughing you are in no danger; but as soon as anyone begins to smile she throws away her drum, seizes him, hurls him to the earth, takes her knife and rips him up, tears out his entrails, throws them into the trough, and then greedily devours them (Propp, [1939] 1984, p. 257-258).

This taboo on laughter in the realm of the dead is a characteristic not only of numerous tales around the world, but also of initiation rites in which initiants undergo a symbolic death. The dead cannot laugh and the living could reveal their presence and imperil themselves by this sign of life. Laughter is not only an indication of life but also, in many myths,

the source of creation. Propp mentions a Greco-Egyptian treatise on the creation of the world: "Seven times the god laughed, and seven gods embracing the world were born. The seventh time he laughed the laugh of joy and Psyche was born" (Propp, [1939] 1984, p. 133). Agricultural rituals are frequently accompanied by laughter, the singing of obscene songs, and gestures of exposing oneself. In the myth of Demeter and Persephone, the mother, searching a barren world for her daughter who has been abducted by the god of the underworld, is called "the one who does not laugh" and it is only when the servant, Iambe, raises her skirt to reveal her genitals that Demeter laughs. Laughter, Propp concludes, is a charm or device to ensure fertility which is why it is so important for the unsmiling Princess Nesmejana, to have a husband who can make her laugh.

The topic of laughter was expanded by the author and a posthumous book, *Problems of Laughter and the Comic*, appeared in 1976, six years after his death. Though his methodology has been criticised, and Propp has been labelled a 'formalist' (notably in a review of the *Morphology* by the structural anthropologist, Claude Lévi-Strauss, in 1960), the structuralists, Roland Barthes, Algirdas Greimas, Tzvetan Todorov and Claude Bremond, have discussed *Morphology* in terms of semiotics, and the plots of contemporary films and soap operas have been analysed according to his scheme.

References

Propp, Vladimir. [1928] 1979. *Morphology of the Folktale.* trans. Laurence Scott. Austin, Texas: University of Texas Press.

Propp, Vladimir. [1939] 1984. "Ritual Laughter in Folklore". In *Theory and History of Folklore.* trans. Ariadna Y. Martin and Richard P. Martin, p. 124-146. Minnesota: University of Minnesota Press.

R

Radcliffe-Brown, Alfred Reginald (1881-1955)

When the British anthropologist, A. R. Radcliffe-Brown was invited to deliver a lecture commemorating the work of James Frazer in 1939, he chose taboo as his topic. His lecture, drawing on fieldwork conducted in Polynesia, Australia, Africa and North America, was later reprinted in *Structure and Function in Primitive Society*. His other publications include *The Andaman Islanders: A Study in Social Anthropology* (1922); "The Social Organisation of Australian Tribes" (1930-1931), which appeared in the first issue of the journal *Oceania* that he founded; *The Social Anthropology of North American Tribes* (1937); and *African Systems of Kinship and Marriage*, which he edited together with Daryll Forde in 1950. He also wrote essays exploring social sanctions and laws, totemic and kinship systems, religion and society and joking relationships.

Radcliffe-Brown's thoughts on taboo owe a debt to Herbert Spencer and Émile Durkheim. Spencer believed in structural functionalism, the idea that social structures are important because of their function in maintaining and regulating society as a whole. Durkheim argued that religious rituals create a sense of community and identity which is personified in the deity or totem. Through the ceremony, an individual comes to realise his debt to, and reliance upon, the social group to which he belongs; the worship of the spirit, god or totem is no more than the worship of society itself. At the end of his lecture on taboo, Radcliffe-Brown reveals how his own ideas on taboo and ritual avoidance reject those of his predecessors:

> My own view is that the negative and positive rites of savages exist and persist because they are part of the mechanism by which an orderly society maintains itself in existence, serving as they do to establish certain fundamental social values. The beliefs by which the rites themselves are justified and given some sort of consistency are the rationalisations of symbolic actions and of the sentiments associated with them (Radcliffe-Brown, p. 152).

Speaking specifically about taboos, Radcliffe-Brown begins by defining his terms. Because the Polynesian meaning of the word *tabu* differs from the term *taboo* used by anthropologists (the former means simply "to forbid", "forbidden" while *taboo* has been applied to a special kind of prohibition), he adopts the terms "ritual avoidance" or "ritual prohibition" which he uses to describe "a rule of behaviour which is associated with a belief that an infraction will result in an undesirable change in the ritual status of the person who fails to keep the rule" (Radcliffe-Brown, p. 134-35). This change in the ritual status (another term adopted by Radcliffe-Brown) places the person in a situation of danger, vulnerable to illness, death or some other misfortune. However, by taking certain precautions which may include some kind of ceremony, the person can avoid disaster and regain his former ritual status. In Polynesia the touching of a corpse changed a person's ritual status but equilibrium could be regained if he observed special restrictions such as not using his hands to feed himself. A British analogy is the spilling of salt which is unlucky unless a pinch is thrown over one's shoulder. Within Catholicism the ritual avoidance of meat on Fridays, if flouted, requires confession and absolution so that the ritual status (or "State of Grace") may be restored.

The rules of behaviour tend to concern things that must be avoided, things which have, as Radcliffe-Brown puts it, "ritual value". Things which have ritual value are dangerous either because they are too holy to be approached or too impure and polluting. In many societies (as Robertson Smith and James Frazer have shown), the distinction between holy and unclean does not exist: in Polynesia a chief or temple is not seen as holy and neither is a corpse unclean, but both are hazardous. Moreover, what is polluting for one person may be sanctifying for another. In Hawaii if a person commits incest with his sister he becomes *kapu* (Hawaiian for tabu) and is so dangerous for the community he must be killed. But if a high-ranking chief (who is sacred because of his status) marries his sister he becomes even more sacred, and this sanctity increases if he is the descendant of siblings. The same word, *kapu*, applies to both commoner and chief but the values attached to their deed are diametrically opposed.

Anything, whether a name, day, place, object, animal, food or person, which is the object of a ritual avoidance has ritual value. A ritual value is exhibited in ritual behaviour which may occur in positive as well as negative rites; many positive rites, like consecration, are designed to imbue an object with ritual value.

Radcliffe-Brown considers that most ritual values are also social values. The meaning of the rites cannot be explained simply by their stated purpose:

The very common tendency to look for the explanation of ritual actions in their purpose is the result of a false assimilation of them to what may be called technical acts. In any technical activity an adequate statement of the purpose ... constitutes by itself a sufficient explanation. But ritual acts differ from technical acts in having in all instances some expressive or symbolic element in them. A second approach to the study of ritual is therefore by a consideration not of their purpose or reason but of their meaning ... Whatever has a meaning is a symbol and the meaning is whatever is expressed by the symbol (Radcliffe-Brown, p. 143).

Like Durkheim, Radcliffe-Brown believes that the primary function of Australian totemic rituals is not the ostensible reason given by the participants themselves – to renew or maintain a species of plant or animal or influence the weather – but they are symbolic acts that serve to bind the individuals in the form of a clan. In other words, ritual behaviour establishes certain social values that are essential to the maintenance of an orderly society. It achieves this by symbolically expressing the social value of a thing or event.

To consider how this operates in the case of ritual avoidances, the anthropologist turns to his fieldwork with the Andaman islanders. Among these people, a name is given to a baby while it is still in the womb but from then until several weeks after the birth no-one may use the personal names of the parents – they can only be referred to by teknonymy, that is, in terms of their relation to the child. Moreover, the parents are subject to certain food taboos. Another occasion on which the Andaman islanders refrain from mentioning a personal name is after a death: during the period of mourning the deceased may not be named and the mourners must avoid certain foods. The parallels are significant: both instances involve the loss of a name and, for the Andamese, "a personal name is a symbol of the social personality, i.e. of the position that a person occupies in the social structure" (Radcliffe-Brown, p. 146-147). The temporary lack of a personal name signifies an abnormal social and ritual status. During this time the group of mourners or friends of the prospective parents are united in the ritual prohibitions – should the naming or food taboos be violated, they will become ill. These avoidances therefore confer a social value on the event. In emphasising the anxiety created by the ritual behaviour Radcliffe-Brown differs from Bronislaw Malinowski who thought ritual behaviour generated confidence in a situation of anxiety and uncertainty. Instead Radcliffe-Brown argues that it is the rites themselves that create a sense of insecurity and danger: if the ritual prohibitions, or taboos, did not exist, neither would the dangers attached to their violation.

Whereas moral and legal sanctions are sufficient to restrain a person from committing crimes that would directly affect other people, ritual obligations, social conformity and rationalism are enforced by ritual sanctions. The perceived danger of not adhering to the sanctions, for instance the threat of sickness, death or some other calamity if a taboo is violated, is sufficient to ensure compliance. On the other hand, correct participation in a ritual will, it is hoped, bring its own rewards.

Humans, Radcliffe-Brown argues, rely upon the efficacy of the symbolic element of the ritual to maintain social cohesion:

> By this theory the Andamanese taboos relating to childbirth are the obligatory recognition in the standardised symbolic form of the significance and importance of the events to the parents and to the community at large. They thus serve to fix the social value of occasions of this kind (Radcliffe-Brown, p. 150-151).

Things to which ritual prohibitions are attached are chosen either because they have an intrinsic value or because they are symbolically representative of prized things. Thus the Andaman food taboos are a necessary means of emphasising the social importance of food and the cicada has ritual value because, though it has no social importance itself, "it symbolically represents the seasons of the year which do have importance" (Radcliffe-Brown, p. 151). Taboos are necessary to guide individuals towards the sentiments and behaviour that are appropriate for a particular occasion. Social coercion, argues Radcliffe-Brown, is their primary function.

References

Goody, Jack. 1995. *The Expansive Movement: The Rise of Social Anthropology in Britain and Africa 1918-1970.* Cambridge: Cambridge University Press.

Radcliffe-Brown, A. R. [1952] 1961. *Structure and Function in Primitive Society.* London: Cohen and West.

Ragas

Ragas, which form the basis for both northern and southern Indian music, must only be played at certain times. As Ravi Shankar, the master of the northern, Hindustani tradition explains:

> There are thousands of ragas. They're classified as early or late morning, early or late evening, and so on. Then there are seasonal ragas of spring or the rainy season; and there are others for special occasions (Quoted in Schafer, p. 136).

Often the mood and subject of the raga determine when it must be played; for example, the *Shri* or *Shri-raga* should only be performed during the winter, in the early evening, after sunset. Shri is personified as a calm, dignified, royal hero but Shri also refers to the harvest season of early winter, hence the winter performance. *Miyan ki malhhar* is a melancholy raga associated with ascetic meditation and the rainy season and is to be played either during the rainy season or around midnight. The *Basant* is an old raga celebrating Krishna or Kama, the god of love, in his incarnation as *Basant* (spring or the god of spring). It is therefore to be played any time during the spring season. Though a northern musician will strictly avoid playing a particular raga at the wrong time of day or out of season, the injunction, while recognised, is not so strong in the Carnatic tradition of the south. This may have something to do with certain differences between northern and southern ragas.

A raga combines scale, melody and key but must also belong to one of seventy-two full-octave "parent" scales. The parent scales were codified between the 16th and 18th centuries and consist of seven notes, the first and fifth of which (corresponding to C and G) never change position. The fourth note, dividing the scale in half, may be either F or F#. This means that there are only two variable notes in each half of the scale. But in the southern tradition there is a prominent use of ornaments of various notes, making it difficult to determine the precise parent scale and a Carnatic raga may exhibit features of more than one of the seventy-two parent scales. Because it cannot be so easily classified, it is more difficult to assign a Carnatic raga to a particular time of day, which may explain why the rules governing time of performance are more lax in the south.

References

Kaufmann, W. 1968. *The Ragas of North India.* Bloomington: University of Indiana Press.

Rowell, L. 1992. *Music and Musical Thought in Early India.* Chicago, Illinois: University of Chicago Press.

The Raga Guide: A Survey of 74 Hindustani Ragas. 1999. ed. Joep Bor. Nimbus Records. Monmouth, England.

Schafer, John. [1987] 1990. *New Sounds.* London: W. H. Allen and Co./Virgin.

Widdes, R. 1995. *The Ragas of Early Indian Music: Modes, Melodies and Musical Notations from the Gupta Period to c.1250.* Oxford: Clarendon Press.

Red

Red, the most salient of colours, is linked with passion, shame and danger. One is red-hot, attracted to a scarlet woman, red-faced, caught red-handed (perhaps in a red-light district), red in tooth and claw, seeing red, waving a red rag, put on a red alert, frustrated by red tape, a red traffic-light or a red herring. Red-heads are famous in European folklore for their fiery tempers and wilful witchcraft, while the ardent Mary Magdalene, sinner turned saint, is traditionally painted with flowing auburn locks. Another biblical character, Esau, was born with a ruddy complexion and hairy – a sign of his bestial nature – and he sold his birthright for a bowl of broth made from red lentils. Red is the colour of revolution, of fire, of love, of vitality, but also of blood, of wounds and of sacrifice.

Because it is the colour of blood, red shares many of the taboos surrounding bloodshed. The anthropologist, James Frazer, relates how Native American Indians, after slaughtering Inuit, would take red earth or ochre, and paint the lower parts of their faces with it before touching food (Frazer, p. 185). Red ochre was also daubed on the unfortunate Maori man whose duty it was to feed a fellow citizen who had been tainted through contact with a corpse, and in New Zealand, a canoe which had carried a corpse was never used again, but was pulled up onto the shore and painted red (Frazer, p. 139). In Madagascar, the funeral colour is red and the brightly coloured striped shrouds are referred to as "red rags" (Huntington and Metcalf, p. 45).

Blood is also shed during menstruation and the Hua women of New Guinea avoid eating red plants as they fear it will lead to an excessive menstrual flow. For Hua males, at the time of initiation, red pandanus oil is tabooed because of its menstrual associations. A Hua myth explains how the original pandanus plant grew at the site of an abandoned menstrual hut in the Gimi area and was nourished by polluted material dumped there. To consume the plant or its oil would be tantamount to absorbing menstrual pollution and would weaken the initiate. For a similar reason, Hua initiates must avoid reddish spinach-like vegetables, reddish taros, the reddish banana, red birds, and two reddish mushrooms. However, it is sometimes wise for the Hua to drink the red pandanus juices. Men and post-menopausal women may be susceptible to *kupa*, a condition in which a blood clot is believed to grow and resemble a foetus. If the red pandanus liquid is drunk it will break up the clot of blood and force it through the intestines. In Japan, it is traditional for girls celebrating the onset of menarche to eat a dish of *sekihan*, rice boiled with red beans.

Curiously, among the Baktaman of New Guinea, the red pandanus plant signifies not weakness but virility. In the secret fourth-degree initiation rituals, which the women are forbidden to see, seniors mix red pandanus juice with red *berber* bark and melted pork fat, to the accompaniment of war cries, and pour the solution on red ochre which they smear all over the novices, chanting "I paint you red". For the Baktaman, red is a colour that betokens strength, secrecy, and the sacred. It is identified with blood lineage and the ancestors, life, growth, increase, strength and maleness (Barth, p. 172-179).

Sometimes red is chosen as a colour because it is so noticeable. Hutton Webster records that a priest in the Hawaiian islands declared everything red to be sacred to his spirit, banning people from wearing red clothes or eating red foods, while in New Zealand red was the sacred colour of the Maori and if a chief laid a taboo on anything he set up a post and painted it red (Webster, p. 33). Red light is thought to stimulate and excite the heart and, after black and white, red is the colour identified in the simplest societies. This became apparent in 1969, when Brent Berlin and Paul Kay published *Basic Colour Terms*, a work that set out to show that the perception of colour is not cultural-rel-

ativist, but that colour perception is innate and stable and that all societies can recognise the most salient colour, red, before other hues. Although the theories of Berlin and Kay have since been challenged (see Willis, p. 26-27), the predominance of red, along with black and white, as a symbolic colour has been recorded by anthropologists in south-west Iran, Africa, Peru, New Guinea and India.

References

Barth, Fredrik. 1975. *Ritual and Knowledge among the Baktaman of New Guinea*. Oslo: Universitetsforlaget; New Haven, Connecticut: Yale University Press.

Berlin, Brent and Paul Kay. 1969. *Basic Colour Terms*. Berkeley: University of California Press.

Frazer, James George. [1911] 1935. *Taboo and the Perils of the Soul*. New York: Macmillan.

Huntington, Richard and Peter Metcalf. [1979] 1987. *Celebrations of Death: The Anthropology of Mortuary Ritual*. Cambridge: Cambridge University Press.

Meigs, Anna S. 1984. *Food, Sex and Pollution: A New Guinea Religion*. New Brunswick, New Jersey: Rutgers University Press.

Turner, Victor. 1967. *The Forest of Symbols*. Ithaca, New York: Cornell University Press.

Webster, Hutton. 1942. *Taboo: A Sociological Study*. Stanford, California: Stanford University Press; London: Oxford University Press.

Willis, Roy. 1985. "Colour Perception: Universal or Culturally Relative?" *Shadow*, vol. 2, no. 1, p. 24-29.

Rough Music

"Rough music" is a manifestation of social disapproval directed at those who have transgressed the culture's norms or violated taboos. It is similar, as the scholar E. P. Thompson notes, to *charivari* in France, to the German traditions of *haberfeld-treiben*, *thierjagen* and *katzenmusik* and to the Italian *scampanate* (Thompson, p. 3-26). The "music" is a discordant clamour made by the clashing of pots and pans, shovels, the rattling of stones in a tin kettle, tongs, cleavers, tambourines, ram's horns, whatever is to hand, accompanied by laughter, ridicule and obscenities. Recorded in Britain since the 17th century, this opprobrious conduct had the aim of humiliating those deemed guilty of such crimes as wife-beating, husband-hitting, squabbling between couples, cruelty to children, adultery, homosexuality, complacency when cuckolded, marrying someone considerably older or younger or otherwise deemed unsuitable, and petty theft. In an industrial context, those guilty of working during a strike, the blacklegs, were targets for rough music (a practice that has continued into the 20th century) as were those who undermined working conditions by accepting low wages or unpaid overtime. Moreover, the police, informers, body snatchers, gamekeepers, unpopular preachers and ruthless employers were all, on occasion, regaled in this way.

Together with the jibes and raucous music, rituals were commonly enacted involving effigies or masquerades, and in some instances the victim was made to ride a pole or donkey. Thompson has identified four distinct categories:

> a) "riding the stang", widely distributed in the Scottish Lowlands and northern England; b) "skimmington" or "skimmety" riding, entrenched still, in the West Country but surviving elsewhere in the South; c) the *ceffyl pren* (Welsh for "wooden horse") associated with "Rebecca Riots" in several parts of Wales; and d) plain rough music, unaccompanied by any riding, although very often accompanied by the burning of the victims in effigy, found almost everywhere, and commonly in the Midlands and the South (Thompson. 1992, p. 4).

The stang was a long pole or wooden bar on which the transgressor, or his representative or an effigy, was carried through the streets and publicly derided. Sometimes the pole was replaced by an old horse or a donkey. A colourful example of this form of derision was recorded in Cheshire towards the end of the 18th century when the wife of a weaver, Alice Evans, had the audacity to attack her husband for some misdemeanour.

> This conduct (of hers) the neighbouring lords of creation were determined to punish, fearing their own spouses might assume the same authority. They therefore mounted one of their body, dressed in female apparel, on the back of an old donkey, the man holding a spinning wheel on his lap, and his back towards the donkey's head. Two men led the animal through the neighbourhood, followed by scores of boys and idle men, tinkling kettles and frying pans, roaring with cows' horns and making a most hideous hullabaloo, stopping every now and then while the exhibitioner on the donkey made the following proclamation:
> Ran a dan, ran a dan, ran a dan,
> Mrs Alice Evans has beat her good man;
> It was neither with sword, spear, pistol or knife
> But with a pair of tongs she vowed to take his life … (Thompson, 1992, p. 5).

Despite the avowed desire to punish the woman, the satire is as much directed at her husband who, in not countering the attack, assumes a "female" role; hence the transvestism and the spinning wheel. 18th-century broadsides throughout Europe regularly depicted such role reversals – in which the woman literally wears the trousers while the man holds the baby and performs household duties – under the category of "human folly" or "the world upside-down" (as in plate 17, Burke, p. 96). Riding an animal backwards, facing the tail, was a humiliation imposed in London in the 16th and 17th centuries upon criminals guilty of pecuniary offences and corruption. "Riding the skimmington" entailed an elaborate and ludicrous procession intended to ridicule a husband or wife after one of them had been unfaithful, or had ill-treated the other, or upon an "unsuitable" marriage.

That it was not only private individuals but also public officials and municipal authorities that were subjected to rough music has already been mentioned. In the 1840s, the rituals of the *ceffyl pren* were employed in the protests against the turnpike tolls in South Wales. Known as the "Rebecca Riots" (after the mythical champion of agrarian reform), the disturbances were not only a protest against turnpike tolls and agricultural malpractices, but also espoused feminist causes.

The French *charivari* is more circumscribed than the British rough music, and is limited to marital transgressions: remarriage, marriage to someone in a different age group, marriage following a pregnancy and sexual promiscuity. If the breaking of social taboos is the motivation for the noise, the *charivari*, in turn, generates a carnival atmosphere in which social rules are breached: transvestism, blasphemy and licentious behaviour are the norm. Claude Lévi-Strauss has even linked the social violations to cosmic phenomena:

> Charivari punishes reprehensible unions, while an eclipse would seem to be the result of a dangerous conjunction – that of a devouring monster taking a heavenly body as its prey. The current interpretation of the din that occurs at the time of an eclipse would seem to complete the proof that the noise is supposed to drive away, in one case, the cosmological monster who is devouring the sun and moon and, in the other, the sociological "monster" who is "devouring" his or her no less innocent prey (Lévi-Strauss, p. 287).

He goes on to modify this statement, arguing that it is the breaking of a natural order through the introduction of an "unnatural" or foreign element that constitutes the real breach.

Elements of the charivari and rough music have survived into the 20th century. Women who slept with enemy soldiers during the occupation of Europe by the Germans in the Second World War had their heads shaved and were "tarred and feathered" after the liberation. The burning of effigies and hooded disguises, which themselves hark back to the terrors of the Inquisition, find echoes in the cross-burnings and sinister rituals of the Ku Klux Klan. Moreover, Thompson cites the case of Bavaria in the early decades of this century where "the last manifestations of *haberfeldtreiben* were linked to mafia-like blackmail, anti-semitism and, in the final stage, to ascendant Nazism" (Thompson, 1992, p. 20).

Just as the relaxation of social conventions during Carnival allowed people the freedom to contest religious and secular authority, so rough music was an opportunity for popular protest. Unfortunately (also like Carnival), hostilities were directed towards those deemed unacceptable either because they did not conform or because they were members of a different race or country. On the positive side, Carnival was (and still is) fun and it is fair to say that rough music has also bestowed a joyful legacy. The "blackenings" that take place during stag nights in Scotland, when the groom is coated with treacle and flour, or the old cans that are tied to the cars of newly-weds in England, are not forms of censure and are (usually) accepted with good humour by the victims themselves.

See also

Carnival; Transvestism

References

Burke, Peter. [1978] 1979. *Popular Culture in Early Modern Europe.* London: Temple Smith.

le Goff, Jacques and Jean Claude Schmitt, eds. 1981. *Le Charivari.* Paris: École des Hautes Études en Sciences Sociales.

Lévi-Strauss, Claude. [1964] 1975. *The Raw and the Cooked.* trans. John and Doreen Weightman. New York: Harper and Row.

Thompson, E. P. 1991. *Customs in Common.* Rendlesham: Merlin Press.

Thompson, E. P. 1992. "Rough Music Reconsidered". *Folklore*, no. 1, p. 3-26.

Sacher-Masoch, Leopold (1835-95)

Masochism, the sexual perversion in which pleasure is derived from the abuse and cruelty of a partner, takes its name from the respected Galician writer, Leopold Sacher-Masoch. That his name had been used to describe this perversion by Richard von Krafft-Ebing in his *Psychopathia Sexualis* (1886-1903) was a source of great annoyance to Masoch. His famous novel, *Venus in Furs* (*Venus im Pelz*, 1870), contains scenes of flagellation but the work cannot be reduced to a chronicle of sexual aberrations. As Gilles Deleuze remarks, "In the language of Masoch's folklore, history, politics, mysticism, eroticism, nationalism and perversion are closely intermingled" (Deleuze, p. 10).

Leopold Sacher-Masoch was born in 1835 in Lemberg, Galicia (then part of the Austro-Hungarian Empire) of Slav, Spanish and Bohemian descent. He was concerned with the oppression of minority groups within the Empire and the struggle of the peasants against the landowners. Appointed Professor of History at Graz, Masoch's literary career began with the writing of historical novels; an early work, *The Divorced Woman* (1870), met with much success. In 1886 he was decorated in Paris and honoured by the *Figaro* and the *Revue des Deux Mondes*. Masoch's sexual proclivities fused fantasy and fetish: in the role of a bear or

bandit, he was chased and beaten; he liked to be tied up, humiliated and whipped, preferably by a woman dressed in furs; and disguised as a servant he would await humiliation and punishment.

Fellow players were acquired through newspaper advertisements and Masoch would enter into official contracts with the women in his life. A relationship with Anna von Kottowitz inspired *The Divorced Woman* and another woman, Fanny von Pistor, prompted *Venus in Furs*. In the contract signed with Fanny von Pistor, he undertook to be her slave for a period of six months and agreed to be punished in whichever way she pleased, while she undertook to wear furs, especially when behaving cruelly (Deleuze, p. 277). In 1873 Masoch married Aurore Rümelin, who took the pseudonym Wanda, and after parting from her in 1886, he married his children's governess. He died in 1895 and is unfortunately remembered more for the sexual perversion he gave his name to than for his writings.

The works of Masoch are imbued with the spirit of German Romanticism. His writings were conceived as a series of cycles, the principle one being *The Heritage of Cain*. The folktales and ethnic tales form secondary cycles and include the novels *The Fisher of Souls* and *The Mother of God*, anguished works about mystical sects in Galicia. The main theme of *The Heritage of Cain* cycle is the crime and suffering that man is heir to, the cold indifference of Nature and of the stern and cruel Mother figure. *Venus in Furs*, Masoch's most famous novel, forms part of the first volume of *The Heritage of Cain*. It is a sad tale of misguided love; the hero, Severin, wishes to worship a woman as distant and awesome as a Greek goddess, someone who will coldly disdain him or, should the whim take her, bestow her grace. His chosen "Venus" desires to love him as an equal but when he insists on becoming her slave, being whipped and maltreated by her, she loses all respect for him. Gradually she learns selfishness, pride and cruelty, lashing the poor Severin while enveloped in furs, "lest she catch cold in [the] abstract northern climate, in the icy realm of Christianity" (Sacher-Moloch, p. 149). By the end of the novel Severin has been "cured" of his subservience but, unfortunately, he turns tyrant. As he relates to his friend, woman cannot be the companion to man: "This she can only be when she has the same rights as he and is his equal in education and work. For the time being there is only one alternative: to be the hammer or the anvil" (Sacher-Moloch, p. 271).

A desire to be the anvil is characteristic of the sexual deviancy known as masochism. Other typical features have been defined by the psychoanalyst, Theodore Reik. They include:

1. The "special significance of fantasy", that is the form of the fantasy (the fantasy experienced for its own sake, or the scene which is dreamed, dramatised, ritualised and which is an indispensable element of masochism).

2. The "suspense factor" (the waiting, the delay, expressing the way in which anxiety affects sexual tension and inhibits its discharge).

3. The "demonstrative" or, more accurately, the persuasive feature (the particular way in which the masochist exhibits his suffering, embarrassment and humiliation).

4. The "provocative fear" (the masochist aggressively demands punishment since it resolves anxiety and

allows him to enjoy the forbidden pleasure) (Deleuze, p. 74).

Masochism and sadism are closely associated and their practice has frequently led to prosecution. However, in 1995 the Law Commission for England and Wales recommended that acts of sado-masochism, when performed in private by consenting adults, should no longer be viewed as criminal offences.

See also

De Sade, Marquis D. A. F.; Pornography

References

Deleuze, Gilles. [1967] 1989. "Coldness and Cruelty". In *Masochism*, p. 9-138. New York: Zone Books.

Krafft-Ebing, R. von. [1886-1903] 1931. *Psychopathia Sexualis*. Brooklyn: Physicians and Surgeons Book Co.

Reik, Theodore. 1962. *Masochism in Sex and Society*. trans. M. H. Beigel and G. M. Kurth. New York: Grove Press.

Sacher-Masoch, Leopold von. [1870] 1989. "Venus in Furs". In *Masochism*, p. 143-271. New York: Zone Books.

Salt

Although salt has always been highly valued as a seasoning, and Roman soldiers were paid money, a salary (Latin *salarium*), to buy salt, it is nonetheless subject to taboos in certain parts of the world. Male initiates among the Hua people of the Eastern Highlands of New Guinea may not eat certain forms of salt. The Hua extract salt from either the leaves of the grasslands or the leaves of the forest; the leaves are burned to ashes, water is poured on the ashes and this brew is boiled till it becomes salt. In the case of salt made from leaves of the grassland, the last liquid to be drawn from the salt is known as the *ai'a* (faeces) of the salt, and is tabooed. Salt made from the leaves of the forest is forbidden to initiates because these saltcakes have a curve which resembles a possum's tail and the Hua regard the possum as the most taboo of all creatures. Furthermore, the liquid form of salt is banned because it resembles women's urine.

In Indian tradition, the saline sea is due to the anger of the sage named Mare's Mouth (Vadavamukha) who cursed the Ocean to become salty because he refused to come at the sage's bidding (*Mahabharata* 12.329.48). Despite this etiology, the sea provided a useful source of salt for Mohandas Karamchand Gandhi and his followers during their campaign for independence. When the British imposed such high taxes on salt that it became unavailable to the masses, Gandhi organised a Salt March in which he and thousands of his followers walked to the sea and began, illegally, to make salt.

See also

Faeces; Food Taboos; Possum; Urine

References

The Mahabharata. A shortened modern prose version of the Indian epic. ed. R. K. Narayan. 1978. London: Heinemann.

Meigs, Anna S. 1984. *Food, Sex and Pollution: A New Guinea Religion*, p. 142. New Brunswick, New Jersey: Rutgers University Press.

Sartorial Taboos

Taboos relating to clothes are amongst the most pervasive of all. The motivation for forbidding or requiring certain garments may be religious or secular, to identify a certain group or to deny individual identity within a group, to establish solidarity or to deny involvement, to renounce the world or to suit the world. Clothes may be forbidden to members of a certain class, status, age or sex and what is permissible in one place at one time may be forbidden in a different place or at a different time.

Biblical injunctions warn against three things: dressing immodestly, wearing the clothes of the opposite sex (*Deuteronomy* 22: 5) which would be tantamount to a mixing of gender, and, more curiously, mixing wool and linen in a single garment (perhaps because of the difference in shrinkage) (*Deuteronomy* 22: 11). As a sign of modesty before God, Jews cover the head during prayer and Orthodox women may wear a wig. Saint Paul decreed that while a woman should pray with her head covered, a man should not:

A man should certainly not cover his head, since he is the image of God and reflects God's glory; but woman is the reflection of man's glory. For ... man was not created for the sake of woman, but woman was created for the sake of man. That is the argument for women's covering their heads with a symbol of the authority over them, out of respect for the angels (1 *Corinthians* 11: 7-11).

In *Sura* 24: 31 of the *Koran,* women are enjoined to reveal their beauty to none but close relatives, although there is no stipulation that they must wear a veil. Muslim fundamentalists have taken the verse to mean that women must be hidden from view, and have adopted the practice of purdah. Purdah (from the Hindu *parda* – screen or veil) involves the use of enclosures to conceal the women within the home and clothes to enshroud and veil the body when outside the home. It is thought that the Persians inaugurated the custom of purdah which was adopted by Muslims after the Arab conquest of Iraq in the 7th century CE. The Muslims, in turn, influenced the Hindu upper classes of northern India when they dominated the area and purdah remained pervasive among Muslims in India under British rule. Although Hinduism has now abandoned the tradition, it is still common in many Islamic countries. In Iran, the Islamic revolution of 1979 led to a disparaging of Western clothes and traditions and an embracing of religious precepts: once again women covered their heads. Sikhs are also required to cover their heads and wear turbans, beneath which their long hair is coiled. Another religious injunction relates to shoes.

Moses was told to remove his sandals because he was standing on a holy spot, and although Jews remain shod during services, Muslims remove their shoes and wash their feet before entering a mosque.

Certain religious Jewish women never wear trousers because of the ban on wearing clothes of the opposite sex, but clothes today, like hairstyles, are commonly shared by both sexes. Transvestism is more noticeable when a man adopts the traditional dress or make-up of a female, either because of a specific sexual orientation or to provoke humour, to flout conventions, or simply for the fun of dressing up. Cross-dressing is part of the joy of carnival (along with masquerades) and *charivari*, of English pantomines and drag-queen competitions. This is not confined to Western countries: the transvestite, along with the clown, is a prominent player in Javanese drama. James Peacock, who studied the plays in which a male transvestite plays a female, suggests that it is the Javanese preoccupation with order, on both a social and cosmic plane, that allows them to "enjoy abnormal combinations that suggest disorder or that transcend superficial order" (Peacock, p. 217). Embracing disorder provides a temporary respite from the rigours of conformity, yet it presents no threat to traditional values as the transvestism is contained within the staging of the drama. Nonetheless, the Indonesian authorities have recently put pressure on the transvestite thespians to cut their hair and to refrain from their homosexual practices offstage.

When women don breaches, the motive is often to appropriate male rights or functions which are denied to them as females. Joan of Arc dressed in male clothes in 1429, claiming that God, the angels and saints had instructed her to do so. Despite such prestigious backing, she was accused by the bishop of Beauvais of flouting the divine law of female modesty, especially since she wore such "short, tight and dissolute garments as tabards, cottes and elaborate hats" and shaved her head. In 1745 the British

woman, Hannah Snell, put on a male uniform and joined the marines, serving in India for five years, and in 1818 Helen Oliver borrowed clothes from her brother to gain employment as a plasterer. As women were not allowed to study medicine until the 20th century, Miranda Barry, born in the 19th century, needed male clothes to study at Edinburgh University. Successful in her subterfuge, she obtained her degree and worked as an army surgeon, and inspector general of military hospitals in Canada, and served in the Crimean War.

The ban on mixing different fabrics within a single garment is not widely recorded outside Judaism but limitations on the use of certain materials are common. The Roman Republic tried to curb spending by introducing sumptuary laws like the *Lex Oppia* of 215 BCE which decreed that women should wear no more than a half ounce of gold on their tunics. The emperor Tiberius forbade silk for men although this may have been to avoid a perceived effeminacy, rather than for pecuniary gains. Sumptuary laws were widespread in Europe during the Middle Ages and Renaissance. In 1322 the citizens of Florence were forbidden to wear silk or scarlet cloth outside their homes and in 1366 Perugia outlawed the wearing of velvet, silk and satin. With its typical penchant for hierarchies and class distinctions, Britain restricted the wearing of rich fabrics to the aristocracy. Edward III determined in 1337 that fur was not to be worn by anyone below the rank of knight, esquires and gentlemen were not allowed to wear velvet, satin, ermines or silver damask, while silk, silver cloth, jewels and buttons were tabooed to yeomen. At the bottom of the pecking order, the agricultural labourers – swineherds, shepherds and ploughmen – were restricted to russet cloth and undyed blanket cloth. In a move of blatant protectionism, the king also placed embargoes on imported cloth.

Henry III of France claimed divine authority for his decree of 1583 that confined jewel and pearl-studded garments to princes. God, he reported, was displeased because he could not recognise a person's quality from his clothes. Such a statement would appear to seriously question God's omniscience and perhaps Edward IV of England was wiser in 1463 when he instituted his sumptuary laws on the grounds that God was angered by costly and superfluous dress. Class restrictions on dress continued in Italy and Spain until the beginning of the 19th century but in other European countries sumptuary laws were increasingly used to restrict the import of foreign goods.

Just as various clothes are forbidden to certain people, so some garments are mandatory for particular groups. In Rome in 1215 the Lateran Council ruled that lepers must wear a grey or black cloak, a scarlet cap and hood and sometimes a wooden rattle and Jews were required to display a yellow, red or green disc upon their clothes so that they might be immediately recognised. Distinctive hats have also stigmatised Jews in medieval and early modern Europe. The dress code was reinforced by words. Above the door of the Parisian cemetery of the Holy Innocents is the inscription "Beware of the friendship of a lunatic, of a Jew or of a leper" (Ginzberg, p. 38).

Those who withdraw from the world tend to express this in their clothes; monks, whether Buddhist or Greek Orthodox, and nuns, take on the robes of their order. Secular life has been abandoned and the robes – often devoid of colour, a stark black or white – express this, as well as conferring identification with the community. Individuality is of less importance than the aims of the group. Even a temporary withdrawal from social life, during death or mourning, has traditionally involved a change of dress: bright colours are proscribed and replaced by dull or black hues. Uniforms, like religious vestments, attenuate the individual identity: a common outfit not only allows for easy identification (useful in the case of the police or airline employees), but is also a means of social control – prisoners and soldiers are

depersonalised in this way, especially when a number replaces the name.

Just as monarchs and republics sought to control dress for pecuniary reasons, so, in the 20th century governments have sought to control dress, with either revolutionary or reactionary motives, or to modernise the country. After the revolution, the Chinese Chairman Mao inaugurated a simple unisex outfit of trousers and tunic which embodied the communist ideals of modesty, industry and uniformity. With the Iranian revolution, of course, there was a movement in the opposite direction, towards traditional Islamic dress, and during the British Raj, Mahatma Gandhi advocated the wearing of classical Indian attire as a sign of resistance to British imperialism. Tsar Peter I of Russia, on the other hand, in an attempt to modernise the country, decreed in 1701 that his subjects must don Western clothes.

Mustafa Kemal of Turkey (known as Atatürk) had the same idea when, in the 1920s, he forbade the fez and introduced Panama hats. This Turkish law is mentioned by the French author, Antoine de Saint-Exupéry, in his book, *The Little Prince*. In this fable for children, the eponymous hero is believed to have descended to earth from the asteroid B612:

> This asteroid has only once been seen through the telescope: by a Turkish astronomer, in 1909. At the time, this astronomer made a grand presentation of his discovery before an International Congress of Astronomy. But since he was wearing Turkish national costume nobody would believe him, grown-ups are like that. Fortunately for the reputation of Asteroid B612, a Turkish dictator ordered his subjects, on pain of death, to convert to European dress. In 1920 our astronomer repeated his demonstration, wearing elegant evening dress. This time everyone accepted his proofs (Saint-Exupéry, p. 14-16).

As in Iran, the rise of Islamic fundamentalism in Turkey in the late 20th century led to a renewed call for veils. The government responded by imposing fines on women who assumed Muslim dress. But Saint-Exupéry is less concerned with the debate over modernisation than with the strength, and the absurdity, of sartorial taboos, which remain as strong as ever.

Throughout the Western world the suit and tie has become the mandatory attire for businessmen, politicians, television presenters and all those who aspire to "respectability". Even the radical Czech playwright and dissident, Vaclav Havel, abandoned his black leather jacket and put on a suit once he became president. Women have more leeway and will not be refused entrance to restaurants if they fail to sport a tie, but suits and jackets are still important to those with high aspirations.

Dissent in past decades has come, mainly, from the young. During the late 1960s ethnic dress became popular in Europe and North America; this was due to a feeling of solidarity with, and interest in, maligned minorities and exotic cultures, a renewal of pride in one's personal background (hence the frizzy "Afro" hairstyle which defied decades of hair-straightening), and a delight in the beauty of the actual garments. At the same time, army uniforms were appropriated and parodied in a manner reminiscent of the donning of clerical robes during European carnivals. Black was revived as a sign of dissent; for the "beats" of the 1950s, it signified a withdrawal from conventional life, and the colour's rich associations, with death, sex, fascism and violence, has assured its continued popularity. Black leather, in particular, has been commandeered by the militant "Hell's Angels", sado-masochistic groups, and left-wing intellectuals. "Punk" fashion of the 1970s attacked both bourgeois society and aestheticism. Characterised by brightly-hued and strangely cut hair, slit jeans and pierced bodies, the clothes reflected the aim of the movement which employed violent imagery and subversive music in order to shock a complacent society that had consistently undervalued the working classes.

It is surprising how emotive the subject of dress remains. A debate in French schools in the late 1980s centred on the right of Muslim women to wear the chadour (veil); this assertion of religious rights clashed with both the ideology of a secular republic and feminist principles that saw in the headwear a manifestation of female suppression. Nor is the absence of clothes a solution: nudity is, in most societies, the most tabooed state of all.

See also
Hair; Transvestism

References
Dress, Rebellion. 1994-1998. Britannica© CD2000: Encyclopædia Britannica, Inc.

Ginzberg, Carlo. [1989] 1991. *Ecstasies: Deciphering the Witches' Sabbath*. trans. Raymond Rosenthal. London: Penguin.

Hebdige, Dick. 1979. *Subculture: The Meaning of Style*. London: Routledge.

Peacock, James L. 1978. "Symbolic Reversal and Social History: Transvestites and Clowns of Java". In *The Reversible World*. ed. Barbara Babcock. Ithaca, New York; London: Cornell University Press.

Saint-Exupéry, Antoine de. [1943] 1995. trans. T. V. F. Cuffe. London: Penguin.

Wilson, Kathryn E. 1997. "Folk Costume". In *Folklore: An Encyclopedia of Beliefs, Customs, Tales, Music and Art*, p. 147-152. Santa Barbara, California; Denver, Colorado; Oxford: ABC-CLIO.

Sex and the Anthropologist

While anthropologists generally spend considerable time studying the sexual habits of the people amongst whom they conduct their fieldwork, they have traditionally refrained from mentioning their own sexual needs. Though they may be away from their partners for many months at a time, there is a taboo upon mentioning how they cope or how the sexual identity that they have in their own culture affects that which they are allowed to express in other cultures. This reticence has stimulated two anthropologists, Don Kulick and Margaret Wilson, to broach the subject, confronting the issue from differing perspectives. As well as considering the fieldworkers' sexuality from the viewpoint of the people they are studying, they look at the incidence of sexual violence and intimidation in the field and consider the influence of this topic on anthropological research.

Reference

Kulick, Don, and Margaret Wilson. 1995. *Taboo: Sex, Identity and Erotic Subjectivity*. London: Routledge.

Shinto Purification

Shinto developed out of the earliest Japanese traditions and grew into a religion under the influence of Buddhism and Chinese culture. Its earliest texts, the *Kojiki* and *Nihongi*, compiled from oral sources in the 7th century CE, describe the creation of the universe and, on a smaller scale, the Japanese people, by many *kami* (deities, spirits or powers, often abiding in, and worshipped at, the shrines). One of the most important Shinto rituals is known as the Grand Purification or Exorcism (*oho-harahe*) when the "sins", or more accurately, pollutions, of the people are transferred onto "sin-bearers", narrow pieces of wood, sedge reeds, or, in more recent times, paper dolls, which are taken and thrown into the river. The ceremony takes place twice a year, on the last day of the sixth and twelfth months, when the *kami* are invoked to descend to earth and purify the land. In the *norito* (ancient Japanese Shinto ritual prayers), recited at these times by the Nakatomi priest, the "sins" that pollute the land and its people are enumerated:

First, the heavenly sins:
Breaking down the ridges,

Covering up the ditches,
Releasing the irrigation sluices,
Double-planting,
Skinning alive, skinning backwards.
The earthly sins:
Cutting living flesh, Cutting dead flesh,
White leprosy, skin excrescences,
The sin of violating one's own mother,
The sin of violating one's own child,
The sin of violating a mother and her child ...
The sin of transgression with animals,
Woes from creeping insects,
Woes from deities on high,
Woes from the birds on high,
Killing animals, the sin of witchcraft
(Norito in Earhart, p. 164-165).

The *norito* goes on to describe how the heavenly *kami*, pushing open the rock door of heaven, hear and receive the sins and how the water *kami* swallow them and the wind *kami* blow them away.

The exorcisms restore a state of ritual purity and cosmic harmony. Traditionally, as well as the "sins" mentioned above, childbirth, death, menstrual blood, disease and deficient rituals were all sources of contagion, disturbing the ideal unity between humans, *kami* and nature, and were surrounded with taboos.

See also

Dolls and Puppets; Pollution

References

Earhart, H. Byron. 1974. *Religion in the Japanese Experience: Sources and Interpretations*. Encino, California: Dickenson Publishing.

Hori, Ichiro. 1968. *Folk Religion in Japan: Continuity and Change*. Chicago, Illinois: University of Chicago Press.

Ichiro Hori, Ikado Fujio, Wakimoto Tsuneya, and Yanagawa Keiichi. ed. 1972. *Japanese Religion: A Survey by the Agency for Cultural Affairs*. Tokyo: Kodansha International.

Sin-Eater

A sin-eater was a person, usually a social out-cast, someone who was extremely poor or leading a dissident life, who for a small payment of food or money, would appropriate the sins of another. A sin, in traditional Christian belief, is similar to the pollution that results from violating a taboo in many non-Christian religions. Those who die with uncleansed sins have difficulty in entering the kingdom of heaven. For this reason a Roman Catholic priest grants sacramental absolution to a dying man and, in medieval times, indulgences were sold by unscrupulous charlatans to a gullible public. Sin-eating was another method of avoiding punishment in the afterlife, by employing a scapegoat to take on the sins. Just as Christ assumed this role and took on the iniquities of mankind, so in the British Isles a sin-eater accepted another man's guilt. The Reverend James Napier gives an account of the custom in his description of folklore in Western Scotland in the late 19th century:

> When the corpse was laid out, a plate of salt was placed upon the breast, ostensibly to prevent the body swelling. Many did so in this belief, but its original purpose was to act as a charm against the devil to prevent him from disturbing the body. In some localities the plate of salt was supplemented with another filled with earth. A symbolical meaning was given for this; that the earth represented the corporal body, the earthly house – the salt the heavenly state of the soul. But there was an older superstition which gave another explanation for the plate of salt on the breast. There were persons calling themselves *sin-eaters* who, when a person died, were sent for to come and eat the sins of the deceased. When they came, their *modus operandi* was to place a plate of salt and a plate of bread on the breast of the corpse, and repeat a series of incantations, after which they ate the contents of the plates, and so relieved the dead person of such sins as would have kept him hovering around his relations, haunting them with his imperfectly purified spirit, to their great annoyance and without satisfaction to himself (Napier, p. 60-61).

The earliest records of sin-eating are from Wales, Herefordshire and Shropshire, in the 17th century, and although there is no living memory of sin-eating, as recently as the 1970s people have been found in North and South Uist who remember dishes filled with salt and earth. In the Scottish Hebrides, the custom was said to be performed by both Catholics and Protestants (Bennett, p. 234).

From the surviving documentation, it is possible to construct an image of the person who took on the unsavoury task. The sin-eater could be either male or female; in one account such a person is described as a "long, lean, lamentable, rascal", in another the term "old Sire" is used, but the participant was always poor, willing to perform the funeral custom in return for a little food. In Herefordshire a loaf of bread, a bowl of beer and sixpence were offered over the corpse; in North Wales the beer was replaced with milk; in Beaumaris on Anglesey, the sin-eater received cake, cheese, beer and milk but no money; in Shropshire, bread and ale were accompanied by a groat (a small coin). Through the accepting and consuming of the food, the sins were transferred from the corpse which would be freed from walking after death and disturbing the living (Kvideland, p. 87).

Although an account from Shropshire has the sin-eater declare that he would pawn his own soul for the ease and rest of the departed soul, little attention is given to the fate of the poor unfortunate who ends his life with the accumulated sins of others. Only in a work of fiction is this problem addressed. The Scottish writer, William Sharp, published a story in

1895, "The Sin Eater", under the name of Fiona Macleod. In the tale, the protagonist returns penniless to his native village and is forced to take on the sins of his greatest enemy. Unable to free himself, the hero dies in agony, tormented in this world and the next.

See also
Death; Pollution

References
Bennett, Margaret. 1992. *Scottish Customs from the Cradle to the Grave*. Edinburgh: Polygon.

Kvideland, Karin. 1993. "Boundaries and the Sin-Eater". In *Boundaries and Thresholds*. ed. Hilda Ellis Davidson, p. 84-90. Stroud: The Thimble Press.

Napier, Rev. James. 1879. *Folk Lore: or, Superstitious Beliefs in the West of Scotland within this Century*. Paisley.

Macleod, Fiona (William Sharp). 1899. *Sin-Eater: The Washer of the Ford and Other Legendary Moralities*. London: Heinemann.

Smith, William Robertson (1846-94)

William Robertson Smith was a Semitic scholar of the late 19th century, best known for his book *Lectures on the Religion of the Semites* ([1889] 1927). Smith considered Israelite practices such as the casting of sins onto a scapegoat and the rules of impurity and defilement surrounding birth, death, disease and menstruation, mentioned in *Leviticus*, to be primitive survivals. This belief in dangerous, contaminating, supernatural agents, capable of inflicting severe penalties on those unwise enough to ignore the rules, differed from Semitic rules of holiness such as those pertaining to sanctuaries and priests. He considered the former to be magical superstition while Semitic rules of holiness were founded on respect for a benevolent god. The inability to distinguish between taboos relating to impurity and those applied

to the sacred was a sign of an unsophisticated religious sensibility:

> The person under taboo is not regarded as holy, for he is separated from approach to the sanctuary as well as from contact with men, but his act or condition is somehow associated with supernatural dangers, arising, according to the common savage explanation, from the presence of invisible spirits which are shunned like an infectious disease. In most savage societies, no sharp line seems to be drawn between the two kinds of taboo ... and even in more advanced nations the notions of holiness and uncleanness often touch ... the fact that the Semites ... distinguish between holy and the unclean, marks a real advance upon savagery. All taboos are inspired by awe of the supernatural, but there is a great moral difference between precautions against the invasion of mysterious hostile powers and precautions founded on respect for the prerogative of a friendly god (Smith, 1929, p. 153).

Smith argued that magical thought preceded religion and that the latter was a social phenomenon with the god and his worshippers forming a single community. Those social laws determining ethical behaviour among the clansmen also governed their relations to the god.

References
Beidelman, Thomas O. 1974. *W. Robertson Smith and the Sociological Study of Religion*. Chicago, Illinois: University of Chicago Press.

Smith, William Robertson. [1882] 1982. *The Prophets of Israel and their Place in History to the Close of the Eighth Century B.C.* New York: AMS Press.

Smith, William Robertson. [1885] 1967. *Kinship and Marriage in Early Arabia*. Cambridge: Cambridge University Press.

Smith, William Robertson. [1889] 1927. *Lectures on the Religion of the Semites*. Edinburgh: Black.

Snails

Snails are taboo for male initiates among the Hua people of the highlands of New Guinea. The Hua attribute this prohibition to the snails' female characteristics:

They are prohibited because the slime they secrete is said to be like female vaginal secretions. Also its *korogo* (wet, soft, fertile, cool) quality is said to resemble the vagina (Meigs, p. 158).

Eating something with female attributes is thought to weaken the initiate.

Reference

Meigs, Anna S. 1984. *Food, Sex and Pollution: A New Guinea Religion*. New Brunswick, New Jersey: Rutgers University Press.

Solitude

While many religions value solitude as an opportunity for religious contemplation, Judaism, with its emphasis on family life, is wary of it. "It is not good that man should be alone", states God (*Genesis* 2.18) before creating Eve. The dangers of solitude are elaborated by the Rabbis. In the 1st century CE Rabbi Hanina warned "It is forbidden for a man to sleep alone in a house lest Lilith get hold of him". Lilith, in Jewish folk belief, was a wild-haired succuba who had once been the wife of Adam. She had refused to lie beneath him, as she claimed she was his equal, and was banished to the Dead Sea where she procreated demons. But her lust for humans continued and a passage in the Zohar, a 13th-century Kabbalistic text, describes her mode of operation:

She roams at night, and goes all about the world and makes sport with men and causes them to emit seed. In every place where a man sleeps alone in a house, she visits him and grabs him and attaches herself to him and has her desire from him, and bears from him. And she also afflicts him with sickness, and he knows it not, and all this takes place when the moon is on the wane (Patai, p. 233).

Afterward, she shows no remorse:

... she removes her ornaments and turns into a menacing figure. She stands before him clothed in garments of flaming fire, inspiring terror and making body and soul tremble, full of frightening eyes, in her hand a drawn sword dripping bitter drops. And she kills that fool and casts him into Gehenna [hell] (Patai, p. 233-34).

It is perhaps not so surprising that nocturnal emissions and lascivious thoughts should be blamed on the evil machinations of a female since, despite the injunction not to sleep alone, and the decree forbidding onanism, the Old Testament does not view women in a favourable light.

Reference

Patai, Raphael. 1990. *The Hebrew Goddess*. Detroit: Wayne State University Press.

Soma

Soma is an Indo-Iranian sacred hallucinogen, known by the term *soma* in Indian religious tradition and as *haoma* in Iran (*sauma* in Proto-Indo-Iranian). An invocation from the ancient Iranian *Avesta*, dating back to the first millennium BCE, stresses its virtues:

O, Yellowish One, I call down thy intoxication. Indeed all other intoxications are accompanied by Violence of the Bloody Club, but the intoxication of *Haoma* is accompanied by bliss-bringing Rightness. The intoxication of *Haoma* goes lightly (From *Hom Yasht,* the part of the *Avesta* devoted to the worship or invocation of *Haoma*. Quoted in Flattery and Schwartz, p. 13).

In the earlier hymns of the Indian *Rig Veda* (c.1200-900 BCE), *soma* is visualised as both a god and as the drink of immortality. The whole of the ninth book of the *Rig Veda* is dedicated to the intoxicant. The texts describe, in metaphors that are by turn cosmic, biological and sexual, how the plant is ground by stones in wooden bowls and the juices poured through a woollen filter. Though the drinking of *soma* can be dangerous, it is thought to confer power, immortality, freedom and ecstasy. It also induces battle fury in the god, Indra.

Myths about the substance are rare, but two important hymns relate how the elixir, like so many precious substances in tales, was stolen from the fortresses of the demons by an eagle bearing Indra on its back (or, alternatively, an eagle brings the *soma* to Indra, losing a wing-feather when the demon Krsanu releases his bow). The eagle is praised for bringing to man the oblation loved by the gods but Soma is not to be outdone, eager to brag about his part in the escapade:

He [the eagle, or Indra riding on its back] did not drag me out against my will, for I surpassed him in energy and manly strength. In a flash, the bringer of abundance left his enemies behind as he outran the winds, swelling with power (*Rig Veda* 4.27).

Other hymns describe *soma* as growing in the mountains. From the time of the *Rig Veda* it was the most popular sacrifice. Hymn 8.48 celebrates its effects:

I have tasted the sweet drink of life, knowing that it inspires good thoughts and joyous expansiveness to the extreme, that all the gods and mortals seek it together ... We have drunk the *soma*; we have become immortal; we have gone to the light; we have found the gods. What can malice and the hatred of a mortal do to us now, O Immortal one? ... The glorious drops

that I have drunk set me free in space. You have bound me together in my limbs as thongs bind a chariot ... Inflame me like a fire kindled by friction; make us see far, make us richer, better ... Passion and fury are stirred up ... Weaknesses and diseases have gone; the forces of darkness have fled in terror. Soma has climbed up inside us ... an immortal inside mortals (*Rig Veda* 8.48).

Delightful and potent as *soma* appears to be, there is a dispute as to its botanical identity. Though it is clearly referred to as an ecstasy-inducing plant in the *Rig Veda,* the plants used in the present-day ceremonies associated with this text and with those of the Zoroastrians, the surviving practitioners of the ancient Iranian religion, are not intoxicating. At some point the plants must have been replaced by non-potent substitutes, either because the intoxicants were no longer available or because they were tabooed.

A lively argument has been advanced by R. Gordon Wasson, indicating that the plant of the *Rig Veda* is in fact a mushroom, the *Amita muscaria*, or fly-agaric, that beautiful crimson, white-spotted fungus ingested by Siberian shamans to help induce their ecstatic trances. Wasson reasons that there is no mention of roots, branches, seed or blossom in the Vedic descriptions of *soma* and that the figurative language that is employed in the hymns is concordant with the fly-agaric. Moreover, the mushroom is quite possibly the only psychotropic plant to be found at high altitudes in the Indo-Iranian area and, as he ingeniously remarks, "no word in the RigVeda is inconsistent with this plant" (Wasson, 1968, p. 171).

The mushroom hypothesis is rejected by two researchers, David Stophlet Flattery and Martin Schwartz, who find Wasson's evidence too slim. The Vedic descriptions of *soma* could apply to any psychotropic plant and the absence of any mention of roots or seed is unremarkable: the *soma* often pertains to the liquid extract of the plant or to the deity, Soma. Moreover, Wasson's attempt to find references to the drinking of urine in the text (a practice of Siberian shamans who got high on the urine of reindeer who had eaten the fly-agaric) is similarly dismissed as being too tenuous. Flattery and Schwartz think that *soma* or *haoma* is actually harmel or wild rue, *Perganum harmala L.* (Zygophyllaceae), which grows in the Central Asian Steppes and on the Iranian Plateau. Not only does *Perganum harmala* contain the visionary drugs harmaline and harmine, but it also has all the non-intoxicating uses attributed to the elixir: it was employed as an aphrodisiac, as incense, to help healing and for apotropaic purposes, to ward off evil spirits. For their evidence, the two authors turn towards Iran; although the Iranian *Avesta* is later than the *Rig Veda*, it is more conservative and is believed to more accurately reflect the Proto-Indo-Iranian culture in which the hallucinogen was probably first drunk. In ancient times, and in a continuing tradition reaching to the present day, harmel has been revered as a sacred plant among the Iranians. In present day Zoroastrian rituals, where sauma is burned instead of being consumed, the plant used is harmel.

Flattery and Schwartz also offer an explanation as to why the intoxicant became taboo and was replaced by a non-inebriating substance. Gordon Wasson assumes that the original *soma* became unavailable shortly after the creation of the *Rig Veda* hymns. But if, as he assumes, ecstasy was such an essential component of the priestly rituals, another intoxicating substance could surely have been used instead. Flattery and Schwartz think that, even before the completion of the Vedic hymns, intoxication of the priests was probably less important than their knowledge of the hymns and rituals, which were used for magical purposes and to secure supremacy. If its hallucinogenic qualities were no longer necessarily required by the priests for their rites, access to the plant became less crucial. Nevertheless, to retain their power, it was necessary for the priests to deny access to the

plant to non-priests and non-Aryans, and for this reason they deliberately obscured its identity. This involved a conscious blurring of details when the drug's components and effects were invoked in the Vedic hymns and a similar confusion in the *Brahmanas* (approx. 600 BCE) when they spoke of *soma* substitutes.

But even after the priests no longer needed to use it, the servants of the priests would still be aware of the true nature of the sacred plant and it was in danger of being defiled. At this point, the sacred substance became tabooed. This, claim Flattery and Schwartz, explains reports by E. Balfour that *Perganum harmala* was "the plant sacred to the Pariah caste … not to be touched by Sikhs or Hindus" (Flattery and Schwartz, p. 93-94). It also illustrates why *Perganum harmala* disappeared from all Hindu folk traditions and rituals.

In Iran, the circumstances were different. The hallucinogen was used by priests to obtain information about the spiritual world and it was probably also taken at the inauguration of pre-Islamic Iranian rulers. The *Hom Yasht* suggests that the plant was once used as a kind of truth-drug at the initiation of priests. The *Yasna* ritual, still performed by priests in Iran in Zoroastrian fire temples, once included a ceremony during which the priest had to consume a *haoma* extract. At the beginning of the ceremony, the *zaotor* priest was handed a cup without knowing its contents as it was prepared in his absence. It was believed to contain a powerful drug which he must drink while all the other priests scrutinised him and observed the effects. Obviously, once a priest had demonstrated his spiritual integrity by exposing his soul to judgement by spirits, it was unnecessary to repeat the process, and less potent solutions could be used. Moreover, initiation into the priesthood in both Iran and India came to be determined by social factors, such as kinship, rather than by tests in which harmel could be employed. To hand a fellow priest the intoxicant would be tantamount to doubting his fitness for the post and would constitute a major breach in courtesy. The plant therefore became taboo in the sauma ceremonies and was replaced by harmless substitutes.

References

Flattery, David Stophlet and Martin Schwartz. 1989. *Haoma and Harmaline: The Botanical Identity of the Indo-Iranian Sacred Hallucinogen "Soma" and its Legacy in Religion, Language, and Middle Eastern Folklore*. Berkeley; Los Angeles: University of California Press.

The Rig Veda. trans. Wendy Doniger O'Flaherty. [1981] 1983. Harmondsworth, Middlesex: Penguin.

Wasson, R. Gordon. 1972. "The Divine Mushroom of Immortality". In *Flesh of the Gods: The Ritual Use of Hallucinogens*. ed. Peter T. Furst, p. 185-200. London: George Allen and Unwin.

Wasson, R. Gordon. 1972. "What Was the Soma of the Aryans?" In *Flesh of the Gods: The Ritual Use of Hallucinogens*. ed. Peter T. Furst, p. 201-213. London: George Allen and Unwin.

Song of the Siren

The song of the Siren is of such haunting beauty that no-one who hears it can fail to be enchanted and lured to his death. In Homer's *Odyssey* Circe, herself no mean enchantress, warns the Greek hero, Odysseus, of the dangers and offers advice:

> Square in your ship's path are Sirens, crying beauty to bewitch men coasting by;
> woe to the innocent who hears that sound!
> He will not see his lady nor his children in joy, crowding about him, home from the sea;
> The Sirens will sing his mind away on their sweet meadow lolling.
> There are bones of dead men rotting in a pile beside them
> and flayed skins shrivel around the spot
> Steer wide; keep well to seaward; plug your oarsmen's ears with beeswax kneaded soft, none of the rest should hear that song.

> But if you wish to listen, let the men tie you in the lugger, hand and foot,
> back to the mast, lashed to the mast,
> so you may hear those harpies' thrilling voices;
> shout as you will, begging to be untied, your crew must only twist more line around you
> and keep their stroke up, till the singers fade (*The Odyssey*. XII).

Odysseus heeds the injunction and fills the ears of his crew with melted wax so that they will not be charmed by the voices that bring death. He himself is bound to the mast and though the Sirens really do "sing his mind away", and he begs to be untied, he lives to tell the tale.

According to Robert Graves, the Sirens of Greek mythology have the faces of women attached to birds' feet and feathers. They are believed to be the offspring of either Achelous or Phorcys and the muse Terpsichore or Sterope, Porthaön's daughter. Just as their parentage is in doubt, so too is the origin of their unusual physiognomies. Either they had been turned into birds by the goddess Demeter because she was angry at their passivity when her daughter, Persephone, was abducted by Hades, or Aphrodite transformed them because they were too proud to submit to the power of love. As a final blow, the ability to fly was taken from them by the Muses who defeated them in a musical contest and plucked out their wing-feathers to make themselves crowns (Graves, p. 249 n.3; p. 361; p. 368 n.7).

References

Graves, Robert. [1955] 1960. *The Greek Myths: 2*. Harmondsworth, Middlesex: Penguin.

Kahn-Lyotard, Laurence and Nicole Loraux. [1981] 1991. "Death in Greek Myths". In *Greek and Egyptian Mythologies* compiled by Yves Bonnefoy. trans. under the direction of Wendy Doniger, p. 105-112. Chicago, Illinois; London: University of Chicago Press.

The Odyssey. trans. Robert Fitzgerald. 1961. London: William Heinemann Ltd.

Spittle

Saliva, like urine, faeces, sweat and all the other substances emitted by the body (with the notable exception of tears), is surrounded by taboos. Even today, spitting is expressly forbidden on trains and buses in many European countries and to spit at someone is a sign of utter contempt. In Edinburgh, some citizens still spit on "the heart of Lothian", outside St. Giles Cathedral, the spot from which prisoners were formerly taken out of jail to be executed.

Within Hinduism saliva has always been particularly polluting and because it could be transmitted from the lips to the fingers, a Brahmin who inadvertently touched his lips had to bathe and change. The anthropologist, Mary Douglas, relates a myth told by a Hindu caste, the Coogs (Srinivas), which demonstrates their horror of contamination: a goddess consistently defeated her two brothers in trials of strength and cunning. Since the order of precedence was to be determined by the outcome of these tests, her brothers grew anxious and decided to try trickery where strength had failed. They asked her if the betel she was chewing was redder than theirs. The goddess took it from her mouth to look, but then replaced it and became defiled by her own saliva. Devastated, she resigned herself to a subordinate position, lorded over by her wily siblings (Douglas, p. 123).

It is precisely because it is so tabooed that saliva is used in tantric yoga. The aim of this discipline is to transcend physical, cultural and religious conditioning and so reach enlightenment. Control and subordination of the body is achieved through techniques of yoga, such as stopping the breath:

> One of the most frequently used methods of arresting the breath is ... obstructing the cavum by turning the tongue back and inserting the tip of it into the throat. The abundant salival

secretion thus produced is interpreted as celestial ambrosia (*amrta*) and the flesh of the tongue itself as the "flesh of the cow" ... the yogin already participates in "transcendence" he transgresses the strictest of Hindu prohibitions (eating cow flesh) – that is, he is no longer conditioned, is no longer in the world; hence he tastes the celestial ambrosia (Eliade, p. 247).

The yogin breaks one taboo by eating cow flesh (at least figuratively) and transforms another reviled substance – spittle – into the divine ambrosia.

Christianity, too, with its emphasis on exalting the lowly, finds a positive use for spittle. When Christ performs a miracle he uses the reviled substance in a divine cure. The gospel according to Mark (*Mark*. 7, 32-35) describes how a deaf man with a speech impediment is brought before Christ. Jesus places his fingers in the man's ears and touches the man's tongue with spittle. Then, looking up to heaven, Christ sighs and turns back to the man proclaiming "Ephphatha" (Be opened), and the man is able both to hear and to speak.

In a way, there is something logical about putting saliva on the tongue to cure a speech impediment. Certainly spit can be efficacious in magic rituals and in many regions people fear the consequences of their spittle getting into the wrong hands. James Frazer believes that this works through a form of "sympathetic" magic:

> For on the principles of sympathetic magic the spittle is part of the man, and whatever is done to it will have a corresponding effect on him ... When a Cherokee sorcerer desires to destroy a man, he gathers up his victim's spittle on a stick and puts it in a joint of wild parsnip, together with seven earthworms beaten to a paste and several splinters from a tree which has been struck by lightning ... he then goes into the forest, digs a hole ... and

deposits in the hole the joint of wild parsnip (Frazer, p. 287).

Mary Douglas, on the other hand, sees the saliva as a bodily effluent which, like all such excretions, confuses the body's borders and is therefore both dangerous and powerful (the confusion in the physical body having repercussions in the social body).

If saliva in the wrong hands can be dangerous, then exchanging saliva is the perfect way to guarantee that a deal will be honoured:

> Thus when the Wajagga of East Africa desire to make a covenant, the two parties will sometimes sit down with a bowl of milk or beer between them, and after uttering an incantation over the beverage they each take a mouthful of the milk or beer and spit it into the other's mouth (Frazer, p. 290).

A similar custom is still extant in Scotland and other European countries where spitting on the palms and then shaking hands seals an agreement. In the *Skáldskaparmál*, part of the *Prose Edda*, a collection of Norse mythology written by the Icelandic scholar Snorri Sturluson in the 13th century, there is mention of saliva being used to seal a truce between two warring factions. The two factions are the Aesir (the gods) and the Vanir. Having decided on peace, both sides go up to a crock and spit into it. Then the gods take the truce token and make of it a man of spittle named Kvasir. This man is so wise that he can answer any question that is put to him and he travels the world to teach men truth and wisdom. Unfortunately, he comes one time to dine with two dwarfs, Fjalar and Galar, who kill him and catch his blood. They mix the blood with honey to make mead, a magical drink that turns the drinker into a poet or scholar. To conceal their crime, the dwarfs tell the Aesir that Kvasir has choked with learning because no-one was able to compete with him in knowledge.

See also

Douglas, Mary (1921-); Urine

References

Douglas, Mary. [1966] 1984. *Purity and Danger: An Analysis of the Concepts of Pollution and Taboo*. London: Ark/ Routledge and Kegan Paul.

Eliade, Mircea. [1954] 1973. *Yoga: Immortality and Freedom*. trans. Willard R. Trask. Princeton, New Jersey: Princeton University Press.

Frazer, James George. [1911] 1935. *Taboo and the Perils of the Soul – The Golden Bough*. New York: The Macmillan Company.

Sturluson, Snorri. [c.1320] 1954. *The Prose Edda: Tales from Norse Mythology*. trans. Jean I. Young. Cambridge: Bowes and Bowes.

Steiner, Franz Baermann (1909-52)

Franz Steiner was born in the former Czechoslovakia in 1909 and, after completing a PhD in Semitic Languages and Ethnology, came to England to study under Radcliffe-Brown at Oxford University. His influential book, *Taboo*, began as a series of lectures and was revised, after his death in 1952, by Laura Bohannan. The present work, published in 1956 with a preface by E. E. Evans-Pritchard, is a critical study of the theories of taboo proposed by Captain James Cook, William Robertson Smith, James Frazer, Sigmund Freud, Lucien Lévy-Bruhl, Arnold van Gennep, A. R. Radcliffe-Brown and others. As Evans-Pritchard remarks, Dr Steiner

> subjects the sources on which they relied to the closest scrutiny. He shows how inadequate most of these theories are and, though he does not reach any positive conclusions himself, his book will be found to be of great value to anyone interested in the idea of taboo and to those who in the future tackle once more the problems it raises (Steiner, p. 12 13).

This has indeed been the case and *Taboo* remains a seminal work on the subject.

References

Evans-Pritchard. 1956. "Preface". In *Taboo* by Franz Steiner, p. 11-13. London: Cohen and West Ltd.

Steiner, Franz. 1956. *Taboo*. London: Cohen and West Ltd.

Strangers

Xenophobia, the irrational fear of the stranger or foreigner, seems to be a universal human characteristic, manifest today in the suspicion of refugees and immigrants, racist abuse and attacks and the exaggerated nationalism of certain football fans. The stranger is considered to be dangerous, malicious, the possessor of the evil eye, out to infect the citizens, to undermine morality, to rape the women; the stranger is a cannibal, a monster, a magician, a witch, a spy, an infidel, a drug peddler, whatever is feared by the community; and the stranger all too often becomes the useful scapegoat towards whom all the aggression of the populace can be directed.

In his book, *Taboo. A Sociological Study,* Hutton Webster devotes an entire chapter to the taboo on strangers. While anthropological reports are not always reliable (William Arens has revealed that native testimonies relating the cannibalistic habits of alien tribes were often erroneous although the field-workers believed what they were told), it is surprising how similar the reactions to strangers are in different parts of the world. The stranger or foreigner is assimilated to the "other world", a region of chaos inhabited by demons, ghosts and the souls of the dead and possessed of fearful powers:

> The inhabitants of Niue, or Savage Island, invariably put to death natives of other islands who drifted to their shores ... "This was occasioned by a dread of disease" ... [Among] the tribes of central and northern Australia ... if a member of an unknown tribe made his appearance, he would most probably be promptly speared ... The Mailu, a Papuan tribe, do not like to

have a stranger enter one of their villages unbidden or unconducted. They fear lest his shadow may fasten itself upon them ... For the Mountain Arapesh sexual relations with a stranger are dangerous ... A man who goes abroad should keep away from all women except those who are related to him and in whose houses he can therefore sleep without fear of sorcery ... The Kayan of Borneo are very careful that no stranger shall handle a young child ... The Lhota forbid speech between parents and strangers for six days after the birth of a boy and for five days in the case of a girl ... The Bakaïri of Brazil attribute sickness, death and other evils to the sorcery practised by strangers ... The Siberian Chukchi whose fire has gone out on the cold and timberless tundra cannot borrow fire from his neighbour, for the fire of a strange family is regarded as infectious and as harbouring evil spirits (Webster, p. 230-236).

Given the widespread infection of indigenous peoples by European colonisers, against whose diseases they often had no natural immunity, it was not unwise to mistrust at least this group of strangers.

Strangers, though disliked and feared, have not always been mistreated. In many cases a strict rule of hospitality towards foreigners has prevailed, despite, or more precisely, because of, the fear; this was apparently in order to wrest a blessing and avoid a curse. The stranger came to symbolise all that was unknown, secret, hidden and mysterious, and could bestow blessings as well as causing calamities. Often, initial caution and respect towards the stranger, who was entertained with banquets and ceremonies, changed over time into a grudging acceptance with the foreigner occupying an ambiguous, marginal status within the community. Even when the stranger was accepted, any problems arising within the community were immediately blamed upon the stranger who became the focus of prejudice and violence.

Literate societies have exhibited a dislike of strangers and foreigners equal to that of preliterate societies. In classical Greece all non Greek-speakers were regarded as barbarians and were generally not allowed to participate in festivals. This is exemplified by the Greek use of the *pharmakós*, the scapegoat, whose human representative was a criminal or slave, to carry the contagion of the society's sins beyond its borders to the savage lands beyond. Not even the gods were immune from mistrust. At Troezen the stoning to death of two foreign goddesses, Damia and Auxesia, who came from Crete, was commemorated each year at the temple of Hippolytos (Girard, p. 94). Those living further afield were not even believed to have human physiognomies. Herodotus, in the 5th century BCE, described the strange inhabitants of India and Ctesias the Cnidian, in his *Indika*, written while he was a physician to the court of the Persian Achaemenidian Artaxerxes Mnemon II in 398-7 BCE, described hybrid races which included the Cynocephali (with dog heads), the Antipodes (whose feet faced backwards), the Blemmyes (with faces set in their chests), the Monoculi (Cyclops), the Sciapoda (with a huge foot which could be used to shade them), the Panotii (with enormous ears) and the Bragamanni (Brahmins). Reports by succeeding travellers, such as Alexander the Great and scholars like Pliny the Elder, assured the continued belief in these races in the ancient and medieval Western world.

The Chinese, too, had their monsters. The Dog Jung (*jung* meaning 'wild', 'warlike', 'barbaric') were deemed to have been descended from dogs and located, according to the "Geography of the Tribute of Yü", to the northwest of Shang China (the traditional dates of the Shang dynasty were 1783-1122 BCE). A later account by the Chinese traveller, Hu Chiao, who was detained by the Turko-Mongol Ch'i-tan in the 10th century CE, describes the inhabitants of the Kingdom of Dogs to the north of the Ch'i-tan:

> Further to the north is the Kingdom of Dogs [*Kou kuo*], where the inhabitants have the bodies of men and the heads of dogs. They have long hair, they have no clothes, they overcome wild beasts with their bare hands, their language is the barking of dogs (White, p. 130-133).

Strangers could be demons, animal hybrids, or monsters, anything but fellow human beings. In medieval Europe, lepers, Jews, Muslims and witches were the principal scapegoats, seen as marginal beings, both outside of, yet living within (except for the Muslims) a Christian society. In the 13th and 14th centuries lepers were considered to be in league with the devil and Jews were thought to poison wells and food and spread contagion. It was decreed in the Lateran Council of 1215 that they should wear special clothes for easy identification and Jews, in a chilling anticipation of the Nazi injunctions, were required to wear a yellow disc on their clothes. Each of these groups suffered appalling massacres and Jews were confined to ghettos while lepers went to asylums (Ginzburg, p. 33-86). In India, those known as the 'Untouchables' have suffered a similar exclusion from the social body. Considered impure from birth, they were further rendered contagious and unclean by the polluting substances they were made to handle.

Unfortunately, at the beginning of the 21st century, he who is a stranger, whether by geography, race, religion, political persuasion or temperament, is still feared and discriminated against. Despite legislation and the International Declaration of Human Rights, genocide and what is euphemistically called "ethnic cleansing" continue unabated. The only way to stop the endless persecutions is to radically change our attitudes, as David White so eloquently argues:

> At the heart of this perverse state of affairs lies the ancient problem of "us,

not them". *They* are the mad dogs, the great Satans … while *we* are the … saviours of a threatened world. It is such logic which has permitted such human monsters as Hitler and McCarthy to present themselves as defenders of the general welfare against generally non-existent "lists of names" and anonymous aggregates. How are we to respond to such violence to others, to ourselves? In the end, there can be no clear divisions between "us" and "them", between humans and monsters, or civilisation and barbary. Only through an openness to meaningful encounter, to dialogue, and to interaction can we hope to find a path to authentic self-understanding, and hope for the continued existence of our fragile blue planet (White, p. 209).

See also
Evil Eye; Miasma; Untouchables

References
Ginzburg, Carlo. [1989] 1992. *Ecstasies: Deciphering the Witches' Sabbath.* trans. Raymond Rosenthal. London: Penguin.

Girard, René. [1972] 1977. *Violence and the Sacred.* trans. Patrick Gregory. Baltimore, Maryland: Johns Hopkins University Press.

Law, Jane Marie. 1997. *Puppets of Nostalgia: The Life, Death, and Rebirth of the Japanese Awaji Ningyo Tradition.* Princeton, New Jersey: Princeton University Press.

Webster, Hutton. 1942. *Taboo. A Sociological Study.* Stanford, California: University of Stanford Press.

White, David Gordon. 1991. *Myths of the Dog-Man.* Chicago, Illinois: University of Chicago Press.

Suicide

Since 1961, suicide is no longer an offence under the criminal law in Britain, but the survivor of a suicide pact is still open to a charge of manslaughter, and although the stigma of a suicide within a family has now decreased somewhat (a coroner often used to record a verdict of accidental death rather than suicide), the act is still condemned by Judaism, Christianity and Islam. Nonetheless, in some cultures suicide is tolerated and even viewed as an honourable form of death. In India the Brahmins accept suicide and the Jains practised such an extreme form of asceticism that they regarded suicide as the supreme form of death. In India it used to be the custom for a Hindu widow, or *sutee*, to die with her husband, a practice that is now outlawed. Greeks, during the classical period, permitted criminals to take their own lives (the fate of Socrates and the poisoned chalice comes to mind) but the Romans, towards the end of the empire, were less sympathetic, having lost too many valuable slaves this way.

Perhaps the most famous example of honourable suicide comes from Japan where the custom of *seppuku* (self-disembowelment), also known as *hari-kiri* (belly-cutting), was practised by the samurai, or warrior, class in feudal times. In a ceremonial rite, a short sword would be plunged into the left side of the abdomen, drawn across to the right, and then turned upwards. This might be followed by another stab below the chest and the piercing of the throat. *Seppuku* could be voluntary or compulsory. Voluntary *seppuku* evolved during the wars of the 12th century, when it was seen as preferable to falling captive to the enemy, and it was also a means of atoning for dishonour. Involuntary *seppuku*, common from the 15th century until its abolition in 1873, was a way in which the death sentence could be administered to samurai without the indignity of a common beheading.

In more recent times Japanese pilots have embraced certain death for military purposes: during the Second World War, Japanese *kamikaze* (wind/divinity) pilots would deliberately crash an aircraft loaded with explosives on its target to inflict maximum damage. The same motivation is found among Islamic suicide squads operating in the Middle East. Followers of the Islamic Jihad and Hamas movements tie explosives to their bodies and detonate them in public places in order to spread terror among the Israelis. Different intentions lay behind the actions of a Buddhist monk who set fire to himself as a protest against the Vietnam war, a gesture that has since been repeated by other pacifists.

Personal suicide, not motivated by politics or religious belief, has been studied by the French sociologist, Émile Durkheim who in 1879 published the seminal work *Suicide: A Study in Sociology* [1879] 1951. Durkheim was concerned with rates of occurrence which he found differed according to social circumstance. He discovered that strong social regulation, or the lack of it, influenced suicide rates. Those with strong religious convictions, such as Roman Catholics and Jews, were less likely to commit suicide. Social isolation increased the risk of someone killing themselves. Marcel Mauss followed up Durkheim's *Suicide* by showing the physiological effectiveness of social imperatives to abandon life.

It is difficult today to imagine the horror evinced by suicide in the past. Those who had killed themselves were refused burial by the church and could not therefore be interred in consecrated ground. In the 19th century, the Reverend Walter Gregor recorded an account of the burial of a suicide in the north-east of Scotland:

> It is not much over half a century since a fierce fight took place in a churchyard in the middle of Banffshire, to prevent the burial of a suicide in it. By an early hour all the strong men of the parish who were opposed to an act so sacrilegious were astir and hastening to the churchyard with their weapons of defence – strong sticks. The churchyard was taken possession of and the walls manned ... In due time the suicide's coffin appeared, surrounded by an excited crowd, for the most part

armed with sticks ... Fierce and long was the fight at the gate, and not a few rolled in the dust. The assailing party was beaten off. A grave was dug outside the churchyard, close beneath the wall, and the coffin laid in it. The lid was lifted, and a bottle of vitriol poured over the body. Before the lid could be again closed, the fumes of the dissolving body were rising thickly over the heads of actors and spectators. This was done to prevent the body from being lifted during the coming night from its resting place, conveyed back to its abode when in life, and placed against the door, to fall at the feet of the member of the family that was the first to open the door in the morning (Bennett, p. 199).

Suicides were buried at crossroads or on the boundary of two lairds' lands, the spot marked by a single large stone or stone cairn. The folklorist, Margaret Bennett, mentions the prevailing belief that nothing would grow on the grave of a suicide and that the suicide's body, if permitted to be buried in the churchyard, was laid below the wall so that no-one could step over it, as a pregnant woman who did so would miscarry (Bennett, p. 200). In some parts of Europe it was believed that a person who had killed himself could return as a vampire.

In France, during the Middle Ages and early modern times if a person committed suicide, the dead man was prosecuted in court and his body expelled from the cemetery. Gabriel Le Bras reports that in Brittany at the beginning of this century, special cemeteries still existed for suicides "where the coffin was passed over a wall that had no opening" (Ariès, p. 44). In Judaism too, suicides are still buried outside the cemetery.

References

Ariès, Philippe. [1977] 1983. *The Hour of Our Death*, trans. Helen Weaver. Harmondsworth, Middlesex: Penguin.

Bennett, Margaret. 1992. *Scottish Customs from the Cradle to the Grave*. Edinburgh: Polygon.

Durkheim, Émile. [1879] 1951. *Suicide: A Study in Sociology*. Glencoe, Illinois: Free Press.

Mauss, Marcel. [1924] 1979. *Sociology and Psychology: Essays*. London: Routledge.

Minois, Georges. 1999. *History of Suicide: Voluntary Death in Western Culture*. trans. Lydia G. Cochrane. Baltimore, Maryland; London: Johns Hopkins University Press.

Surrealism

The artistic movement known as Surrealism was inspired by the theories of the psychoanalyst, Sigmund Freud, and aimed at the liberation of the repressed forces of the subconscious through both art and political action. In 1924, in his First Surrealist Manifesto, the French poet and critic, André Breton, defined the term:

> SURREALISM, n. Pure psychic automatism, by which it is intended to express, verbally, in writing, or by other means, the real process of thought. Thought's dictation, in the absence of all control exercised by the reason and outside all aesthetic or moral preoccupations.
>
> ENCYCL. *Philos.* Surrealism rests in the belief in the superior reality of certain forms of association neglected heretofore; in the omnipotence of the dream and in the disinterested play of thought. It tends definitely to do away with all other psychic mechanisms and to substitute itself for them in the solution of the principal problems of life (Chipp, p. 412).

Breton had visited Freud in Vienna in 1921 and hailed him as the greatest psychologist of the time. He had occasionally used Freud's methods of investigation while treating patients injured in the First World War, encouraging them to pour out a monologue as quickly as possible. Together with the writer Philippe Soupault, he began an experiment in automatic writing, to release his own proscribed thoughts, uncensored by his conscious mind. Dreams, those receptacles of unconscious desire, were also of paramount importance but unlike Freud, who interpreted the dream as the manifestation of unconscious fears and desires, Breton insisted on the objective reality of the dream and its effect on conscious life. He hoped to fuse dream and reality into an absolute reality, a surreality.

Although surrealism began as a literary movement, championed by writers and poets such as Louis Aragon, René Crevel, Robert Desnos and Paul Eluard, it soon came to embrace the visual artists Giorgio de Chirico, Paul Klee, Max Ernst, André Masson, Joan Miró, Paul Delvaux, René Magritte, Yves Tanguy and Salvador Dali. Together they explored all that was repressed or taboo, whether primordial sexual drives, sadism, incest, paedophilia and blasphemy, or, equally unmentionable, paranoia and insanity.

Max Ernst paid a direct tribute to Freud in 1941 with his painting *Totem and Taboo*, in which giant-beaked birds devour a hollowed out totem while a woman with huge breasts watches passively and the stern face of an older man, no doubt the father, stares anxiously from the peak of another totem, surmounted by an eagle. The technique employed, decalcomania, was invented by the surrealist artist, Oscar Dominguez, and consists of compressing fluid paint between two surfaces and then peeling off one layer to reveal complex configurations in which the artist deciphers hidden images – a typical surrealist technique in which chance is manipulated to reveal the unconscious. Ernst also constructed collages, a technique culled from Dadaism, a nihilistic precursor of surrealism, using prints from 19th-century novels. Typical in its use of Freudian themes is *Germinal, my Sister, the Hundred Headless Woman* in which an adolescent girl with an exposed breast pokes at the eye of a severed head while a caged father-figure reaches out to her.

Though he was later to be expelled from the surrealist movement, Salvador Dali was the only artist in the group admired by Freud. In 1929 he collaborated with the film-maker, Luis Buñuel in the film *Le Chien Andalou*, which includes shots of a girl's eye being sliced open with a razor blade and a donkey putrefying in a grand piano, in a sequence of images as randomly and tentatively connected as those in a dream. They exemplify Dali's declared obsession with images of blood, decay and excrement. In 1930 he proposed what he termed a 'paranoid-critical' method, in *La Femme Visible*:

> I believe the moment is at hand when, by a paranoic and active advance of the mind, it will be possible (simultaneously with automatism and other passive states) to systematise confusion and thus to help to discredit completely the world of reality (Chipp, p. 415).

Dali had practised, together with Paul Eluard, the simulation of mental diseases to reach "the condemned places of the human mind" and was intrigued by the ability of the paranoiac who, considering the external world unstable and threatening, was able to convince others of the veracity of his vision. Dali defined painting as "Hand-done colour 'photography' of 'concrete irrationality' and of the imaginative world in general", and his meticulous technique rendered the irrational concrete and convincing.

While Dali shared a preoccupation with sexual deviancy with many of the other surrealists, a deviancy manifest in the *Young Virgin Autosodomized by her own Chastity* (1954) in which the buttocks of a young girl leaning out of a window are threatened by, and transformed into, phallus-like objects, the fascination with sexual taboos reached its peak in the works of the German artist and sculptor, Hans Bellmer. His most notorious object was the female doll made of wood, metal and paper mâché which could be twisted and contorted in accordance with erotic and sadistic fantasies, fantasies that recur in his graphic depictions of sexual permutations and drawings of young girls.

See also

Dolls and Puppets

References

Chipp, Herschel B. [1968] 1975. *Theories of Modern Art: A Source Book by Artists and Critics.* Berkeley; Los Angeles; London: University of California Press.

Nadeau, Maurice. [1948] 1965. *The History of Surrealism.* trans. Richard Howard. New York: Wittenborn.

Table Manners

Table manners and social proscriptions at meal times no doubt preceded the use of tables. The ostensible reasons for such observances are a fear of pollution (both spiritual and material), to indicate good breeding, and to manifest solidarity with a particular class or ethnic group (such as eating with chopsticks in a Chinese restaurant). Hinduism, for example, has traditionally maintained intricate rules on the harvesting, preparation and serving of food. The principle aim was to avoid pollution through contact with "impure" food and to prevent the contamination which might ensue from contact with a lower caste. The complex rules were accompanied by rules for eating. Only the fingers of the right, or pure, hand were to be used for taking food. Furthermore, as J. Jolly wrote of Hindu law in 1928:

> one cannot eat standing, lying naked, or in wet clothes, nor out of a broken or impure vessel, nor out of the hand ... nor can one eat during a period of indigestion or to surfeit (J. Jolly's account of Hindu Law quoted in Goody, p. 124).

Saliva was particularly polluting and could be transmitted from the lips to the fingers. For this reason, if a Brahmin accidentally touched his lips, he needed to bathe and change. Furthermore, certain materials also acted as conduits. E. B. Harper explains how:

> These two beliefs have led to the practice of drinking water by pouring it into the mouth instead of putting the lips on the edge of the cup, and of smoking cigarettes ... through the hand so that they never directly touch the lips ... Eating of any food – even drinking coffee – should be preceded by washing the hands and feet (Douglas, Mary. [1966] 1984, p. 33).

Though the fear of pollution may not be as strong, in Britain, at the beginning of the 21st century, table rules still apply. Mary Douglas analyses the components of an acceptable meal and the taboos involved:

> Meals properly require the use of at least one mouth-entering utensil per head ... A spoon on a saucer is for stirring, not sucking. Meals require a table, a seating order, restriction on movement and on alternative occupations. There is no question of knitting during a meal. Even at Sunday breakfast, reaching for the newspapers is a signal that the meal is over. The meal puts its frame on the gathering (Douglas, 1977, p. 41).

Mary Douglas emphasises the different levels of formality that meals embrace, from the casual breakfast to the ordered dinner, each accompanied by appropriate rules of cutlery and dress. Eating utensils, beyond the communal bowl, goblet and knife, began to appear on European tables around the 16th century. Forks and small, individual knives are depicted in paintings from about 1600. The knife, a potential weapon as well as a necessary tool, had restrictions placed upon it: it was not to be placed near the face, held by the point, lifted unnecessarily, or used for cutting boiled eggs, fish or potatoes. In China knives had been banned altogether from the table: when the scholar replaced the warrior as the ideal citizen, chopsticks replaced knives, and the cultivated Chinese looked with disdain upon the European barbarians who "eat with swords" (Farb and Armelagos, p. 204-208). In both China and Europe, meat was increasingly carved away from the table, out of sight of the guests. Nevertheless, the custom of carving at table has continued in Britain and its colonies, hence the familiar threat to those who indulge in the reprehensible habit of placing their elbows on the table: "Any joints on the table will be carved". After the development of the fork, all kinds of utensils began to appear: soup spoons, oyster forks, fish knives, flat butter knives, cake knives, serving implements and napkins (which became common by the beginning of the 19th century), resulting in the bewildering array seen at formal dinners today.

Obviously, in an age when people wash their hands before eating, the implements are not strictly necessary for hygiene. But this is not their function: eating correctly and table manners are an indication of good breeding, a sign of social class. While Douglas' observations may seem dated in our more liberal times, and newspapers are commonly acceptable at breakfast, oafish behaviour at table is still frowned upon. In fact it is curious how relevant the ancient Chinese food manual, *Li chi*, largely composed before the 2nd century BCE, still seems today:

Do not roll the [grain] into a ball; do not bolt down the various dishes; do not swill down (the soup) ... Do not make a noise in eating; do not crunch

the bones with the teeth; do not put back fish you have been eating; do not throw bones to the dogs; do not snatch (at what you want) ... do not use chopsticks in eating millet ... do not keep picking the teeth (Chang, p. 38-39).

These rules prescribe the correct etiquette for a member of the late Chou (12th century BCE to 221 BCE) upper class. Sinologist K. C. Chang wisely observes that poor people no doubt had their own rules but unfortunately they are not preserved in the available records. As with language, the norms of the social élite are deemed more acceptable than those of the poor.

The Arabs also had elaborate manuals prescribing table manners, which, as in China, differed according to class. A surviving 13th-century text describes meals during the Abbassid dynasty (750 CE to 1258 CE). Washing before and after the repast was essential and, after cleansing and praising God, the rich folk would be presented with a menu detailing what was available while the masses had all the food placed on the table simultaneously. As in India, food was to be taken with the fingers of the right hand, but knives, spoons and napkins were popular with princes and courtiers. All ate from a communal bowl and herein lies the crux of good behaviour:

A man of taste should encourage his neighbour to eat first and avoid offending the assembled company in any particular, making no noise or mess, taking small portions, not reaching out in front. Jahiz recommends as a table companion one who does not pick marrow from the bone or grab at the egg lying on top of the vegetables or make for the choice morsels (Goody, p. 130-131).

The Chinese injunction not to bolt down the food or eat noisily strikes a cord; a wolf guzzles his food, and therefore a human must not. Nonetheless, there are times and places when the noisy slurping of soup, or the smacking of lips, is a sign of satisfaction (or the converse). Claude Lévi-Strauss is particularly interested in the alimentary customs of preliterate societies and examines two Native American myths, in one of which the hero must chew quietly, while in the other the heroine must eat noisily. A myth is not reality but even in real life noise is prohibited or allowed depending on the circumstances:

> the Omaha [a Sioux tribe of eastern Nebraska] scolded children who made noises or faces while eating but silence with the lips when eating was not exacted, except from the chiefs when they were taking their soup. This act must be done very quietly. It was said there was a religious reason attached to this custom … The Ingalik [of Alaska] had more prosaic motives. They usually ate quietly, but smacked their lips a little if they did not like the taste of the food (Lévi-Strauss, p. 498).

This behaviour is described by Lévi-Strauss as "a kind of adjustable code, the terms of which could be combined in such a way as to transmit different messages" (Lévi-Strauss, p. 489). In the Western world, by contrast, table manners have become uniform so that while it was acceptable for a 19th-century Spaniard to belch, and a 16th-century Frenchman could munch vigorously and with impunity, all now conform to a common code in order, says Lévi-Strauss, "to transmit a *compulsory message*" (Lévi-Strauss, p. 499). Noisy eating, in the West, signals bad breeding. The implication is that noise indicates disruption and violence; this is inimical because the moral aim of table manners is to protect against disorder and chaos. This is accompanied by the hygienic aim (not eating out of a common dish and using individual eating utensils) to protect against germs and diseases.

For Lévi Strauss the preliterate societies were more admirable because they would use hollow tubes and other implements for drinking and eating in order to protect other people from the pollution that they themselves emitted whereas Westerners use straws and cutlery to protect themselves from the viruses of others. This argument is rather disingenuous because there is no reason to suppose that the fear of transmitting pollution negates the fear of contracting it. Mary Douglas sees no essential difference between the moral and hygienic aims of table manners, maintaining that the sanitary requirements of Westerners differ little from customs enacted by other cultures to counteract impurity and that our supposed fear of dirt is really a fear of disorder that operates on both a social and metaphysical plane (Douglas, Mary. [1966] 1984, p. 32).

References

Chang, K. C. 1977. "Ancient China". In *Food in Chinese Culture: Anthropological and Historical Perspectives*. ed. K. C. Chang, p. 23-52. New Haven, Connecticut; London: Yale University Press.

Douglas, Mary. [1966] 1984. *Purity and Danger: An Analysis of the Concepts of Pollution and Taboo*. London: Ark, Routledge and Kegan Paul.

Douglas, Mary. 1977. "Deciphering a Meal". In *Food and Culture: A Reader*. ed. Carole Counihan and Penny van Esterik, p. 36-54. New York; London: Routledge.

Farb, Peter and George Armelagos. 1980. *Consuming Passions: The Anthropology of Eating*. Boston, Massachusetts; Houghton Mifflin Company.

Goody, Jack. 1982. *Cooking, Cuisine and Class: A Study in Comparative Sociology*. Cambridge: Cambridge University Press.

Lévi-Strauss. [1968] 1978. *The Origin of Table Manners: Introduction to a Science of Mythology 3*. trans. John and Doreen Weightman. New York: Harper & Row.

Taoism – Japanese

Taoism, along with other aspects of Chinese culture, only began to influence Japanese life around the 6th century CE despite the fact that the major text of philosophical Taoism, the *Tao Te Ching*, attributed to Lao-t'zu, had arrived in

247

Japan much earlier. It was religious, rather than philosophical, Taoism that appealed to the general public. Religious Taoism, rooted in ancient China and replete with a complex network of cosmological and calendrical rituals and taboos, fused with the native Japanese Shinto, with its belief in *kami* (spirits or powers), and Buddhism. Many taboos deriving from these traditions still survive and tend to cluster around sacred occasions, times, places and directions.

Taboos concerning dates

Certain days are considered auspicious, whereas others are unlucky. The traditional concept of luck comes from the *ommyodo*, the "Way of Positive and Negative Principles", the yin and yang. Many Japanese still rely on an almanac, based on an ancient astrological scheme, to decide on which day to begin an activity. Days to be avoided include *sanrinbo* (three-neighbour destroying), because house-building started on this day results in the house and the three neighbouring dwellings being burnt to ashes, and, for a funeral, *tomobiko* (friend-pulling) lest another be also brought down by death. Conversely, a day named *dai'an* (Great security) is safe for marriage, but not a day known as *butsumetsu* (Buddha's death). The Day of the Horary Sign of the Horse is bad for rice-planting and cloth cut for clothes on the Day of the Monkey or of the Horse will cause holes to be burnt in the dress – the auspicious day for cutting cloth is the Day of the Rabbit. Once made, the clothes must not be washed on the first, fifteenth and twenty-eighth of each month as these days are devoted to deities.

Taboos pertaining to place

The precincts of shrines and sacred buildings are holy and must be kept free from pollution. Urinating on the ground and the use of manure on fields surrounding a Shinto shrine is forbidden. Some fields in the village and certain forest regions are set aside and no-one can own or cultivate them for private purposes without incurring the risk of sickness or death. Taboos also surround cemeteries, reducing the price of residential lots in the area.

Taboos of direction

In the Heian Era (around the 11th century CE), a custom known as *katatagai* (changing the directions) was observed. This involved taking a circuitous route to avoid travelling in an inauspicious direction. An architectural practice still observed today is based on the "Way of Positive and Negative Principles". According to this tradition, the north-easterly direction is the *kimon* (devil's gate), the entrance and exit for demons; it is dangerous to build kitchens or toilets in this direction. The north-west is also inauspicious and to protect this part of the house a shrine of the household god is often built.

Auspicious directions may change by years and months: *kami*, both malicious and benign, are thought to circle the heavens, controlling the points of the compass. Every year has its own *eho* (propitious direction) or *akinokata* (direction which is open). Inauspicious is a direction governed by the dreadful Konjin, the golden *kami*. As Konjin changes his position each month, careful calculation is necessary before beginning any journey or enterprise.

Agricultural taboos

Agricultural taboos include a ban on the sowing of crops on the day known as *fujuku-nichi* (unripe day), lest they fail to ripen, while straw taken from wheat sown on *jika-no-hi* (the day of fire on earth), if used to thatch a roof, will ignite.

See also

Mountains; North-East; Shinto Purification

References

Earhart, H. Byron. 1974. *Religion in the Japanese Experience: Sources and Interpretations*, p. 80-84. Encino, California: Dickenson Publishing.

Ichiro Hori, Ikado Fujio, Wakimoto Tsuneya, and Yanagawa Keiichi ed. 1972. *Japanese Religion: A*

Survey by the Agency for Cultural Affairs, p. 125-126. Tokyo: Kodansha International.

Ikawa, Eri. Personal communication.

Theory of Evolution – Darwin

Darwin's theory of natural evolution opposed the theological view of creation and even today there are groups of religious fundamentalists who refuse to teach the doctrine. But ideas on evolution did not begin with Charles Darwin's *On the Origin of Species* which was first published in 1859. In ancient Greece both Anaximander and Empedocles had had some thoughts on the subject in the 5th century BCE and J. B. Lamarck had proposed a comprehensive theory of natural development including the adaptation and transmission of acquired characteristics, in his *Zoological Philosophy* of 1809. Lamarck, for example, supposed that the efforts of giraffes to reach the leaves of trees caused their necks to gradually lengthen until they reached their present size. The French biologist, Georges Buffon (1707-88) considered "transformism" possible and even Darwin's grandfather, Erasmus Darwin, had included a chapter on transmutation in his *Zoonomia* of 1794-96.

Darwin, however, proposed a mechanism for evolution. He believed it happened by means of chance variations (mutations) which, if they were adaptive, survived to give new species. He was influenced by the parson Thomas R. Malthus' 1798 *Essay on the Principle of Population* which he read in 1838. Malthus drew attention to the fact that the population increases faster than the food supply, creating a stimulus for adaptation and self-improvement if one is to survive. The theory of individualism which such a notion implies is in many ways repellent (it influenced 19th-century notions of poverty being the fault of the poor and was indirectly responsible for non interference in the Irish potato famine in which millions starved). Nonetheless, it helped Darwin formulate his thesis that animals had to compete to survive; the inadequate would be killed off and those better suited to their environment would persist and breed. Savage competition would lead to the survival of the fittest.

Unlike his predecessors, Darwin provided a body of evidence to support his theory. His first evidence came while he travelled the world on a voyage that began in 1831 as a naturalist on the survey ship, the HMS *Beagle*. The *Beagle* sailed down and up the coasts of South America, through the Galapagos Islands and across the Pacific to Tahiti, New Zealand, Australia, Mauritius, Ascension Island and South Africa. He noticed the variety of species and their adaptations, collected fossils of recently extinct animals and compared them with living specimens. He returned in 1836 and began a series of investigations to see whether a natural mechanism of transmutation was possible and in 1838 he first conceived the idea of natural selection. Curiously, Alfred Russel Wallace was working on a very similar theory to Darwin's and in 1858 offered it to the Linnaean Society where it was published along with extracts of Darwin's model.

The *Origin of Species* aroused enormous controversy. In arguing that God was unnecessary (and that humans were descended from an extinct species of ape), Darwin antagonised many theologians and scientists, although the more enlightened among them could accept his views. Charles Kingsley humorously remarked:

> We know of old that God was so wise that he could make all things; but, behold, he is so much wiser than even that, that he can make all things make themselves (Tolstoy, p. 204).

But the opposition was vocal. A clergyman in the British museum pointed Darwin out as "the most dangerous man in England" (Bowler, p. 3). Bishop Samuel Wilberforce came up with anti-evolutionary arguments at the British Association meeting in Oxford in 1860. In sardonic mood, Wilberforce asked Thomas Henry Huxley, who was defending Darwin, whether he claimed to be descended from an ape from his mother's or his father's side. Theistic evolutionists emerged, who believed that God intervened in the evolutionary process: if the divine still had a role, then religious leaders could retain their social authority. The anatomist, Richard Owen, in an article in the *Edinburgh Review*, fiercely criticised Darwin, at the same time suggesting that there was nothing new in the book. The physicist, William Thomson (Lord Kelvin), disputed Darwin's model because he calculated that the earth would not have maintained its steady state over an immense period of time as its hot interior would gradually have cooled – in no more than forty million years – and Darwin knew that evolution would have taken longer. (When, in 1896 radioactivity was discovered – a source of energy that has kept the earth warm over vast periods of time – the conundrum was resolved.) In the *Genesis of Species,* a further attack on Darwinism was mounted by St George Jackson Mivart. Mivart argued that the development of complex organs through a series of intermediate stages was problematic; for instance, the intermediate stages between a leg and a wing would not allow for walking or flight.

In 1871, Darwin published the *Descent of Man* which placed the white male at the pinnacle of the evolutionary tree. Though females, blacks and other creatures were not so perfect, Darwin was at pains to show that even dogs, apes and higher mammals possessed rudimentary intelligence and morality. His *Expression of the Emotions in Man and the Animals*, which appeared the following year, imputed emotions to the lower animals. The reason for man's greater intelligence was due to a change in lifestyle: having left the trees for the plains and adapting an upright posture, the hands were free to fashion tools and manipulate the environment. Typically, perhaps, those aspects of Darwin's theory that were considered reprehensible in Victorian times are often different from those that are tabooed today. No-one but a religious fundamentalist would question man's

descent from apes while Darwin's belief in white supremacy (Europeans were thought to have larger brains and greater intelligence than other races) is abhorrent to most people.

The theory of evolution was to influence other disciplines. Anthropologists posited a cultural evolution with preliterate people as "cultural fossils", manifesting an earlier stage in the process. Some, such as Lévy-Bruhl, even suggested that the thought processes of "primitives" were different and prelogical, an idea that has since been discredited. Herbert Spencer, who coined the phrase the "survival of the fittest", has been termed a "social Darwinist". Spencer extolled free enterprise to enable the individual to adapt to an ever-changing society. But he was not especially influenced by Darwin's theory of natural selection; rather, he supported Lamarck's mechanism of the inheritance of acquired characteristics. Advocating non-intervention by the State, he supposed that sufferings that are due to repeated failure would stimulate the individual to do better next time and that the acquired virtues would be passed on to succeeding generations. Unfortunately, someone in dire need who was not helped would have no "next time" to improve in.

Just as alarming as the views of Herbert Spencer are those of Francis Galton to whom we owe the concept of "eugenics". In his *Hereditary Genius* of 1869, Galton argued that intelligence was hereditary and that the human race could be improved by way of artificial selection: the professional (superior) classes should be encouraged to procreate while the poor (inferior) classes were to be prevented from doing so. Darwin agreed in principle with Galton's ideas:

> Though I see so much difficulty, the object seems a grand one; and you have pointed out the sole feasible, yet I fear utopian, plan of procedure in improving the human race (Bowler, p. 200).

Though the Victorians did not adopt the "procedure", during the Nazi régime eugenics was practised to "purify" the "Aryan race". The mentally ill, criminals and those considered "racially impure" were sterilised or killed while selected "perfect" couples were brought together for procreation. This chilling experience has been a salutory lesson and has made eugenics a taboo topic.

In 1865 Gregor Mendel published reports of his experiments on heredity in peas and it was Mendel's experiments which became the foundation for modern genetics. The existence of genes – information carriers that exist within the nucleus of each cell – provides a key to understanding the mechanics of Darwin's theory of natural selection. At the beginning of the 21st century a new controversy has arisen over the morality of genetic engineering – though it may help eliminate hereditary conditions and benefit agriculture, the cloning of humans (just as Dolly the Sheep resulted from cloning in Scotland) bestows upon mankind superhuman powers. If Darwin's *Origin of Species* argued that God was unnecessary for evolution, the ability to modify genes has given man a God-like role.

References

Bowler, Peter J. 1990. *Charles Darwin: The Man and His Influence*. Oxford: Basil Blackwell.

Numbers, Ronald L. 1998. *Darwin Comes to America*. Cambridge, Massachusetts; London: Harvard University Press

Rose, Michael R. 1998. *Darwin Spectre. Evolutionary Biology and the Modern World*. Princeton, New Jersey: Princeton University Press.

Tolstoy, Ivan. 1990. *The Knowledge and the Power: Reflections on the History of Science*. Edinburgh: Canongate.

Tobacco

There are seventy-four species of the genus *Nicotiana* or tobacco; some, such as *Nicotiana rustica* and the less potent *N. tabacum* were cultivated hybrids (the latter is the progenitor of the modern, commercial varieties) while others, including *N. attenuata*, *N. bigelovii* and *N. trigonophylla*, initially grew wild. Tobacco is viewed now as a pernicious, addictive substance, incontrovertibly linked to such medical conditions as lung cancer and respiratory diseases. Smoking in public places is increasingly prohibited, advertisements for cigarettes banned in many Western countries and the act itself considered anti-social. Yet in other cultures tobacco has the seal of the sacred, and is believed to have been bestowed upon mankind by benevolent gods. It has played a central role in North and South American shamanism and in purification ceremonies and supernatural healing. The tobacco may be smoked in pipes, rolled into cigarettes or cigars, chewed, eaten, drunk as tobacco juice, sucked or sniffed. This ritual use of tobacco goes back a long way; in Mexico the earliest clay tobacco pipes date to Olmec times (*ca*. 1200-900 BCE) but conical stone pipes have been excavated in California that are probably over a thousand years older.

The ethnologist Johannes Wilbert has spent considerable time conducting field research among the Warao tribe of the Orinoco Delta in eastern Venezuela, for whom tobacco is a vehicle of shamanic ecstasy. Warao shamans smoke it in enormous "cigars", fifty to seventy-five centimetres long, to induce a trance in which they visit the Supreme Spirits (*Kanobos*) who inhabit the mountains at the end of the world and who need nourishment in the form of tobacco smoke. If provided with the gift of tobacco which they crave, the *Kanobos* will ensure health and abundance on earth. If denied it, they will spitefully send invisible pains and death to humans. Although now most of the Warao population smoke tobacco, in the past they were wary, fearing a dangerous encounter with tobacco-craving spirits. Even today the long "cigars", rolled leaves of black tobacco mixed with a fragrant resin, remain the preserve of the shamans, taboo to all others.

To reach the realm of the *Kanobos*, the *bahanarotu* or "light" shaman must travel a bridge of smoke till he reaches the House of

Tobacco Smoke in the Eastern part of the universe. A myth describes how the first *bahanarotu* shaman crosses the bridge and becomes a shaman. In the beginning, it is told, a youth arises in the East, spreads out his arms and proclaims himself Creator Bird Of the Dawn. Under his wings he holds a bow and a shaman's rattle. He creates a white house of tobacco smoke which becomes "the birthplace of *bahana*, the shamanistic practice of blowing smoke and sucking out sickness" (Wilbert, p. 66-67).

One day, a four-year-old boy decides to visit the East. He fasts, then ascends on fire-smoke and is met by a spirit guide:

> Soon the boy found himself on a bridge made of thick white ropes of tobacco smoke. He followed the invisible spirit guide until, a short distance from the centre of the celestial dome, he reached a point where marvellous flowers began meandering alongside the bridge in a rainbow of brilliant colours – a row of red and a row of yellow flowers on the left, and lines of blue and green flowers on the right. A gentle breeze wafted them back and forth. Like the bridge they adorned, the flowers were made of solidified tobacco smoke. Everything was bright and tranquil. The invisible guide ushered the boy toward the House of Smoke (Wilbert, p. 67).

Entering the House of Smoke, the boy is presented with a sparkling rock crystal, a ball of white hair, white rocks and tobacco smoke. These are the essential elements of the Game of *Bahana*: ingested by malevolent *bahanarotus*, they are sent out as projectiles through a hole in the hand and have the magical ability to transmit sickness. This sickness can be cured by benevolent *bahanarotus* who inhale vast quantities of tobacco and then suck out the foreign bodies from the patient. The boy is also given the shaman's bow and arrows. Now a *bahanarotu*, he awakens from his trance. For four days he fasts, desiring only smoke. On the fifth day he is transfigured, his entire body begins to glow and he turns a brilliant white.

At the other end of the universe, in the West, live the souls of the dead "dark" shamans, the *hoarotus*, half-human, half-animal, with their Supreme spirit, the Scarlet Macaw and his *hoarao* companions. To sustain themselves, they need the cadavers and blood of humans. The blood was formerly provided through a form of benign vampirism, through an artery that reached from the dark Western realm to the hearts of the Warao villagers, with the result that the spirits were nourished and the villagers merely felt weakened but soon recovered. Unfortunately, this bridge of blood was severed and now the carcasses must be provided by *a hoarotu* shaman who kills his victim by means of his *Kaidoko* snare of tobacco smoke.

The initiation of a *hoarotu* shaman is long and gruelling. A novice is taken to a small hut in the forest by his master and the two remain secluded for five days. Smoking incessantly, the novice must learn the requisite songs, one to cause sickness, another to cure it. Then his master blows into a cigar and two demonic spirits enter the body of the novice and try to tear it apart. For a month, the novice must fast and smoke. He dreams he is killed by spirits, but is not dead. Then he dreams that he is offered a corpse to eat but is revolted by it. By now emaciated, and near death himself, he dreams he is placed in a grave of stone slabs. Should he awake at this stage, he would truly die. But he escapes through a crack in the stone slabs and is gradually brought back to life (Wilbert, p. 55-83).

Shamanic initiation by means of tobacco is not the sole preserve of the Warao. Among the Carib of the lowland northern South America, initiates are starved till they are virtual skeletons, during which time they are fed large quantities of liquid tobacco through the nose and mouth to induce trances. Thus prepared, they make their first ascent to the spirit world. In North America, too, tobacco is an important intermediary between the human and supernatural worlds. The Iroquois and Algonquin tribes of the Eastern Woodlands and the Plains and the Plains and Prairie tribes all placate the spirits with tobacco. An Iroquois Seneca myth tells of a meeting between a youth and an emaciated Skeleton Man who sits surrounded by human bones and who requests tobacco. To satisfy him, the young man must go on a perilous journey and outwit the Seven Sisters and their fiendish mother who guard the elixir. When the youth returns with the tobacco and fills Skeleton Man's pipe, the bones of the dead take on flesh and return to life.

The pipes of the Native Americans of the Plains are made of catlinite, a red clay stone mined in south-western Minnesota, which is thought to represent the petrified flesh and blood of dead ancestors and their buffalo. It was impossible for the tribes of the Plains to enact any ceremony or ritual without first smoking the pipes which were often beautifully carved and decorated. The powerful, flat pipe of the Plains Arapaho is believed to have existed before the great flood which poured out over the earth with the felling of the world tree. As the pipe represents the Supreme Deity of the Arapaho, it may neither come close to the earth nor be looked upon. To prevent these taboos being violated, during the Sun Dance, for instance, the pipe is kept on a plinth and wrapped in several blankets. Throughout North America, the pipe is a successor to the shaman's sucking straw, through which he extracted the spirits of disease from the patient's body and inhaled tobacco smoke to induce ecstasy. The indigenous people of the Northwest Coast initially chewed their tobacco together with lime at commemorative feasts for the dead. Once introduced to smoking by Western explorers, they carved pipes from wood and ivory and decorated them with animals and mythological scenes.

Pipe smoking is not depicted in Mesoamerican Mayan art but tobacco in the form of cigars, and also cigarettes, is well documented. The word *cigar* is of Mayan origin and *tobacco* may be derived from an Arawak word for cigar. When the Spanish arrived in the early 16th century they reported cigars varnished with clay, and decorated, as well as tubes of cane and clay which were stuffed with tobacco and were either smoked or used to blow smoke. The pre-Columbian Maya portrayed their deities, rulers and nobles smoking (one god being shown with a smoking cigar stuck through his forehead), as well as mythological animals, usually representing gods: monkeys, jaguars, frogs and toads all enjoyed the tobacco. Present-day Maya continue to treat tobacco as a magical substance, efficacious in the dispelling of demons and shamanic healing. Maya travellers protect themselves from malevolent forces by chewing tobacco and carrying tobacco-filled gourds. Moreover, in many areas of Central America tobacco and smoking implements are placed in graves to accompany the deceased on the journey to the otherworld.

Detailed information about the use of tobacco among the Aztecs is available from the writings of the Spanish chroniclers. Juan de Torquemada (1615) wrote of Cihuacoatl, the earth goddess and creator of mankind, who had a body composed of tobacco and was an incarnation of the plant. Hernando Ruiz de Alarcón (1629) described offerings of tobacco to the war god, Huitzilopochtli, while Fray Diego Durán (c. 1581) related how tobacco and incense were regularly sprinkled onto the fire of the fire god, Xiuhtecuhtli. Priests who served Tezcatlipoca, possessor of the "smoking mirror" used for divination, wore small tobacco gourds (*yequachtli*) on their backs as insignia of their priestly status, and in both the Codex Mendoza and the Codex Florentine some of the figures performing the sacrificial rites are shown carrying tobacco gourds and pouches (*yequachtli*) or incense ladles (*tlemaitl*). Tobacco was carried in the form of powder or moulded into balls and burnt as incense. When it was smoked, it was mixed with other herbs and intoxicants.

Certainly tobacco had an apotropaic function in pre-Columbian America. It averted witchcraft and the malevolence of the dead. The Totonac of Papantla de Olarte offered it to the guardians of the forest and Mazatec healers would make a paste of powder and lime to protect pregnant woman from witchcraft. The Tlaxcalan presented it to their war god, Camaxtli, and the cacique (chiefs or pinces) of Michoacán declared war by sending bowls of tobacco, along with eagle feathers and blood-stained arrows, to their enemies. Fray Bernardino de Sahagún (1569-82) described a further use of tobacco: when hunting snakes, the Mexicans would aim powdered tobacco at the reptiles to render them powerless.

Even when, as is commonly the case, a society combines the use of tobacco with other intoxicants, it retains its sacred character. The Huichol Indians of Mexico are known for the sanctity which they attach to the hallucinogenic cactus known as peyote. But during the pilgrimage to collect the peyote, the potent native tobacco, *Nicotiana rustica*, is indispensable. The tobacco is carried in gourds; it is sacred, said to impart visions, and is only used ceremonially when all the men smoke in unison. It belongs to Our Grandfather, the Fire Shaman, who led the first peyote hunt and cured the participants of their afflictions with its help. Native American groups in California combine tobacco with *Datura inoxia*, a plant with powerful psychotropic and narcotic properties. In lowland South America, shaman initiates take infusions of liquid tobacco as a prelude to inbibing *Banisteriopsis Caapi*, an hallucinogenic plant, also known as *yajé*; in eastern Bolivia Tacana shamans employ *Banisteriopsis* to induce trances and rely on tobacco to keep the demons at bay; and in northern Peru tobacco is combined with the San Pedro (*Trichocereus pachanoi*) cactus, which contains hallucinogens, in folk healing.

It is clear that traditional societies have not treated tobacco as a profane substance. However, like anything that is believed to be powerful and sacred, it is not without its dangers and its use is carefully circumscribed. Among Europeans, who were introduced to the substance through the travels of Christopher Columbus, tobacco has served no religious ends and European influence has resulted in the increasing secularisation of tobacco among Native Americans. Nevertheless, when tobacco reached Siberia, probably towards the end of the 16th century, it was quickly adopted by Siberian shamans who recognised its potential as a pathway to the stars.

See also
Cannabis Sativa L.

References
Arents, George. 1937-1952 *Tobacco*. 5 vols. ed. Jerome E. Brooks. New York: Rosenbach Co.

Furst, Peter T. 1987. "Tobacco". In *The Encyclopedia of Religion*. Vol 14. ed. Mircea Eliade. New York: Macmillan.

Hultkrantz, Åke. [1967] 1980. *The Religions of the American Indians*. trans. Monica Setterwall. Berkeley; Los Angeles: University of California Press.

Paper, Jordan. 1987. "Cosmological Implications of Pan-Indian Sacred Pipe Ritual". In *Amerindian Cosmology*. ed. Don McCaskill. *The Canadian Journal of Native Studies*, vol. VII, no. 2, p. 297-306.

Robicsek, Francis. 1978. *The Smoking Gods: Tobacco in Maya Art, History and Religion*. Norman, Oklahoma: University of Oklahoma Press.

Wilbert, Johannes. 1972. "Tobacco and Shamanistic Ecstasy Among the Warao Indians of Venezuela". In *Flesh of the Gods: The Ritual Use of Hallucinogens*. ed. Peter T. Furst, p. 55-83. London: George Allen and Unwin.

Wilbert, Johannes. 1987. *Tobacco and Shamanism in South America*. New Haven, Connecticut: Yale University Press.

Tortoises

One type of tortoise, known as both *taw phii* (tortoise belonging to the spirit) and *taw san lang diaw* (tortoise with a single stripe on its shell) is tabooed in Phraan Muan village in northeastern Thailand. Those tortoises with more stripes are readily eaten but the *taw phii*, associated with the spirit of the swamp and symbolising water, is forbidden by the intermediary (*cham*) of its guardian spirit. It may be the sacred nature of the turtle that saves it from being eaten or it may be its association with sex, for the shell of the tortoise (*daung*) is identified with the female sex organ. In Bangkok the word for tortoise, "taw", also means "vagina" but this is not the case in Phraan Muan (where the shell is more significant).

The shell is also used in corrective rituals, for example when second cousins marry. Marriages between second cousins are discouraged within the village (being seen as too close), especially if there is a great disparity in age between the betrothed. To avert the terrible consequences that could ensue from such a union, a rite is performed in which the couple are made to eat rice from a tortoise shell. The underlying idea is that dogs commit incest and ignore age differences, therefore by also eating like dogs the couple will mislead the punitive moral agents into thinking that they are not humans but animals. S. J. Tambiah explains how this works on a linguistic level. The term for marriage ceremony is *kin daung* with *kin* meaning "to eat" and *daung* referring to the tortoise shell and, both literally and metaphorically, to the vagina:

> The words and metaphor which are normally associated with acceptable marriage, are now used instrumentally in an unacceptable marriage. The ritual implies that the couple are eating from (born of) the same tortoise shell (the same vagina), and in thus themselves eating together (having sexual intercourse) they are behaving like incestuous dogs (Tambiah, p. 428).

See also

Food Taboos

Reference

Tambiah, S. J. 1969. "Animals are Good to Think and Good to Prohibit". *Ethnology*, no. 8, p. 423-459.

Trade

Embargoes on trade are a common feature of contemporary life, established for economic, political or moral purposes – because a particular country is out of favour or for reasons of narrow protectionism. They are not new and neither are they limited to western, industrialised societies. At the end of the 18th century, a Hawaiian chief named Kamehameha placed a taboo on the selling of pigs to foreigners. The animals were only to be exchanged for guns and ammunition. Kamehameha and subsequent chiefs also used taboos to monopolise their trade with Europeans, denying commerce to their own commoners:

> Trade goods received from foreigners might be seized immediately by the chiefs' enforcers, or a taboo placed on commerce so as to reserve the trade for the chiefs. The chiefs' taboos could be quite selective and were employed both to deter the commoners and to pressure the shippers (Linnekin, p. 161)

In 1786 a trader by the name of Dixon described how he had had his ships tabooed by the chief, Kehekili, who had built a storehouse:

> for such articles as the natives might obtain in the course of their traffic with our vessels: when this was completed, he caused the bay to be tabooed … [and directed the inhabitants] to bring whatever trade they had got, that it might be deposited in his new-erected edifice. This being effected, he found means … to appropriate one-half of these stores to his own use (Linnekin, p. 162).

Unfortunately the citizens of Hawai'i suffered great hardship at the hands of their chiefs and in Hawai'i, like elsewhere, the term "free trade" came to be something of a misnomer as not everyone had the freedom and power to trade.

Reference

Linnekin, Jocelyn. [1990] 1993. *Sacred Queens and Women of Consequence: Rank, Gender and Colonialism in the Hawaiian Islands.* Ann Arbor, Michigan: University of Michigan Press.

Transvestism

Transvestism, or cross-dressing, is condemned in *Deuteronomy* which emphatically states that "A woman must not wear men's clothes nor a man put on women's dress" (22:5). The prohibition still exists among Orthodox Jews and certain Christian sects like the Amish. During the 13th century, at the time of the Crusades, the Church began a campaign against cross-dressing as a reaction to what it considered an Islamic practice of using feminised boys for sexual gratification (Bolin, p. 22-51). In 1620 King James I ordered the clergy to condemn the donning of male clothes by women; this was common practice during female protests against enclosures and food restrictions (Ramet, p. 1-21). In past centuries, women have also donned the garb of men as a disguise so that they could participate in activities that were forbidden to them: they became soldiers, surgeons and pirates. The Dutch social historians, Rudolf Dekker and Lotte van de Pol, found that female transvestism was particularly prevalent in Europe from the late 16th century to the 19th century. One 17th-century Spanish woman, Catalina de Erauso, joined the Spanish army and, after her discovery, was granted a license by Philip IV of Spain to wear male clothes. Less fortunate was the Dutch woman, Catherine Rosenbrock, who, after spending twelve years as a sailor and soldier, was imprisoned by her own mother. In recent times, cross-dressing has been seen as a sign of sexual deviancy and treated with ridicule or used for entertainment: performers in British pantomime cross-dress and make sexual innuendoes, and role reversal is a common feature of carnivals. The Hungarians, Romanians and German Schwabs celebrate a women's carnival (*asszonyfarsang*) which frequently involves the wearing of male attire, the singing of bawdy songs and the performance of male dances (Kürti, p. 148-163), and in Javanese drama a male transvestite commonly adopts the social role of a female in the plays. Transvestism can also play a vital role in rituals.

Ritual transvestism

Ritual transvestism, performed on specific occasions as a group activity, has been a favourite study of anthropologists who have searched for its underlying causes. Max Gluckman sees the primary function of the transvestism and assertive behaviour of Zulu women of the Bantu tribe, during the Nomkubulwana festival, as a means of catharsis. During the "little ceremony", the women wear men's clothes and herd and milk the cattle which are normally taboo to them. Any passing male is derided and mistreated. Gluckman thinks the festival offers an opportunity for open rebellion for the women, suppressed as they normally are by a rigid patriarchal society. The festival acts as a "safety valve" to release pent-up frustrations but the dissent is circumscribed and does not disturb the status quo (Gluckman, p. 112-123).

Inconsistencies in Gluckman's theory are criticised by Edward Norbeck; for instance, during the Wiko circumcision rites both females and males cross-dress but Gluckman does not think that male transvestism constitutes rebellion. Male transvestism occurs in initiation ceremonies in many parts of Africa. Among the Turkana, boys from "conservative families" wear their hair like women. During the period of recovery from circumcision, the Masai youths dress like women and Nandi boys at initiation to manhood wear some article of female clothing (Norbeck, p. 201-217). It is possible that transvestism during initiation ceremonies is a means of separating the boys from the profane world, by making them sexless or bisexual, while they are initiated into the sacred mysteries of the tribe. Certainly some Tantric sects of Hinduism use male transvestism "as a way of transcending one's own sex, a prerequisite to achieving salvation" (Nanda, Serena, p. 376). This is similar to Edmund Leach's formulation that role reversals during festivals and rites of passage are "symbolic of a complete transfer from the secular to the sacred" (Leach, p. 249).

Peter Rigby, while not denying that Gluckman's theory of ritual catharsis may explain the behaviour of Zulu women, finds it inadequate to explain female transvestism among the Gogo of Tanzania. The Gogo women perform their rituals at times of crisis, such as the birth of twins or a cattle disease. Such disturbances are thought to be caused by a "bad ritual state" (*mbeho ibeho*) of the area around the village, an area that is symbolically associated with the women of the village. When the cattle disease known as *masaho* strikes, the women are called upon to purify the area, an act that involves donning male attire, including the men's dancing bells, and driving out the cattle on two consecutive days (normally the work of men). Normal taboos are lifted so that the women may handle the weapons of their husbands, even when they are menstruating, and demonstrate sexual aggression (although sexual relations are prohibited). After returning the cattle to the homesteads at the end of the second day, the women dance, singing, to the western boundary of the area around the village, where they "throw away" the disease into a swamp and return home. Rigby explains the transvestism and associated features of the ritual as a deliberate reversal of action and event in the human sphere which will bring about a corresponding reversal in the cosmic sphere so that the *mbeho ibeho*, the dangerous ritual state, can be transformed into a

positive auspicious state, or *mbeho swanu*. During the ceremony, the women are in a sense "sacred", outside the sphere of normal society and conventional time. At the end of the ritual, the *ibeho* is thrown away to the west as the Gogo identify this area with death, sorcery and evil spirits (Rigby, p. 164-171).

Like Rigby, Victor Turner believes that the social life of men is intricately linked to that of the cosmos. When a "bad ritual state" exists in an area, causing such disasters as cattle disease, it is thought to be caused by an abnormality in man's social structure. According to Turner, society is characterised by a hierarchical social structure and the division of roles is necessary for its proper functioning. But underlying this structure is a universal desire for what he terms "communitas", a state in which all are equal and part of one homogeneous whole. If those in authority, through self-interest and disregard for others, have caused some calamity in the environment, it is up to the structural inferiors of the community, namely the women, to restore normal conditions. The women symbolically adopt masculine roles, dressing as men and carrying their weapons. In this way, according to Turner, "authority is wielded by communitas itself, masquerading as structure. Structural form is thereby divested of selfish attributes and purified by association with the values of communitas" (Turner, p. 183). The social unity which has been disrupted by the selfish interests of men is restored, and the "bad ritual state" is dispersed.

Turner's concept is also applicable to role reversals that occur at Saturnalian festivals and carnivals, where social distinctions are dissolved, and to the liminal stage of an initiation ceremony, where the wearing of female clothes by the initiate may symbolise his passive attitude and loss of social status. Another anthropologist, Gregory Bateson, looks at the temporary reversal of gender roles during the Naven celebrations of the Iatmul tribe of Papua New Guinea. Among the Iatmul, men are valued for their pride, independence and self-assertion but find it difficult to express joy at the achievement of another. Women, on the other hand, are expected to exhibit humility and co-operation. During a Naven situation celebrating a child's notable feat, the relatives are expected to express joy – difficult for the men because of their own egos and for the women who are unaccustomed to the demonstrative behaviour expected of them. The embarrassment which both sexes feel is somewhat mitigated by the adoption of the clothes of the opposite sex. These clothes act as a type of mask, disguising the individual sexes and allowing the participants to act out unfamiliar roles.

The Naven transvestism fulfils another, more complex, role. It helps cement a potentially fraught relationship between a *wau* (a mother's brother) and his *laua* (sister's child). Throughout the initiation ceremonies, the *wau* acts as a kind of foster-mother to his *laua*. During the Naven celebrations the *wau* is particularly demonstrative in his adoption of the female role, rubbing the male *laua*'s shin with his buttocks and acting as substitute mother. Such bonding averts any animosity that might exist between a mother's brother and her husband. For although in economic matters the boy is grouped with his father's clan, it is the mother's clan who takes the credit for the youth's achievements. The Naven transvestism of the *wau* is a symbolic means by which, as a "surrogate mother", he can lay claim to the *laua*'s success.

In certain cultures individuals may exhibit transsexual behaviour on a more or less permanent basis. Shamans in Siberia are often capable of harnessing the sexual potential of both male and female. The ethnographer Waldemar Bogoras has written about remarkable Chukchi shamans who assumed the identities of the opposite sex and, though socially stigmatised, were believed to possess tremendous spirit power. Assisted by spirits, a male shaman would plait his hair, wear female clothes, forsake his harpoon, rifle and lasso and take up needle and skin-scraper. Female shamans cut their hair, adopted male dress and pronunciation and learned how to handle a spear and shoot a rifle (Balzer, p. 164-182). A number of Native American cultures have what anthropologists have referred to as the *berdache*, individuals who cross-dress and adopt character traits that are not generally associated with their own gender. Sabine Lang rejects the term *berdache*, seeing it as pejorative because it derives from the Arab term for a male prostitute, *bardaj*. Instead she speaks of women-men (men who adopt women's clothes and assume traditional female roles) and men-women (women who seek to look and behave as men, hunting and joining men on their raids). Usually these character traits are manifest in early childhood and the reversals are voluntary. Sometimes both male and female characteristics exist within the same person (Lang, p. 183-196).

Although, within traditional societies, the practice of transvestism does not always confer sanctity, it is often treated with more reverence than in the industrialised West.

See also

Carnival; Liminality; Sartorial Taboos

References

Balzer, Marjorie Mandelstam. 1996. "Sacred Genders in Siberia: Shamans, Bear Festivals and Androgyny". In *Gender Reversals and Gender Cultures: Anthropological and Historical Perspectives*. ed. Sabrina Petra Ramet, p. 164-182. London; New York: Routledge.

Bateson, Gregory. [1936] 1958. *Naven*. Stanford, California: Stanford University Press.

Bolin, Anne. 1996. "Traversing Gender: Cultural Context and Gender Practices". In *Gender Reversals and Gender Cultures: Anthropological and Historical Perspectives*. ed. Sabrina Petra Ramet, p. 22-51. London; New York: Routledge.

Gluckman, Max. 1963. "Rituals of Rebellion in South-East Africa". In *Order and Rebellion in Tribal Africa*. London: Cohen and West.

Kürti, László. 1996. "Eroticism, Sexuality and Gender Reversal in Hungarian Culture". In *Gender Reversals and Gender Cultures: Anthropological and Historical Perspectives*. ed. Sabrina Petra Ramet, p. 148-163. London; New York: Routledge.

Lang, Sabina. 1996. "There is More than Just Women and Men: Gender Variance in North American Indian Cultures". In *Gender Reversals and Gender Cultures: Anthropological and Historical Perspectives*. ed. Sabrina Petra Ramet, p. 183-196. London; New York: Routledge.

Leach, Edmund. 1965. "Two Essays Concerning the Symbolic Representation of Time". In *Reader in Comparative Religion*. ed. William A. Lessa. New York: Harper and Row.

Nanda, Serena. 1994. "Hijras: An Alternative Sex and Gender Role in India". In *Third Sex, Third Gender: Beyond Sexual Dimorphism in Culture and History*. ed. Gilbert Herdt. New York: Zone Books.

Norbeck, Edward. 1967. "African Rituals of Conflict". In *Gods and Rituals*. ed. John Middleton. Austin, Texas; London: University of Texas Press.

Peacock, James, L. 1978. "Symbolic Reversal and Social History: Transvestites and Clowns of Java". In *The Reversible World*. ed. Barbara Babcock. Ithaca, New York; London: Cornell University Press.

Ramet, Sabrina Petra ed. 1996. *Gender Reversals and Gender Cultures: Anthropological and Historical Perspectives*. London; New York: Routledge.

Ramet, Sabrina Petra. 1996. "Gender Reversals and Gender Culture: An Introduction". In *Gender Reversals and Gender Cultures: Anthropological and Historical Perspectives*, p. 1-21. London; New York: Routledge.

Rigby, Peter. 1968. "Some Gogo Rituals of Purification: An Essay on Social and Moral Categories". In *Cambridge Papers in Social Anthropology*. ed. E. R. Leach, p. 164-171. Cambridge: Cambridge University Press.

Turner, Victor W. 1977. *The Ritual Process: Structure and Anti-Structure*. Ithaca, New York: Cornell University Press.

Twins

Taboos on twins have arisen because, among humans, twin births are an anomaly. Anything that deviates from the norm is traditionally accorded a special status, as either auspicious or dangerous. Twins of different sexes have been considered especially hazardous because, sharing the same womb, they are thought to have an almost incestuous relationship. Another rea-son for the anxiety of twins is related to the fear of the "double"; it was believed that one of the twins may have incarnated the spirit of a dead person or that the twins would cause their father to lose his entire soul (a portion of which is lost with each birth) and die. Obviously, the potential dangers caused by the birth of twins had to be averted, often by drastic means. The ethnologist, Hutton Webster, recorded many historical instances of the exposure of twins or infanticide: in Borneo, South Africa, Central and East Africa and among certain Native American tribes, either one or both twins were killed. In some instances it was sufficient to merely purify the mother or her offspring, or to isolate or expel the mother from the community (Webster, p. 61-65). A more recent cross-cultural study of infanticide after the birth of twins, conducted in 1973 by Gary Granzberg, has found that the killing of both twins is extremely rare and that the killing of one twin generally only occurs in those societies where the mother must cope alone, unsupported by female relatives (Granzberg, p. 405-412). This would imply a pragmatic approach; only when the rearing of twins places an unacceptable burden on the mother are the superstitious beliefs invoked to justify the killing.

Moreover, twins have not been tabooed in every culture. Webster mentions the Kpelle of Liberia who treated twins as sorcerers and regaled them with gifts, and the Nilotic tribes of Uganda who believed that dual births signified divine intervention and augured well for the prosperity of the entire village (Webster, p. 66-67). Certainly twins are a manifestation of exceptional fecundity. The ancient Assyrians thought that twins were a blessing when born to royalty (although inauspicious for everyone else) while the Ashanti of West Africa welcomed twin births except in the case of royalty – twins might initiate a dispute over the right of succession and to forestall this they were smothered at birth (Gonzalez-Crussi, p. 15-16).

In mythology twins are often rivals, fighting for ascendancy. A biblical legend tells how

Jacob and Esau wrestle together while still in the womb with Esau grabbing his brother by the heel to prevent him being born first. Esau even threatens to tear their mother's womb rather than allow Jacob to emerge before him (Ginzberg, p. 313-317). The evil twin who struggles for control also plays a role in the religion of Zoroastrianism, which emerged in Iran at the beginning of the first millennium BCE. In the Zurvanite strain of Zoroastrianism, a myth of creation describes Ahriman, the spirit of darkness, fighting with Ohrmazd, the spirit of light, before they are born from Zurvan, the god of time (Zaehner, p. 409-411). An African origin myth from the Mande-speaking people of Mali echoes this theme. In the Mande tale, the treacherous twin, Pemba, tries to dominate creation by emerging prematurely from his primordial egg. He plants seeds inside the earth, which is his mother, and thereby commits incest and brings evil into the world. Goodness is only restored when Pemba's twin, Faro, atones for his brother's sins and purifies the earth (Dieterlen, p. 124-138). The twins in these myths express the polarities of good and evil and the struggle between the two forces. Other tales emphasise the bounteousness of a double birth. George Dumézil, a scholar of Indo-European society, sees mythical twins such as the Greek Dioscuri, Castor and Polydeuces (also known as Pollux), the legendary founder of Rome, Romulus, and his brother Remus and the Asvins of the Vedas as representatives of fertility and prosperity. They therefore embody what he interprets as the third function within Indo-European society (the second function being that of the warrior while the priest/legislator typifies the first function).

Nowadays, twins are not seen as unnatural although conjoined twins still arouse the curiosity of the prurient. The Siamese twins, Chang and Chen, who were joined at the abdomen, married and agreed to spend three days in the house of each spouse in succession, and one of a pair of Hungarian sisters who were joined at the pelvis gave birth to a healthy baby at the end of the 19th century. Multiple births have become more common in the West as a result of infertility treatment but the recently developed technique of cloning – the reproduction of an identical specimen from a single cell – although not yet practised on humans, remains a subject of controversy.

References

Dieterlen, Germaine. 1957. "The Mande Creation Myth". *Africa*, no. 17 (2), p. 124-138.

Dumézil, Georges. 1970. *Archaic Roman Religion*. Chicago, Illinois; London: University of Chicago Press.

Ginzberg, Louis. 1909-1938. *The Legends of the Jews Vol 1*. Philadelphia: Jewish Publication Society of America.

Gonzalez-Crussi, Franz. [1985] 1986. "Twins". In *Notes of an Anatomist*, p. 14-23. London: Picador-Pan Books.

Granzberg, Gary. 1973. "Twin infanticide: a cross-cultural test of a materialistic explanation". *Ethos*, no. 1, p. 405-412.

Lyle, Emily. 1986. "The Place of the Hostile Twins in a Proposed Theogonic Structure". In *Duality. Cosmos*. ed. E. Lyle, p. 1-14. Edinburgh: Traditional Cosmology Society.

Puhvel, Jaan. [1987] 1989. *Comparative Mythology*. Baltimore, Maryland; London: The Johns Hopkins University Press.

Ward, Donald. 1968. *The Divine Twins: An Indo-European Myth in Germanic Tradition*. Berkeley; Los Angeles: University of California Press.

Webster, Hutton. 1942. *Taboo: A Sociological Study*. Stanford, California: Stanford University Press, London: Oxford University Press.

Zaehner, R. C. 1955. *Zurvan: A Zoroastrian Dilemma*. Oxford: Clarendon Press.

Untouchables

Untouchables were members of the group of social outcasts in India, known as "untouchables" because their traditional occupations of leather tanning and street cleaning were considered unclean, rendering them ritually impure and capable of polluting others. They were also sometimes known as panchamas (fifths). To understand this designation, and their low status, it is necessary to know something of the Hindu caste (Sanskrit: *jati*) system. The social structure that was later to become ossified in the caste system already existed during the Vedic period (from 1200 BCE) and consisted of four classes, or *varnas* (each *varna* contained many castes): Brahmans (priests, sacrificers), Ksatriyas (soldiers, protectors of the community), Vaisyas (farmers and producers) and Sudras (artisans and labourers). The Brahmans integrated the caste system into Hindu religious law and claimed divine justification for their decision. In the *Purusasukta* (*Rig Veda* 10.90) the gods create the world by dismembering the cosmic giant, Purusa (primal man), who becomes the victim in a Vedic sacrifice: 'His mouth became the Brahman, The Warrior was the product of his arms, his thighs were the Artisan, from his feet the Servant was born'. Thus each *varna* has its place in the social hierarchy determined by the creation myth. The *Manu Smriti*, or *Law of Manu*, var

iously dated from 600 BCE to 300 CE and composed by a legendary progenitor of humanity, systematised the social and religious laws and further specified the duties of each of the four *varnas*. But there remained a fifth group of castes consisting of those who had no *varna* designation, whose position was not sanctified by the scriptures, and who were, quite literally, the outcasts (*apasadas*). The *Manu Smriti* decrees:

... the dwellings of 'Fierce' Untouchables and 'Dog-cookers' (a caste of Untouchables) should be outside the village; they must use discarded bowls, and dogs and donkeys should be their wealth. Their clothing should be the clothes of the dead, and their food should be in broken dishes; their ornaments should be made of black iron, and they should wander constantly. A man who carries out his duties should not seek contact with them; they should do business with one another and marry with those who are like them. Their food, dependent upon others, should be given to them in a broken dish, and they should not walk about in villages and cities at night. They may move about by day to do their work, recognisable by distinctive marks in accordance with the king's decrees; and they should carry out the corpses of people who have no relatives; this is a fixed rule. By the king's command, they should execute those condemned to death, always in accordance with the teachings, and they should take for themselves the clothing, beds, and ornaments of those condemned to death (*Manu* 10. 51-56).

It is sometimes claimed that this group was composed of the indigenous Dravidian population who inhabited India before the Aryans arrived from central Asia, but the Sudras, an accepted *varna,* were also deemed non-Aryan.

The Indian caste system is characterised by extreme rigidity; membership is hereditary, marriage is restricted to members of the same caste, and the choice of occupation and social relationships is carefully circumscribed. It is validated by the Hindu idea of karma, a belief that all people on earth are reincarnated and the caste into which someone is born is determined by the conduct in previous existences. To be born an Untouchable is therefore a punishment for previous transgressions, but as Hindus place all living things in a hierarchy according to the degree of purity, the violation of certain laws of purity can cause contagion and result in a person of a higher caste becoming an outcast during his life. The *Manu Smriti* refers to pollution from contact with an Untouchable as well as from birth, death and menstruation. A law states:

> If a man has touched a 'Notorious by Day' Untouchable, a menstruating woman, anyone who has fallen (from his caste), a woman who has just given birth, a corpse, or anyone who has touched any of these objects, he can be cleaned by a bath (*Manu* 5.85).

Ritual bathing can cleanse pollution but one of the Buddhist *Jataka* tales tells how a Brahman eats food from a Candala (an Untouchable) and goes off into the forest to die because such internal pollution cannot be cleansed.

The rules for avoiding pollution are intricate. Generally cooked food is more liable to pass on pollution than raw food, so members of any caste may handle uncooked food. Meat, and especially beef, is forbidden to all but lower castes. Certain substances such as faeces and left over food are particularly polluting and can only be removed by an Untouchable. While the ground does not transmit contagion, the straw that covers it does. Professor Edward Harper, who studied Havik Brahmin pollution rules, observed:

> A Brahmin should not be in the same part of his cattle shed as his Untouchable servant, for fear that they may both step on places connected through overlapping straws on the floor. Even though a Havik and an Untouchable simultaneously bathe in the village pond, the Havik is able to maintain a state of *Madi* (purity) because the water goes to the ground, and the ground does not transmit impurity (Harper, 1964, p. 173).

Untouchables, who numbered about fifteen per cent of the population, were condemned to live in isolation from other castes, either on the outskirts of a village or in a separate hamlet, were not allowed to study or hear the sacred texts and were subject to considerable prejudice. However, by the late 1940s the caste system was breaking down. The nationalist leader, Mohandas K. Gandhi called Untouchables *Harijan* (children of God, although now they designate themselves *Dalits*, or "oppressed") and helped to politicise them. The drafted constitution of India, published a few days after Gandhi's assassination in 1948, stated that 'Untouchability is abolished and its practice in any form is forbidden' and the Constitution of 1950 outlaws untouchability.

See also

Foods Forbidden to Brahmins; Laws of Manu; Pollution

References

Anand, Mulk Raj. 1935. *Untouchable* (A novel describing the life of a sweeper and latrine cleaner in 1930s' India).

Douglas, Mary. [1966] 1984. *Purity and Danger*. London: Ark.

Dumont, Louis. [1966] 1970. *Homo Hierarchicus: An Essay on the Caste System*. Chicago, Illinois: University of Chicago Press.

Harper, Edward B. 1964. "Ritual Pollution as an Integrator of Caste and Religion". *Journal of Asian Studies* XXIII. *Religion in South Asia*. ed. Edward B. Harper, p. 151-196. Seattle, Washington: University of Washington Press.

Kolenda, Pauline. [1978] 1985. *Caste in Contemporary India*. Prospect Heights, Illinois: Waveland Press.

The Laws of Manu. trans. Wendy Doniger and Brian K. Smith. 1991. London: Penguin.

Levy, Robert I. 1990. *Mesocosm: Hinduism and the Organization of a Traditional Newar City in the Nepal*. Berkeley: University of California Press.

Quigley, Declan. 1993. *The Interpretation of Caste*. Oxford: Oxford University Press.

The Rig Veda. trans. Wendy Doniger O'Flaherty. 1983. Harmondsworth, Middlesex: Penguin.

Urine

Urine, like most bodily effluents, tends to be seen as a pollutant. The Hindu law-code, *The Laws of Manu*, is unequivocal in this respect. To avoid contamination, a person is enjoined not to urinate "on the road, on ashes, in a cow-pen, on ploughed land, in water, on a hill, on the ruins of a temple, nor on an ant hill, ever, nor in a cave inhabited by living creatures, while moving or standing up, from the bank of a river, or on the summit of a mountain" (*Manu* 4.45-47). The consequences of transgression can be dire: "Urinating on fire, or at the sun or moon, or in water, or at a twice-born man, or on a cow, or into the wind, destroys a man's wits" (*Manu* 4.52).

Urine, though, like most substances is not without its uses. Cow's urine is commonly used to shrink cloth and the potent plant *haoma*, named in the Ancient Zoroastrian *Avesta*, and ingested as *soma* by the Vedic priests of India, was still more powerful when drunk in the urine of an animal that had consumed the plant.

Also renowned is the *gomez* or bull-urine remedy of Mazdean Iran, still practised in certain orthodox Yazdi villages in 20th-century Iran and by the Parsi of India. In Parsi Gujerati, bull's urine is used in the *Nahn* (bath) purification ceremony, performed on ritual occasions such as initiation, marriage, and during the *Frawardigan* holy days at the end of the year, to cleanse the soul, mind and body. After prayers, ablutions and the chewing of a pomegranate leaf (a token of fecundity), the candidate must sip a small quantity of *nirangdin* (ritually consecrated bull's urine) mixed with *bhasam* (ash taken from a temple fire). When ingested, these two holy substances will internally cleanse the soul. A prayer of repentance, *patet*, is then recited to purify the mind. Finally a ritual bath is taken, enclosing *baj* prayers are spoken, and the priest passes the purifying agents to the candidate on a long-handled ladle. These include consecrated bull's urine, which must be rubbed over the body three times, sand, which must also be rubbed in three times, and consecrated water. The body is then washed with water into which a few drops of consecrated water have been added. Following the body's purification, the candidate dresses and ties the *kusti* (consecrated thread) over the *sudra* (sacred undershirt).

Consecrated bull's urine is also drunk in the *Barasnom-i no sab* (purification of the nine [days and] nights) exorcism and cleansing ceremony, designed to drive out the corpse demoness from those who have suffered serious pollution from contact with a corpse, or from similar bodily pollutions such as a miscarriage. The ceremony is long and complex, requiring nine days of seclusion during which the polluted person, or *riman*, must both imbibe *nirang*, the consecrated bull's urine, and rub the body with *gomez*, unconsecrated bull's urine, as well as sand and water. Starting with the head, the *riman* rubs the *gomez* over the entire body, finally reaching the toes, aware that the corpse demoness is being chased down the body. Two priests perform the ritual, one of whom tethers a dog whose gaze is purifying to the *riman* but anathema to the corpse demoness (Williams, p. 160-163).

Although the institution of the *gomez* rite is attributed in the *Avesta* to the divine Airyaman, a later Parsi commentary offers a novel, somewhat bawdy, etiology:

> The demon Ahriman, is tied up for thirty years by his adversary, Taxmoruw, and saddled three times each day to ride around the world. Tired of this humiliation, Ahriman bribes Taxmoruw's wife with jewellery so that she reveals her husband's flaws; in particular, his fear of acrophobia when he is riding in high places. When the wily Ahriman is next saddled, he waits till they reach dizzying heights before throwing Taxmoruw and swallowing him. Taxmoruw's brother, Jamshid, sets out to search for him and is advised of his lamentable fate. Learning, also, of the devil's homoerotic inclinations, Jamshid arouses Ahriman with the prospect of anal penetration, but instead inserts his hand and pulls out the body of his brother. Jamshid flees from Ahriman and builds a "tower of silence" [in which corpses are exposed to be eaten by vultures] for Taxmoruw. But his own hand has become vile and leprous after its contact with the diabolic innards and as its

condition worsens he withdraws to the solitude of the desert. However, by chance, the hand is urinated upon by a bovine while Jamshid sleeps and is miraculously cured (Puhvel, p. 119).

The magical functions of urine may have decreased in recent years, but the dangers of urinating in the wrong place are still valid. The pathologist, F. Gonzalez-Crussi, recounts how the bodies of several men were found on or near the tracks of the New York City underground. Curiously, the penis of each of the men was completely carbonised, a detail that provided the clue to their sudden demise. They had urinated onto the electrified track and the liquid had formed a continuous arc between their genitals and the track, transmitting thousands of volts of electricity and electrocuting them (Gonzalez-Crussi, p. 65-70).

References

Gonzalez-Crussi, F. [1986] 1987. "Mors Repentina: An Essay on Three Forms of Sudden Death". In *Three Forms of Sudden Death and Other Reflections on the Grandeur and Misery of the Body*, p. 65-84. London: Picador.

The Laws of Manu. trans. Wendy Doniger and Brian K. Smith. 1991. London: Penguin.

Puhvel, Jaan. [1987] 1989. *Comparative Mythology*. Baltimore, Maryland; London: Johns Hopkins University Press.

Williams, Alan. 1997. "Zoroastrianism and the body". In *Religion and the Body*. ed. Sarah Coakley, p. 155-166. Cambridge: Cambridge University Press.

Vagina

The vagina, according to many feminist writers, is so taboo as to be virtually invisible in Western culture. The French writer, Simone de Beauvoir, wrote in *The Second Sex*, "The feminine sex organ is mysterious even to the woman herself ... Woman does not recognise herself in it and this explains in part why she does not recognise its desires as hers" (quoted in Ardener, p. 124). Germaine Greer similarly complained, "The vagina is obliterated from the imagery of femininity in the same way that signs of independence and vigour in the rest of her body are suppressed" (Greer, p. 15). A myth from an entirely different culture, the Kuttla Kond people from the tribal areas of Orissa, India, suggests that the organ was not always so obscure:

> Originally the vagina was in the middle of the forehead. The only cloth worn by women then was a turban. Sona-aru and Rupa-aru were like this. One day they said to Nirantali, "So long as it's in the forehead, there is danger that some man may pull it out." Nirantali put it in the armpit instead. But it was too obvious there and people used to giggle when they saw it. Sona-aru and Rupa-aru went again to their mother and said, "This is no use; people giggle when they see it."

This time Nirantali fixed it between their thighs with wax, and in time it stuck there (Elwin, p. 474-475).

The vagina in the forehead, like a third eye, is reversed in another tale from the same area in which a woman has an eye in her vulva. The face in the genitals, the dark forbidden face, is common in medieval depictions of witches and demons. More pertinent, though, is yet another story told by the Konds in which the woman has teeth in her vagina which are subsequently pulled out by her husband. Versions of this myth, the *vagina dentata*, are found in cultures scattered around the world. Often, the men trying to make love to this menacing organ are castrated and die until a culture-hero, either by extracting the teeth or by giving the "mouth" sour fruit to eat, renders the vagina safe for sex. Sigmund Freud supposed that the fear of castration is prevalent in boys because they have seen the penis-free genitalia of a nurse or mother and imagine such a fate is in store for them or because they have been explicitly threatened with it as a punishment for masturbation.

Whatever the reasons for the concealment of the vagina (and male fear could underlie it), feminists think that it is symptomatic of the way women themselves are disregarded and undervalued. It follows that by making the vagina visible, by defying the taboos, a woman can reaffirm her identity. Shirley Ardener offers a few examples from her own field research, from that of others, and from classical Greece.

When she lived in Cameroon, she observed how insults to a woman's vulva would incur the wrath of all the females who would surround the culprit, singing obscene songs, making vulgar gestures, and demanding a pig as recompense. Although not unseen, in this instance, the vagina had certainly been devalued. Among the Balong, another Cameroon people, a gross insult by a male, if not atoned for, would cause all the women to undress before him and shame him, while the Kom, who live several hundred miles up-country, have a practice known as *anlu* reserved for such occasions. If the vagina is insulted – told that it smells or is rotten – the village women gather together before dawn, dressed in vines and shreds of male clothes, and with painted faces:

> the women pour into the compound of the offender singing and dancing and, it being early in the morning, there would be enough excreta and urine to turn the compound and houses into a public latrine. No person looks human in that wild crowd, nor do their actions suggest sane thinking. Vulgar parts of the body are exhibited as the chant rises in weird depth (F. Nkwain in Ardener, p. 116).

For a classical example, Shirley Ardener turns to the women's festival of the Thesmophoria which celebrated the cult of Demeter, the goddess of agriculture. This festival, which was observed in Athens, Syracuse, Mykonos, Sparta and other Greek cities, was notable for its exclusion of men and pig sacrifice. (According to myth, when Demeter's daughter, Kore, was abducted, the pigs of the swineherd of Eubouleus were also swallowed up. Demeter, searching for her daughter, instituted the Thesmophoria, the death-marriage being re-enacted in the sacrifice.) The festival involved women carrying "unspeakable sacred things made of dough" on their heads in closed baskets (Burkert, p. 243). Moreover, the cult was characterised by obscenity and blood. The classical scholar, Walter Burkert, elaborates:

The women indulge in indecent speech, *aischrologia*, they may split into groups and abuse one another, but there must also have been occasions on which men and women derided each other. The *iambos* as a mocking poem has its origin here; Baubo, who makes the goddess laugh by exposing herself, belongs to the Thesmophoria. According to a late source, the women worship a model of the female pudenda. In Sicily, cakes in this shape are baked ... In fantasy ... the hostility to men is greatly exaggerated. In Cyrene it is said that slaughterers (*sphaktriai*), their faces smeared with blood and swords in hand, castrated the man who came to spy on them at the festival ... In reality the women at the Thesmophoria eat pomegranate pips whose deep red juice is associated with blood; if a pip falls on the ground it belongs to the dead (Burkert, p. 244).

The festival of the Thesmophoria has direct agrarian functions (lewd behaviour by females in fertility rites being well attested in anthropological literature) but it also places emphasis on the solidarity of women. The seclusion of women throughout the event has been compared with the periodic isolation of females in menstrual huts; the atmosphere of blood and sexuality suggests this, as does the taboo on all sexual activity. Shirley Ardener focuses on the spirit of rebellion in which the forbidden is revealed and the male reviled. She turns to 20th-century artists who, in an act of defiance, repeatedly paint precisely that female organ that is so repressed: the vagina. In the late 1970s, Judy Chicago created *The Dinner Table*, a triangular structure with, on each of the three sides, thirteen place settings each depicting a stylised vulva representing a particular woman. The aim was to celebrate the female identity, in particular that of the female artist, for so long excluded from art academies and denied space in exhibitions. The problem is that such depictions, as feminists have pointed out, while being admirable for breaking taboos, can also inadvertently contribute to pornography. After all, for centuries men have viewed women as mere sexual ciphers (or as vessels of reproduction), valued for their corporal, but not their intellectual attributes. And the vagina, while absent from polite society, is by no means absent from the titillating pages of men's magazines.

See also

Clitoris; Cunnilingus

References

Ardener, Shirley. [1987] 1996. "A note on gender iconography: the vagina". In *The Cultural Construction of Sexuality*. ed. Pat Caplan, p. 113-142. London: Routledge.

Burkert, Walter. [1977] 1987. *Greek Religion*. Oxford: Basil Blackwell.

Elwin, Verrier. 1954. *Tribal Myths of Orissa*. Bombay; New York: Oxford University Press, Indian Branch.

Greer, Germaine. 1970. *The Female Eunuch*. London: McGibbon & Kee.

van Gennep, Arnold (1873-1957)

In 1904 the French ethnographer and folklorist, Arnold van Gennep, began his study of taboos with *Tabou et Totémisme à Madagascar* (Totem and Taboo in Madagascar), a work which examines taboos in their social contexts. In his analysis of the *fady* (taboo) in Madagascar, van Gennep explores two concepts: that of *tohina* (contagion); and the notion of *hasina* (*mana*, or supernatural power). The concept of contagion implies that anyone who comes into contact with a tabooed person or object will be "infected" and become as dangerous to the community as the original object. The second notion envisages a dangerous force, *hasina* or *mana*, which is immanent in certain things which must therefore be

"insulated" by taboos to prevent them from harming others. This work was followed, in 1906, by a study of Australian totemism in which van Gennep questions the theories of Andrew Lang and Émile Durkheim that attempt to construct models of social evolution. Inspired by the seminal work of Robert Hertz, van Gennep concludes that taboo and totemism can be better understood as systems of classification.

In 1909, van Gennep published his seminal work, *Rites de Passage*, in which he describes the proscribed behaviour involved in the passage from one social status to another, whether this be pregnancy, childbirth, puberty, initiation, betrothal, marriage, death or mourning. He also studies territorial transitions, social incorporation and seasonal customs. Each transition in the life cycle involves a period during which the initiate has no distinct status and is in a state of danger as well as being dangerous to others. The danger is alleviated by ritual abstentions and taboos, often involving segregation from the community and dietary restrictions. The rites of passage are subdivided into what van Gennep defines as "rites of separation", "transition or liminal rites" and "rites of incorporation". These can be seen in the pregnancy and childbirth rites among the Todas of India:

> When a woman becomes pregnant, she is forbidden to enter the villages or the sacred places. In the fifth month there is a ceremony called 'village we leave'. At this time the woman must live in a special hut, and she is ritually separated from the dairy, the sacred industry which is the heart of Toda social life. She invokes two deities, Pirn and Piri. She burns each hand in two places. A ceremony marks the leaving of the hut; the woman drinks sacred milk. She goes back to live in her home till the seventh month. During the seventh month 'the ceremony of the bow and arrow' establishes a social father for the

unborn child (the Todas practise polyandry). The woman returns to her home, performing the appropriate rites … The woman is delivered in her house, in anyone's presence and without special ceremonies. Two or three days later, mother and child go to live in a special hut; the rites performed for the departure from the house, the departure from the hut, and the return to the house are the same as those marking the woman's previous trip. While in the hut, the woman, her husband, and the child are tainted with the impurity called *ichchil*. Ceremonies are performed to protect them against the evil spirit *keirt*. They return to ordinary life by drinking sacred milk (van Gennep, [1909] 1977, p. 42-43).

The rites of separation are manifest in the rites performed while leaving the village and the ritual separation from the dairy. The periods within the hut represent the transition or liminal rites during which she (and later her husband and child) is considered impure, and susceptible to evil spirits. She must invoke protective deities and is physically marked by the burning. Drinking the sacred milk, as drinking and eating invariably are, is a rite of incorporation. Once more she is a part of the community, as she has symbolically 'died' to her old status and has been 'reborn' to her new role.

At the other end of the life cycle, death places a person in a sacred, impure state and touching the corpse is considered polluting in many societies. The function of funerary rituals is to separate the dead person from the living and then incorporate him into the realm of the dead. For the living, the transitional period includes the time of mourning during which the mourners are excluded from normal social activities.

The threefold pattern of separation, transition and incorporation has a spatial as well as a temporal dimension. Entry into a temple, or even into a house, is marked by certain procedures such as the removal of shoes, the washing of feet, or blessing with holy water. Moreover, every new house is taboo until the requisite rites are performed.

Finally, seasonal customs are scrutinised and here again the pattern is observed; the expulsion of an effigy of winter from the village and the welcoming in of summer are, respectively, rites of separation and rites of incorporation.

Van Gennep is eager to point out that taboos, or negative rites, cannot be used in isolation from positive rites within a ceremony. The command not to act must be accompanied by rules of action or there would be no ritual. Similarly, taboos placed upon people or things must be lifted by means of certain actions. In *L'État actuel du problème totémique*, while considering marriage restrictions, van Gennep reiterates the need to view prohibitions in the light of positive actions:

> … the result, and probably the aim, of exogamy is to link together certain societies which without it would no more come into contact than the masons of Rouen and the hairdressers of Marseille. If we examine the marriage diagrams from this point of view … we see that the positive element in exogamy is quite as powerful as the negative, but that, as in all codes, only what is forbidden is specified … (van Gennep, 1920, p. 351).

The pattern of the rites, identified by Arnold van Gennep, influenced the anthropologist Victor Turner who focused on the liminal stage and especially the social reversals, breaking of taboos and chaos characteristic of this stage.

See also

Liminality

References

Turner, Victor. 1964. "Betwixt and Between". In *Proceedings of the American Ethnographic Society*, ed. June Helm. Seattle, Washington: University of Washington Press.

Turner, Victor. 1969. *The Ritual Process*. Chicago, Illinois: Aldine.

van Gennep, Arnold. [1909] 1977. *The Rites of Passage*. London: Routledge.

van Gennep, Arnold. 1904. *Tabou et totémisme à Madagascar*. Paris: E. Leroux.

van Gennep, Arnold. 1920. *L'État actuel du problème totémique*. Paris: E. Leroux.

Zumwalt, Rosemary Lévy. 1988. *The Enigma of Arnold van Gennep*. Helsinki: Suomalainen Tiedeakatemia.

Webster, Hutton (1875-1955)

In 1942 Hutton Webster published *Taboo: A Sociological Study,* a compilation of accounts of taboos culled from preliterate societies. After an initial chapter examining the nature of taboos, Webster orders his material according to theme. The subsequent sections cover: the reproductive life, separation of the sexes, sexual intercourse, death and the dead, strangers and strange phenomena, sacred persons, sacred things, sin and ritual defilement, economic aspects of taboo and social aspects of taboo. As Webster states in his preface, given the wealth of information on the subject, it is impossible to include everything, but he does make use of extensive footnotes which refer to further sources of information.

As a sociologist and anthropologist, Webster is interested in the social importance of taboos:

An inquiry of this sort might be conducted along various lines: ethnographically, by an effort to trace the diffusion of taboos; or historically, by a search for the contacts between peoples which may explain this diffusion; or psychologically, by the attempt to formulate the ideas underlying the system of taboo in its many ramifications. I have not wholly neglected these various approaches to the subject, but my main concern has been to show ...

how important a place taboos hold in the cultural history of mankind (Webster, p. vii).

Although Webster's work is now somewhat dated, it is full of interesting details and anecdotes.

Reference

Webster, Hutton. 1942. *Taboo: A Sociological Study.* Stanford, California: Stanford University Press; London: Humphrey Milford – Oxford University Press.

Whistling

Whistling is forbidden in Islam because of its association with sorcery and the casting of spells in pre-Islamic times. Whistling is also a means of "communication with the *Jinn*". The *Jinn* (from which the English word "genie" derives) inhabit the subtle or immaterial world. In the Koran it is stated that the *jinn* were created from "smokeless fire" (55:15) while man was made of clay and angels were formed from light. Some *jinn* are benevolent and beautiful, others, such as the *'ifrit* and *ghul* (the source of the English "ghoul"), are vindictive and hideous (Glassé, p. 210-211).

The French anthropologist, Claude Lévi-Strauss, has also uncovered a link between whistling and sorcery. In two myths from the Bororo tribes of Central Brazil, whistled speech:

allows access from the cultural level (that of articulate speech) to the supernatural level, since gods or spirits use it to communicate with supernatural plants (those which once grew spontaneously) or with stars, which are supernatural beings (Lévi-Strauss, p. 329).

It is perhaps for this reason that whistling at sea is deemed unlucky in countries from Scotland to Japan.

Because it can easily be mistaken for natural sounds such as a bird's cry, whistling is also a useful means of signalling between members of clandestine groups and resistance fighters. Speaking of the song, *Le Chant des Partisans* (Underground Song), which was whistled by French prisoners in Ravensbrück concentration camp, and used by the French Resistance to indicate that the coast was clear, Maurice Druon comments:

> It is natural for those who take part in a secret struggle in the shadows to use whistling as a signal. It is possible that *Underground Song* contributed to making this one of the classical representative elements of the resistance fighter (Raskin, p. 75).

References

Glassé, Cyril. 1989. *The Concise Encyclopedia of Islam*. London: Stacey Publications.

Lévi-Strauss, Claude. [1966] 1973. *From Honey to Ashes: Introduction to a Science of Mythology* 2. trans. John and Doreen Weightman. New York: Harper and Row.

Raskin, Richard. 1991. "Le Chant des Partisans: Functions of a Wartime Song". *Folklore*, no. 102, p. 62-76.

Wine

Wine (*al-khamr* in Arabic) and other fermented drinks are forbidden to Muslims. This is expressly stated in *Sura* 2:219 of the *Qur'an* while *Sura* 5.92 asserts:

> O believers, wine and arrow-shuffling,
> idols and divining-arrows are an abomination,
> Some of Satan's work; so avoid it, haply so you will prosper (*Koran*. 5.92).

Nonetheless, the prohibition is only temporary. While on earth the devout Muslim must refrain from drinking because he will become inebriated but in paradise there are rivers of wine and the wine of paradise does not cloud the understanding. It flows in celestial fountains along with pure water and milk.

Despite the general Islamic ban on wine, for the Sufi mystics wine was a symbol of divine knowledge and invocation (*dhikr*). The most famous Arab Sufi poet, Ibn al-Farid (1181-1235 CE), wrote an ode to wine, *al-Khamriyyah*, in which the full moon represents the spiritual master and the crescent moon the aspirant to divine knowledge:

> We quaffed upon the remembrance of the Beloved a wine wherewith we were drunken, before ever the vine was created.
> The moon at the full its cup was; itself was a sun that a crescent moon passes round.

Ibn al-Farid goes on to describe the potency of the wine:

> had they sprinkled therewith the dust of a dead man's tomb, the spirit would surely have returned unto him and his body been quickened ...
> And had they brought nigh to its tavern one paralysed, he would have walked ... and the dumb would have spoken upon the mention of its flavour;
> And had the breaths of its perfume been wafted through the East, and in the West were one whose nostrils were stopped, the sense of smell would have returned to him ...
> And had an enchanter drawn its name on the forehead of one afflicted with madness, the letters drawn would have cured his sickness ...

And had its name been inscribed above the banner of an army, surely that superscription would have inebriated all beneath the banner ...

More ancient than all existing things was the tale of it told in eternity, when neither was shape nor trace to be seen (Glassé, p. 221).

Away from the heady atmosphere of Sufism, in the chambers of medieval Arab physicians, a concoction of wine mixed with herbs was considered efficacious in healing the sick.

References

Glassé, Cyril. 1989. *The Concise Encyclopedia of Islam*. London: Stacey Publications.

Koran. trans. A. J. Arberry. 1964. Oxford: Oxford University Press.

Writing

While a deep suspicion of what is written has consistently characterised dictators, moralists and, for opposite reasons, liberals and members of minority groups, the actual technology of writing is seldom seen as subversive today. Although it is true that in recent years there has been a new appreciation of the spontaneity of traditional oral culture with live storytelling and folksong sessions (and the Canadian, Herbert Marshall McLuhan, has even maintained that the 20th-century proliferation of non-literate modes of communication such as radio and television has meant that we are living – at least in a technical if not literal sense – in a post-literate era), this has not detracted from the value attached to literacy.

The invention of writing was generally considered to be of divine origin: the Egyptians claim it was invented by the god, Thoth or Theuth, while a Greek myth relates how his counterpart, Hermes, watching the flight of cranes, deciphered patterns suggesting the shape of the letters. Another Greek legend records how Cadmus introduced the

Phoenician letters to Greece – a tale which agrees with the accepted opinion of scholars that Greek letters derive from the Phoenician alphabet. According to Islamic tradition, Allah secretly gave the alphabet to Adam, the Indians credit Brahma with its invention, the Scandinavians believed the magical runes were obtained by Odin, while in China Ts'ang Chieh, a dragon-faced, four-eyed sage or demigod who lived during the reign of the Emperor Huang Ti (2698-2598 BCE), is said to have discovered the characters in the stars, in tortoise-shell markings and in the footprints of birds in sand. At the invention of writing in China, "heaven caused showers of grain to fall from on high, the disembodied spirits wept in the darkness, and the dragons withdrew themselves from sight" (Firmage, p. 8-9).

Whether or not the disappearance of the dragons is auspicious, it is only when the Egyptian myth of Theuth's invention of writing is recounted by the philosopher, Socrates, in Plato's *Phaedrus* that the benefits of the technology are called into question. Socrates relates how the talented (if such a word can be applied to a deity) Egyptian god journeys from his native Naucratis to the city of Thebes in Upper Egypt to show his invention to the god Thamus (or Ammon). Theuth praises the art, which will make the Egyptians wiser and give them better memories. Thamus disagrees.

> ... the parent or inventor of an art is not always the best judge of the utility or inutility of his own inventions ... you who are the father of letters, from a paternal love of your own children, have been led to attribute to them a quality which they cannot have; for this discovery of yours will create forgetfulness in the learners' souls, because they will not use their memories; they will trust to the external written characters and not remember of themselves ... [This] is an aid not to memory but to reminiscence, and you give your disciples not truth, but only the semblance of truth; they

will be hearers of many things and will have learned nothing; they will appear to be omniscient and will generally know nothing ... having the show of wisdom without the reality (Plato. *Phaedrus*, p. 274-275).

Socrates goes on to persuade his companion, Phaedrus, of the supremacy of speech, a position perhaps surprising in 5th-century Greece where many contemporary authors were stressing the necessity for a written code of law, accessible to all, to ensure justice and equality. That Plato's position was not unique is demonstrated by Deborah Tarn Steiner in her book *The Tyrant's Writ: Myths and Images of Writing in Ancient Greece*. She shows how many other 5th-century Greek writers manifest a deep suspicion of writing which they equate with tyranny and despotic oriental kings. In Herodotus' *Histories* the Egyptian, Persian and Lydian kings use writing as a personal instrument of despotism and self-aggrandisement, issuing harsh decrees and recording victories on engraved columns, while engaged in the related activities of branding slaves, stamping coins and mapping and altering the landscape. The Greek sources contrast this with the power of speech, manifest in public assemblies in which the citizens can declare their will – a communal activity and the foundation of democracy. Those who write, it is proposed, are "outsiders", foreigners or private individuals who do not fully participate in civic life.

Similar views are expressed by Jean-Jacques Rousseau, writing in 18th-century France, who sees written documents as an emblem of a society which has lost popular sovereignty. Furthermore, he contrasts those languages of the north, English, French and German which, reflecting harsh and cold climates, are characterised by a stark clarity, and lose little when transcribed, with the passion of oriental and southern languages which need to be heard if their sonority and harmonies are to be appreciated. In a poetic flight of fancy, Rousseau claims that the more "writerly" languages of the

north encourage a system of political oppression while the speech of the south, with its capacity to carry over long distances, favours the public assembly and an open exchange of views. Unfortunately for mankind, the language of tyranny is universal and no major civilisation, whatever its language, has achieved supremacy without the subjugation of others.

It is no doubt a recognition of this fact that has led the anthropologist, Claude Lévi-Strauss, to question the values of civilisation itself. The appearance of great empires, he observes, coincides with the introduction of writing which was the property of a political or religious minority. It was used not so much for communication and the dissemination of knowledge as for dominating and enslaving men. He agrees with Rousseau that in the simplest society it is mutual consent, not coercion by the powerful, that codifies the laws. In what can only be described as a parable, Lévi-Strauss recalls an incident in which an illiterate Nambikwara chief in Mato Grosso, Brazil, imitates the anthropologist, pretending to write out a list of gifts to be used in bartering with another tribe. The chief then pretends to read back the list to his company, hesitating as he deciphers certain words and hoping to astonish the group with his powers. The act:

> ... had not been a question of acquiring knowledge, of remembering or understanding, but rather of increasing the authority and prestige of one individual – or function – at the expense of others (Lévi-Strauss, p. 298).

Writing, Lévi-Strauss concludes, supports hierarchies and suppresses dialogue. An interesting critique of Lévi-Strauss' views on writing is that of Jacques Derrida in *L'écriture et la différence*, in which Derrida argues that violence precedes writing and exists in the spoken language.

While one would expect the printing press, developed by Johann Gutenberg in the 15th century, to have changed this situation, liberating men from their superstition of the written word by making texts available to the masses, Marshall McLuhan finds that it also "... detribalizes or decollectivizes man ... Print is the technology of individualism" (Firmage, p. 153-54). However, McLuhan's aforementioned dream of a return to an oral culture, and the creation of a humane, interactive community or "global village" through the mass media, is somewhat naive. After all, while Hitler's pernicious book, *Mein Kampf*, had some influence, it was the mass rallies attended by tens of thousands of Germans, and transmitted through the media, that persuaded the German people to follow one particular demagogue. The media, rather than sharing control with the entire population, place greater power in the hands of a few disseminators. Perhaps the World Wide Web creates a "global village" but at the present time it relies on text. Moreover, like writing or any other technology, it can be used for evil as well as for good.

Ironically, it is the most literate section of society, philosophers and writers, who most fear the written word. The Czech writer, Franz Kafka, wrote a tale, "In the Penal Colony", in which the execution of justice is perpetrated by a huge writing machine that engraves the text of the person's crime, the law he has broken, on his body. There is no trial of the accused and neither is he told of his offence. He only learns it as it is carved into him:

> ... around that sixth hour! The dimmest begin to catch on ... the man is simply beginning to decipher the text, pursing his lips as if listening. It's

not easy ... to decipher the text when looking at it; our man remember, is doing it with his wounds ... he needs six hours to complete the job. But then the harrow [containing the needles] runs him right through ... Judgement is then complete (Kafka, p. 757).

The fable ends with the machine malfunctioning and destroying the very officer who had extolled its virtues. It is perhaps not surprising that Kafka, before he died, gave instructions that all his writings be burned.

References

Firmage, Richard A. 1993. *The Alphabet Abecedarium. Some Notes on Letters*. Boston, Massachusetts: David R. Godine.

Kafka, Franz. 1983. "In the Penal Colony". trans. J. A. Underwood. In *Black Water: The Anthology of Fantastic Literature*. ed. Alberto Manguel. London: Pan Books.

Lévi-Strauss, Claude. [1955] 1973. *Tristes Tropiques*. London: Jonathan Cape Ltd.

Plato. 1997. *Phaedrus*. trans R. Hackforth. Cambridge: Cambridge University Press.

Puhvel, Jan. [1987] 1989. *Comparative Mythology*. Baltimore, Maryland; London: Johns Hopkins University Press.

Rousseau, Jean-Jacques. [1966] 1986. "Essay on the Origin of Languages". In *On the origin of language: Jean-Jacques Rousseau, Essay on the Origin of Languages; Johann Gottfried Herder, Essay on the Origin of Language*. trans. John H. Moran and Alexander Gode. Chicago, Illinois; London: University of Chicago Press.

Steiner, Deborah Tarn. 1994. *The Tyrant's Writ: Myths and Images of Writing in Ancient Greece*. Princeton, New Jersey: Princeton University Press.

Yellow

In German-occupied countries, during the Third Reich, it became mandatory for Jews to wear a yellow star so that they might be identified as "tabooed" persons. Those wearing the yellow star were denied food, society, work, education, and finally, life itself. The star represents the 'Shield of David', a traditional Jewish symbol, but the colour plays no significant role in Jewish iconography. Yellow is traditionally associated with brightness and sunlight. However, Christianity, in an effort to distance itself from classical idealism, has spurned the colour. As Havelock Ellis explains:

> It was clearly the advent of Christianity that introduced a new feeling in regard to yellow ... In very large measure, no doubt, this was clearly the outcome of the whole Christian revulsion against the classic world and the rejection of everything which stood as a symbol of joy and pride. Red and yellow were the favourite colours of that world. The love of red was too firmly rooted in human nature for even Christianity to overcome it altogether, but yellow was a point of less resistance and here the new religion triumphed. Yellow became the colour of envy.

Yellow became the colour of jealousy, of envy, of treachery. Judas was painted in yellow garments and in some countries Jews were compelled to be so dressed. In France, in the sixteenth century the doors of traitors and felons were daubed with yellow. In Spain heretics who recanted were enjoined to wear a yellow cross as a penance and the Inquisition required them to appear at public *autos da fe* in penitential garments and carrying a yellow candle.

There is a special reason why Christianity should have viewed yellow with suspicion. It had been associated with wanton love. In the beginning the association was with legitimate love ... but in Greece, and to a still more marked extent in Rome, the courtesan began to take advantage of this association (Quoted in Eisenstein, p. 95-96).

The common European prejudice against yellow can be confirmed by such expressions as "yellow-livered" and "yellow streak" to denote cowardice. During the reign of Francis I of France, the traitor Charles de Bourbon had yellow paint smeared on his door and an executioner in medieval Spain wore a garment of yellow and red – yellow to symbolise the treachery of the accused and red for the retribution of society. Jews in medieval Spain identified the forbidden fruit in the Garden of Eden as a lemon, a sour fruit, and Johann Wolfgang von Goethe, in his *Theory of Colours*, is aware of the disagreeable effect of the colour yellow when it appears on course surfaces such as cloth or felt:

> By a slight and scarcely perceptible change, the beautiful impression of fire and gold is transformed into one not undeserving the epithet foul; and the colour of honour and joy reversed to that of ignominy and aversion. To this impression the yellow hats of bankrupts and the yellow circles on the mantles of Jews, may have owed their origin (Goethe, p. 308).

The Jews are not the only race to have been maligned by this colour. As recently as the 20th century warmongers have spoken of the "yellow peril", the supposed danger of the invasion of Europe by Asiatic people.

Yellow also signifies disease. A yellow flag flown on a ship was a warning that its crew were in quarantine, infected with the "yellow plague" or jaundice. Illness, more psychological than physical, also underlies a novel by Charlotte Perkins Gilman, *The Yellow Wallpaper*. In this feminist tale, a young mother is oppressed by the social restraints of a patriarchal society. Forbidden by her husband to continue with her writing, she is trapped within a room which has hideous yellow wallpaper. As she observes, "The colour is repellent, almost revolting; a smouldering unclean yellow" (Gilman, p. 765) and "It makes me think of all the yellow things I ever saw – not beautiful ones like buttercups, but old foul, bad yellow things" (Gilman, p. 774). The wallpaper, with its twisted patterns, evokes nightmarish visions of contorted shapes. Behind the yellow paper, a woman, trapped like herself, crawls around the room and struggles to escape: "I pulled and she shook, I shook and she pulled, and before

morning we had peeled off yards of that paper" (Gilman, p. 776).

Yellow was also the colour that symbolised social revolution in China in the millenarian revolt of the Yellow Turbans in 182 CE. Already during the 1st century, Taoist-inspired messianic and millenarian movements had appeared, with the aim of establishing the Great Peace (*T'ai-p'ing*) which was believed to have existed before civilisation – akin to the Golden Age of the Greeks. The state, governed at the time by a Confucian ideology, predictably resisted such utopian movements but the 2nd-century revolt was on such a scale that it drained the Han dynasty and allowed local Taoist organisations to set up regional democracies (Schipper, p. 9). Naturally, Taoism does not have the Christian aversion to yellow and in Chinese mythology the Yellow Emperor (*Huang-ti*), who was supposed to have lived in the first half of the 3rd millennium BCE, was esteemed as the father of civilisation and master of metallurgy, and his teacher was believed to have been an incarnation of the Taoist sage, Lao Tzu.

References

Armitt, Lucy. 1996. *Theorising the Fantastic*. London: Arnold.

Eisenstein, Sergei M. 1943. *The Film Sense*. trans. Jay Leyda. London: Faber and Faber.

Ellis, Havelock. May 1906. *Popular Science Monthly*.

Gilman, Charlotte Perkins. [1895] 1991. "The Yellow Wallpaper". In *White Fire. Further Fantastic Literature*. ed. Alberto Manguel. London: Pan Books.

Goethe, Johann Wolfgang von. [1810] 1973. *Theory of Colours*. trans. Charles Lock Eastlake. Cambridge, Massachusetts: MIT Press.

Schipper, Kristofer. [1982] 1993. *The Taoist Body*. trans. Karen C. Duval. Berkeley; Los Angeles: University of California Press.

Z

Zoroastrian Purification Rituals

Zoroastrian purification rituals are described (and prescribed) in the sacred text known as the *Avesta,* parts of which date back to the first millennium BCE. Zoroaster is the Greek form of Zarathustra, the reformer credited with composing parts of the *Avesta* and establishing Ahura Mazda, "Lord Wise", as the one god. Much of the *Avesta* has been lost and the present texts were only edited during the Sasanian empire (3rd to 7th century CE) when Zoroastrianism was the state religion. The *Avesta* comprises three parts: the *Yasna*, cult or liturgy, which includes the oldest material, the *Gathas*; the *Yasts*, or sacrificial hymns; and the *Videvdat*, the "Anti-Demon Law".

The *Videvdat* is particularly concerned with ritual pollution. The greatest pollutant was the decomposing corpse, therefore great towers, known as "towers of silence", were built for the dead, frequented by carrion birds who could devour the putrefying flesh and prevent the pollution of the sacred fire, earth or water. For the living, cures often involved vicious beatings, even for problems such as irregular menstruation. If one was possessed by the demoness Nasu (cognate with the Greek word for corpse), which could come about after a miscarriage or contact with a corpse, it was necessary to suffer *citha* (restitution or fine), *aprtis* (corporal punishment), and *yaos-da* (weal setting), which involved a complex purification ceremony to cleanse the individual of the taint of death.

See also

Urine

References

Boyce, Mary. 1984. *Textual Sources for the Study of Zoroastrianism.* Manchester: Manchester University Press.

Duchesne-Guillemin, Jacques. 1973. *Religion of Ancient Iran.* Bombay: Tata Press.

Puhvel, Jaan. [1987] 1989. *Comparative Mythology.* Baltimore, Maryland; London: Johns Hopkins University Press.

Zaehner, R. C. 1976. *The Teachings of the Magi: A Compendium of Zoroastrian Beliefs.* London: Oxford University Press.

Index